ATTENTION, BALANCE, AND COORDINATION

ATTENTION, BALANCE, AND COORDINATION

The A.B.C. of Learning Success

Sally Goddard Blythe

With contributions from

Lawrence J. Beuret, MD

Peter Blythe, PhD

WILEY-BLACKWELL

A John Wiley & Sons, Ltd., Publication

This edition first published 2009

© 2009 John Wiley & Sons Ltd, except for appendix I, which is a revised and adapted version of a study published by the College of Occupational Therapists; and appendix II, which is revised and adapted from www.listenhear.co.uk, published by Steven Brown, for which permission has been kindly granted.

Wiley-Blackwell is an imprint of John Wiley & Sons, formed by the merger of Wiley's global Scientific, Technical, and Medical business with Blackwell Publishing.

Registered Office
John Wiley & Sons Ltd, The Atrium, Southern Gate, Chichester, West Sussex, PO19 8SQ, UK

Editorial Offices
The Atrium, Southern Gate, Chichester, West Sussex, PO19 8SQ, UK
9600 Garsington Road, Oxford, OX4 2DQ, UK
350 Main Street, Malden, MA 02148-5020, USA

For details of our global editorial offices, for customer services, and for information about how to apply for permission to reuse the copyright material in this book please see our website at www.wiley.com/wiley-blackwell.

The right of the author to be identified as the author of this work has been asserted in accordance with the Copyright, Designs and Patents Act 1988.

Library of Congress Cataloging-in-Publication Data
Goddard, Sally, 1957–
  Attention, balance, and co-ordination: the A.B.C. of learning success /
Sally Goddard Blythe; with contributions from Lawrence J Beuret and
Peter Blythe.
     p. cm.
  Includes bibliographical references and index.
  ISBN 978-0-470-74098-9 (cloth) – ISBN 978-0-470-51623-2 (pbk.)
  1. Reflexes–Handbooks, manuals, etc. 2. Child development–Handbooks, manuals, etc.
3. Developmental disabilities–Physiological aspects–Handbooks, manuals, etc. 4. Learning–
Physiological aspects–Handbooks, manuals, etc. I. Beuret, Lawrence J.
II. Blythe, Peter. III. Title.

QP372.G57 2009
612.6'5 – dc22

                                                                          2008047079

Set in 10 on 12 pt Palatino by SNP Best-set Typesetter Ltd., Hong Kong
Printed and bound in Singapore by C.O.S. Printers Pte Ltd

6 2014

CONTENTS

ABOUT THE AUTHOR

Sally Goddard Blythe is a Consultant in Neuro-Developmental Education and currently the Director of The Institute for Neuro-Physiological Psychology (INPP) in Chester, England.

She has worked in the area of neuro-development for more than 20 years and is the author of several books and published papers on child development and neuro-developmental factors in specific learning difficulties. Her first book, *Reflexes, Learning and Behavior*, has provided the basic information for many other professions throughout the world now using reflex assessment. Her subsequent books, *The Well Balanced Child* and *What Babies and Children Really Need*, examine the importance of physical development for later learning success, health, well-being, and social integration.

She is the author of The INPP Test Battery and Developmental Exercise Programme for Use in Schools – a programme of daily exercises designed to be used in schools with a whole class of children over one academic year – this programme has been the subject of published research initially involving 810 children across schools in the UK. The aim of the programme is to provide teachers with a method to enable them to identify physical readiness for learning and how to use a physical intervention programme designed to encourage physical readiness for learning in children of all ages.

CONTRIBUTORS

Peter Blythe, PhD was formerly a Senior Lecturer in Applied Psychology/Education at the College of Education in Lancashire. In 1969, he became aware that many children with average to above-average intelligence who have specific learning difficulties in the classroom still had a cluster of primitive reflexes that should not be present above the first year of life and underdeveloped postural reflexes, which are necessary to support all aspects of education. These developmental 'signposts' of maturity in the functioning of the central nervous system were connected to inability to demonstrate their intelligence in an acceptable academic way.

In 1975, he established The Institute for Neuro-Physiological Psychology (INPP) where he developed protocols of assessment and effective remedial intervention. He was the Director of INPP until 2000.

The INPP in Chester is the international training centre for professionals seeking access to The INPP Method.

Lawrence J. Beuret, MD graduated from the Loyola Stritch School of Medicine in Chicago, Illinois. During a fellowship at the Mayo Clinic, he observed a high incidence of learning disabilities in the adolescent psychiatric population. Following two years as an emergency room physician, he entered a private practice in the treatment of psychosomatic and post-traumatic stress disorders (PTSD). In 1985, he trained in Chester, England with Dr Peter Blythe in the INPP treatment techniques for neuro-developmental delay (NDD). In the course of his practice, he has extended the diagnostic and treatment techniques of INPP to include pre-school ages, as well as adolescents and adults with reading and learning difficulties. He is currently active in developing courses for therapists in the recognition and treatment of subconscious aspects of PTSD. His medical practice is in the Chicago suburb of Palatine.

PREFACE

In my years of practice, I have continued to hear a similar story told by parents several times a week. The story is of families who have struggled, usually for several years, to find help for their child but to no avail, despite the fact that they, the school, teachers, and often other professional agencies have been aware that a problem exists for several years. It is all so depressingly familiar.

The story begins something like this. A happy child starts school just prior to his or her fifth birthday. The child may have had a series of minor problems in the early years, such as difficulty with feeding, sleeping, frequent ear, nose, or throat infections, or delay in achieving some developmental milestones such as learning to talk and learning to walk, but these early signs are rarely considered as possible precursors to the problems that may arise in the classroom in the years to come. Because medicine as a profession tends to be focused on the treatment of immediate, short-term outcomes, the longer-term sequelae of these developmental indicators do not re-enter their ken. The early warning signs that were evident in developmental records simply become buried in the system when the handover of responsibility for the developmental progress of the young child is transferred from health visitor and doctor to education at the time of school entry.

Towards the end of the first year of schooling, the teacher may inform the parents that their child is having problems either in relation to difficulties with reading and fine motor skills, or, more often at this stage, problems with attention, ability to sit still, compliance, and social skills. These are often viewed as being primarily behavioural problems requiring behavioural management, but in the developmentally delayed child, the behaviours are usually *symptomatic* of physical immaturity which is affecting posture, the ability to sit still, the development of freedom from distractibility, control impulsivity, and the ability to read and to react appropriately to the body language of others. It is at this stage that the special needs team may be brought in to provide additional support. Specialist teaching in smaller groups helps as long as it is ongoing but does not necessarily sustain itself over time.

It may take a further two to three years of education before the child is referred to an educational psychologist for formal evaluation of cognitive strengths, weaknesses, and IQ. Generally, a child must be at least two years behind his or her chronological age in reading before referral to an educational psychologist takes place with subsequent recommendations being made for specific support in the educational setting. In severe cases, referral back to the medical profession may be made with recommendations that further investigations should be carried out to see if a diagnosis of developmental coordination disorder (formerly dyspraxia) or attention deficit (hyperactivity) disorder is relevant. By this time, the child is at least eight years of age, and three years of formal education have already passed without anyone investigating whether there might be a physical or neurological basis to the child's educational difficulties. Even when the child is referred on for occupational therapy or physiotherapy, there is often a wait of several months for assessment and follow-up remedial intervention. Therapy is often carried out in a group setting for a finite period of time, and, while undoubtedly the child benefits from therapy, therapy either does not continue for long enough or is not carried out on a sufficiently regular basis (i.e. daily) to effect change not only in physical coordination but also in cognitive performance.

In effect, these children who are not 'bad enough' to qualify for a medical diagnosis, but who are nevertheless delayed in aspects of neurological development, simply fall through the net of services which should be in place to identify their difficulties at an early stage and to provide effective remedial assistance. Teachers recognize the symptoms but struggle to identify the *cause* or *how to help*, because the *physical* development of the child does not constitute a major part of teacher training at the time of writing. I have been increasingly reminded of this when delivering training in The Institute for Neuro-Physiological Psychology (INPP) Method to probationary teachers in the UK. When asked, at the beginning of the lecture, how much time students spent in their training on physical infant development, not one hand in the group goes up. A few hands may be raised at the mention of Piagetian stages of development, but only the early years specialists have a good understanding of the importance of sensory-motor development to support later cognitive skills. A child's learning throughout education is rooted in its own physical development from conception. Mastery of balance, posture, coordination, and adequate vision and hearing are crucial to learning success but do not form a part of statutory assessments when a child starts school. In my view, this constitutes a major deficit in the current education system.

The INPP was originally set up by Peter Blythe in 1975 to research into the effects of central nervous system dysfunction in specific learning difficulties (and adults with anxiety, agoraphobia, and panic disorder that have failed to respond to intervention or therapies of choice), and to devise effective methods of assessment and subsequent remedial intervention. Although the clinical assessment and supervision of remedial programmes for individual cases remain as the main focus of INPP's work some 30 years later, the INPP also provides training to allied professions in the administration of school-based programmes and ongoing research. As the scope of the work carried out at the INPP has broadened, it has become increasingly apparent that there are gaps between the professional services which should be in place to provide help for individuals experiencing a range of problems linked to developmental delay, also sometimes referred to as central nervous system immaturity or neurological dysfunction.

This book is an attempt to bring together a body of knowledge and to make it available to *all* professions that are involved, in one way or another, in helping to treat the symptoms of specific learning difficulties and emotional problems. For this reason, different parts of the book are aimed at different readerships. Chapter 1 examines the links between the symptoms of specific learning difficulties and underlying physical dysfunctions. The connections between these two are relevant to the professions of education, psychology, and medicine. The chapters on the role of reflexes in development may be familiar ground for those working within the field of medicine, but the impact of aberrant reflexes on subsequent learning and behaviour is often new ground for doctors, teachers, and psychologists. The effect of aberrant reflexes and vestibular dysfunction in secondary neuroses is relevant to psychiatrists, while the general concept of a neuro-developmental basis for learning difficulties and emotional problems is of interest to parents, teachers, doctors, psychologists, and to anyone involved in planning and implementing educational policy in the future. The *application* of The INPP Method is to the resolution of educational, emotional, and behavioural problems for which there is an underlying physical cause.

While modern technology has advanced our understanding of a wide range of diseases and the prevention of disease, and has increasingly enabled scientists to look into the functioning of the brain, technology cannot yet reveal everything. Just as gaps exist between professional domains in the investigation and treatment of subclinical disorders, so gaps also exist between what modern scanning equipment, posturography, etc. can detect, and what old-fashioned, less sophisticated methods of assessing the nervous system can show. In many cases, advanced technology does not detect a specific area of abnormality, but simple tests carried out to assess static balance, proprioception, and oculomotor functioning reveal that functional abnormalities are present. These will affect performance on a wide range of skills.

Additionally, findings obtained from clinical practice or field observation are frequently treated as the 'poor relations' of research, and can take many years to be accepted in academic circles or to become integrated into general professional practice. In this sense, what is taught to the next generation of professionals as students in universities today are the tried and tested clinical techniques of yesterday, not the developments of the present. This statement should not be misinterpreted to mean that rigorous attention to the scientific method is not an essential part of research and clinical practice; it is, but the scientific methodology also has limitations, and there is a danger that each individual profession becomes so specialized and focused on the minutiae of its own disciplines that it loses the ability to see the bigger picture. Children's difficulties do not exist in specialist departments; they exist within the context of the whole child.

The techniques used by the INPP cross a number of professional boundaries: The *diagnostic techniques* and scoring
systems are based on tests originally developed by mainstream medicine. This means that if the same tests were
carried out by a doctor, physiotherapist, or occupational
therapist, they would find identical results. However, the
methods of *intervention* used at the INPP are different from
conventional methods used by physiotherapists or by those
occupational therapists trained in the techniques of sensory
integration; finally, the *application* of physical tests and physical remediation programmes is to problems of an educational or psychological nature.

The purpose of this book was to bring together the different
professional domains and to reach a common understanding of *the role that physical factors can play* in learning and in
emotional problems.

It is not within the scope of a book to provide training in
The INPP Method, rather to offer a solid basis to the underlying theories and current research so that professionals can
work more closely together for the benefit of children and
patients.

Sally Goddard Blythe
March 2008

ACKNOWLEDGEMENTS

Hawthorn Press for permission to include sections relating to The Institute for Neuro-Physiological Psychology Questionnaire originally published in *What Babies and Children Really Need – How Mothers and Fathers Can Nurture Children's Growth for Health and Well being* and examples of children's drawings originally published in *The Well Balanced Child.*

Paul Madaule, Director of The Listening Centre in Toronto, Canada for permission to include *The Listening Check List* in Chapter 11.

Svea Gold for permission to include an extract from 'Using the Head Righting Reflex to Check for Warning Symptoms That Something Is Wrong with the Child's "Gaze Control" and How to Proceed from There', and for having the faith to publish my first book, *A Teacher's Window into the Child's Mind*, from which all my subsequent books have grown, and for her tireless curiosity and hard work in seeking to understand and to resolve the problems of children struggling to learn.

Peter Blythe and *The British Journal of Occupational Therapy* for permission to include The INPP Questionnaire for Children and research based upon the use of the questionnaire instrument.

Dr Harold Levinson for information and advice.

Peter Blythe and Dr Lawrence Beuret for their invaluable contributions to this book.

Sheila Dobie OBE, Dr Kjeld Johansen, Dr Lutz E Koch, and Dr Heiner Biedermann for developing and sharing their work.

For parents and colleagues who have donated pictures from their personal collections of their own children as babies and in the childhood years.

For many other people whose ideas, research and scholarship over many years have provided the information on which this book is based, and also those people whose contributions through discussion and the sharing of information have been silently woven in to the fabric of knowledge which has supported the development of The INPP Method over many years.

To everyone at Wiley-Blackwell involved in the editing, picture sourcing and production of the book.

CHAPTER 1

WINDOWS ON THE BRAIN

INTRODUCTION

Although all learning ultimately takes place in the brain, it is often forgotten that it is through the body that the brain receives sensory information from the environment and reveals its experience of the environment. Postural control reflects integration of functioning within the central nervous system (CNS) and supports brain–body functioning. Immaturity or conflict in brain–body functioning affects the brain's ability to assimilate and process information and to express itself in an organized way.

One method of assessing maturity and integrity in the functioning of the CNS is through the examination of primitive and postural reflexes. The presence or absence of primitive and postural reflexes at key stages in development provides 'windows' into the functioning of the CNS, enabling the trained professional to identify signs of neurological dysfunction or immaturity.

This book, I hope, will give the reader an understanding of why early *reflexes* are important, their functions in early development, their effects on learning and behaviour if retained, and the possible effects on other aspects of development such as posture, balance, and motor skills if they are not integrated at the correct time in development.

Reflexes *will be described in detail in subsequent chapters.*

There is an increasing body of scientific evidence to support the theory that physical skills support academic learning and are involved in emotional regulation and behaviour. Since its foundation in 1975, The Institute for Neuro-Physiological Psychology (INPP) in Chester has been the pioneer in researching the effects of immature primitive and postural reflexes on learning and behaviour, developing protocols for the assessment of abnormal reflexes and related functions, and has devised a specific method of effective remediation (The INPP Method).

Research carried out both independently and by The Institute over the last 30 years has shown that there is a direct link between immature infant reflexes, academic underachievement and increased anxiety in adult life, and that a remedial programme aimed directly at stimulating and integrating primitive and postural reflexes can effect positive change in these areas. This book will outline the underlying theory, mechanisms, developmental markers, and effects of immature reflexes in the older child to assist professionals involved in education and child welfare to recognize the signs of neurological dysfunction and their implications.

The book will also explore interdisciplinary shortcomings endemic in the current system for identifying, assessing, and providing effective remedial intervention for learning and behavioural problems. In this context, the book will propose that there is a need within education for a new profession to bridge the present gaps – a neuro-educator – trained specifically to assess children's developmental readiness for education.

DEVELOPMENTAL READINESS FOR EDUCATION

Chronological age and intelligence are not the only criteria for learning success. Developmental readiness for formal education is equally important. Developmental testing of motor skills is carried out regularly in the first year of life, but when responsibility for the young child moves from the domain of medicine (midwife, paediatrician, and health visitor) to education at the time of school entry, a child's developmental readiness in terms of *physical* development is not assessed as a matter of routine. Once a child enters formal education at rising five years of age in the UK, assessment of physical development only takes place if problems of a medical nature arise. Assessment within the school system tends to focus on the educational problems or the presenting symptoms rather than on the investigation of underlying causes.

The INPP in Chester was set up in 1975 by psychologist Peter Blythe, PhD, with the aim of investigating whether underlying physical factors could play a part in specific learning difficulties and in some phobic disorders. In the 1970s, Peter Blythe and David McGlown devised, first, systems of assessment to identify areas of impaired functioning, and second, physical remediation programmes to correct the underlying dysfunctions. These methods of assessment, which involve examining the neuro-developmental level of the child and the subsequent physical programmes of remedial intervention, are now known as The INPP Method of Developmental Training.

By their very nature, symptoms of specific learning difficulties tend to cross diagnostic boundaries, with different categories sharing a number of symptoms in common (co-morbidity). This is particularly true of many of the symptoms of dyslexia, developmental coordination disorder (DCD), attention deficit disorder (ADD), and some aspects of autistic spectrum disorders. A number of the symptoms shared in common are a direct result of immaturity in the functioning of the CNS and are sometimes referred to as neurological dysfunction or neuro-developmental delay.

WHAT IS NEURO-DEVELOPMENTAL DELAY?

Every normal human baby, born at full term (40 weeks' gestation) is equipped with a series of primitive reflexes to help it survive the first few weeks and months of life. If one side of the mouth is gently stroked, the neonate will turn its head in the direction of the stimulus and the mouth will open, searching or 'rooting' for the breast; if a finger is placed inside the baby's mouth, it will reflexively start to suck, and if an object is placed in the palm of its hand, it will grip and not be able to let go at will. These primitive reflexes are hard-wired into the brainstem at birth. They are active for the first six months of life, but from the moment of birth, they start a gradual process of inhibition by higher centres in the brain as neurological connections to higher centres develop. As the primitive reflexes are inhibited, the postural reflexes emerge, which gradually take over many of the functions of the primitive reflexes. Postural reflexes take up to three and a half years of age to be fully developed.

Neuro-developmental delay, *sometimes also referred to as neurological dysfunction, is defined by the INPP as (1) the continued presence of a cluster of aberrant primitive reflexes above six months of age and (2) absent or underdeveloped postural reflexes above the age of three and a half years.*

The vestibular system *is a system responsible for maintaining balance, posture, and the body's orientation in space. This system also regulates locomotion and other movements and keeps objects in visual focus as the body moves. The* cerebellum *is the control centre for balance and movement coordination. As part of the nervous system, it receives two types of input: one locating the body's position in space and the other indicating whether the muscle is*

Neuro-developmental delay describes the continued presence of a cluster of primitive reflexes in a child above six months of age together with absent or underdeveloped postural reflexes above the age of three and a half years. The presence or absence of primitive and postural reflexes at key stages in development provides evidence of immaturity in the functioning of the CNS and will influence the development and control of posture, balance, and motor skills.

WHAT IS THE CONNECTION BETWEEN NEURO-DEVELOPMENTAL DELAY AND SPECIFIC LEARNING DIFFICULTIES?

Successful academic learning relies upon adequate mastery of motor skills: reading, for example, involves development and control of smooth eye movements to send an orderly flow of sequential information to the brain; eye movements are a motor skill. In order to write, a child needs to have developed hand–eye coordination; this is also a motor skill. Sitting still and paying attention require postural control, balance, and orientation, in addition to the involvement of cortical centres implicated in the maintenance of attention; aspects of mathematics require spatial skills and cooperation between the two sides of the cerebral cortex (left and right hemispheres) to cooperate in solving problems in a sequential fashion. Many of these 'higher' cognitive processes are rooted neurophysiologically in systems involved in postural control, and the reflexes play a crucial part in supporting and facilitating stability and flexibility in postural control.

Spatial skills develop directly from physical awareness of the body position in space. Secure balance is fundamental to navigation in space because it provides the physical basis for a secure internal reference point from which spatial judgements about the external environment are formed. Dr Harold Levinson described the *vestibular-cerebellar system* as acting as 'a compass system. It reflexively tells us spatial relationships such as right and left, up and down, front and back, east and west, north and south'.[1] Research has shown that perception and differentiation of sequences of mobile stimuli, known to be related to vestibular and cerebellar mediation and postural stability, are faulty in children with reading difficulties.[2] The cerebellum is also linked to the ability to sequence not only motor tasks but also associated cognitive processes.[3]

Inter-hemispheric functioning, which is essential for problem solving, is reflected in a child's ability to use the two sides of the body in different ways. In addition to the specific brain centres which are involved in the mediation and control of balance, integration in the use of the two sides of the body both reflects and supports the use of balance, *bilateral integration*. While many of the areas of the brain are involved in different types of learning, higher cognitive functions rely upon the integrated functioning of lower centres to support and to feed information to the cortex.

Primitive and postural reflexes at key stages in development provide a 'window' into the structural and functional integrity of the hierarchy of the brain. Abnormal primitive and postural reflexes provide diagnostic signs of immaturity in the functioning of the CNS which can interfere with optimal cortical functioning. 'The central nervous system acts as a coordinating organ for the multitude of incoming sensory stimuli, producing integrated motor responses adequate to the requirements of the environment.'[4] When the CNS is working well, the cortex is free to concentrate on 'higher' functions, being involved in intention and motor planning, but not the detailed mechanics of movement. 'The cortex knows nothing of muscles, it only knows of movement.'[5]

This is because voluntary movements, particularly those associated with postural adjustment, are largely automatic and function outside of consciousness. The maintenance of posture and equilibrium is carried out by the CNS recruiting lower centres in the brainstem, midbrain, cerebellum, and basal ganglia in the service of the cortex.

contracted or relaxed. Based on this information, and depending on the desired action (move forward, grasp, etc.), the cerebellum triggers, adjusts, or stops a movement.

Bilateral integration *is the ability to carry out movements on one side of the body independently of the other side and the ability to coordinate both sides of the body in many different combinations.*

PRIMITIVE AND POSTURAL REFLEXES – THE MEDICAL MODEL

It is medically accepted that abnormal reflexes can persist as a direct result of pathology such as in cases of cerebral palsy when damage to higher brain centres prevents the cortex from completely inhibiting the primitive reflexes in the first year of life or from releasing postural reflexes.

Primitive reflexes may also reappear as a result of progressive pathology such as in multiple sclerosis when pinhead-sized hardened patches develop and scatter irregularly through the brain and the spinal cord, causing the insulating sheaths of the nerve fibres in the hardened patches to break up and become absorbed, leaving the nerve fibres bare. When this happens, postural reflexes become impaired and the primitive reflexes re-emerge as a direct result of loss of integration within the functioning of the nervous system and loss of control from higher centres. A similar regression of reflex integration can be seen in Alzheimer's disease, when degeneration within the cerebral cortex results in gradual loss of higher cortical function and the release of primitive reflexes as primitive, protective, survival mechanisms.

Structural development of the nervous system takes places as a result of maturation and interaction with the environment. Every species begins life with a common tool kit of genes involved in bodybuilding, but the development of the nervous system in each individual is the product of using the same genes in different ways.

The transition from primitive to postural reflex in the first year(s) of life is a gradual one. It occurs as a result of *maturation* within the CNS, but it is also partly environmentally dependent. While the reflexes are hard-wired into the system at birth, physical interaction with the environment is like the software through which the potential of the nervous system is entrained. In the early months of life, primitive reflex actions provide rudimentary physical training through movement at a time in development before the cortex and connections to the cortex are sufficiently mature to orchestrate a controlled response. In other words, through the feedback or movement experience of early reflex actions, neurological pathways are developed and strengthened. As connections between higher and lower centres become established, primitive reflexes are inhibited to make way for more advanced systems of voluntary movement and postural control.

At this stage of development, postural reflexes lay the foundations for automatic reactions needed for the maintenance of posture and balance in a gravity-based environment (preconscious), as well as support the control of voluntary movement. The importance of postural reflexes in supporting automatic reactions and in reducing the workload of the cortex was described as early as 1898 by Reuben Halleck in a book *Education of the Nervous System* when he explained how 'reflex action is the deputy of the brain, and directs myriad movements, thus leaving the higher powers free to attend to weightier things.'[6]

It should be stressed that the primitive reflexes never entirely desert us. The process of inhibition puts them to sleep in the brainstem only to be reawakened if disease, accident, or injury results in damage to higher brain centres. In this way, primitive reflexes continue to remain available to fulfil a protective function if required. However, the concept that abnormal primitive and postural reflexes can persist in the general population is still controversial, despite an increasing body of evidence to support the theory that abnormal primitive and postural reflexes can and do exist in the absence of *identified* pathology.[7–15]

The *effects* of retained primitive reflexes and underdeveloped postural reflexes in the older child are well documented.[16–19] It is also recognized that aberrant reflexes can affect higher cortical functioning particularly in the area of education,[17,20,21] but 30 years after much of this research has been published, the concept that reflex status can interfere with cognitive performance still remains controversial. The role of abnormal reflexes in dyslexia as a discreet entity has never been conclusively established despite the fact that dyslexia is sometimes categorized as a developmental and neurological disorder.[22]

How Can Testing of Primitive and Postural Reflexes Be Used?

Primitive and postural reflexes can be used as clinical tools to

- identify signs of immaturity in the CNS (diagnosis);
- provide indications as to type and developmental level of intervention (appropriate treatment);
- measure change (clinical evaluation).

NEUROLOGICAL DYSFUNCTION IN SPECIFIC LEARNING DIFFICULTIES

By their very nature, symptoms of specific learning difficulties tend to cross diagnostic boundaries, with different categories sharing a number of symptoms in common. This is because 'common neurophysiological functions which feed and control postural mechanisms are fundamental to higher cognitive processes.'[23] They affect developmental aspects of motor, vestibular, and postural functions including

- visual and acoustic sequence processing;
- inadequate perception;
- graphic representation of geometrical forms;
- confused spatial organization;
- poor short-term memory;
- clumsiness;
- deficits in surface and deep structure language.

While the individual features of each category are unique to the condition, there is often an overlap in many presenting symptoms (co-morbidity). When areas of shared dysfunction are present, they are indicative of immaturity in the functioning of the CNS.

A number of years ago, a cluster of some of these signs and symptoms would have been described collectively under the more general and now redundant term of minimal brain dysfunction (MBD). This term was discarded in the 1960s and early 1970s, partly because there were over 99 symptoms listed under MBD with at least 10 major symptoms, making it too broad a definition on which to base or select effective clinical intervention. Nevertheless, MBD was an attempt to describe a 'grey area' between the disciplines of medicine, psychology, and education by listing a cluster of symptoms for which there was no clear pathology at the time.

The first ABC a child learns is the ABC of the body – the foundation on which cognitive learning is built and the mode through which it is expressed:

A = Attention
B = Balance
C = Coordination = developmental readiness for educational achievement.

In many cases, when co-morbidity is present, further investigations do reveal a general immaturity in the functioning of the CNS, which can be confirmed by a cluster of aberrant reflexes in the older child. The reasons for immature reflex development in the first year or years of life are generally multifactorial, but possible early signs of delay in reflex integration can be seen in a child's developmental profile, and some of these developmental markers will be explored further in Chapters 6 and 7. In the same way, the effects of aberrant reflexes on a child vary according to age and reflex profile of the individual child. Individual reflexes, their functions, and effects will be the subject of Chapters 2–5, which will examine the role of reflexes in early development and their impact on learning. Immaturity in the control of the body can affect educational achievement and behaviour in a number of ways. *Attention*, *balance*, and *coordination* are the first *ABC* on which *d*evelopmental readiness for *e*ducation is built.

DIAGNOSTIC CRITERIA, SIGNS, AND SYMPTOMS OF SPECIFIC LEARNING DIFFICULTIES

When parents first become aware that their child is experiencing difficulties, they are usually anxious to find a reason and/or a term to describe their child's problem. The child may be referred for assessment, and if the combination of problems fits into a recognized category, a diagnosis or label will be given. This diagnosis provides a description of a specific group of symptoms and indicates which types of intervention are likely to be helpful, but diagnosis in the area of specific learning difficulties does not always explain *why* the problem has developed, nor does it identify specific underlying mechanisms at fault. In other words, diagnosis in the area of educational difficulties frequently tells us *what* is wrong, but rarely reveals *why* it has happened.

In order to understand how and why postural problems can be factors in many specific learning difficulties, it is necessary to look at some of the individual features of specific learning difficulties and some of the possible underlying factors at a physical level which may be playing a part in the presenting symptoms (Figures 1.1 and 1.2).

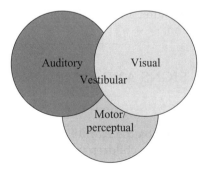

Figure 1.1   Co-morbidity of symptoms in specific learning difficulties: dyslexia

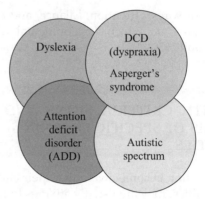

Figure 1.2 Co-morbidity in underlying problems in dyslexia, DCD, ADD, and in some aspects of autistic spectrum disorders

Each of the specific learning difficulties mentioned above shares impairment in the perception, organization, or execution of controlled movement: attention deficit hyperactivity disorder (ADHD), for example, involves inadequate inhibition of movement and inhibition of arousal to competing sensory stimuli. An important feature of dyspraxia or DCD is the inability to integrate sensory-motor experience and to organize motor output; children with dyslexia who have visual processing and motor-perceptual problems have difficulty with understanding direction, sequencing, and control of eye movements. Additionally, a large percentage of children with dyslexia also have phonological processing problems. Phonological and visual processing problems are often treated as discrete entities, even though hearing and listening *also* involve the perception of *motion* within a specific range of frequencies. Children diagnosed on the autistic spectrum suffer from disintegrated or fragmented sensory perception.

DYSLEXIA – SIGNS AND SYMPTOMS

Dyslexia

Dyslexia was defined by the World Federation of Neurology in 1968 as 'a disorder in children who, despite conventional classroom experience, fail to attain the language skills of reading, writing and spelling commensurate with their intellectual abilities.'[24] More recently, this definition has been expanded and described as 'a complex neurological condition which is constitutional in origin. The symptoms may affect many areas of learning and function and may be described as a specific difficulty in reading, spelling and written language. Additionally, one or more of the following areas may be affected: Numeracy, notational skills (music), motor function and organisational skills. However, dyslexia is particularly related to mastering written language, although oral language may be affected to some degree.'[25]

Associated symptoms

In addition to problems with reading, spelling, and written language expression, children with dyslexia often manifest problems with motor skills such as hopping and skipping, catching and throwing a ball; learning to ride a bicycle, coordination at gym and sometimes at swimming; and problems with directionality, such as telling left from right, laying a table correctly, and telling the time from an analogue clock. Problems with fine muscle skills may include difficulties tying shoelaces, doing buttons up, and manipulating a writing instrument. Sequencing, visual memory, and auditory perception may also be affected, and there may be ambiguity of laterality.[26] Performance in these areas is dependent upon the maturity of the reflex system which underlies motor learning, vestibular functioning, and kinaesthetic integration.

Neurological factors in dyslexia

Ever since dyslexia was first identified, it has been hypothesized that structural abnormalities in the brain may underlie the disorder. Post-mortem examination of the brains of five male and three females who had dyslexia revealed two consistent findings in the group: developmental neuropathology and symmetry of language-related regions of the brain.[27-29]

Over the last 40 years, research into dyslexia has focused upon four main areas of difficulty:

1. Difficulties with automatic balance originating from dysfunction in the vestibular-cerebellar loop;[30-33]
2. Immature motor skills;[34-38]

3. Auditory processing problems[39,40] and the phonological deficit theory;[41-45]
4. Abnormal processing of visual information.[46-48]

In 1996, Fawcett and Nicolson[33] concluded that 'children with dyslexia have deficits in phonological skill, speed of processing and motor skills. These deficits are well characterised as problems in skill automisation, which are normally masked by the process of conscious compensation.' Many other causal and contributory factors have also been suggested including differences in left hemisphere functioning, structure of the thalamus[49] – an area of the brain involved in processing and filtering sensory information – and genetic susceptibility for developmental dyslexia.[50]

Inheritable tendency through the male line has been associated with phonological processing problems. This may be because men have only one gene responsible for phonological processing, whereas women have two. If the gene responsible for phonological awareness, rapid naming, and verbal short-term memory is affected, males are less able to compensate for the problem. Females tend to use the language centres located in each cerebral hemisphere with greater flexibility than males. This may be in part due to the fact that the *corpus callosum* has been found to be larger in relation to brain weight and is more bulbous in females than in males, presumably facilitating increased inter-hemispheric communication.

Corpus callosum – the bundle of nerve fibres which allow for the exchange of information between the two cerebral hemispheres.

The automization of skills depends upon the maturity of the subcortical supporting systems within the brain, of which the primitive and postural reflex system (mediated at the level of the brainstem and the midbrain) is one of those underlying structures. Postural reflexes are important for maintenance of posture and the execution of controlled movements in cooperation with other centres such as the cerebellum, basal ganglia, and motor cortex.

Features of dyslexia:

• More common in males;
• Tends to run in families;
• Developmental history of clumsiness and minor speech impairments in rote learning (sequencing) such as learning the alphabet, days of the week, months of the year, multiplication tables, etc.

• Marginally late developmental milestones such as crawling (may have omitted crawling stage), walking, talking,
  and reading.

Difficulty with the following:

• ambi- or cross-laterality;
• telling left from right;
• letter and number reversals when reading and writing
  above the age of eight years;
• spatial reversals, mirror writing, and misordered letters;
• losing place when reading;
• following instructions (Tables 1.1–1.6).

Laterality

There is ambiguity of laterality or cross-laterality. Lack of
lateral preference can occur for many reasons. Some of these
will be covered in subsequent chapters (Tables 1.7 and 1.8).

DCD (DYSPRAXIA)

Dyspraxia means difficulty with praxis, praxis being a deri-
vation of the Greek word for 'action'. Formerly described as
the clumsy child syndrome, the term dyspraxia has currently been replaced by DCD. DCD is defined by the *Diagnostic Statistical Manual of Mental Disorders*[53] as

> A marked impairment in the development of motor coordi-
> nation (criterion A). The diagnosis is made only if this
> impairment significantly interferes with academic achieve-
> ment or activities of daily living (criterion B). The diagnosis
> is made if the coordination difficulties are not due to a
> general medical condition.
>
> **Criterion A**
>
> Performance in daily activities that require motor coordina-
> tion is substantially below that expected given the person's
> chronological age and measured intelligence. This may
> be manifested by marked delays in achieving motor mile-
> stones, dropping things, poor performance in sports or poor
> handwriting.

Table 1.1   Physical symptoms in dyslexia

Motor skills	Symptom	Subcortical mechanisms/ systems involved
Gross motor skills	Hopping, skipping, forward rolls	Balance, sequencing of movements (cerebellum), and upper/lower body integration
	Catching, throwing, and kicking a ball	Hand/eye, eye/foot coordination
	Clumsy when going upstairs	Left/right, upper- and lower-body coordination
	Marginally late developmental milestones, e.g. crawling, walking, talking, and reading	Balance, posture, bilateral integration
	Learning to ride a bicycle	Vestibular, postural and bilateral integration
	Learning to swim	Poor upper- and lower-body and left/ right coordination
	Coordination at gym, climbing a rope, working with an apparatus	Vestibular, postural, hypotonic, upper- and lower-body integration
Fine motor skills	Difficulty using equipment, e.g. scissors, cutlery	Fine motor skills, dysdiadochokinesis (cerebellum and motor cortex)
	Immature or awkward pencil grip	Retained reflexes affecting manual dexterity
	Difficulty learning to tie shoelaces, do buttons up, etc.	Fine motor skills, directionality (vestibular), left/right integration

Table 1.2 Directionality problems in dyslexia

Symptoms	Underlying mechanisms/systems involved
Left/right, up/down, before/after discrimination	Spatial (vestibular)
Orientation	Vestibular
Laying a table correctly	Spatial (vestibular)
Putting clothes on the right way round	Spatial (vestibular)
Following or giving directions	Auditory processing, sequential processing (cerebellum), directional (vestibular)
Jigsaw puzzles and mazes	Spatial (vestibular)
Learning to tell the time from an analogue clock	Spatial (vestibular)
History of motion sickness which continues beyond puberty	Vestibular-visual-proprioceptive mismatch

Table 1.3 Speech and language symptoms in dyslexia

Symptoms	Underlying mechanisms/systems involved
Letter, number, and word reversals	Directionality (vestibular), auditory discrimination and/or sequencing (phonological/cerebellum), lateral organization
Word-naming problems	Visual and/or auditory recognition and recall; inter-hemispheric communication
Mispronunciation	Auditory and oral-motor discrimination
Confusion/substitution of wrong words	Auditory and/or visual discrimination (reading)
Poor use of syntax	
Difficulties with rhyme and alliteration	Sequencing, auditory discrimination, inter-hemispheric communication
Hesitant speech	
Poor memory for new words and word recall	Coding and retrieval

Table 1.4   Sequencing problems in dyslexia

Symptoms	Underlying mechanisms/systems
Rote learning	Cerebellum, inter-hemispheric communication
Board games that involve planning a series of moves	Spatial (vestibular), procedural (cerebellum); forward planning (frontal lobes), procedural memory

Table 1.5   Visual symptoms in dyslexia

Symptom	Underlying mechanisms/systems
Letter, word, number reversals	Directional (vestibular), visual (unstable supporting postural mechanisms), laterality, auditory delay
Mirror writing	Directional (vestibular)
Poor memory for word shape and pattern	Visual processing (right hemisphere)
Poor memory for detailed features of words	Left hemisphere, phonological processing
Scotopic sensitivity syndrome (SSS)	Immaturity in the visual system's response to light
Difficulties with visual tracking	Underdeveloped postural mechanisms which support oculomotor functioning
Letter, word blurring/movement/omission	Poor near-point convergence

SSS
The nerve endings at the back of the retina of the eye are relayed to the thalamus, an area of the brain involved in filtering sensory information before it reaches the cortex, by two specialized types:

1. small cell bodies concerned mostly with colour hues and contrast (parvocellular pathways);
2. large cell bodies concerned mostly with movement *detection (magnocellular pathways).*

A body of research indicates that in dyslexia, these cell bodies do not differentiate their functions adequately, resulting in visual dysfunctions and *overlapping of functions between the two pathways.*

Evidence suggests that dysfunctions in the magnocellular pathways are responsible for difficulties with visual motion detection in dyslexia. *The effect of dysfunction in the relationship between the two pathways is problems with perception of form when there is high contrast between dark print on a white background.*

Table 1.6 Auditory symptoms in dyslexia

Symptom	Underlying mechanisms/systems
Confusion or inability to hear the difference between different sounds	Auditory discrimination – may be connected to a history of frequent ear, nose, or throat infections in the first 3–5 years of life
Difficulty in processing auditory information	Laterality of auditory processing
Difficulty repeating rhymes	Sequencing (cerebellum), music of language (right hemisphere)
Difficulty following sequential instructions	Auditory delay (laterality of auditory processing), cerebellum, short-term memory
Difficulty in clapping or tapping out rhythms	Vestibular

Table 1.7 Phobic disorders in dyslexia

Symptom	Underlying mechanisms/systems
Fear of the dark, heights, new places	Poor orientation in the absence of visual points of reference (vestibular/proprioceptive)
Fear/avoidance of motor-related activities	Immature coordination and postural control
Mood disturbances	Performance anxiety, frustration, orientation problems, biochemical, hormonal
Obsessive–compulsive tendencies	Increased metabolic activity in left orbital gyrus,[51] deficiency in availability of the neurotransmitter serotonin,[52] heightened glucose metabolism in the frontal lobes

Table 1.8 Psychosomatic symptoms in dyslexia

Symptom	Underlying mechanisms/systems
Headaches	Visual stress, structural misalignment (skeletal)
Dizziness	Vestibular, visual, low blood pressure
Motion sickness	Vestibular-ocular-proprioceptive mismatch
Bed-wetting	Neurological immaturity; persistent ear, nose, or throat infections resulting in congestion; retained spinal Galant reflex
Free-floating anxiety	Vestibular dysfunction and/or postural control resulting in gravitational insecurity, poor spatial awareness, perceptual problems, and difficulty coding environmental stimuli

Criterion B

- The disturbance in Criterion A significantly interferes with academic achievement or activities of daily
living.
- The disturbance is not due to a medical condition and does
not meet the criteria for a pervasive developmental
disorder.
- If mental retardation is present, the motor difficulties are in
excess of those usually associated with it.

DCD is characterized by impairment or immaturity in the
organization of movement. This involves problems with
coordination of sensory-motor functions. Jean Ayres, an
American occupational therapist who developed the system
of sensory-motor training known as *Sensory Integration*,
explained the problems of the clumsy child as stemming
from difficulty with the *visualization*, *ideation* (motor planning), and *execution* of voluntary movement. In addition
to motor problems, the child with DCD can also have associated problems with perception, language, thought, and
behaviour. These are usually a secondary outcome of the
primary sensory-motor coordination problem. Symptoms of
DCD fall into three main categories: motor coordination,
perceptual functioning, and learning abilities (Tables 1.9
and 1.10).

This combination of motor and sensory problems can then
affect learning ability in a number of ways.

Learning Problems

- Attention and concentration;
- Organizational difficulties;
- Poor visual and auditory coding and memory;
- Writing;
- Coping;
- Reading;
- Presentation of work.

Some signs and symptoms are specific to one
particular diagnostic category, while others are shared
by all.

Table 1.9   Motor coordination symptoms in DCD

Symptoms	Underlying mechanisms/systems
Hypotonia (low muscle tone), which can manifest itself in poor posture and fatigue	Vestibular/postural, often linked to a retained symmetrical tonic neck reflex
Lack of coordination in the use of the two sides of the body	Bilateral integration, sometimes linked to a retained asymmetrical tonic neck reflex
Vertical midline problems	Retained asymmetrical tonic neck reflex
Poor balance	Vestibular, postural, and immature righting reflexes and equilibrium reactions
Lack of truncal differentiation	Upper- and lower-body integration (symmetrical tonic neck reflex)
Need to learn and practise motor tasks; practice does not make permanent	Cortical compensation for immature postural control, poor bilateral integration
Directionality problems, e.g. up/down, left/right, front/back, before/after	Spatial (vestibular)
Gross and fine motor coordination difficulties, e.g. learning to ride a bicycle, do buttons up, tie shoelaces, etc.	Vestibular, proprioceptive, visual and visual-motor integration
Hand–eye coordination difficulties, e.g. throwing or catching a ball, threading a needle, copying writing, and drawing	Primary or secondary visual problems: Primary problems resulting from eyesight; secondary resulting from oculomotor problems resulting from immaturity in the functioning of the CNS and from a cluster of immature primitive and postural reflexes
Poor manual dexterity particularly with *dysdiadochokinesis*	Poor fine motor control – can be impaired as a result of retained palmar or oral reflexes
Speed and clarity of speech	Can result from many areas in the brain; motor aspects of speech can be affected by retained oral reflexes

Dysdiadochokinesis – *difficulty with rapid alternate movements; can affect the fingers, hands, feet, and the speech apparatus.*

Table 1.10   Sensory processing problems in DCD

Symptoms	Underlying mechanisms/systems
Hyper- or hyposensitive in one or several sensory modalities	Poor integration between the sensory systems – there can be a number of causes for this; developmental history is important to identify specific underlying factors
Tactile hypersensitivity with a tendency to withdraw from contact, or hyposensitivity, which can result in poorly developed sense of body image and in difficulty recognizing shapes and textures	Can result from retained Moro or infant tactile reflexes
Vestibular problems resulting in poor balance, awareness of position in space, ability to make accurate spatial judgements, and sense of direction, speed and rhythm	Hyper- or hypovestibular; may be a primary or secondary dysfunction resulting from retained vestibular reflexes in the older child, and underdeveloped righting and equilibrium reactions resulting in a mismatch in the feedback loop from the proprioceptive system to the vestibular system
Auditory processing problems: discrimination, orientation, speed of processing, filtering out background noise	Developmental history of hearing impairment; unilateral hearing impairment, poorly developed auditory laterality, retained Moro reflex
Visual: control of eye movements, visual discrimination, spatial organization, form constancy, figure-ground effect, stimulus-bound effect	Primary refractive problems (eyesight); in the absence of refractive problems, oculomotor problems resulting in visual-perceptual problems are likely to stem from underlying postural dysfunction; specific visual-perceptual problems can result from damage to the right frontal lobe

ATTENTION DEFICIT DISORDER (ADD)

The essential feature of ADD is a persistent pattern of inattention that is more frequent and severe than is typically observed in individuals at a comparable level of development.

ADHD is now classified as a separate category from ADD, the additional criteria being a persistent pattern of inattention and hyperactivity/impulsivity that is more frequent and severe than typically observed in individuals at a comparable level of development. Symptoms that cause impairment must have been present before seven years of age, and the symptoms must be present in at least two settings (e.g. home and school). There must be clear evidence of interference with developmentally appropriate social, academic, or occupational functioning.

ADD and ADHD appear to involve many layers within the hierarchy of the brain from the cortex's inability to focus and to maintain attention on tasks at the top, down to supporting systems involved in spatial organization, sensory integration, and auditory processing, which should support the higher cognitive functions.

The clinical criteria for ADD have been established as the presence of six or more of the following signs, which have persisted for at least six months and to a degree that is maladaptive and inconsistent with the developmental level:

- Often fails to give close attention to details or makes careless mistakes in schoolwork, work, or other activities;
- Often has difficulty sustaining attention or tasks or play activities;
- Often does not seem to listen when spoken to directly;
- Often does not follow through on instructions and fails to finish schoolwork, chores, or duties in the workplace;
- Often has difficulty organizing tasks and activities;
- Often avoids, dislikes, or is reluctant to engage in tasks that require sustained mental effort;
- Often loses things necessary for tasks or activities;
- Is often easily distracted by extraneous stimuli;
- Is often forgetful in daily activities;
- Excessive daydreaming;

- Frequent staring;
- Lethargic;
- Confusion;
- Memory problems.

ADD is currently thought to be the result of a problem with the brain's processing system, whereas ADHD is connected with the behavioural motor system.[54]

Symptoms of ADHD

Six or more of the following must have persisted for more than six months to a degree that is inconsistent or maladaptive with the developmental level (Table 1.11):

Table 1.11   Criteria for ADHD

Symptoms	Physical mechanisms/systems involved
Often fidgets with hands or feet or squirms in seat	Immature postural control, inability to inhibit extraneous movement when at rest, may involve poor regulation of the neurotransmitter dopamine
Often leaves seat in class or in other situations in which it is inappropriate	Reticular activating system (RAS) involved in arousal and attention, frontal lobes (voluntary control of attention), temporal-parietal regions (involuntary attention[55])
Often runs about, climbs excessively in situations in which it is inappropriate	Poor inhibition of movement or poor ability to maintain 'stillness', immature posture and motor skills, continuous need to provide stimulation to the vestibular system (hypoactive vestibular)
Often has difficulty playing or engaging in leisure activities quietly	Needs continuous sensory (auditory and vocal) feedback, seems unable to 'internalize' thoughts
Is often 'on the go' or acts as if 'driven by a motor'	Unable to inhibit excess movement; needs constant motor and sensory feedback; needs to change down a gear (up the revs) to keep going; thought to be related to slower firing rate in the beta brainwaves; probably stems from a combination of hypovestibular functioning, immature motor skills, and hyperarousal (RAS) differences in the availability of neurotransmitters and abnormal brainwave variants

UNDERACHIEVEMENT

There also exists a group of children who do not qualify for assessment nor do they fit into any diagnostic category. These are usually children of above-average intelligence who are able to compensate for their underlying motor and postural problems to produce academic work that is commensurate with their chronological age or 'good enough' to meet the minimum requirements of standard educational assessments. These bright children are held back by their unrecognized motor and postural problems and tend to become 'lost in the system' because it is assumed they are performing reasonably well. Examination of this group for neurological dysfunction frequently reveals a profile of neurological immaturity which is masked by the processes of conscious compensation. When the underlying problems are identified and corrected, cognitive educational performance exceeds previous expectations.

THE SENSORY-MOTOR CONNECTION

All forms of life share the characteristic of motion, and movement is the vital ingredient of all forms of sensory perception and motor output. For example, the vestibular system (balance mechanism) comprises specialized receptors that respond to *slow* movements of the head. The sense of touch arises from the sensation of movement across fine hairs bedded into the dermis of the skin or of pressure applied to skin. The sense of hearing detects vibrations which travel at speeds from 20 to 20,000 Hz shortly after birth, narrowing down to a smaller range of frequencies in the first three to six years of life. What we perceive as sound is the ability of sound receptors to detect a specific range of motion frequencies. Similarly, at a simplistic level, vision is the response of specialized receptors in the eye which detect photons and waves of light travelling at faster frequencies still. While the senses keep the brain informed about momentary changes in the internal and external environments, each specializing in a different type of movement, it is the job of the CNS to conduct and to convert those impulses into meaningful sensations. Sensory experience and arousal are just the first phases of perception.

While the sensory systems provide information about the environment (feeling), *integration* of sensory experience takes place as a result of action or motor output in response to sensory signals (doing). Mastery of motor skills is supported by posture, and good postural control is the product of an integrated reflex system. In this way, the reflex system is the foundation on which higher postural- and motor-dependent skills are built. The significance of feedback from the motor system to the sensory systems is illustrated by the development of vision.

'Nothing that is seen is understood by the sense of vision alone.'[56] In other words, what we experience through vision as adults is actually the product of years of *multi*sensory experience – a compound sense – which has developed as a result of sight combined with moving, touching, and proprioceptive feedback from the muscles, tendons, and joints of the body in response to movement of the body through space. A newborn baby knows nothing of distance, speed, or depth. He or she can only focus at a distance of approximately 17 cm from the face, and the internal features of objects have little meaning until they have also been experienced through the other senses. The mother's voice and the taste of her milk are more familiar to the neonate than how she looks in the first days of life, but the senses of smell, sound, and touch will all help the baby to recognize her visually within a few days.

I mentioned the infant rooting reflex earlier as a well-recognized example of a primitive reflex in the newborn. It also serves as an example of how one sensory system combined with movement experience helps to train another sense. The rooting reflex ensures that when the side of the neonate's mouth is touched, the mouth opens, the head turns, and the baby will nuzzle against an object, searching for the breast (cats do something similar when they are hungry, brushing up against an object). Provided the baby receives satisfaction for its rooting attempts, within a few short weeks, the *sight* of the breast or bottle alone will be enough to elicit sucking movements.

It is also of interest to realize that a baby's focusing distance at birth is approximately the same as the distance between the breast and its mother's face. When a baby sucks, his eyes tend to converge at near distance, helping to train the eye muscles to line up together to focus on the object at near distance and to 'fuse' the two separate objects seen by each into one clear image instead of two. In other words, the *action* of sucking assists in a process of oculomotor training which will later support the more complex visual-perceptual skills needed for reading, writing, and judging the speed of moving objects in a more advanced form. The eyes are but a window for the brain. In order to 'make sense' of what is seen, the brain must receive additional information from other senses combined with motor experience. A child's reflex profile can provide additional information about motor competency in relation to chronological age and may help to explain why a child's oculomotor skills, for example, are immature.

THEORIES OF MOTOR CONTROL

The brain comprises many separate entities which are all interlinked and interdependent. At birth, connections to the superficial layer of the cortex are only tenuously formed and in the first months and years of life, the developing nervous system forms millions of new connections between the nerve cells which provide a network of communication or neural circuitry of almost unimaginable complexity. It is on this neural circuitry – a circuitry that will adapt and change all through life – that behaviour and learning will be based. The layering of connections between motor areas is sometimes viewed as a hierarchy of systems, which involves multiple levels of control and is open to modification as a result of many influences – developmental, biochemical, and environmental. Reflex assessment provides one method of assessing maturity in hierarchical functioning.

During the process of normal development, functional direction and organized control of movement proceeds from the lowest regions of the brain (the brainstem) to the highest level of the CNS, the cortex. This process of corticalization is characterized by the emergence of behaviours organized at sequentially higher levels in the CNS with lower levels being recruited into the service of higher functions as maturation takes place. Each level of the nervous system can act upon other levels, higher and lower, in either direction, depending on the task. Reflex status can therefore provide indications of integration in how the brain functions as well as point to specific receptors which may be involved in presenting symptoms. In order to gain an understanding of what primitive and postural reflexes can tell us, it is necessary to know what they do, both individually and collectively in early development, when they are inhibited, the interrelationship between inhibition and the development of new skills, and the possible effects if primitive reflexes fail to be inhibited or if postural reflexes do not develop fully. In Chapters 2–5, we will examine reflexes according to their main sensory receptors: the Moro reflex, a multi-sensory reflex; reflexes of position; reflexes of touch; and postural reflexes.

REFERENCES

1 Levinson HN. 1984. *Smart but Feeling Dumb*. Warner Books Inc., New York.
2 Frank J, Levinson HN. 1976. Compensatory mechanisms in cerebellar-vestibular dysfunction, dysmetric dyslexia and dyspraxia. *Academic Therapy* 12:1–14.
3 Leiner HC et al. 1993. Cognitive and language functions of the human cerebellum. *Trends in Neuroscience* 16:444–447.
4 Bobath B. 1978. *Abnormal Postural Reflex Activity Caused by Brain Lesions, 3rd ed*. William Heinemann Medical Books Ltd, London.
5 Hughlings Jackson J. 1946. Cited in: Walshe FMR. 1923. On certain tonic or postural reflexes in hemiplegia with special reference to the so-called associated movements. *Brain* Part 1.46/2,14:16–23.
6 Halleck RP. 1898. *Education of the Nervous System*. Macmillan and Company Ltd, New York.
7 Gustafsson D. 1971. A comparison of basis reflexes with the subtests of the Purdue-Perceptual-Motor Survey. Unpublished Master's Thesis. University of Kansas.
8 Rider B. 1976. Relationship of postural reflexes to learning disabilities. *American Journal of Occupational Therapy* 26/5: 239–243.
9 Bender ML. 1976. *Bender-Purdue Reflex Test and Training Manual*. Academic Publications, San Rafael, CA.
10 Blythe P, McGlown DJ. 1979. *An Organic Basis for Neuroses and Educational Difficulties*. Insight Publications, Chester.
11 Wilkinson G. 1994. The relationship of primitive and postural reflexes to learning difficulty and under-achievement. Unpublished MEd Thesis. University of Newcastle-upon-Tyne.

12 Goddard Blythe S. 2001. Neurological dysfunction as a significant factor in children diagnosed with dyslexia. *Proceedings of The 5th International British Dyslexia Association Conference.* University of York, April, 2001.

13 Taylor M et al. 2004. Primitive reflexes and attention-deficit/ hyperactivity disorder: developmental origins of classroom dysfunction. *International Journal of Special Education* 19/1: 23–37.

14 McPhillips M, Sheehy N. 2004. Prevalence of persistent primary reflexes and motor problems in children with reading difficulties. *Dyslexia* 10/4:316–338.

15 Goddard Blythe SA. 2005. Releasing educational potential through movement. A summary of individual studies carried out using the INPP Test Battery and Developmental Exercise Programme for use in schools with children with special needs. *Child Care in Practice* 11/4:415–432.

16 Bobath K, Bobath B. 1965. *Abnormal Postural Reflex Activity Caused by Brain Lesions.* William Heinemann, London.

17 Ayres AJ. 1972. Improving academic scores through sensory integration. *Journal of Learning Disabilities* 5:338–343.

18 Fiorentino MR. 1981. *Reflex Testing Methods for Evaluating C.N.S. Development.* Charles C Thomas, Springfield, IL.

19 Levitt S. 1984. *Treatment of Cerebral Palsy and Motor Delay.* Oxford, Blackwell Scientific Publications.

20 Bender ML. 1976. *Bender-Purdue Reflex Test and Training Manual.* Academic Publications, San Rafael, CA.

21 Blythe P, McGlown DJ. 1979. *An Organic Basis for Neuroses and Educational Difficulties.* Insight Publications, Chester.

22 Rosen GD et al. 1993. Dyslexia and brain pathology: experimental animal models. In: Galaburda AM (Ed.). *Dyslexia and Development. Neurobiological Aspects of Extraordinary Brains.* Harvard University Press, Cambridge, MA.

23 Kohen-Raz R. 1986. *Learning Disabilities and Postural Control.* Freund Publishing House, London.

24 World Federation of Neurology. 1968. Report of research group on developmental dyslexia and world illiteracy. *Bulletin of the Orton Society* 18:21–22.

25 British Dyslexia Association. 1998. *The Dyslexia Handbook.* The British Dyslexia Association, Reading.

26 Ott P. 1997. *How to Detect and Manage Dyslexia. A Resource Manual.* Heinemann, Oxford.

27 Galaburda AM, Kemper TL. 1979. Cytoarchitectonic abnormalities in developmental dyslexia: A case study. *Annals of Neurology* 6:94–100.

28 Galaburda AM et al. 1985. Developmental dyslexia: four consecutive patients with cortical anomalies. *Annals of Neurology* 18:222–223.

29 Humphreys P et al. 1990. Developmental dyslexia in women: neuropathological findings in three cases. *Annals of Neurology* 28:727–738.

30 Levinson HN. 1974. Dyslexia: does this unusual childhood syndrome begin as an ear infection? *Infectious Diseases* 15.

31 De Quirós JB, Schrager OL. 1978. *Neurological Fundamentals in Learning Disabilities.* Academic Therapy Publications Inc., Novato, CA.

32 Nicolson RI, Fawcett AJ. 1990. A new framework for dyslexia research? *Cognition* 35:159–182.

33 Fawcett AJ et al. 1996. Impaired performance of children with dyslexia on a range of cerebellar tests. *Annals of Dyslexia* 46:259–283.

34 Blythe P, McGlown DJ. 1979. *An Organic Basis for Neuroses and Educational Difficulties.* Insight Publications, Chester.

35 Augur J. 1985. Guidelines for teachers, parents and learners. In: Snowling M (Ed.). *Children's Written Language Difficulties.* NFER Nelson, Windsor.

36 Denckla MB et al. 1985. Motor performance in dyslexic children with and without attentional disorders. *Archives of Neurology* 42:228–231.

37 Goddard SA. 1996. *A Teacher's Window into the Child's Mind.* Fern Ridge Press, Eugene, OR.

38 Goddard Blythe SA. 2001. Neurological dysfunction as a significant factor in children diagnosed with dyslexia. *The 5th BDA International Conference.* University of York, April, 2001.

39 Geschwind N, Levitsky W. 1968. Left-right asymmetries in the temporal speech region. *Science* 161:186–87.

40 Tallal P, Piercy M. 1974. Developmental aphasia: rate of auditory processing and selective impairment of consonant perception. *Neuropsychologia* 12:83–98.

41 Geschwind N, Galaburda AM. 1985. *Cerebral Lateralisation.* MIT Press, Cambridge, MA.

42 Dalby MA. 1986. Aspects in reading processes. In: Troudhjem K (Ed.). *12th Danavox Symposium.* Danavox, Denmark.

43 Johansen KV. 1988. Sensory deprivation – a possible cause of dyslexia. *Nordisk Tidsskrift for Spesialpedagogikk.* Scandinavian University Press, Oslo.

44 Shaywitz SE. 1996. Dyslexia. *Scientific American,* November, pp. 98–104.

45 Tallal P. 1996. Language learning impairment: integrating research and remediation. *Orton Dyslexia Society 47th Annual Conference Commemorative Booklet.* Orton Dyslexia Society, Boston, MA.

46 Galaburda AM et al. 1986. Histological asymmetry in the primary visual cortex of the rat: implications for mechanisms of cerebral asymmetry. *Cortex* 22:151–160.

47 Pavlidis G, Miles T. 1987. *Dyslexia Research and its Applications to Education.* Wiley, Chichester.

48 Chase C, Jenner A. 1993. Magnocellular visual deficits affect temporal processing of dyslexics. In: Tallal P et al. (Eds). *Temporal Information Processing in the Nervous System, with Special Reference to Dyslexia and Dysphasia.* New York Academy of Sciences, New York.

49 Galaburda AL. 2001. Dyslexia and the brain. *The 5th International BDA Conference Proceedings.* University of York, April, 2001.

50 Nopola-Hemme et al. 2001. A dominant gene for developmental dyslexia on chromosome 3. *Journal of Medical Genetics* 38:658–664.

51 Bower B. 1987. Images of obsession. *Science News* 131:236–237.

52 Jenike et al. 1989. Obsessive compulsive disorder: a double blind, placebo controlled trial of clomiprimine in 27 patients. *American Journal of Psychiatry* 146:1328–1330.

53 *Diagnostic and Statistical Manual of Mental Disorders – DSM-IV.* 1994. American Psychiatric Association, Washington, DC.

54 Barkley RA. 1995. *Taking Charge of ADHD: the Complete, Authoritative Guide for Parents.* Guilford, New York.

55 Schaughnecy EA, Hynd GW. 1989. Attention and impulse control in attention deficit disorders (ADD). *Learning and Individual Differences* 1:423–449.

56 Alhazen BC. Cited in: Arnheim R. 1969. *Visual Thinking.* University of California Press, Berkeley, CA.

CHAPTER 2

THE SIGNIFICANCE OF PRIMITIVE AND POSTURAL REFLEXES

Reflexes were described as early as the 17th century by physician Thomas Willis when he used the term 'motus reflexus' and 'reflexion' to describe how impulses of spirits in the nerves to the central nervous system could be 'reflected' back to the muscles. He described the automatic action as being similar to light bouncing off a mirror.

There are many different types of reflex. Although they differ in many respects, they share the common property of being stereotyped and constant 'because the same stimulus always gives the same kind of response.'[1] Some reflexes like the blink reflex are simple; others like the swallowing reflex are more complex, involving the cooperation of many structures. Some reflexes only involve lower parts of the central nervous system such as the spinal cord and the brainstem, whereas others, such as the oculo-head righting reflexes (OHRRs), involve higher parts of the nervous system, including the cortex. 'Many of the tasks of the nervous system are carried out reflexively – that is, independent of our consciousness. This, of course, frees the higher levels of the brain from handling numerous trivial every-day tasks.'[1] Although reflexes largely operate independently of will, some, such as reflexes for emptying the bladder and rectum, can be suppressed voluntarily; others, such as reflexes involved in the control or *visceral* functions, take place without any conscious awareness. Primitive and postural reflexes provide useful tools with which to assess the central nervous system, because they are *developmental* in terms of when they should be active and *hierarchical* in terms of the level of the nervous system involved.

The viscera *are the soft internal organs of the body, including the lungs, the heart, and the organs of the digestive system. Visceral functions are functions involving these systems.*

WHAT ARE PRIMITIVE AND POSTURAL REFLEXES?

Primitive reflexes develop in the womb, are present at birth in the full-term neonate, and are inhibited by higher centres in the developing brain in the first six months of post-natal life.

Postural reflexes emerge after birth and take up to three and a half years to be fully developed. By the time a child reaches school age, in theory at least, the postural reflexes should be developed, and no obvious signs of continued primitive reflex activity should be evident.

WHAT CAN PRIMITIVE AND POSTURAL REFLEXES TELL US?

Collectively, abnormality in the profile of these two groups of reflexes provides indications of neurological dysfunction or neurological immaturity.

1. Assessment of primitive and postural reflexes at key stages in development can be used to identify signs of *immaturity* in the functioning of the nervous system (identification). Many of the primitive reflexes are tested as a matter of routine at birth, as part of the neonatal neurological examination, but are rarely carried out later in development unless a neurological problem is suspected.
2. Reflex tests can be used again at later stages of development on the school-aged child, but when they are used on the older child, the examiner will be looking for signs of inappropriately *retained* primitive reflexes and *under-developed* postural reflexes (assessment).
3. Reflex evaluation can also provide indications of the type and developmental level of intervention needed to integrate abnormal reflexes (remediation).
4. Reflex tests can also be used during and after an intervention programme to measure the changes that have occurred as a result of remedial intervention (evaluation).

In order to understand how reflex testing can be used in these ways, it is necessary to examine reflex development in the broader context of general development and also individually in more specific detail.

THE DEVELOPING BRAIN

The nervous system begins to develop very early in embryonic life. In fact, just three weeks after fertilization, the ectoderm, the outer layer of the three sheets of cells that make up the embryo at this very early stage, thickens to form a neural plate. The neural plate then develops a neural groove; neural crest cells form, and the neural grove deepens to form the neural folds. One week later, the neural folds fuse to form a neural tube, which dilates to form the beginning of the forebrain, midbrain, and hindbrain, while the remainder of the tube elongates to form what will become the spinal cord. At five weeks, the forebrain and hindbrain (vesicles) divide, and the cerebral hemispheres begin to expand. At six weeks, the thalamus, which will later act as a central 'relay' and processing station for all sensory information with the exception of smell, and the cerebellum or 'little brain', which will be involved in the coordination of movement and automization of motor output, appear (Figure 2.1).

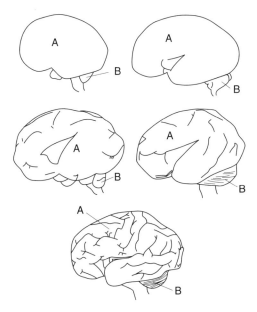

Figure 2.1 The maturing brain from four to eight months' gestation. A, cerebral hemisphere; B, cerebellum

At eight weeks, the brain starts to take on a human appearance and the first reflex arc becomes functional. Reflex actions, described by Sherrington[2] in the early 1900s, are a functional unit comprising an effector (sense organ), conductor (at least two or more nerve cells), and a receptor. These components make up the reflex arc:

Action potential – the change in membrane potential occurring in nerve, muscle, or other excitable tissue when excitation occurs.

• A *receptor* – which registers the stimulus and translates the stimulus to *action potentials*;
• An *afferent link*, comprising a sensory neuron, which conducts the action potential to the nervous system;
• A *reflex centre* in which the signals from the receptor may be modified (increased or decreased) by signals from other receptors and from parts of the central nervous system before signals are passed on to *effectors*;
• An *efferent link* comprising neurons passing *out* of the central nervous system, which conducts action potentials to the organ producing the response;
• An *effector*, which is the responding muscle(s) or glands.

One of the functions of the *receptor* is to lower the threshold for a particular type of stimulus while raising the threshold for all others. In this way, reflexes are responses to specific types of stimulation. Because they are largely carried out below the level of conscious awareness, reflexes provide information about the integrity of the nervous system free from interference from the psyche.

THE EMERGENCE OF SPINAL REFLEXES

The earliest reflex-type response appears at five to seven and a half weeks after conception in response to tactile stimulation of the area which will eventually form the upper lip. Stroking with a fine hair elicits withdrawal of the head, neck, and trunk.[3,4] Over the course of the succeeding weeks, tactile sensitivity and reactivity spreads from the upper lip in an outward spiral pattern to encompass more of the area around the mouth, the palms of the hands, and the soles of the feet until eventually, by 13–14 weeks post-conception, the whole body surface will become responsive to touch. The initial reaction to this type of stimulation is one of withdrawal and is an example of a *spinal reflex*.

Spinal reflexes function at the base of the hierarchical control system. They are somatic reflexes mediated by the spinal cord, but they can involve higher brain centres. When a spinal reflex is elicited, the message is simultaneously sent to the spinal cord and the brain, but the reflex triggers the response from the spinal level without waiting for higher brain analysis. Withdrawal reflexes such as the *flexor withdrawal reflex* and the *crossed extensor reflex* are other examples of spinal reflexes.

REFLEXES MEDIATED AT THE SPINAL LEVEL

Flexor Withdrawal Reflex

The flexor withdrawal reflex is sometimes referred to as the 'flight reflex', the defence reflex, or the negative supporting reaction. Reflex movement at this level is used as a protective defence against threatening stimuli at the only level the infant has available at the time – withdrawal. The flexor withdrawal reflex can be elicited with the neonate lying in the supine position by stimulating the sole of the foot with a sharp instrument (pin prick). The response is extension of the toes, dorsiflexion of the foot, and flexion of the limb from the knee and the hip (withdrawal). The opposite leg may also be involved in the response. The flexor withdrawal reflex is present at birth and may remain active until independent walking is established.[5]

Crossed Extensor Reflex

The crossed extensor reflex emerges at 28 weeks' gestation and is inhibited at four months of post-natal life.

The crossed extensor reflex is elicited by applying pressure to the ball of the foot on one side, which results in extension (kicking) of the leg on the other side. This reflex is tested in the supine position with the head at midline. One leg is extended and held at the knee, while firm pressure is applied to the ball of the foot. The response is flexion in the opposite leg followed by adduction and then extension. Inhibition normally takes place by four months of post-natal life as the sequence of the response changes to adduction – extension

– flexion. However, the cross extensor reflex may reappear as a defence response in adults when walking on rough terrain, such as walking barefoot on a shingle beach. If it remains active after four months of age, it is associated with gravitational instability from the base when standing, an unusually narrow base of support, and poor reciprocal kicking movements in the baby.

REFLEXES MEDIATED IN THE BRAINSTEM

Between 9 and 12 weeks, the first of the *primitive reflexes* emerges, but it will take many more weeks for each individual reflex to mature. The first of the primitive reflexes to emerge – the Moro reflex – starts as a withdrawal reaction, but as it develops, the nature of the response begins to change from an initial withdrawal phase to one of 'embrace'.

In the past, observation of preterm infants used to be limited to examining viable premature infants or non-viable aborted embryos placed in a body-warm saline bath for the remainder of their short extra-uterine life.[3] During the 1970s, the development of ultrasound techniques made it possible to carry out less invasive and more direct observation of foetal behaviour using more systematic investigations. More recently, the development of four-dimensional ultrasound has made more detailed observation of prenatal development possible including observation of eye movements, hand and finger movements, and foetal breathing movements.

The emergence of the Moro reflex at 9 to 12 weeks after conception is followed by development of reflexes related to grasping and feeding.[3,4,6] The grasp reflexes become evident in the hands at 10.5 weeks and involve closing of the fingers when the palm of the hand is stroked; by 11.5 weeks, the toes flex in response to stimulation of the sole of the foot (plantar grasp reflex). The feeding reflexes first appear with opening of the mouth at 9.5 weeks and with ipsilateral rotation of the head in response to stimulation of the outside edge of the mouth by 11.5 weeks. Momentary lip closure and swallowing in response to stimulation of the lip can be seen at 12.5 weeks. Signs of the Babkin and pal-momental reflexes (details of which are given later) can be elicited at 13 weeks, tongue movements at 14 weeks, the gag reflex at 18 weeks, and protrusion and pursing of the lips by 20–22 weeks. Sucking movements develop between 20 and 24 weeks.[7] A feature of both grasping and feeding reflexes is that as they mature, they seek to 'hold on' to the stimulus. In other words, whereas the earliest reflex responses were ones of avoidance (withdrawal), as the primitive reflexes mature, they supersede the earlier response (unless the stimulus is noxious), and the *nature* of the response changes. The emergence of individual primitive reflexes heralds the development of increase in connections within the developing nervous system.

Sherrington[2] described each reflex as having an integrative function with coordination resulting from the compounding of individual reflexes. Although this is now considered to be an overly simplistic and mechanistic view of the functioning of the nervous system, it has, nevertheless, provided a theoretical and practical basis for the use of evaluation of reflexes as 'markers' of development and for hierarchical integrity in the functioning of the nervous system.

Once the main organs have been formed in the first trimester of pregnancy, a spurt of foetal brain growth takes place from mid-gestation onwards, but 85 per cent of brain growth takes place *post*-natally. This is because of a combination of bipedalism (upright posture), which is unique to humans, and the growth of the size of the cranium, necessary to house the human brain. 'It is the price we pay for the human brain and intelligence. Humans have exceptionally big heads relative to the size of their bodies, and the opening in the female human pelvis through which the baby must pass is limited in size by our upright posture.'[8] Compared to other species of mammals, the human infant is born at an immature stage of development, making it totally dependent on its mother to fulfil its every need for the first weeks of life, unable, for example, even to stand or to walk until the end of the first year of post-natal life. This has led certain authors to describe the first nine months of post-natal life as being an extended period of extra-uterine gestation.

Certain periods of development involve more active growth than others. In this respect, the brain is particularly sensitive to environmental and internal influences at times of *rapid* growth and development. External influences at times of rapid growth can result in changes or deviations in the developing architecture of the brain. This neural 'plasticity' can have positive or negative outcomes, and is a reminder that child development occurs as a result of both nature and nurture, maturation and environmental influences, and growth and interaction.

At birth, some areas of the brain are more advanced in their development than others. The cerebral cortex of the neonate is only half its eventual thickness with posterior regions more developed than anterior regions. The increase in the thickness of the cortex that takes place over the next few years occurs as a result of an increase in the size of the nerve cells and of sprouting of numerous connections between nerve cells (*dendritic* growth). Lower brain regions are more developed than higher ones at the time of birth, but as connections between the higher and lower centres in the brain develop rapidly in the first 6–12 months of post-natal life, lower centres surrender increasing control to higher centres while, at the same time, taking on various unconscious functions. Therefore, reflexes provide direct reflections of maturity in hierarchical control.

Dendrite – branched extension of a nerve cell neuron that receives electrical signals from other neurons and that conducts those signals to the cell body.

REFLEXES AS REFLECTIONS OF HIERARCHICAL DEVELOPMENT

It should be noted that early reflexes never disappear. They are 'inhibited' as higher centres, and more mature reflex systems develop. They may be 'disinhibited' if there is trauma or deterioration to higher centres, or if later reflexes fail to develop (see Figure 2.1).

Capute[7] described three groups of reflexes present in the first three and a half years of life:

1. Intrauterine (spinal);
2. Primitive (brainstem);
3. Postural (midbrain and cortex).

Intrauterine Reflexes

As described above, intrauterine reflexes emerge at five to seven and a half weeks after conception. Capute[7] suggested that these early reflexes, sometimes referred to as the 'mass cutaneous reflexes', should be modified and largely inhibited in utero as they are supplanted by the developing primitive reflexes. The characteristics of the intrauterine reflexes are that they are withdrawal in nature and that they involve the entire body in the response. This is in contrast to the developing primitive reflexes, which, with the exception of the Moro reflex, are characterized by *differentiated* response in a particular part(s) of the body. Specific tactile primitive reflexes such as the suck, palmar, and plantar reflexes elicit a grasp response (Figure 2.2).

Primitive Reflexes

Primitive reflexes emerge in the womb beginning with the Moro reflex at 9–12 weeks after conception; primitive reflexes are fully present at birth in the healthy neonate born at 40 weeks' gestation, and then they are gradually inhibited by the developing brain during the first six months of post-natal life. Their continued presence in the older individual is a recognized sign of pathology in conditions such as cerebral palsy when damage to higher centres in the brain prevents full inhibition from taking place, and they are later seen as a sign of developing pathology in demyelination conditions such as multiple sclerosis and Alzheimer's disease.

The primitive reflexes are mediated at the level of the brainstem. They help a baby to survive the first months of life before connections to higher centres in the brain have become established, and they also provide rudimentary training for many later voluntary skills. They are involuntary stereotyped responses to specific stimuli, and they allow no leeway for variation or choice of action. If they remain active beyond the normal developmental period, they can interfere with the development of later voluntary skills.

Early reflex patterns never entirely disappear. They can reappear to facilitate survival if higher centres are damaged through injury or progressive disease – in this sense, once inhibited, they become 'dormant', only to be reawakened if higher systems fail – and they should not be elicited by general stimuli. However, primitive reflexes can also be *intentionally* accessed by higher centres in the brain to assist in the execution of specific skills. Examples of intentional release of a primitive reflex can be seen in the basketball player who may utilize the asymmetrical tonic neck reflex (ATNR) when shooting a goal or in the attitude of the fencer

Development of the
Reflex System

WITHDRAWAL
REFLEXES

Vulnerability to any invasive outside stimuli.

Automatic reaction involving the whole body.

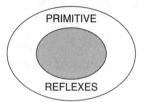

PRIMITIVE

REFLEXES

Involuntary reactions to external stimuli or motor activity.
Automatic stereotyped response—allow
no leeway for variation or choice of action.

Vulnerability and over-reaction—limited systems of response.

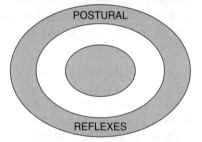

POSTURAL

REFLEXES

Automatic reactions for the maintenance of balance,
stability and flexibility throughout the body.

Provide the foundations for voluntary, adaptive
responses to environmental changes.

Figure 2.2 Model to illustrate the interrelationship between different reflexes in development. As each succeeding group of reflexes develops, it provides a protective outer zone which helps to prevent inappropriate activation of the more primitive reaction. However, if there is a gap in the development of the outer layer(s), then certain types or intensity of stimuli may elicit a deeper and less mature response
Source: Goddard SA. 2002. *Reflexes, Learning and Behavior* (p. 37). Fern Ridge Press, Eugene, OR.

in the 'on guard' position. The difference between these examples of when a reflex is deliberately used for a specific purpose and the child who has a cluster of retained reflexes is that the former is the *master* of his reflexes, whereas the child with neuro-developmental immaturity is *servant* to his or her reflexes.

Postural Reflexes

The postural reflexes emerge after birth, mostly during the course of the first 12 months of life, but some can take up to three and a half years to be fully developed. This is because each time a child learns a new postural and related motor skill (sitting, four-point kneeling, standing, walking, running, jumping, etc.), the postural reflexes need to be re-calibrated to accommodate a new postural relationship with gravity and to support the new movement pattern. Postural reflexes emerge as connections to higher centres in the brain are established to provide the basis for automatic (unconscious) control of posture and movement in a gravity-based environment. Postural reflex development begins with control of the head.

Postural development follows a general cephalocaudal (head to toe) and proximo-distal (from the centre outwards) pattern, although after the first few weeks of life, development of posture and coordinated movement also progresses from the caudal end (bottom up). Integration through the truncal section of the body develops towards the middle of the first year. The postural reflexes are largely mediated at the level of the midbrain with the exception of the OHRRs. OHRRs are controlled from the cerebral cortex and are dependent on visual cues.

Many motor training programmes are aimed at trying to improve the functioning of postural reflexes (even if this is not taken into consideration by those using them). The theory is that by stimulating postural reflexes through specific types of exercise and physical training, secure postural reflexes will naturally override or inhibit earlier primitive reflexes. Motor training programmes of this type tend to have mixed success. They generally have positive results with children who have poor balance, postural control, and motor skills combined with little or no evidence of abnormal primitive reflex activity. In this group, they tend to improve balance and coordination as long as the programme continues, but do not necessarily cross over to affect higher cognitive skills (academic performance, for example) if primitive reflexes also persist beneath. In those cases where a cluster of primitive reflexes persist in the school-aged child, physical exercises should be aimed at the developmental and then at the postural level of the reflex abnormality rather than trying to impose direct training on higher skills. This is where the INPP programmes differ from other motor training programmes in *the level of development* from where remediation begins (Table 2.1).

AREAS OF THE BRAIN INVOLVED IN THE MEDIATION OF PRIMITIVE AND POSTURAL REFLEXES

Brainstem

The brainstem connects the spinal cord to the rest of the brain. It comprises three parts: the *medulla*, the *pons* (bridge), and the *midbrain*. The brainstem contains the cluster of nerve cells necessary for survival, which function outside of con-

Table 2.1   Development and characteristics of early reflexes

Development	Intrauterine	Primitive	Postural
Emerge	5.0–7.5 weeks post-conception	From 9 to 12 weeks post-conception	Post-natal
Inhibited		6 months post-natal	Remain for life
Transformed	Prenatal and at birth	6 months post-natal	Birth to 3.5 years
Characteristic	Involuntary withdrawal	Involuntary; tactile reflexes seek to maintain contact	Adaptive righting, equilibrium, and locomotion reactions – the basis for voluntary control of movement
Mediated	Spinal level	Brainstem	Midbrain and cortex (OHRRs)

scious control or awareness, to regulate breathing, heart rate, blood pressure, and digestive processes. The brainstem receives all the sensory inputs from the body, including the sense of pain, joint position, and motor output from the cortex. These pathways are grouped in discrete, tightly organized bundles of nerve fibres, which pass down through the base of the skull to the spinal cord (Figure 2.3).

Moving upwards from the spinal cord is the *medulla oblongata*, which forms part of the brainstem and contains the nerve cell bodies of the 9th to the 12th cranial nerves. These nerves receive and relay taste sensations from the tongue to the speech muscles, and control swallowing and movements of the tongue and the neck. The medulla is the point where pathways involved in movement and sensation cross over (decussation) to the opposite side of the body. The medulla also contains the group of nerve cells that control the automatic activities of heartbeat, breathing, blood pressure, and digestion, sending and receiving information about these

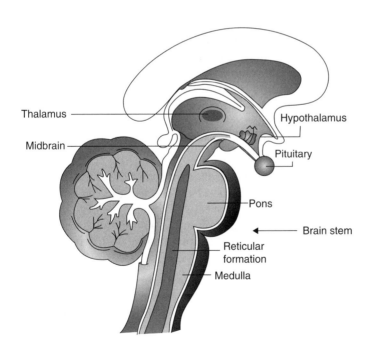

Figure 2.3 The brainstem, midbrain, and part of the limbic system

Vagus nerve – the 10th cranial nerve, taking its name from the word 'vagrant', meaning 'wanderer'. This is because it is the longest of all the cranial nerves and affects many vital functions including innervation of the parasympathetic nervous system. Blythe (1990) suggested that stimulation of the vagus nerve as a result of vestibular dysfunction probably plays a part in the physiological changes that take place in panic disorder (see Chapter 9).

automatic functions via the *vagus nerve*.[i] The *pyramids*, special bundles of nerve fibres, which carry messages necessary for skilled, controlled movements from the cerebral cortex, cross at the medulla. This is also where the *reticular formation* – known as the reticular activating system (RAS) – an intricate network of nerve fibres, runs through the back of the brainstem and extends upwards to the cortex.

The RAS is like the brain's own alarm clock. It monitors incoming sensory signals, passing them on to either alert or calm down, testing information carried by the sensory, motor, and autonomic nervous system (ANS) pathways before it is passed on. It also plays an important part in maintaining consciousness, the regulation of the sleep–wake cycle, and how much sensation, particularly pain, is admitted further up into the brain. The efferent (downward) pathways go down the spinal cord to affect certain aspects of movement, including sensitivity of the spinal reflexes. Afferent (upward) pathways affect arousal and consciousness, keeping the brain awake. The RAS also acts as a filter for the intensity of sensory information, which is given access to higher centres in the brain. In this way, 99 per cent of information that reaches consciousness has first been filtered by the reticular formation, leading to it being described as the 'gatekeeper' of consciousness. It has an important role in supporting attention, both in regulating levels of arousal and also in shutting out distracting information, making it possible to focus attention on one aspect of a task. We will return to this later when we examine problems of attention, distractibility, and sensory overload in subsequent chapters.

The *pons* links the medulla to the midbrain and is chiefly made up of nerve tracts which connect the cerebral cortex to the spinal cord and the cerebellum. It is involved with the control of sleep and dreams, and it also contains a centre for the cranial nerves which supply the face with sensation and movement.

The *midbrain* contains the highest number of motor neurons in the central nervous system. It is the point at which the large efferent (downward) motor pathways, the *corticospinal*

[i] Blythe P. 1990. Paper presented to the 4th European Conference of Neurodevelopmental Delay in Children with Specific Learning Difficulties, Guernsey, September 1990.

tracts, merge into the brainstem. It coordinates head and eye movements, and certain of the postural reflexes particularly the labyrinthine head righting reflexes, which are instrumental in enabling the midbrain to carry out its functions in relation to effective control of head and eye movements.

The *cortex* (derived from the Latin word for rind or bark of a tree) is the most highly developed area of the brain in humans. It is the elaboration and complexity of the cerebral and the cerebellar cortices that separates man from other vertebrate species, even from our closest cousins, the apes, enabling man to develop a whole range of skills unique to humankind, including the ability to make and use tools, speech, the use of symbolic language, and abstract thinking.

THE MULTISENSORY REFLEX –
THE MORO REFLEX

In medicine, the person who identifies or discovers something new often has their name conferred upon the discovery. Moro, a professor of paediatrics in Heidelberg, was the first to describe in detail in 1918 the reaction pattern now known as the Moro reflex. It was Moro's belief that the reflex is *phylogenetically* a clasping reflex, the early human equivalent of the grasping reflex seen in young apes who cling to their mother's fur. Moro gave the reflex the name *umklammerungsreflex*, meaning 'clasping', but today it is by his name that it is commonly known (Figure 2.4).

The Moro reflex is present in the healthy full-term neonate. Testing of the Moro reflex usually forms part of the neonate paediatric assessment, which is carried out shortly after birth. A weak or absent Moro reflex is seen in cases of upper motor neuron lesions; an asymmetrical Moro reflex at birth may indicate a fractured clavicle or an *Erb's palsy*.

If the Moro reflex persists beyond four to six months of postnatal life, it is considered an indication of delay in neurological maturation.[9,10] Chasnoff and Burns[11] found delay in the

Phylogeny – *the evolutionary history of a species, genus, or group, in contrast with the development of an individual.*

Ontogeny – *the development of an individual from a fertilized ovum to maturity.*

Erb's palsy *involves varying amounts of injury to the fifth and sixth cranial nerves as they pass through the brachial plexus.*

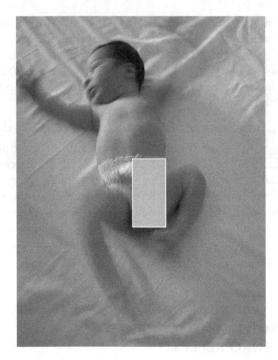

Figure 2.4   The Moro reflex
Note: The Moro reflex is asymmetrical in the example above, because the baby's head is turned to one side. When the head is at the midline, the reflex reaction is symmetrical

inhibition of the Moro reflex in infants born to narcotic-dependent mothers, suggesting that general irritability of the central nervous system resulting from drug exposure in the womb might be an early indication of cerebral damage. At another level, persistence of the Moro reflex can also delay the establishment of head control, voluntary sitting, and other developmental motor milestones.

Kernicterus *is the staining of the basal nuclei of the brain with bile, with toxic degeneration of the nerve cells which sometimes occurs in haemolytic disease of the newborn.*

However, even more important than persistence of the Moro reflex beyond the first four to six months of post-natal life is its absence *in the first few weeks* of life. Infants who are deeply sedated or those who have suffered a severe cerebral insult either prenatally or during birth generally lack the Moro reflex. If the reflex is present then disappears, it may indicate *kernicterus*. Absence of the response in the neonate does not necessarily indicate brain disease, and it can be difficult to elicit in premature babies.[12] 'The response is generally regarded as a mass reflex that occurs when normal reticular brain stem mechanisms are not yet under significant inhibitory control from higher centres.'[12]

The Moro reflex is usually tested by placing the palm of the hand under the baby's head and by lowering the head below the level of the spine. Unexpected vestibular stimulation such as rapidly lowering the whole body or striking the surface on which the baby is lying will also activate the Moro reflex. When the head is lowered, the arms open out and extend (abduct), the legs abduct to a lesser degree; there is a sudden intake of breath; the neonate 'freezes' momentarily in this position before the arms return across the body (adduct), and the baby will usually start to whimper or cry (Figure 2.4).

Although the Moro reflex is most sensitive to vestibular stimulation in the first days of life, it can also be activated by any form of sudden or unexpected sensory event. Inhibition of response to certain types of stimulus occurs slightly earlier in development than others. It can be elicited by a sudden loud noise, change of light, noxious tactile stimulation, change of temperature, or the baby's own vigorous movements such as shaking of the head, kicking, coughing, and sneezing. In other words it has multisensory receptors.

The Moro reflex undergoes inhibition in the first four months of post-natal life, when it is gradually replaced by a more adult 'startle' response. Whereas the Moro reflex is primarily an extensor (withdrawal) movement followed by a flexion or clasping phase, the adult startle response consists of a brief startle reaction, *intake* of breath, blink, lifting of the shoulders, and a moment to scan the environment, orient to the stimulus, and decide whether to react to the stimulus or to ignore it. Whereas the more mature startle response involves higher centres in the brain in attention, orientation, and directed response, the Moro reflex acts as a primitive alarm response with the reaction taking place first and awareness of the context only reaching consciousness a few seconds later.

All reflexes presumably have a function at the time in development when they are active. Just as behaviours such as thumb sucking or bed-wetting are considered normal at one stage in life but become inappropriate if they persist at a later stage, so primitive reflexes have a positive influence in the first six months of life, but their influence becomes increasingly negative if they remain active beyond the normal period of inhibition.

In the first months of life, the Moro reflex acts as an alarm reflex to protect the defenceless infant before it develops the postural control either to flee from a frightening stimulus towards an attachment figure or to fight for itself.[ii] The first withdrawal phase is one of avoidance; the second 'clasping' phase seems to be an ancient throwback to a time earlier in evolution when the infant could cling to its mother using the grasping reflex for protection. The distressed cry which usually follows the clasping phase is an effective way of gaining the mother's immediate attention. The withdrawal phase (abduction) throws the infant into a position of extreme muscle weakness and momentary 'freeze'; the clasping phase (adduction) is associated with some recovery of muscle tone. Emotionally, the Moro reflex is an alarm reaction associated with helplessness. This has implications for emotional development if it persists into later life.

At birth, the process of normal delivery helps to prepare a baby for breathing after birth. Some of the mechanisms involved will be discussed further in Chapter 6 when

[ii] The long-term effects of significance of flight *towards* an attachment figure have been discussed in relation to attachment theory. 'Babies and toddlers tend to live in the present, and when unable to access any well-known and trusted attachment figure, they usually (but not always) protest and become highly aroused, and if their *flight towards* an attachment figure is barred, they may try to *fight* by struggling and crying to various degrees, some may cry briefly and others more-so, but some become visibly distressed and scream long and loud. When fight and flight behaviours are unsuccessful, babies and toddlers tend to use *freeze* or disassociation as *psychological flight*. The level of dissociation will depend on intensity and duration of the real or perceived threat, and can temporarily *de-activate* babies' attachment seeking response; their senses become blunted or numbed allowing them to function again but at a subdued level' (Bowlby R. 2007. Babies and toddlers in non-parental day care can avoid stress and anxiety if they develop a lasting secondary attachment bond with one carer who is consistently accessible to them. *Attachment and Human Development* 4/4:307–319). This provides a psychological example of the stages of *disinhibition* which can occur as a result of both physical and emotional events; that is, when a regulatory response is not available, the individual is forced to search for a deeper, more primitive reaction. This also has implications for emotional trauma later in life.

we will examine developmental indicators of neuro-developmental delay, particularly events surrounding birth in more detail. However, not all babies start to breathe spontaneously at birth and may need additional stimulation to initiate breathing. Some of the techniques used to stimulate breathing at birth such as change of position (inversion), tactile stimulation, and change of light or temperature are also triggers for the Moro reflex. The first phase of the Moro reflex is a rapid *in*take of breath followed, in the second phase, by *ex*piration. In the Moro reflex, nature has provided a second fail-safe mechanism to stimulate breathing if breathing has not started naturally as a result of a combination of mild hypoxia and release of chest compression at birth.

The Moro reflex is also associated with increased physiological arousal, resulting in stimulation of the sympathetic division of the ANS, which is involved in all our basic survival functions such as breathing, heart rate, blood pressure, and digestion. The ANS has two main divisions – sympathetic and parasympathetic.

When the sympathetic division of the ANS is stimulated, it results in increased activity, which prepares the body for fight or flight using adrenaline as the principal chemical transmitter involved. Stimulation of the sympathetic division results in immediate physiological changes including increase in heart rate, narrowing of blood vessels to increase blood pressure, and diverting blood away from digestion to the muscles.

The second division of the ANS, the parasympathetic nervous system, is involved in the conservation of energy resources, the maintenance of blood flow to the digestive system to safeguard absorption of energy from food, slowing of heart and breathing rates, and lowering of blood pressure. The two divisions of the ANS operate to balance one another in order to maintain homeostasis in physiological functions. However, at times of stress, one division will increase its influence, tuning physiological processes to meet the immediate demands of the environment. One of the effects of the Moro reflex is to increase arousal in response to specific stimuli, by increasing sympathetic activity and by temporarily suppressing parasympathetic activity.

This is thought to have a protective function in the first months of life, when the immature nervous system is less able to regulate itself, particularly during sleep. It has been suggested[13] that the Moro reflex is available to increase arousal if breathing becomes depressed. Lipsitt suggested that underdeveloped reflexes in the first months of life may be linked to sudden infant death syndrome (SIDS). Babies usually exhibit a 'rage reaction' in the first two to four months of life if there is a threat to breathing. 'If respiratory blocking occurs while eating, or from mucous in the nose, for example, the infant exhibits useful counter-reactions; It pulls its head back, shakes it to and fro, flailing its arms and legs about as though trying to remove an offending object. Such reflexive defence against respiratory blocks gradually evolves into more deliberate, skilled behaviour . . . infants who for some reason do not display such strong reflex actions are less likely to learn more mature defences.'[14]

Also the asymmetrical tonic neck reflex (see Chapter 3).

Others[15] have suggested that the Moro reflex might be underdeveloped in babies who succumb to SIDS; Goddard[16] suggested that there may be an interrelationship between the Moro reflex and the fear paralysis reflex in the first four months of life whereby if the Moro reflex is weak or cannot be accessed for any reason, the fear paralysis reflex – first discussed by Kaada[17] in connection with SIDS – reacts to threatening events such as respiratory blockage *before* 'higher' systems can be activated. This is important because the Moro reflex and fear paralysis response trigger *opposite* physiological reactions to stress, particularly in relation to breathing and cardiovascular responses.

The Fear Paralysis Reflex

The fear paralysis reflex was described by Kaada as 'an innate atavistic fear paralysis reflex' which is present in the entire animal kingdom in response to situations which evoke extreme fear. When an animal is exposed to danger such as a potential predator, it can react with fight or with flight (active avoidance), or 'when actions are not possible, with a sudden and prolonged state of immobility (passive avoidance). This may be observed either as freezing on approach of the predator, or as fear paralysis (animal hypnosis).'[15]

The fear paralysis response can be observed in certain animals, rabbits, for example, if they are unexpectedly caught in the headlights of a car at night. Instead of running away to avoid being hit by the approaching vehicle, the startled animal will freeze and remain rooted to the spot. While feigning death may be effective in avoiding detection by living predators, this mechanism has not adapted to the invention of the modern motor car. The same response at work can be seen in animal hypnosis. If a chalk line is drawn along the ground and a chicken is placed with its beak on the line, the chicken is unable to move.[18] Entertainers such as stage magicians use the reflex to 'conjure' doves out of the air. One of the triggers to the fear paralysis reflex in animals is inversion; birds can be put into a state of temporary immobility by hanging them upside down from hooks hidden inside the magician's coat. When the bird is turned the right way up with a flamboyant gesture of the magician's hand, the bird is freed from the temporary state of immobility and appears to fly, as if from nowhere, up into the air.

Potential activators of the fear paralysis reflex are multisensory and psychological as well as physical. Kaada suggested that the reflex may set in motion a chain reaction involving other reflexes involving 'the respiratory and gastro-intestinal tracts as well as from the chemo- and baro-receptors, all working in the same direction and contributing to excessive vagal cardiac innervation.' Although the reflex can be activated by thoughts as well as by external events and can therefore be elicited from any level in the brain, its effects on subsequent behaviour are significant because in the long term, it appears to result in *reduced* neocortical control with greater susceptibility to less mature reaction patterns which are mutually reinforcing in activating inappropriate reactions to 'startle'.

The various phases of startle reaction are well recognized:

- Freeze.
- Fight or flight (flight may be away from the threat or towards a source of security).
- Conscious response, which involves the ability to orient, pay attention to, identify, and decide how to react to the stimulus.
- Each phase or level of response has a corresponding emotional association as well as characteristic *changes* in the functioning of the ANS.

These phases may also be viewed within the developmental context of intrauterine and post-natal reflex development, with primitive startle reactions being transformed into more mature ones as the brain develops from the earliest withdrawal response to the adult startle response. The Moro reflex with its characteristic features of arousal and reaction acts as an intermediary between the primitive withdrawal response and a more mature adult startle reflex.[19] All levels remain potentially active within the system throughout life, so that if the organism is exposed to extreme danger with no capability of defending itself, the fear paralysis reaction may come into play. If the threat is such that an aggressive defence reaction (fight) or flight is appropriate, the Moro reflex may be released, but for most of the time, the mature adult is able to make a conscious, thinking decision about how to react to events in the environment – *unless* – the early sequence of development has been disturbed and primitive reactions remain overreactive (Table 2.2).

Each phase of development should increase the organism's resilience to shock as higher systems mature, but all levels remain potentially active in the system.

In an article, Lipsitt referred to the earlier of work of Myrtle McGraw[20] who had carried out studies on the neuromuscular maturation of infants in the 1940s, showing that, 'during the time an infant is shifting from purely reflexive to volun-

Table 2.2   Development and characteristics of startle reflexes

Category of reflex	Time of emergence	Characteristic motor/ behavioural response	Level of mediation	Type of startle reflex
Intrauterine	5.0–7.5 weeks post-conception	Withdrawal and temporary freeze	Spinal	Fear paralysis reflex
Primitive (tactile)	From 9 to 12 weeks post-conception	Development of vestibular, clasping, and grasping reflexes	Brainstem	Moro reflex
Postural	From birth to 3.5 years of age	Preconscious control and adaptation of posture, support the control of voluntary movement	Midbrain	Adult startle response (Strauss reflex)

tary responses, its neurological system is quite disorganised. This is true even of completely normal infants, but those prone to SIDS (which occurs most often during this transition period – two to four months of post-natal life) have an added handicap, they may have incurred some minimal brain damage around the time of birth, probably from a temporary loss of oxygen. The accident leaves their central nervous systems not quite prepared for the critical shift from reflexive to voluntary control. When such an infant is faced with an air blockage, it may not move its head or cry, or take whatever action is required before lack of oxygen leads to unconsciousness or even death.'[13] This is important because activation of the more primitive fear paralysis response elicits a series of immediate physiological changes.

CHARACTERISTICS OF THE FEAR PARALYSIS REFLEX

The fear paralysis reflex is described as a highly alert but immobile state involving one or several physical changes:

- Immobility as if 'frozen to the spot';
- Respiratory arrest;
- Flaccid, floppy muscle tone;
- Inability to respond to external events despite a high level of internal excitation;
- Immediate deceleration of heart rate resulting in cardiac arrhythmia;
- Pallor;
- Rise in blood pressure;
- Lowered seizure threshold (shock);
- Difficulty swallowing, temporary paralysis of the muscles of the pharynx and larynx necessary for speech.

Activating events	*Type of stimulus*
Predator approach	Fear
Restraint of movement	Inability to react
Separation	Helplessness
Inversion	Vestibular
Sudden noise/sound frequency	Auditory
Distant movement or shadows	Peripheral vision

Pain	Noxious sensation
Smoke	Olfactory
Sudden change of temperature	Thermo-receptors
Opiates	Biochemical
Helplessness or hopelessness	Emotional
Inability to react	Defeat

Antinociception – *a reduction in pain sensitivity produced within neurons when an endorphin or similar opium-containing substance, opioid, combines with a receptor, tending to reduce the perception and behavioural effects of nociceptive stimuli.*

Bradycardia – *slowness of the heart rate, usually measured as fewer than 60 beats per minute in an adult.*

The fear paralysis reflex has a survival function in *extreme* situations in humans as well as in animals. For example, the response of 'motor quieting makes it difficult to discover the prey, the *antinociception* is favourable in case of wounding, and the *bradycardia* is part of a complex oxygen conserving cardiovascular response involving regional shifts of blood supply with constriction of most vascular beds, maintaining central arterial perfusion pressure, and reserving the limited oxygen stores for the vital organs, as in spontaneously prolonged apnoeic attacks.' Kaada[17] expressed his view that the fear paralysis reflex acts as a trigger mechanism to a chain reaction involving 'other reflexes with the same final path such as reflexes affecting respiratory and gastro-intestinal tracts, chemo and baro-receptors all working in the same directions and contributing to excessive vagal cardiac innervation.' This trigger mechanism can occur in an upward or downward direction, i.e. from the spine up to the cortex, or from the cortex down. He also suggested that the respiratory and cardiovascular responses involved were related to the mammalian diving and smoke reflexes, which 'appear to utilize the same brainstem mechanisms and the same peripheral efferent paths as the former.'

The dive reflex is present in aquatic mammals such as seals, otters, and dolphins, and exists in a weaker form in humans. It is triggered by cold water contacting the face or the face being submerged, when receptors in the nasal cavity and areas of the face supplied by the trigeminal nerve relay information to the brain, which activates the vagus nerve. This causes immediate bradycardia or slowing of the heart rate, which lessens the need for bloodstream oxygen, and peripheral vasoconstriction of blood vessels, which removes blood from the limbs and from all organs except the heart and the brain, thereby protecting the vital organs of the heart and the brain from damage, making it possible to withstand longer periods under water without damage to the brain. The dive reflex may also appear 'in anticipation of immersion, during submergence and frightening stimuli.'

The foetal diving reflex, which is also a response to stress, is thought to protect the baby from hypoxia during birth. In aquatic animals, deep dives set into motion a blood shift whereby organ and circulatory mechanisms allow plasma or water to pass freely through the thoracic cavity so that its pressure remains constant and the organs are not crushed. Blood plasma is re-absorbed when the animal leaves the pressurized environment, and although this stage of the diving reflex does not occur in humans after birth, it may play a part in enabling the foetus to withstand the pressure of labour during birth.

During uterine life, the dive reflex is inhibitory in nature, while it is not so in post-natal life. While the adult generally reacts to frightening or stressful stimuli with a fight-and-flight response characterized by increased muscular blood flow, increased breathing, and tachycardia (rapid heart rate), the foetus becomes paralysed with decreased muscular blood flow; breathing is suppressed and becomes bradycardic. This so-called foetal diving response is probably a very adequate response to conserve oxygen during the birth process. It is normally reversed at birth, probably as a result of the surge of hormones (the *catecholamine surge*) that occurs moments before birth in a vaginal delivery.[21]

In a series of papers (unpublished) written in the late 1980s early 1990s, based on Kaada's original work, I suggested that a weak Moro reflex may render the infant more susceptible to the fear paralysis reflex under conditions of sleep, separation, or stress.[22] As McGraw had suggested many years earlier, the infant is particularly vulnerable at times when there is a shift from purely reflexive to voluntary responses, and the Moro reflex normally undergoes inhibition between two and four months of post-natal life – the period when the highest incidence of cases of SIDS has been recorded. The Moro reflex may be easily activated when a baby is lying on its back but may be suppressed or temporarily immobilized when the baby is lying on its tummy if the arms are restrained. This may be one reason behind the significant reduction in cases of SIDS since the inception of the 'back to sleep' campaign, which advises parents always to place infants to sleep on the back. When sleeping on the

Catecholamine surge – *sudden increase in catecholamine levels, particularly adrenaline, which occurs when birth is imminent. This surge of hormones is thought to activate the foetal ejection reflex – the final powerful contraction which expels the baby at the moment of birth and prepares the baby for the change from a state of inhibition before birth to arousal after birth.*

back, the Moro reflex is more readily available to arouse the infant and to restore breathing if an apnoea develops.

MORO REFLEX ACTIVATORS

- Sudden unexpected occurrence of any kind;
- Stimulation of the labyrinth (vestibular);
- Noise (auditory);
- Sudden movement or change of light (visual);
- Pain, sudden change of temperature, being handled roughly (tactile).

FUNCTIONS OF THE MORO REFLEX

- (Inhibition and integration of withdrawal responses) Hypothesis;
- Primitive reaction to positional change;
- Arousal;
- Stimulation of the sympathetic nervous system;
- May help to initiate the first breath of life;
- Alert and summon assistance.

PHYSIOLOGICAL RESPONSE TO
THE MORO REFLEX

- Instantaneous arousal;
- Rapid intake of breath – freeze – expiration, often accompanied by a cry;
- Abduction of the arms and the legs to a lesser degree, followed by adduction;
- Dilation of the pupil;
- Alerts the sympathetic nervous system resulting in
  - release of adrenaline and cortisol (the stress hormones)
  - increase in rate of breathing
  - increase in heart rate
  - rise in blood pressure
  - flushing of the skin
  - possible outburst, e.g. crying.

IMPLICATIONS OF A RETAINED
MORO REFLEX

If the Moro reflex remains active beyond the first four to six months of post-natal life, it is associated with hypersensitivity to vestibular stimulation and other unexpected forms of sensory arousal. This fast-acting reflex action comes into play *before* higher centres in the brain have time to filter unwanted sensory stimuli from consciousness or to process relevant sensory information and to direct a response. As a result, the child can become easily 'overloaded' by competing sensory stimuli and reacts without the cortex being involved in deciding if the reaction is appropriate, a case of act first – think later.

Sensory overload linked to a retained Moro reflex occurs for a number of different reasons: while on the one hand, retention of the Moro reflex will tend to result in hypersensitivity and overreactivity to certain types of sensory stimulus, if there is a problem at the sensory (receptor) level, such as a visual problem, hypersensitivity to sound, or immaturity in postural mechanisms, the Moro reflex may persist as a secondary protective mechanism as a result of a primary immaturity or impairment in specific sensory systems.

Vision, hearing, and posture all provide examples of how the Moro reflex can be released and/or retained as a result of a specific impairment. Myopic patients who cannot see at far distance may be more easily startled and upset when not wearing corrective glasses or contact lenses. This is because they cannot see approaching danger until the threat is almost on top of them. The cortex does not have sufficient time to plan a response, so the brainstem steps in first as a 'defence' reaction. Similarly, the patient with a hearing impairment has reduced distance awareness and, therefore, less time for the cortex to defend itself from unpleasant or unexpected noises. The older child or adult who has underdeveloped postural, righting, and equilibrium reflexes is more susceptible to disturbances of balance, and when balance is insecure, the Moro reflex is more easily elicited.

Retention of the Moro reflex can also affect physiological processes and emotional behaviour. Due to its effect upon arousal, not only the reaction itself, but eventually the *anticipation* of an unpleasant reaction can result in hypervigilance. When it is retained, the Moro reflex tends to lower the threshold of response to potentially frightening situations. In an unpublished paper on the relationship between the Moro reflex and asthma, Cottrell[23] described how 'this is done by lowering of the stimulus threshold, making for a very frightened individual who over-responds to potential threats[iii] and who is hypersensitive. This is particularly true of the auditory modality.' It is also true of vestibular and visual stimuli if postural control is immature. In this way, a vicious circle of hypersensitivity – hyper-reaction – increased sensitivity is set up.

The older child with a retained Moro reflex tends to be not only overreactive to certain stimuli but also hypersensitive to events and situations which *might* trigger the reaction. Although he or she can learn to override the *overt* signs of the reflex in most situations, he or she tends to develop a secondary fear of fear, or *anticipatory anxiety* around any situation which might provoke unpleasant feelings associated with the Moro response, often at a subconscious level. This can result in behaviours which seem immature and inappropriate, but which fulfil an adaptive function in accommodating the reflex in everyday life. These children present a paradox – acutely sensitive, perceptive, and imaginative on the one hand – immature, demanding, and manipulative on the other. They may develop two opposing strategies to cope with their daily experience of life:

1. by being a fearful child who shies away (withdraws) from new people and experiences, dislikes robust physical activities such as contact sports, finds it difficult to form peer relationships while appearing to get on well with adults, and has difficulty accepting or demonstrating physical affection;
2. or by being an overactive, excitable child who does not read the body language of others and who needs to dominate situations to fit his or her needs.

Either strategy tends to make for a child who manipulates situations as a result of an impaired capacity to regulate levels of arousal in response to specific stimuli.

[iii]The author has altered the words here from 'every threat' to 'potential threat'.

These are the children who tend to cling to familiarity, dislike change, and who try to manipulate people and situations in an attempt to control their own reactions to novel situations, which usually require the ability to respond spontaneously in a flexible way (adaptability). A discrepancy between verbal, emotional, and social behaviour often exists, causing problems with social integration, particularly peer relationships. The Moro-driven child can appear withdrawn and fearful in social situations or may have a tendency to be overbearing and controlling. They are frequently the children who are 'picked on' in the playground because other children recognize that they are 'different' and that they have a tendency to overreact to provocation. The behavioural traits and longer-term effects of a retained Moro reflex are not confined to children. They can also be present in adults who suffer from anxiety and panic disorder.[24]

Older children with a residual Moro reflex can often have a history of allergies and compromised immune functioning. The Moro reflex is not necessarily the primary cause, although the biochemistry of anxiety – a feature of a retained Moro reflex – can affect the functioning of the immune system over time. Conversely, disorders in functioning of the biochemical system such as leaky gut, food intolerances, and hormonal disturbances can affect the functioning of the central nervous system. Although the Moro reflex will sometimes recede when biochemical problems are corrected, when this happens, it is an indication that the primitive reflex had persisted or has been *dis*inhibited to fulfil a protective function when other systems (in this case the biochemical messenger system) which affect the functioning of the central nervous system are impaired.

Other long-term effects of the Moro reflex are related to its role in stimulating the sympathetic nervous system, resulting not only in arousal but also in secretion of adrenaline and cortisol – hormones most associated with response to stress. Long-term overstimulation of the stress hormones can also result in adrenal fatigue affecting immune functioning either through exhaustion or overstimulation, the former affecting resistance to infection and the latter being associated with the development of allergic reactions.

Retention of primitive reflexes is also linked to developmental lag – certain skills being 'held back' to the level of a much younger child despite normal development in other areas and the existence of average or above-average intelligence. One example of this can be seen in the 'visual stimulus-bound effect'. Stimulus-bound effect describes the inability to ignore irrelevant visual stimuli within a given visual field. Developmentally, a baby is naturally stimulus bound in the first two months of life. The immature visual system of the young baby does not see in the same way as an adult. In the first few weeks of life, a baby's eyes are drawn to the periphery of objects at the expense of central focus. 'With no cortex to direct his gaze, the baby watches whatever part of an object catches his eye, and does not think to examine other areas. Outlines of things are larger than the elements within, and often contrast more against the backgrounds, so they catch the baby's attention to the exclusion of all else.'[25] This means that a baby recognizes the contours of his mother's hairstyle better than the overall 'picture' of her face in the first weeks of life. The baby's eyes tend to be drawn towards anything that is lighter, brighter, or moving within his visual field, and to fix on one point on the perimeter, seeing the world in small pieces, not as a whole. By four months of age, at the time the Moro reflex is inhibited, the baby's ability to maintain central focus improves.

Fragmented sensory perception *is a feature of some autistic spectrum disorders.*

Another effect of the Moro reflex concerns light. Light enters the eye through the pupil, a tiny aperture which constricts or dilates to allow light to be focused on the lens, which lies behind it. Normally, the size of the pupil adapts by constricting or dilating according to the intensity of the light, but when the Moro reflex is elicited, there is a momentary dilation of the pupil, allowing more light to enter the eye. Inside the eyeball is a layer of photosensitive cells – the retina – and the retina comprises two types of light-sensitive cells: long, thin rod-shaped cells which produce electrical impulses in response to light and cone-shaped cells which respond to colour and fine detail. The colour-sensitive cone cells are concentrated at the centre of the retina – the *fovea* or macula – and it is on the fovea at the centre of the retina that the majority of light is focused.

Fovea *– a small pit or central depression in the macula retinae where the retina is very thin so that rays of light have free passage to the layer of photoreceptors, mostly cones. This is the area of most distinct vision to which the visual axis is directed.*

The fovea is immature at birth, and this is significant because it is the part of the retina with the highest image resolution and density of cone (colour-sensitive) cells. Also, the area of most distinct vision is at the centre of the fovea. Peripheral rod cells function better in conditions of low light, but the image is not as sharply focused. Adults prevented from seeing with the fovea (similar to a baby's vision in the first two to four months of life) are more sensitive to blue light in the colour spectrum.

A study which tested the spectral sensitivity of 28 baby girls[26] found that up to four months of age the babies were relatively more sensitive to blue light, but this relative sensitivity changed at about four months of age to yellow light, more in line with adult vision and also with the colour used in many anti-glare devices. Light containing a lot of blue seems to be overwhelming and has the effect of enhancing the brightness of ultraviolet light. Daphne and Charles Maurer,[25] in a book describing the sensory world of the newborn, explain how, when there is relative sensitivity to blue light, 'whites, will often look brighter; for white paints, white papers and white fabrics commonly contain fluorescent brighteners that work by reflecting ultra-violet light.'

Sensitivity to light and dark contrast is a feature of *scotopic sensitivity syndrome* (SSS). SSS describes a syndrome based on the theory first discovered by Helen Irlen in the early 1980s that certain wavelengths of light interfere with the visual pathways between the eye and the brain. Irlen observed that some people with poor reading showed a marked and immediate improvement by simply overlaying the pages with coloured filters or overlays. In other words, by interposing colour between the eye and black and white contrast on the page, visual sharpness, figure-ground effect (the ability to separate foreground from background), and stability of the image on the page were improved. The image is focused more precisely on the centre of the fovea where colour receptors are more prolific.

SYMPTOMS OF SCOTOPIC SENSITIVITY SYNDROME (SSS)

1. Sensitivity to light caused by
   - bright sunlight or bright lighting;
   - fluorescent lights [which contain a high concentration of ultraviolet (blue) light];

- glare from lights, e.g. oncoming headlights, making night driving difficult.
2. Sensitivity to contrast caused by:
   - black print on white paper; the print or the background may appear to move, affecting reading;
   - stripy, zany, or bold patterns on furnishings, clothing, etc; patterns may appear to move or to change shape;
   - vertical or horizontal window blinds where the light shines through the gaps;
   - driving through an avenue of trees on a sunny day (sometimes known as the poplar effect).
3. Restricted field of clear vision:
   - This can result in only some letters of a word or on a page appearing clear, while the remainder are out of focus. This can affect reading and spelling.
4. Poor depth perception affecting:
   - spatial awareness;
   - judging the speed, time, and distance of moving objects such as catching a ball, and going up and down escalators;
   - figure-ground effect, such as when crossing a bridge;
   - objective vertigo.
5. Attention and concentration:
   - difficulty in visual processing affects concentration and attention, distractibility, staying on task, and sustained attention on visual tasks;
   - visual processing problems are also associated with increased anxiety.
6. Somatic symptoms:
   - headaches;
   - migraine;
   - fatigue.

Not all individuals with scotopic sensitivity syndrome have a retained Moro reflex; neither do all people with traces of a Moro reflex suffer from SSS. When the two conditions coexist, in some cases, inhibition of the Moro reflex will reduce photosensitivity and will obviate the need to use coloured filters.

Empirical evidence from clinical observation has revealed that older children and adults who have traces of a *Moro reflex* tend to be hypersensitive to light (photosensitive). Although it cannot be claimed that retention of the Moro reflex is the *cause* of photosensitivity, in some cases when the Moro reflex is inhibited using a specific reflex stimulation and inhibition programme,[iv] children who had previ-

[iv] The INPP Programme.

ously needed to use coloured filters or overlays to help overcome reading problems linked to specific difficulties with blurring of text, text that takes on the appearance of moving or having 'rivers' of white running between the words on the page, have found that they do not need to continue using coloured overlays or tinted lenses as they progress through the reflex programme. In other words, there appears to be an association between light sensitivity, visual stimulus-bound effect, immaturity in visual functioning, and a retained Moro reflex in some cases.

GENERAL SYMPTOMS ASSOCIATED WITH A RETAINED MORO REFLEX

- Hypersensitivity and overreactivity to sudden stimuli;
- Vestibular-related problems such as motion sickness, which continues beyond puberty, gravitational insecurity;
- Poor balance and coordination;
- Difficulty catching a ball or processing rapidly approaching visual stimuli;
- Immature eye movements and visual perceptual abilities, particularly *stimulus-bound effect* (the inability to ignore irrelevant visual information within a given visual field). This can result in difficulty sustaining visual attention and increased distractibility.
- Hypersensitivity to specific sensory stimuli;
- Delayed pupillary constriction to bright light resulting in photosensitivity;
- Adrenal fatigue resulting from easily elicited fight/flight reaction;
- Attention – easily distracted.

Links to Auditory Processing

Many children and adults who have a retained Moro reflex also have an increased tendency to be hypersensitive to sound. This may be to loud noise, unexpected noises, or specific frequencies of sound. The latter is particularly true of some children diagnosed on the autistic spectrum. A specific form of sound therapy known as auditory integrative training (AIT), which selects specific sound frequencies and randomizes stimulation to each ear, has been found to be useful in reducing auditory hypersensitivity in some cases. Why might this be? And what is the possible link to the Moro reflex?

To answer these questions, it is necessary to revisit the concept that retention of primitive reflexes beyond the first year of life is linked to developmental lag in associated functions. This is illustrated by the fact that inhibition of the Moro reflex at circa four months of post-natal life and the parallel development of another reflex, the acoustic stapedius reflex (which helps to protect the ear from loud noises), is normally associated with improved ability to filter out or occlude irrelevant or unpleasant sounds.

The acoustic stapedius reflex develops between two and four months of age, and it consists of a contraction of the stapedius muscle of the middle ear in response to loud noise. The stapedius muscle, the smallest muscle in the human body, is attached to the stapes (stirrup) bone, and when the ear is exposed to loud noise, the acoustic stapedius reflex causes the stapedius muscle to contract involuntarily within 30 milliseconds of exposure to the sound. This contraction of the stapedius muscle reduces the movement of the stapes, decreasing the intensity of the vibration transmitted to the *cochlea*. When the contraction occurs, it effectively reduces the intensity of sound transmitted to the inner ear by as much as 20 decibels. This reflex should also come into play just before a person vocalizes to prevent interference from the sound of one's own voice. (When we hear sounds from outside, they are chiefly received via air conduction, but when we use the voice, the ear receives vibrations internally via bone conduction *and*, fractionally later, externally via air conduction.) To summarize, the main function of the acoustic stapedius reflex is to protect the ear from loud and intrusive noises and from distraction from the sounds of one's own voice.

Cochlea – the hearing apparatus located in the inner ear.

If the acoustic stapedius reflex does not develop adequately, the child can be hypersensitive to loud noises, to specific frequencies of sound, or to the sound of his or her own voice. There can be many reasons why this might occur: development of the reflex may be affected by a history of *frequent ear, nose, or throat infections* in the first three years of

Hearing can continue to be affected for up to eight weeks after the acute phase of a middle ear infection (otitis media) has cleared up.

life, which can result in periods of intermittent hearing impairment. During the periods of reduced hearing, the reflex is not activated at the same threshold of sensitivity so that when hearing is restored, the reflex appears to have become slack or 'lazy'. Lacking an adequate defence mechanism against loud or unwelcome sounds, the Moro reflex is then easily elicited by acoustic stimuli. It is also important to record that the acoustic stapedius reflex cannot protect against very sharp sounds such as a gunshot, because very sharp sounds travel at faster speeds than the time it takes for the reflex to effect a complete contraction of the stapedius mucle (100–200 milliseconds), but it should operate under most other conditions. Cantrell et al.[27] reported abnormalities in neurological disorders. The processing of sound by the brain can also be perceived as a human stressor. The auditory orienting response, startle reflex, and defensive response all translate sound stimuli into action and sometimes into stress-induced bodily changes through 'fight-or-flight' neural mechanisms,[28] which can involve activation of the Moro reflex.

The method of auditory training known as AIT probably helps to reduce hypersensitivity to sounds by 'exercising' the acoustic stapedius reflex through randomized stimulation to each ear. Other forms of sound therapy may help by improving tolerance to certain sound frequencies (habituation), improving lateral processing (cortical selectivity), and developing the ability to orient to sound (location). The ability to locate the source of sound is important because it is the first step towards a conscious decision either to continue to pay attention to the sound or to ignore it. We will examine specific problems in auditory processing in further detail in the final chapter when we explore how other types of intervention in addition to a specific reflex stimulation and inhibition programme can also effect changes in an individual's reflex profile.

Effects on Behaviour

Cottrell[23] described how 'All primitive reflexes (if retained[v]) require a compensation mechanism from higher centres of

---

[v] Author's note.

the brain. The Moro, being a startle reflex, requires an overriding effect. This requires several differing types of compensation. First is the normal mechanism of controlling the muscular reaction. As the normal Moro response to a startle is to fling the arms wide and take a deep breath, this must be eliminated. It is done through a considerable amount of tension and rigid control of muscle tone.' In other words, retention of primitive reflexes results in the need to employ a high degree of compensation involving sustained mental and physical effort to override the effects of the reflex(es) in the process of daily living. The effects of the retained reflex may be seen in various characteristic patterns of behaviour. Not all associated problems will be present in one person, and the expression of associated behaviours varies across different age groups and individual circumstances. The effects of a retained Moro reflex on adults will be examined later.

BEHAVIOURAL OUTCOMES ASSOCIATED WITH A RETAINED MORO REFLEX

- Insecurity;
- Generalized anxiety and/or fearfulness;
- Dislike of sudden unexpected events, e.g. loud noises, bright lights;
- Poor adaptability and dislike of change;
- Attention – easily distracted;
- Physical timidity – may dislike or avoid rough contact sports;
- Tendency to hyperventilate under stress;
- Poor regulation of energy levels – tendency to be either 'on the go' or exhausted.

Possible Secondary Psychological Effects[13,29,30]

- Free-floating anxiety;
- Excessive reaction to stimuli:
  1. poor regulation of emotional affect resulting in labile emotions and mood swings;
  2. tense muscle tone (body armouring), resulting in a tendency to 'hold in' emotions, sometimes resulting in emotional outbursts (can no longer contain emotions)

or the development of somatic symptoms such as headaches, digestive problems, or other psychosomatic complaints.

- Lack of confidence resulting in weak ego and low self-esteem, which can then result in
  1. insecurity and/or dependency, need to remain with a safe 'controlled' environment;
  2. need to control or manipulate events.
- Tendency to suffer from sensory overload in busy or novel environments.

The Moro reflex is the only one of the primitive reflexes to have multisensory effectors. Others are responsive to one type of sensory stimulus. Over the course of the next two chapters, we will examine the role of other reflexes in development, which respond specifically to positional change and to touch.

REFERENCES

1 Brodal P. 1998. *The Central Nervous System. Structure and Function*. Oxford University Press, Oxford.
2 Sherrington C. 1906. *The Integrative Function of the Nervous System*. Cambridge University Press, Cambridge.
3 Hooker D. 1952. *The Prenatal Origin of Behaviour*. University of Kansas Press, Lawrence, KS.
4 Humphrey T. 1964. Some correlations between the appearance of human fetal reflexes and the development of the nervous system. *Progress in Brain Research* 4:93–135.
5 Towen B. 1976. *Neurological Development in Infancy*. William Heinemann Medical Books Ltd., London.
6 Hooker D, Hare C. 1954. Early human fetal behaviour with a preliminary note on double simultaneous fetal stimulation. In: Hooker D, Hare C (Eds). *Genetics and inheritance of neuropsychiatric patterns*, Vol. 33, pp. 98–113. Research Publications – Association for Research in Nervous and Mental Disease.
7 Capute AJ, Accardo PJ. 1991. *Developmental Disabilities in Infancy and Childhood*. Paul H Brookes Publishing Co., Baltimore, MD.
8 Rosenberg K, Trevathen WR. 2001. The evolution of human birth. *Scientific American*, November 2001, pp. 77–81.
9 Mitchell RG. 1960. The Moro reflex. *Cerebral Palsy Bulletin* 2:135–141.

10 Parmelee AH. 1964. A critical evaluation of the Moro reflex. *Pediatrics* 33:773–788.

11 Chasnoff IL, Burns WJ. 1984. The Moro reaction: a scoring system for neonatal narcotic withdrawal. *Developmental Medicine and Child Neurology* 26:484–489.

12 Van Allen MW, Rodnitzky RL. 1981. *Pictorial Manual of Neurological Tests*. Year Book Medical Publishers Inc., Chicago, IL.

13 Goddard SA. 2002. *Reflexes, Learning and Behavior*. Fern Ridge Press, Eugene, OR.

14 Lipsitt LP. 1980. Conditioning the rage to live. *Psychology Today*, February 1980, 124.

15 Pucher G et al. 1987. Quantitative assessment of the Moro reflex: an attempt to identify infants at risk for SIDS? *Biomedizinische Technik. Biomedical Engineering* 32/5:112–117.

16 Goddard SA. 1989. The fear paralysis and its interaction with the primitive reflexes. *INPP Monograph Series 1*. Chester.

17 Kaada B. 1986. *Sudden Infant Death Syndrome. The Possible Role of the Fear Paralysis Reflex*. Scandinavian University Press, Oslo.

18 Blythe P. 1988. Personal communication.

19 Strauss H. 1929. *Journal of Psychology* 38:111.

20 McGraw M. 1945. *The Neuromuscular Maturation of the Human Infant*. Hafner Press, New York.

21 Lagercrantz H. 1989. Neurochemical modulation of fetal behaviour and excitation at birth. In: Euler E et al. (Eds). *Neurobiology of Early Infant Behaviour*, Wenner-Gren International Symposium Series, Vol. 55. Stockton Press, New York.

22 Goddard SA. 1990. Developmental milestones: a blueprint for survival. *INPP Monograph Series. 2*. Chester.

23 Cottrell S. 1988. Aetiology, diagnosis and treatment of asthma through primitive reflex inhibition. Paper presented at the 2nd International Conference of Neurological Dysfunction, Stockholm, October 1988.

24 Blythe P. 1974. Somatogenic neuroses and the effect upon health. Monograph. Institute of Psychosomatic Therapy, Chester, August 1974.

25 Maurer D, Maurer C. 1988. *The World of the Newborn*. Viking, London.

26 Moscowitz-Cook A. 1979. The development of photopic spectral sensitivity in human infants. *Vision Research* 19:1133–1142.

27 Cantrell RW et al. 1979. Stapedius muscle function tests in the diagnosis of neuromuscular disorders. *Otolaryngology and Head and Neck Surgery* 87:261–265.

28 Westman JC, Walters JR. 1981. Noise and stress: a comparative approach. *Environmental Health Perspectives* 41:291–309.

29 Goddard SA. 1996. *A Teacher's Window into the Child's Mind.* Fern Ridge Press, Eugene, OR.
30 Goddard SA. 1991. Elective mutism; the unchosen silence. Paper presented at the 5th European Conference of Neuro-Developmental Delay in Children with Specific Learning Difficulties. March 1991. In: Goddard SA. 1996. *A Teacher's Window into the Child's Mind.* Fern Ridge Press, Eugene, OR.

CHAPTER 3

PRIMITIVE REFLEXES OF POSITION

Certain reflexes respond directly to stimulation of the balance mechanism, which occurs when the position of the head is altered as a result of turning, tilting, or moving the head forwards or backwards. Reflexes of position are directly connected to the functioning of balance, and affect posture and muscle tone.

TONIC LABYRINTHINE REFLEX (TLR)

The TLR is a reflex which originates (receptor) in the *otolith* of the internal ear. Stimulation of the labyrinth through movement of the head forwards or backwards through the mid-plane stimulates neurons of the vestibule affecting extensor muscles. Both the TLR and the symmetric tonic neck reflex have been observed as being present from approximately 30 weeks' gestation in normal premature infants.[1]

In the full-term infant, the TLR can be elicited by lowering the head below the level of the spine resulting in increased retraction of the shoulders, adduction of the externally rotated arms, which are flexed at the shoulders so that the fists are up by the ears, and extension and adduction of the legs, which may also be crossed.[2] Capute et al.[3] describe the extensor pose of the TLR as 'mimicking a surrender position'. Descriptions of the TLR in extension vary with some authors describing extension of the arms and legs on head retraction (Figure 3.1).

It can also be tested by raising the head above the level of the spine or by placing the baby in the prone position. Either of these changes in position results in a marked

Otolith – *from Greek word meaning 'ear-stone'. Minute calcium carbonate 'stones' associated with neuromast organs in the labyrinth. The 'stones' deform the villi of the hair cells in response to changes in orientation in the gravity field.*

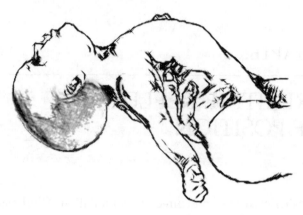

Figure 3.1 TLR in extension (showing extension in the arms as well as in the legs)
Source: Dan Chen. Reproduced by permission of Fern Ridge Press, Eugene, OR.

Figure 3.2 TLR in flexion
Source: Dan Chen. Reproduced by permission of Fern Ridge Press, Eugene, OR.

increase in flexor tone especially at the hips and at the knees. Muscles of the arms and of the legs become flexed, and the neonate curls into a characteristic foetal position (Figure 3.2).

It is thought that the normal flexed posture of the baby in the womb is an early expression of the TLR in flexion, but full extension can only take place after birth. Aspects of the TLR in flexion probably assist in the birth process by helping to facilitate changes in presentation. Presentation describes the position or the situation of the foetus in the womb with the part of the foetus that is closest to the cervix being the presenting part. There are various types of presentation which will affect the course of labour. The most common and safest birth position is described as vertex or cephalic, where the baby's head is the presenting part, with the head flexed forward and the chin on the chest.[4] In this position, pressure from the foetal head on the cervix helps the cervix to dilate, enabling the head to enter the birth canal.

While there are many advantages to upright posture, human beings have paid a price in the design of the birth canal. In order to be born, the human baby has to negotiate two 90° turns to pass safely down the canal. These turning movements involve flexion, internal rotation, extension, and external rotation of the head. It is thought that in addition to being responses to vestibular stimulation *after* birth, some of the primitive reflexes [TLR, asymmetrical tonic neck reflex (ATNR), Pulgar Marx reflex] probably assist mother and baby in the process of birth.

At the beginning of labour, the head should be well flexed as it enters the pelvic brim with the posterior parietal bone presenting. Lateral flexion of the head on the neck (TLR in flexion) enables the head to descend and to become engaged. Further lateral flexion facilitates descent of the head past the pubic symphysis. The baby then needs to make a 90° anterior rotation of the occiput (back of the head) and a 45° rotation towards the front, followed by the shoulders (ATNR). As descent proceeds, the head then needs to extend, and birth of the head is due to head extension with the pubic symphysis acting as a fulcrum. The birth of the head is followed by a 45° restitution which occurs as a result of the twist exerted to the neck, which occurred as a result of internal rotation, being undone. External rotation of the head after it has been born is due to internal rotation of the shoulders at an earlier stage.

Among the many changes that take place at birth, one of the major challenges the baby has to face for the first time is the full force of gravity. While in the womb, the baby is cushioned by surrounding amniotic fluid and the support of its mother's body. In the first weeks after birth, it does not have sufficient muscle tone to support its own posture against gravity. The vestibular system functions as a gravity receptor and vestibular and labyrinthine reflexes provide primitive reactions to gravity, affecting muscle tone.

The vestibular system responds to slow movements of the head (positional change) – being flexed, extended, or rotated – as well as to slow movements of the head and body which occur as a result of external movements that affect the whole body. Muscle tone describes the balance or degree of tension between flexor and extensor muscles, in other words, the 'readiness' for postural support and movement potential.

Bobath (1991)[i] disputed this, stating that 'it is not a primitive reaction and is not seen in normal babies as been stated in American (Snell 1976) or German (Flehmig 1970, 1979) literature. As the labyrinths are fixed within the head, it is the position of the head itself which determines the distribution of hypertonus throughout the affected parts.'

As a *primitive response to gravity*, the TLR is present in early infancy *before* higher, more advanced systems involved in postural control and associated muscle tone have developed. Inhibition of the TLR is a gradual process involving the development of several other righting, protective, and equilibrium reflexes, which emerge over the course of the first year(s) of life. Complete inhibition of the TLR can take up to three and a half years of age.

DEVELOPMENT OF HEAD CONTROL

The development of head control provides one example of the continuous interaction between reflex development and postural control. At birth, a baby has no head control: if held in the ventral position, the head falls forward; if held in the supine position, the head will drop back unless it is supported; and if pulled up to sitting from lying supine, the head lags behind. Head control is the starting point for postural stability and progresses as the labyrinthine *righting* reactions, as opposed to the TLR, develop. Labyrinthine righting reactions start to develop between four and six weeks of age, when the baby begins to lift its head up when placed in the prone position. By 12 weeks, the baby should be able to lift and hold its head up sufficiently to take its weight on its forearms when lying on the tummy. Head control from a supine position takes a little longer; head lag when pulled up into a sitting position disappears by 20 weeks, and by 28 weeks the baby will spontaneously lift its head in anticipation of being lifted and may even be able to

[i] Bobath K. 1991. *A Neurophysiological Basis for the Treatment of Cerebral Palsy.* Cambridge University Press, Cambridge.

sit for a few seconds if supported. In order to gain good control of sitting unaided, the baby needs to be able to recruit the protective reactions that require extension of the arms in response to losing its balance – these develop from about 30 weeks but need to be strengthened and practised before the baby can recover the sitting position by itself.

As each new postural skill is learned, higher postural reactions should come into play, but there is often a period, just as a new skill is being learned, when an earlier reaction will reappear for a short time until the new skill is secure. Between birth and three and a half years of age, children develop a wide range of movement capabilities in the upright posture, from standing to walking; walking to running; hopping, skipping, climbing, jumping. Although the TLR should not be evident in its crude form beyond the first few weeks of life, traces of it may still be seen up to three and a half years of age in normal children if balance or posture is placed under stress or if the child is trying to learn a new skill.

If the TLR is not completely inhibited by three and a half years of age, it provides an indication of immaturity in the functioning of the vestibular apparatus and associated pathways. For instance, if it is still present in flexion or extension, movement of the head forwards or backwards will not only affect muscle tone, but will also result in a 'mismatch' between messages passing from the vestibular system *to* the body and the body's reaction (*proprioceptive feedback*), a discrepancy between intended movement and performance. This is because the neck acts as *the* junction through which signals pass from the vestibular system *to* the body, and information *from* the body is returned. Neck proprioceptors act as important mediators in postural reactions. 'When pressure is exerted on neck muscles, it is possible to produce a greater inhibition of vestibular responses.'[5]

When normal righting reactions are present, a child should be able to maintain postural stability and control of muscle tone without interference from alteration of the head position. When 'mismatch' occurs, the actions of the body do not match the intention of the vestibular system or the motor cortex. It can also affect the control of eye movements necessary for stable visual perception. The result is as if the body has a mind of its own.

Proprioception – *feedback from muscles, tendons, and joints concerning position, movement, or balance of the body or any of its parts. Proprioception and balance provide* internal *information about the body's status relating to balance and position in space (interoceptors). Touch, vision, hearing, and smell inform us about the* external *environment (exteroceptors).*

Synchrony in the timing of messages passing from the vestibular, proprioceptive, and visual systems to other centres in the brain is modulated by the cerebellum and provides the basis for *perceptual* stability in space. When there is mismatch or disassociation in the functioning of these systems, perceptual and/or physical symptoms such as motion sickness, vertigo, and visual-perceptual disturbances appear. Problems in the integration of sensory perception then affect the brain's ability to encode and to interpret information correctly. Stable perception is an important precursor to cognitive understanding (conception) and the more advanced ability to abstract information (to visualize concepts based on earlier concrete experience), and can affect both learning and emotional behaviour.

Stable perception is also in part dependent on congruence in the functional relationship between three interconnecting loops:

1. The vestibular-spinal system;
2. The vestibular-ocular reflex arc;
3. The vestibular-cerebellar system.

Information is passed from the three semicircular canals and the otoliths of the vestibular system via the eighth vestibular-acoustic cranial nerve to the vestibular nuclei, located in the brainstem (Figure 3.3). The vestibular nuclei act rather like a way station through which messages from the vestibular system are sent:

1. to and from the body (vestibular-spinal system);
2. to and from centres involved in the control of eye movements (vestibular-ocular reflex arc);
3. regulation and modification of motor output based on signals received and matched to cortical intent (vestibular-cerebellar system).

Cerebellar dysfunction (difficulty of functioning) as opposed to cerebellar damage.

The cerebellum utilizes the *postural reflexes* to carry out its functions efficiently. If primitive reflexes, elicited as a result of head flexion, extension, or rotation, remain active or succeeding postural reflexes either do not develop fully or are unable to operate effectively under all conditions, the *functioning of the cerebellum* will be affected. In this respect,

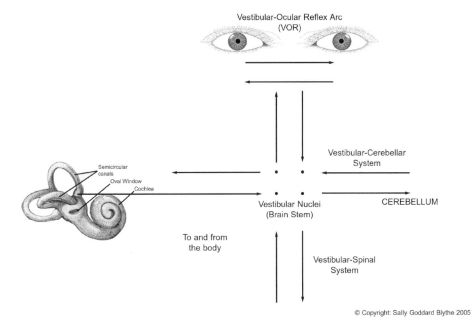

Figure 3.3 Functional links to and from the vestibular system
Source: Goddard SA, 2001. *Reflexes, Learning and Behavior.* Reproduced with permission of Fern Ridge Press, Eugene, OR.

postural reflexes provide *tools* on which the cerebellum relies to carry out its tasks related to posture and motor control effectively. Retained primitive reflexes of position can temporarily block access to these tools, depending on head position.

Centres involved in the control of eye movements are dependent upon having a stable platform in terms of postural control from which to operate. A retained TLR and lack of labyrinthine righting reactions result in an *un*stable platform which can then affect the higher centres involved in the control of eye movements. The effect is similar to trying to read while sitting in the back seat of a car riding over rough terrain at speed or while sitting in a boat on a rough sea. 'In order to achieve posture, positions, purposeful equilibrium, and eventually – locomotion and skilled movements – and in order to develop learning, normal persons must have vestibular impulses integrated with spinal motor activity,'[5] or congruence in the functional relationship between the vestibular system and the spinal system. Retention of the TLR in the older child results in disturbance of this relationship as a result of head movement through the mid-plane.

WHY IS HEAD CONTROL SO IMPORTANT?

In cerebral palsy, primitive reflexes do not become inhibited as a direct result of damage which has affected higher centres in the brain. 'Cerebral defect results in disorders of movement and tone referred to as spasticity, rigidity, flaccidity, athetosis and ataxia. These children show arrested to retarded motor development with a poorly developed postural reflex mechanism and many retain the primitive total movements of early childhood.'[7] The lack of postural adjustment and influence of retained primitive reflexes affects head control and muscle tone in response to head position, which then affects the development of succeeding motor milestones. 'Head control is an important prerequisite for the development of all functions. Until the position of the head in space and against gravity is established, the young baby cannot develop eye-hand control, visual acuity or balance against gravity. He cannot roll over sit up or take his hand to his mouth. He cannot hear properly or vocalise effectively.'[6]

The effects of a residual TLR in a child who does not have cerebral palsy are less severe and may not be immediately obvious. He or she does learn to sit, roll over, stand, walk, and balance in most situations, but the TLR can continue to interfere with some stages of motor development undermining specific higher functions.

THE TONIC LABYRINTHINE REFLEX (TLR) AND EARLY FEEDING

Capute et al.[7] described an additional feature of the TLR in extension when present in cases of central nervous system damage. Extension of the head to 45° elicits adder-like or thrusting movements of the tongue. 'Tongue thrust is the forceful protrusion of the tongue beyond the lips . . . tongue thrust interferes with inserting the nipple and initiating normal feeding pattern.'[7] He further described how expression of the TLR in the supine position determines the position of the extremities, resulting in retraction of the shoulders and extension of the trunk and legs, which is sometimes associated with arching of the back. If this occurs during infant feeding, the baby's posture may seem to be rejecting of the mother, making it difficult to feed. A number of mothers are aware that there are some infants who do not feed well in the most common feeding position with the baby's head nestling in the crook of the mother's arm, but who suck voraciously if the head is placed in the palm of the mother's hand, face on to the breast with the body tucked underneath her arm and the baby's head slightly raised. By changing position and raising the head, arching of the back and any tendency to tongue thrust may be avoided. Early feeding patterns are important because in addition to their obvious role in survival in the first months of life, they affect development of the shape of the mouth and motor aspects of speech such as tongue position and swallow pattern.

Symptoms Suggestive of a Residual TLR

1. TLR in flexion
- Insecure balance
- Posture
- Hypotonus (weak muscle tone)
- Vestibular-related problems including
  - gravitational insecurity;
  - motion sickness;
  - vertigo;
  - visual-perceptual disturbances;
  - spatial problems.
- Visual problems may include
  - lack of near-point convergence;
  - figure-ground effect.
- Vestibular-cerebellar-related problems may include
  - problems with sequencing;
  - time.

2. TLR in extension
- Insecure balance
- Postural problems
- Coordination problems
- Hypertonus (predominance of extensor tone when the head is extended)

- Vestibular-, visual-, and cerebellar-related problems (as above)
- Toe walking
- Articulation problems.

ASYMMETRICAL TONIC NECK REFLEX (ATNR)

The ATNR occurs in response to *rotation* (as opposed to flexion or extension) of the head. It emerges circa 18 weeks' gestation, at about the same time as the mother starts to become aware of her baby's movements. Rotation of the head to one side is followed by extension of the arm and leg on the same side (jaw side) and retraction of the opposite (*occipital*) arm and leg (Figure 3.4).

Occipital *refers to the back of the head. In this context, it means the arm and leg on the side to which the back of the head is directed.*

The reflex grows stronger during the second half of pregnancy and should be fully developed at the time of birth in a full-term pregnancy.

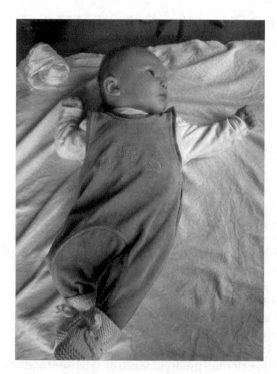

Figure 3.4   The ATNR

While in the womb, the ATNR helps the foetus to move around, to turn, and to adjust its position in response to changes in its mother's posture, to make itself comfortable, to exercise muscles, and to explore its tiny world. It also helps to develop independent movements on each side of the body and may help the baby to take an active role in its own birth.

We have already seen how, during a normal vaginal delivery, the baby has to make two turns of 90° to pass down the birth canal. Maternal contractions alone are not sufficient to enable the baby to turn, but pressure applied to the baby's head encourages the head to turn, probably activating some involvement of the ATNR which helps adjust the position of the shoulders. This may play a part in the sequence of interior rotation of the head, followed by the shoulders in the opposite direction, which should occur during the process of descent. The mechanism will be used again for restitution following the birth of the head. In this way, mother and baby work together as cooperative partners in the birth process, the mother's body stimulating responses in the baby and vice versa. Additionally, it has been suggested that a normal vaginal delivery strengthens the reflexes for the first few weeks of life, and that *intervention* during the birth process such as forceps, ventouse, or caesarean section may disturb the sequence of reflex integration which is reinforced during a normal vaginal delivery. We will return to this theme later when we examine early developmental indicators of neurological dysfunction and the use of the Institute for Neuro-Physiological Psychology Screening Questionnaire.

Conversely, the need for medical intervention at birth may occur in part because the reflexes are not able to assist in the birth process. This could be due to foetal position, foetal maturity, and other factors.

After birth, the ATNR is often released when the baby is placed on its tummy, ensuring that the head turns to one side so that the airway is free and the baby can breathe (Figure 3.5).

As discussed in Chapter 2, research into the incidence of sudden infant death syndrome (SIDS) has consistently found the incidence of SIDS is reduced when parents are advised *not* to place their babies to sleep on their tummy. The current advice is that babies should be placed to sleep on their backs to minimize the risk of SIDS and until research proves otherwise this advice should be followed. However, it does raise a question as to whether babies who succumb to SIDS have

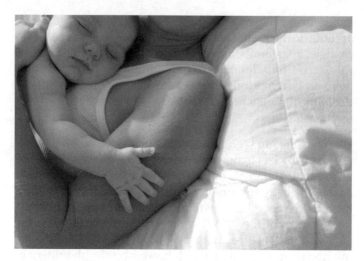

Figure 3.5   Infant under six months of age lying in the ATNR position in prone
Source: Corbis/Jerry Tobias.

an underdeveloped ATNR at just the time when it should be available to fulfil a protective and survival function. We will return to the implications of the 'back to sleep' campaign on other aspects of subsequent development later in the book.

Early Training for Hand–Eye Coordination

In addition to helping to develop differentiated movement on either side of the body, the ATNR provides a mechanism for training early hand–eye coordination. A baby's visual system is immature at birth and can only focus at a distance of approximately 17 cm from the face (the same visual distance needed for most mother and baby interactions in the first few weeks of life, particularly feeding). However, even at this distance, details are not clear and the baby sees more of the outline of an object than the central features. For this reason, babies have to *learn* how to use their vision effectively, and it is *movement* that acts as an elementary teacher in this respect.

For example, in the first weeks of life, a baby does not know that his hands are part of his own body. These mobile 'toys' come and go from his field of vision, reappearing as objects to watch and follow. At this early stage in development, the

ATNR ensures that when the head is turned, not only does the arm stretch out on the same side, but the eyes also move in the same direction as the head and with the arm. In this way, a baby's focusing distance is extended from near point when the head is in the middle and the hands are in front of the face, to arm's length as the head is turned, and the eyes follow the direction of the extending arm and hand (Figure 3.6).

Demyer[8] said that 'since the head and eyes look to the side of the extending hand, we can interpret the ATNR as the forerunner of hand-eye coordination. One's eyes discover one's hand moving in space and learn to grasp visual targets.'

It is equally likely that the ATNR plays a functional part in helping to develop both central and peripheral vision. One study videotaped 14 infants seven times within the first 12 weeks of life to investigate whether the ATNR had a role in placing their hands within their field of vision. They found that when the infants' arms were out of the reflex position,

Figure 3.6 ATNR in baby three weeks old, showing visual convergence just prior to arm extension. ATNR active as her head turns; her arm straightens, and her eyes try to move from near-point convergence to follow her arm
Source: Author's collection. Photograph appeared previously in Goddard Blythe SA. 2008. *What Babies and Children Really Need*, Hawthorn Press, Stroud.

the hands were within the peripheral field of vision, and this situation occurred more often than when the arms and hands were in the reflex position or were completely out of sight. The amount of time that the hands were in a particular visual field varied according to the presence or absence of the reflex with a higher proportion of reflex observations occurring in the focal or central visual field. When the infants were not in the reflex position, hand observations occurred in the peripheral visual field. More focal field observations occurred in the reflex position for the first six of the seven ages. This study confirmed that 'when infants are in the ATNR position, their hands are more likely to be in a position in which they can be visualised or focused on.'[9] Activation of the reflex therefore probably helps to train the eyes to move from peripheral vision to focal vision.

Over the next two to four months, the ATNR gradually diminishes as neck muscles grow stronger, head control improves, visual abilities become more advanced, and the cortex develops. The baby's ability to focus increases as far-distance vision improves. By the time he is four months old, a baby can focus at different distances to the same degree as an adult.[10] This is a remarkable progress from the visual ability of the newborn whose immature cortex left it unable to voluntarily coordinate the muscles moving its eyes with the image it saw, and who watched any part of an object or movement that caught its eye (*stimulus-bound effect*). Observation of newborns and one-month-olds watching an assortment of objects showed that most of the time, their eyes remain on one spot on the perimeter.

Stimulus-bound effect *describes the inability to ignore irrelevant visual stimuli within a given visual field.*

By two months of age, an infant can range broadly with its eyes.[11,12] By four months of age, an infant can see stereoscopically and its vision is sharper, and by six to eight months of age, its vision is sharp enough to see texture. While these visual skills result from the development of the cortex, movement and sensory experience have been important trainers in the process, providing mechanisms through which motor and visual skills work together in training the brain to 'make sense' of what it sees. By the same token, visual understanding of texture is also fed through a combination of touch and oral experience.

A baby's first arena of discovery is its mouth. Through sucking, chewing, and biting, the baby first learns about texture and shape, and in the second half of the first year of life, any object that is small enough and can be reached tends to be taken to the mouth. This is only possible as the ATNR recedes and the hand can be easily brought to the midline of the body even when the head is turned to one side. As long as the ATNR is active, the arm wants to stretch out when the head is turned to the side, making it difficult to bring the hand to the mouth or to the midline unless the hand is already placed in the mouth *before* the head is turned. This is because the action of sucking helps to inhibit the ATNR, allowing a baby to continue to suck its thumb or fingers even when the head is turned to the same side, but the ATNR will prevent the child from *bringing* an object to the mouth if the head is already turned. The simple activities in infancy of reaching and mouthing are important for developing body awareness and body image and for acquiring everyday skills such as self-feeding and dressing.[13]

Functions of the ATNR (18 Weeks in utero to 4–6 Months of Post-natal Life)

- Facilitate movement in utero;
- Develop homolateral movements;
- May assist in the birth process;
- Ensure a free airway when placed in the prone position by turning the head to one side;
- Early hand–eye coordination training.

The ATNR is normally inhibited between four and six months of post-natal life.

Retention of the ATNR beyond four to six months of age can interfere with the development of subsequent motor abilities such as rolling over, commando-style crawling, control of upright balance when the head is turned, the ability to cross the midline of the body affecting bilateral integration, eye movements, and hand–eye coordination. This is a direct consequence of the increase in extensor tone which occurs when the head is turned to one side. In order to be able to roll over, for example, a baby needs to be able to turn its head and to bend the arm and leg on the *same* side as in Figure 3.7.

Commando (cross-pattern) crawling on the tummy requires the ability to turn the head, stretch out the arm on the same side, place it on the floor, and then *bend* the arm to pull the

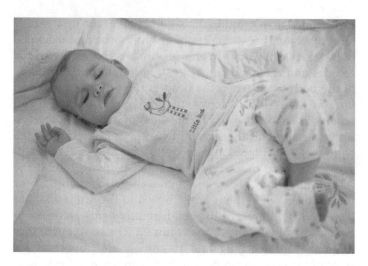

Figure 3.7   ATNR inhibited in supine position in a six-month-old baby. ATNR is substantially inhibited enabling the baby to turn its head and to bend its arm and leg on the same side. Amphibian reflex in the supine position is present. Segmental rolling reflexes are not developed yet in this example
Source: Mother & Baby Picture Library.

body forward while pushing off with the opposite leg. If the ATNR is still strongly present at the time the baby is ready to crawl, it will prevent the arm from bending, making it difficult to pull the body forwards. The baby may use *homologous movements* to try to propel itself forward or may simply miss out the stage of crawling on the tummy. Children who have never crawled on the tummy as babies can find it difficult to carry out the necessary cross-pattern crawling movements if asked to do so later on, as if the brain has never assimilated the movement patterns that are required. The same children may have difficulty with activities that require the same sequence of movements when they are older (e.g. front crawl when swimming, marching using the opposite arm and leg).

Homologous movements – using the two arms together to pull itself forward while either dragging the legs or attempting to push with the two legs at the same time. This is a primitive method of crawling.

Control of upright balance can be affected because head rotation can result in extension of the leg on the same side and flexion of the opposite leg, 'throwing' control of balance off centre. Just as the TLR can have a destabilizing effect on balance when the head is moved through the mid-plane, the ATNR results in a 'mismatch' between intent (motor planning) and body reaction when the head is turned to the affected side(s). Balance is secure as long as the head is positioned at the midline (*static balance*), but is impaired when there is lateral head movement. This is why one of the standard tests for assessing static balance, the Romberg test, is not sufficient to assess a child's balance if used in isolation. Additional tests for dynamic balance should also be included.

The ability to cross the midline can also be affected. The leg, the arm, and/or the eyes may be affected when the head is turned to one side. Ayres[14] observed that children with a retained ATNR have impaired motor planning skills and lack of bilateral integration. Telleus[15] found there was a correlation between a retained ATNR and cross-laterality in a sample of children above the age of eight years.

Difficulty in crossing the midline has implications for writing and reading: writing because a right-handed child finds it difficult to cross the midline of the body with the hand to write on the left side of the page; reading because the eyes do not track smoothly across the midline. Most children learn to 'accommodate' the problem by compensating in a number of ways: they may make adjustments to their sitting posture by pushing the chair back or by leaning back into the chair so that writing can continue without having to bend the arm, as in Figure 3.8.

Children may twist their posture and may rotate the writing page by as much 90° so that they can write with the arm extended; they may use an awkward or very tight pen grip to try to keep the fingers closed and the pen under control (Figure 3.9). Irrespective of the strategy used, the physical action of writing does not become an automatic one. If a physical action is not automated, additional cognitive effort must be recruited to carry out the motor task, and this can interfere with the ability to carry out the action and to process information cognitively at the same time.

Once beyond the early stages of learning to form letters, the educative process requires the ability to think and to write at the same time. The effects of a retained ATNR on written work can occur irrespective of intelligence – indeed, the more intelligent and orally articulate the child, the more likely he or she is to be accused of laziness and to be told 'you could do better if only you tried harder'; 'could do

Static balance – ability to maintain a fixed position. When control of static balance is unstable, more movement or involvement in other body parts is involved in the maintenance of stability. Dynamic balance – ability to maintain equilibrium while moving. Children with poor control of static balance need to move more to maintain an attitude. It is possible to have poor static balance but to have reasonably well-developed dynamic balance. These are children who have good coordination while in motion but who may have difficulty concentrating when sitting still, e.g. good on the sports field but underachieve in class.

Figure 3.8   Example of sitting posture and pencil grip used to 'accommodate' the effect of a retained ATNR when writing
Source: Author's collection.

Figure 3.9   Example of a pencil grip used to 'control' the effect of the ATNR when writing
Source: Author's collection.

better if only you applied yourself', etc., and to under-achieve. If the ATNR is the only aberrant primitive reflex, a child can usually learn to read (managing to compensate for control of eye movements), but handwriting will continue to be a problem because writing involves control of eye *and* hand movements (visual-motor integration). Eye move-ments will also be affected if other reflex immaturities exist such as underdeveloped head righting reflexes *in combina-tion* with an ATNR. Then, 'A child with a dominate ATNR pattern of movement will have difficulty visually tracking an object across an arc of 180°. The infant may be able to focus an object and begin to follow it visually on the chin side of the ATNR, but he appears to have difficulty follow-ing the object to the midline or past the midline. The lack of visual attention and tracking may not only affect reaching and grasping, but in the older child, it could affect reading and writing across a paper. Gesell noted the inability of normal infants to follow objects visually beyond the midline if an ATNR was present.'[13]

Reading comprehension may be affected.[16] This is because additional cognitive effort must be employed in the physical aspects of reading, particularly the control of eye move-ments. Blythe and McGlown[17] found the ATNR to be present in children with reading and writing problems. In a study carried out by the author, which examined the reflex status of 54 children age 8 to 15 years who had been diagnosed with dyslexia, all participants were found to have a residual or retained ATNR and also visual-motor integration diffi-culties.[18] McPhillips and Sheehy[19] found that among a group of children with reading difficulties, the lowest reading group had a significantly higher mean level of persistent ATNR (although the ATNR was also found to a lesser degree among the general population).

SYMMETRICAL TONIC NECK REFLEX (STNR)

The STNR has been observed in premature infants at 30 weeks' gestation;[20] it is present for a short period at birth, only to recede and to re-emerge at circa eight months of post-natal life and to be inhibited at circa 11 months.

The STNR reappears at about eight months of age as the infant prepares to push itself up off the ground from the prone position in preparation for creeping on hands and knees. When the baby lifts its head up (extended), there is extension in the upper limbs accompanied by flexion in the lower limbs; when the head looks down (flexion), the limbs of the upper body flex and the lower limbs extend (Figure 3.10).

Whereas the TLR results in either flexion or extension of the *whole* body in response to change of head position, the STNR helps to break up the pattern of tone in the *middle* of the body, resulting in *opposite* reactions in the upper and lower sections. In this way, the STNR is thought to play a part in helping to integrate and to inhibit the TLR, and to provide the basis for stable positions against gravity in the prone position (prone on elbows) and the ability to bear upper-body weight *ready* for creeping on hands and knees (Figure 3.11).

a

b

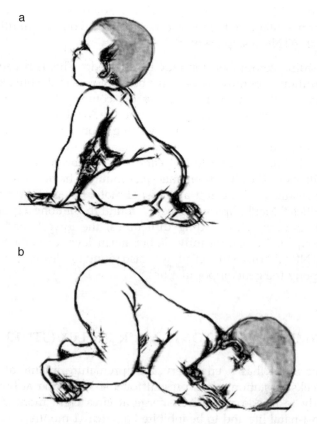

Figure 3.10   (a) STNR in extension. (b) STNR in flexion
Source: Dan Chen. Reproduced by permission of Fern Ridge Press, Eugene, OR.

However, as long as the STNR persists, the infant cannot carry out the necessary coordination of the upper *and* lower body for creeping. It is only possible to bear weight on the extended upper limbs when the head is also extended. In order to bypass this developmental difficulty, some babies will learn to 'bunny hop' in this position (Figure 3.12).

Figure 3.11 Infant using STNR in prone (full arm extension) getting ready to creep
Source: Don Bayley/istockphoto.

Figure 3.12 Infant still under the influence of the STNR prior to learning to creep on hands and knees
Source: Corbis/Laura Doss/Flirt.

When the baby puts its head down, its arms collapse and it cannot continue to bear weight on its arms. Most babies pass through a phase of rocking backwards and forwards on hands and knees, gradually helping to integrate the reflex before they learn to creep.

Another function of the STNR is that it helps the child pull from hand and knees to the standing position. 'The child reaches up to grasp the side of his crib or playpen. "As he pulls himself upward, his elbows bend. The reflex response pulls his head down and forward, and at the same time strongly extends his hips and knees, pushing him toward the erect position. As long as he keeps his head down and holds to the crib side, his legs will continue to provide reflex support. But let him look up and reach out for mother – his legs collapse under him."'[21] (Figure 3.13).

Functions of the STNR

The STNR is thought to fulfil a number of functions: using video footage of babies in the first hour after birth, Righard and Alade[22] showed that babies who had been born to mothers who had not received analgesic or other medication during labour, if placed on the mother's tummy immediately after birth, spontaneously worked their way up towards the breast and started to root and suckle within an hour of being born. To achieve this, the babies used a combination of the infant stepping/crawling reflex (and STNR) to nudge their way up towards the breast. Babies born to mothers who had received medication during labour were too tired to seek and self-attach to the breast, and even if placed at the breast, struggled to latch on and to suckle.

As the head is flexed, the bottom pushes up. As the toes touch the mother's abdomen, extension of one foot and withdrawal of the other, combined with flexion of the arms and legs, enables the neonate to slowly nudge its way up towards the breast.

This newborn crawling is really a 'false' crawling reflex and, rather like the stepping reflex, is only present for a short time at birth. If the newborn is placed on the stomach, it will begin to flex the arms and legs in a motion that simulates crawling. This is partly due to the neonate's earlier foetal curled-up position and will start to recede as the baby is able to lie in a flatter position. False crawling usually starts to recede after about one week. The stepping reflex occurs if the baby is held upright with the feet touching a flat surface. The baby will appear to 'walk' by placing one foot in front of the other. This is not really walking because the neonate

Figure 3.13   Infant aged 10 months, able to support weight with upper body when standing, using the STNR in flexion – with head forward and arms bent, extensor tone in the legs increases – legs not yet able to support posture without hand/arm support
Source: Alamy Images/Lisa Valder/Imagestopshop.

has insufficient antigravity muscle tone with which to support its weight, and the reflex will disappear by about four months of age to reappear between 11 and 16 months as true walking is learned. In the early stages of learning to walk, the infant stepping reflex is present and the infant will tend to walk on its toes.

The STNR may also play a part in helping to align the occipital and sacral regions of the spine in preparation for good skeletal alignment in the upright posture, which is necessary for standing and walking. In this respect, chiropractors refer to 'primary' and 'secondary' curves of the spine. The primary curve develops from the fourth week in utero to form a

Lordosis – to bend the body forward and inward.

simple arc; the first secondary curve (cervical *lordosis*) occurs at three to four months of post-natal life, coinciding with the development of righting reflexes and ocular focus; the second secondary curve occurs between 12 and 18 months of post-natal life as the infant makes the transition from creeping on hands and knees to walking. This is the time when the lumbar lordosis is formed.

Differentiation of upper and lower sections of the body, the quadruped position, and mobility on all fours may play a part in helping the secondary curve to develop (Figure 3.14) so that by the time the infant learns to stand on two feet, the erect infant has one primary and two secondary curves to support upright posture and differentiated movement.

Helping to Train Visual Skills

Blythe[23] suggested that at the time when the STNR is active (8–11 months), it may play a part in helping to develop visual accommodation. This is because when a baby is positioned on all fours, as it puts its head down and as the arms bend, the eyes are forced to focus at near distance (Figure 3.15).

Figure 3.14   Infant (approximately 10 months) creeping on hands and knees. STNR and ATNR are inhibited, enabling the infant to lift and to turn its head and to maintain upper-body support with both arms
Source: Alamy Images/Picture Partners.

Figure 3.15 STNR in flexion still active in an infant getting ready to creep on hands and knees
Source: Corbis/Pete Leonard/Zefa.

Figure 3.16 Residual STNR in extension – visual attention is focused at far distance
Source: Alamy Images/Juniors Bildarchiv.

When the head is extended, the arms extend, and the knees bend, visual focus naturally shifts to far distance (Figure 3.16).

The period of integration (rocking on hands and knees followed by creeping) probably helps to entrain the ability to shift visual focus between near and far distances.

In this respect, it is of interest that the stage in development when a baby learns to creep on hands and knees coincides with the time that a baby starts to perceive depth. Walk and Gibson[24] carried out investigations using a 'visual cliff', which simulated the *appearance* of a steep edge by attaching a piece of glass to a surface about 3 feet above the floor. Part of the underside of the glass had a checkboard pattern, while on the other side, the same pattern was placed on the floor. This gave the visual appearance of a sudden drop in the supporting surface. When babies over six months of age were placed on the visually 'solid' side and their mothers called to them from across the visual cliff, babies would crawl towards mother from the 'shallow' side, but very few would venture from the side which required them to cross the visual precipice.

The action of creeping on hands and knees also helps to integrate vision, proprioception, and balance in a new relationship with gravity, providing yet another stage of entrainment for the integrated functioning of these three systems. This may be one reason why there is a higher incidence of specific learning difficulties in children who did not go through the developmental stages of crawling like a commando and of creeping on hands and knees in the first year of life. This is not to suggest that all children who bypassed crawling and creeping are likely to have later learning problems – rather, if a child is *unable* to crawl or creep at the expected time in development as a result of delayed reflex integration at this important developmental stage, it may have an effect on subsequent related functions, such as balance, posture, and visual perception.

Functions of the STNR

- May help neonate to crawl up to the breast at birth;
- Helps to modify and inhibit the TLR;
- Helps to support upper-body posture in the prone position;
- May help in the formation of secondary spinal curve;
- Helps to train visual accommodation;
- Helps the infant to pull up from sitting to standing.

What happens if the STNR is not inhibited or fully integrated by the end of the first year of life?

Effects of a Retained or Residual STNR

Posture can be one of the first casualties of a residual or retained STNR. This is because head position continues to influence muscle tone in the upper and lower sections of the body. When the head is forward or flexed, there is a tendency for the shoulders to retroflex and for the lower body to extend, which results in a tendency to stand with the head poked forward and to be round-shouldered (Figure 3.17).

Head position is everything when it comes to posture, and posture affects ambulation. In the elderly, skeletal, joint, and muscular problems can all affect posture as a result of skeletal changes, and the first reflex to re-emerge in old age as a result of either structural *or* central nervous system degeneration is the STNR (Figure 3.18).

Whereas structure determines function, bad posture over a long period of time will affect structure, particularly in the developing child at times of rapid growth such as at puberty and during the adolescent years. A retained or residual STNR can affect both stance and gait. Sitting posture will also be affected because a residual STNR interferes with upper- and lower-body integration.

Figure 3.17 Standing posture typical of an adult with a retained STNR
Source: Alamy Images/Itali.

Figure 3.18   Effects of released STNR on standing posture in the elderly
Source: Corbis/Anne W. Krause.

Young children, particularly girls with a retained STNR whose hips are more flexible than boys, tend to sit using a 'W' leg position as in Figure 3.19. They often find it uncomfortable to sit cross-legged on the floor and may be the children who fidget and squirm during 'quiet time', sitting on the floor at school assembly or during story time. This is because when the head is forward, the arms bend and the legs straighten, making it almost impossible to sit cross-legged. When sitting at a desk, as soon as the child bends its head to start writing, the arms also want to bend, making it difficult to maintain good control of upper-body posture (Figure 3.20). As they grow older, these are the children who prefer to do their homework or to watch television lying on the floor rather than sitting in a chair. To sit with the legs straight and the arms bent is uncomfortable, so children will often tuck their feet underneath their legs or wind them

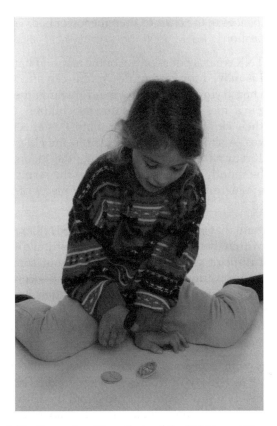

Figure 3.19   Example of the effects of the STNR on sitting posture in older children. W leg position – characteristic of a residual STNR
Source: Corbis/Olivia Baumgartner/Sygma.

Figure 3.20   Example of the effects of the STNR on sitting posture in older children. Sitting position typical of a residual STNR in the upper body – when the head is bent, the arms bend so that the child tends to lie across the writing surface
Source: Author's collection.

Whereas the STNR was found chiefly in children with primary neurological dysfunction when I first started to work with reflex integration programmes in the mid-1980s, over the last 10 years there appears to be an increase in the number of older children who still have retained STNR in the upper body, which is so strong that they have difficulty in carrying out the simplest of reflex integration exercises. The reasons for this increase have not been researched, but empirical evidence suggests that changes in modern child-rearing practices, with children being placed in baby seats from an early age, sleeping on their backs, and spending less time engaged in free play on the floor lying on the tummy may be contributing to the retention of the STNR as a result of environmental factors, as opposed to primary neurological dysfunction.

around the legs of the chair to keep the lower body anchored in one position.

As the STNR creates poor control of the arm and hand when the head is moved forward or down, this can affect coordination when trying to bring the hand towards the mouth, resulting in a 'messy eater'. These are the children who tend to feed their clothes and the floor almost as effectively as themselves. A similar problem is seen in the elderly when the STNR returns. The action of bringing the spoon, fork, or cup to the mouth becomes clumsy, with the result that the mouth is sometimes missed altogether or pieces of food are misplaced.

It can be said that children with a residual STNR are uncomfortable within their own body, and this postural discomfort makes it difficult to sit still and to carry out coordinated actions. Poor posture affects muscle tone and vice versa, so that the child with an STNR in flexion often has poorly developed muscle tone in the upper body and may already have received a diagnosis of hypotonus from an occupational therapist or a physiotherapist.

Problems with coordination, attention, and concentration can all be secondary outcomes of a retained STNR in the older child. Two professors emeritus from the University of Indianapolis, O'Dell and Cook,[25] who had spent more than 30 years working with the Bender Exercise Programme – a special exercise programme devised by Miriam Bender to inhibit the STNR – found that a high percentage of children diagnosed with attention deficit hyperactivity disorder (ADHD) in the USA still had an active STNR. When the STNR was inhibited using a motor programme which involved crawling and creeping against a resistant force, many of the 'symptoms' of ADHD started to recede. In other words, poor control of the body can affect the ability to remain still and to focus attention.

Other factors affected by poor upper- and lower-body integration include many gross motor skills such as learning to climb a rope, leap over a box in gymnastics, do handstands, and breaststroke at swimming. Breaststroke is affected because each time the head is lifted up to keep it above the water, the feet start to sink, making it very difficult to keep the body level on top of the water. Some children with an STNR learn to swim under water more easily because when the head goes down, the feet start to come up, and the weight of the water helps to keep the body level.

Elite athletes will sometimes momentarily recruit certain reflexes such as the STNR or the ATNR to carry out highly skilled actions, particularly those that take place in states of suspended or altered gravity such as when leaping to place the ball in the basket at basketball (ATNR), or when diving from a springboard (STNR) (Figures 3.21 and 3.22).

If, as Blythe suggested,[23] the STNR helps to train visual accommodation in the first year of life, as with other reflexes, if it is not inhibited, it tends to hold related skills back to an earlier developmental stage. In the case of visual skills, a retained STNR is often associated with slower visual accommodation. This affects activities that require rapid

Figure 3.21   Basketball players releasing the ATNR to catch and/ or to reach for the ball
Source: Getty Images/Black 100.

Figure 3.22   Springboard diver using STNR in flexion
Source: Corbis/Erich Schlegel/New Sport.

visual accommodation such as keeping track of an object approaching at speed – needed for catching a ball – or copying from the board or from a book at school.

In cases where there is a combination of a retained ATNR and lack of head righting reflexes, these have been linked to impaired visual *horizontal* tracking (needed for reading and writing). A study which investigated the impact of abnormal reflexes and a reflex integration programme on specific eye movements has found a correlation between a retained STNR and impaired *vertical* tracking.[26] Vertical eye tracking movements are necessary for aligning columns correctly in maths, for judging heights such as when standing near the edge of a cliff, or for stepping on to a descending escalator.

Effects of a Retained or Residual STNR

- Upper- and lower-body integration;
- Attention/concentration;

- Swimming;
- Hand–eye coordination;
- Visual accommodation – copying, catching a ball;
- Vertical eye tracking movements.

Primitive reflexes that respond to changes in position can all have an effect on balance, posture, and coordination, which collectively provide support to higher centres involved in the control of eye movements and in visual perception. These can have an impact on specific aspects of learning, but reflexes of position are only part of the story. Other primitive reflexes respond to tactile stimulation influencing fine motor skills as well as balance, body awareness, sensitivity, and spatial awareness. These are the subject of the next chapter.

REFERENCES

1 Allen MC. 1987. The symmetric tonic neck reflex (STNR) as a normal finding in premature infants prior to term. *Pediatric Research* 20:208A.

2 Drillien CM, Drummond MB. 1977. *Neurodevelopmental Problems in Early Childhood*. Blackwell Scientific Publications, Oxford.

3 Capute AJ et al. 1980. *Primitive Reflex Profile*. University Park Press, Baltimore, MD.

4 Goddard Blythe SA. 2008. *What Babies and Children Really Need. How Mothers and Fathers can Nurture Children's Growth for Health and Well Being*. Hawthorn Press, Stroud.

5 De Quirós JB, Schrager OL. 1978. *Neuropsychological Fundamentals in Learning Disabilities*. Academic Therapy Publications, Novato, CA

6 Shepherd R. 1980. *Physiotherapy in Paediatrics*. Butterworth-Heinemann Limited, Oxford.

7 Capute AJ et al. 1981. Primitive reflexes: a factor in non-verbal language in early infancy. In: Stark RE (Ed.). *Language Behaviour in Infancy and Early Childhood*. Elsevier, North-Holland, New York.

8 Demyer W. 1980. *Technique of the Neurological Examination*. McGraw-Hill Book Company, New York.

9 Coryell J, Henderson A. 1979. Role of the asymmetrical tonic neck reflex in hand visualization in normal infants. *American Journal of Occupational Therapy* 33/4:255–260.

10 Maurer D, Maurer C. 1988. *The World of the Newborn*. Viking, London.

11 Aslin RN. 1985. Oculo-motor measures of visual development. In: Gottlieb G, Krasnegor N (Eds). *Measurement of Audition and Vision During the First Year of Life: a Methodological Overview*, pp. 391–417. Ablex, Norwood, NJ.

12 Maurer D. 1983. The scanning of compound figures by young infants. *Journal of Experimental Child Psychology* 35:437–448.

13 Crutchfield CA, Barnes MR. 1993. *Motor Control and Motor Learning in Rehabilitation*. Stokesville Publishing Company, Atlanta, GA.

14 Ayres AJ. 1973. *Sensory Integration and Learning Disorders*. Western Psychological Services, Los Angeles, CA.

15 Telleus C. 1980. En kompararitiv studie av neurologisk skillnader hos born medoch utan Isoch skrivovarigheter. Unpublished Master's Thesis. Göteborg Universitet Psychologisker Instituktionen.

16 Parmenter C. 1975. The asymmetric tonic neck reflex in normal first and third grade children. *The American Journal of Occupational Therapy* 29:463–468.

17 Blythe P, McGlown DJ. 1979. *An Organic Basis for Neuroses and Educational Difficulties*. Insight Publications, Chester.

18 Goddard Blythe SA. 2001. Neurological dysfunction as a significant factor in children diagnosed with dyslexia. *The 5th International British Dyslexia Association Conference Proceedings*. University of York, April 2001.

19 McPhillips M, Sheehy N. 2004. Prevalence of primary reflexes and motor problems in children reading difficulties. *Dyslexia* 10(4):316–338(23).

20 Capute AJ, Accardo PJ. 1991. *Developmental Disabilities in Infancy and Childhood*. Paul H Brookes Publishing Co., Baltimore, MD.

21 Bender ML. 1976. *Bender-Purdue Reflex Test*. Academic Therapy Publications, San Rafael, CA.

22 Righard L, Alade MO. 1990. Effect of delivery room routine on success of first breast-feed. *Lancet* 3/336(8723):1105–1107.

23 Blythe P. 1990. Lecture for INPP Supervision. October 1990, Chester.

24 Walk RD, Gibson EJ. 1961. A comparative and analytical study of visual depth perception. *Psychological Monographs*, 75.

25 O'Dell NE, Cook PA. 2004. *Stopping ADHD. A Unique and Proven Drug-free Program for Treating ADHD in Children and Adults*. Avery, New York.

26 Bein-Wierzbinski W. 2001. Persistent primitive reflexes in elementary school children. Effect on oculomotor and visual perception. Paper presented at the 13th European Conference of Neuro-Developmental Delay in Children with Specific Learning Difficulties, Chester, UK.

CHAPTER 4

PRIMITIVE TACTILE REFLEXES

PALMAR GRASP REFLEX

First described by Robinson[1] in 1891 as a 'clinging reaction', the palmar grasp reflex is elicited in response to placing an object, such as a finger, crosswise into the palm of a newborn baby's hand. The neonate will grasp the object by curling its fingers successively around the stimulus beginning with the middle finger, followed by the ring and little fingers, index finger and thumb.[2] The thumb usually nestles underneath the index finger. Grasping movements can also occur spontaneously without any object being placed in the hand, as in Figure 4.1. In the first few days after birth, the reflex is strong enough to support the baby's weight if suspended.

The reflex comprises two phases:

1. a grasping or 'catching' phase consisting of rapid flexion and adduction of the fingers and thumb;
2. a holding phase when there is sustained flexion of the fingers maintained by traction on the flexor tendons.[3]

The grasping phase is easily elicited by light touch, but the holding phase requires more proprioceptive input, such as resistance from the object or tugging as in weight suspension.

Giordano[4] examined 282 infants and found that the palmar reflex was always present in healthy infants up to the fifth month of life. It appears to be strongest in the first 12 days,[5] becoming more infrequent between the fourth and sixth months, and is usually inhibited by the end of the first year.

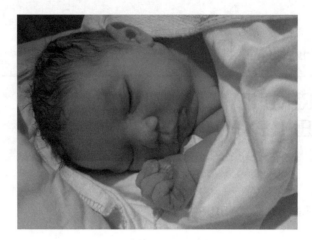

Figure 4.1   Palmar grasp reflex in a newborn baby
Source: Author's collection.

Both the palmar and a similar reflex in the foot – the plantar grasp reflex – are thought to be a continuation of an earlier stage in evolution when it was necessary for the infant to cling to its mother's fur. This can be seen in certain breeds of monkey who use the grasping reflex at birth by clinging to the mother's fur and by crawling on to her abdomen. To this day, the grasping phase of the reflex in humans is most easily elicited by contact with hair.

Developmentally, the palmar reflex appears at the 11th week of pregnancy and has been noted by Hooker[6] in his studies of foetuses removed from the womb. Closing of the fingers (without the thumb) appears at the 11th week; by 16 weeks, tactile stimulation of the hand elicits fist closure, but fingers do not grasp the object; at 20 weeks, the fingers hold on weakly to a thin glass stick, and by 22 weeks, strength of the grasp has increased. Hooker's earlier findings have since been confirmed with the use of ultrasound. After birth, the strength of the palmar grip varies according to feeding times, it being stronger if tested before than after feeding.

The palmar reflex is also linked to feeding movements in the first four months of post-natal life. Prechtl[2] noted that the tonic palmar reflex is coupled with sucking movements in the first four months. At this stage of development, there is a link between excitation of the sucking centre and the centre involved in the palmar grasp reflex. Should this persist into later childhood, it has implications for speech and independent use of the fingers later on. Sucking movements can also be elicited by stimulation of the palmar reflex at this stage. This is because reciprocal movements between sucking and grasping exist as a result of the Babkin reflex, which links movements of the hands to those of the mouth. The Babkin reflex is sometimes used to stimulate sucking in a baby who is unwilling to feed by applying gentle pressure to the palms of the hands, which elicits sucking movements.

The *Babkin reflex* is sometimes referred to as the palmar-mandibular reflex, and is active from birth to approximately four months of age. It is elicited by applying quick pressure to the palms of the hands. The response is rotation of the head to the midline, forward flexion of the head, and opening of the mouth.[7] If the nipple or teat is placed in the mouth, contact with the inside of the mouth – the frontal area of the palate – will stimulate sucking movements. The Babkin reflex is an example of a hand-to-mouth sensorimotor link in the first months of life. A similar response in reverse can be observed in young mammals, particularly hand-reared kittens if they have lost their mother. When sucking from a bottle, they simultaneously knead with their claws.

André Thomas et al.[8] found that the palmar grasp reflex modified the effect of the Moro reflex if it was stimulated on one side prior to eliciting the Moro reflex. If an object was placed in one hand, the Moro reaction would only occur in the arm on the opposite side. If an object was placed in both hands, first eliciting the palmar grasp, then the Moro reaction was inhibited in the arms bilaterally. This example of interaction between reflexes in the first year of life provides the foundations for the principles of remediation used in the Institute for Neuro-Physiological Psychology (INPP) programmes.

As adults, we sometimes utilize this connection when under stress. When about to undertake an unpleasant or difficult task, we often clasp and unclasp our hands in anticipation. Stress balls may be effective based on the same principle.

Functions of the Palmar Grasp Reflex

- In primates, helps the infant to cling to its mother;
- May help to develop traction response;
- Has an inhibitory effect on the Moro reflex if stimulated just prior to eliciting the Moro reflex;
- Is linked to feeding and sucking movements;
- May help to stimulate myelinization of pathways involved in hand and mouth movements in early development.

The palmar reflex is gradually inhibited over the course of the first three to six months of post-natal life. By the fifth month, the infant starts to be able to let go of an object at will, although this will often occur as much by accident as by design. This is the stage when the infant will start to drop its toys or its food. Lacking sufficient mobility to retrieve the object for itself, the dropping phase will often be followed by whimpering or by a more vociferous protest until the object is retrieved by a nearby adult, only to be dropped again a few seconds later. This ability to 'let go' from the palmar grasp is an important precursor to the development of more skilled hand and finger movements.

Difficulty in carrying out fine finger movements (dysdiadochokinesia) is often seen in children who have a history of speech impairment or language delay, indicating that the same motor centres involved in independent finger movements are necessary for motor aspects of speech.

Pyramidal tract – either of two bundles of nerve fibres, shaped like inverted pyramids, running from each cerebral hemisphere down the spinal cord to all voluntary muscles of the body.

As it becomes possible to release an object, the thumb and finger take part in a radial-palmar grasp. Soon, the infant will be able to pick up small objects using all its fingertips; finger coordination improves, and increasingly, it will be able to use one hand without a corresponding or mirroring movement in the other. By nine months, the child will start to use a pincer grip using the thumb and index finger, and skill in the use of the pincer grip will continue to develop over the remainder of the second half of the first year. This increase in manual dexterity is related to maturation of the *pyramidal tract*, one of the areas of the brain which shows the most striking differences between adults and neonates.[9]

Fine motor tasks, such as holding a pencil to write, begin with repetition of earlier patterns. For example, when first learning to write, 'the child's first grasp on a writing tool is cross-palmar grasp. The whole hand clutches the chalk or pencil and usually the arm is turned inwards. The arm is not supported on the table, so the child draws with gross motor movements. A little later, almost the same grasp is used, but the child notices that he can guide the pencil better, if he extends his index finger.'[10] Eventually, the child will learn to hold the pencil using a tripod pincer grip with third finger supporting the pencil and the forearm supported on the writing surface. This allows the arm to be turned outwards rather than inwards, giving greater flexibility, scope, and control to hand and arm movements.

The ability to hold and then to manipulate feeding implements follows a similar pattern. At two to two and a half years of age, children trying to feed themselves will naturally use a turned-in cross-palmar grip. Their early attempts at feeding are clumsy and often miss the mark, but improve as they are gradually able to adapt their grip and arm position. Using two feeding implements together (spoon and fork) will take much longer, and cutting (necessary for effective use of knife and fork) is yet another type of coordination.

What are the implications of a retained or residual palmar reflex in the older child?

Effects of a Retained or Residual Palmar Reflex

- Poor manual dexterity;
- Poorly developed pincer grip, which can affect fine muscle skills such as use of feeding implements, tools such as scissors, and pencil grip for drawing and writing;
- Palm of the hand may remain hypersensitive to tactile stimuli;
- Mouth and hand movements do not become independent. This can affect speech as well as manipulation. There may be an 'overflow' of movements from hand to mouth so that the mouth moves when the hands are engaged in a task, or the hands are involuntarily active while speaking (Figure 4.2).

PLANTAR REFLEX

The plantar reflex was first described by van Woerkom[11] in 1912. It emerges circa 11 weeks in utero and starts to be inhibited between seven and nine months of post-natal life. It should disappear by the age of one year as the infant learns to stand.

The plantar and palmar grasp reflexes correspond to each other in as far as both result in a grasping response to touch or pressure applied to the sole of the foot or to the palm of the hand. The plantar grasp reflex is elicited by pressure applied to the anterior end of the sole of the foot, which results in *flexion* of the toes. Although the plantar grasp is not usually as strong as the palmar grasp, it is strong enough for the toes to grip a slender object (Figure 4.3).

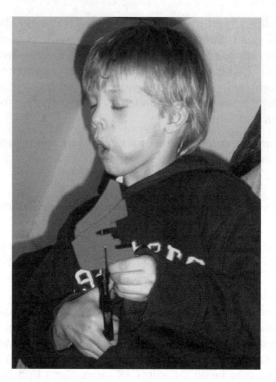

Figure 4.2   An example of an 'overflow' between hand and mouth movements in an older child
Source: Magdalena Zweegman – personal collection.

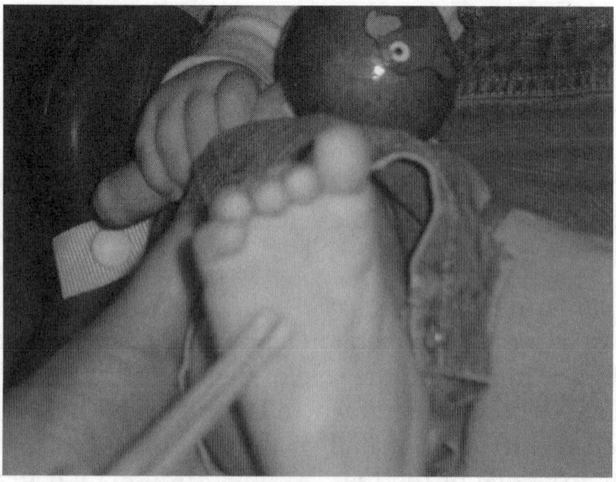

Figure 4.3   Infant plantar reflex
Source: Author's collection.

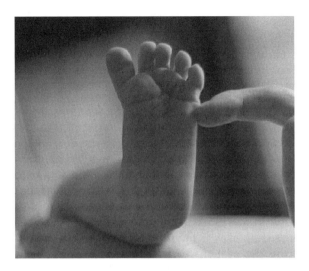

Figure 4.4   Babinski reflex in an infant
Source: Corbis/Jim Craigmyle.

The plantar reflex grasp is thought to play a part in integrating the *Babinksi reflex* during the first year of life. The Babinksi reflex, also present at birth, is elicited by stroking from the outside of the sole of the foot upwards and across from underneath the little toe to the great toe. Babinski's sign consists of an overextension of the big toe, which may be accompanied by fanning of the other toes. It is also sometimes referred to as the *extensor* plantar response (Figure 4.4).

Babinski believed that extension of the toes occurs as a result of immaturity in the pyramidal (corticospinal) tract. The corticospinal tract comprises nerve paths connecting the spinal cord and the brain. Because this tract is right- and left-sided, a Babinski reflex can be present on one side only or on both sides, providing a reflection of the functional status of the corticospinal tract on each side.

Myelination of corticospinal fibres follows a general sequence of the head first, followed by the arms, upper body, and then the legs. Because the corticospinal tract houses some of the longest nerve fibres in the body, the process of myelination and subsequent voluntary control of the feet takes longer to develop. As the pyramidal tract and associated neuromuscular systems mature, the extension reaction changes to one of flexion in response to pressure applied to the lateral sole of the foot. This develops gradually over the course of the second half of the first year of life. Gallahue and Ozmun[12] state that the Babinski reflex 'gives way around the fourth month of life to the plantar grasp reflex, which may persist until about the twelfth month.'

During the second half of the first year of life, the normal baby can be seen spontaneously exercising *both* reflexes in the absence of a pressure stimulus to the sole of the feet. When propped or seated in a chair or a buggy, the infant engages in a game of repeated extension/flexion/extension of the toes. In effect, the toes appear to carry on a 'conversation' at this stage in development, becoming more active when the infant is excited by something or just before it vocalizes, rather as if the motor pathways are involved in preparing the system for the utterances or babble which precedes intelligible speech. It is probable that continuous exercise of the pathways involved also helps to develop connections within the corticospinal (pyramidal) tract.

The extensor plantar reflex (Babinski reflex) is also used when the baby starts to crawl in the prone position. By extending the big toe and bedding the toes into the ground, the infant is able to 'push off' with one foot while pulling itself forward with one or both arms.

Functions of the Babinski Reflex

- Involved in inhibition of the plantar grasp reflex;
- Helps in commando crawling (bedding the toes into the ground);
- Helps exercise/develop the corticospinal tract;
- May be involved in the development of preverbal motor aspects of speech.

Effects of a Residual or Retained Babinski Reflex

Persistence of the Babinski reflex beyond the initial period of learning to stand and to walk will affect the muscle tone at the back of the legs and gait. The effect of this can be seen in cases of multiple sclerosis, when, as a result of demyelination, the Babinski reflex is released; there is elevation of the big toe and the patient develops a characteristic shuffle when walking. Failure to inhibit the Babinski reflex after

24 months of post-natal life is usually considered a pathological sign, signifying the presence of organic interference with the function of the nervous system. An abnormal Babinski reflex can result from a failure of the motor area (area 4) or the related corticospinal projections for a number of reasons.

Here it has to be stated that an abnormal Babinski reflex in the older child can be temporary or permanent. For example, it is a sensitive indicator of an abnormally low blood glucose level (hypoglycaemia) and may become positive (re-emerge) if blood glucose levels fall only to recede some 15 minutes after the administration of intravenous glucose.[13]

It is probable that the plantar grasp and Babinski reflexes work together in the first year of life, one exercising the corticospinal pathways and the other helping to inhibit the reaction. Neither should be present once the child learns to stand and walk, although the flexor response can sometimes be seen when walking barefoot on uneven surfaces such as cobbles or pebbles.

Babinski[14] considered the plantar extensor reflex to be part of a 'réflexe de défense'. Wartenberg[15] saw the overextension of the big toe as part of a larger flexion response involving shortening of the leg and avoidance, the foot being the most sensitive component. In German literature, the plantar extensor reflex is referred to as 'shortening reaction of the leg' or 'withdrawal reflex'.[16] If the infant reflex is still present in the older child, it provides an indication of immaturity in the functioning of the corticospinal tract.

Effects of a Residual or Retained Babinski Reflex

- Indicative of problems in the upper pyramidal tract (motor area 4);
- May be temporarily released under conditions of hypoglycaemia – disappears within 15 minutes of glucose administration;
- Affects muscle tone and coordination in the legs.

Functions of the Plantar (Flexor) Reflex

- Spontaneous exercise of the toes and associated pathways;

- Continuously activated in the middle of the second trimester of the first year of post-natal life – precedes or leads into many larger movements made by the developing infant.

If the plantar (flexor) reflex remains active after the first year of life, it will alter foot position and placement on the supporting surface. As the toes grip in response to pressure exerted on the sole of the foot, the sole retracts, altering those parts of the foot used as the supporting base. This can result to gravitational insecurity and can alter proprioceptive feedback from the foot to the brain centres involved in the control of balance, posture, and locomotion. At best, the child may be hypersensitive when walking on uneven surfaces. At worst, balance, posture, gait, and walking will all be affected. In some cases, the child may try to shift the centre of gravity forward by altering the point of pressure on the foot and by walking on the toes.

Effects of Residual or Retained Plantar (Flexor) Reflex

- Gravitational insecurity from the base;
- Altered proprioceptive feedback from the supporting base to other centres involved in the control of posture and balance;
- Sometimes present in children who 'toe walk'.

Hydramnios – the presence of an abnormally large amount of amniotic fluid for a particular stage in pregnancy. Commonly associated with foetal abnormality, particularly neuromuscular disorders of prenatal onset.

ROOTING REFLEX

Searching, sucking, and swallowing movements all start their development in the womb, beginning with the pharyngeal swallow at about 10–12 weeks after conception.[17] The development of swallowing in utero is important because it helps to equilibrate the volume of amniotic fluid, and if swallowing is absent, *hydramnios* develops. True suckling movements emerge from around the 18th to the 24th week[18] using a forward and backward movement of the tongue, but because at this early stage the tongue fills the oral cavity, it limits more advanced oral motor activity.

The rooting reflex emerges between 24 and 28 weeks in utero. Stimulation of the rooting reflex results in turning of the head and opening of the mouth (usually in response to a touch stimulus). After birth, this reflex leads to the sucking reflexes so that the lips are pursed and the touching object is drawn into the mouth. The final part of the feeding reflex *trio* is a response to the object touching the roof of the mouth, which activates rhythmic sucking movements. It is primarily the sense of touch combined with smell and hunger which leads to the motor activities of searching, suckling, and swallowing, but it is practice of the motor activities involved in feeding which help to coordinate muscular systems, to enhance central nervous system integration, and to innervate gastrointestinal functions necessary for digestion. While touch provides the pathway into feeding, the motor activity then leads into integration with other sensory systems such as vision and hearing (Figure 4.5).

The trio *comprises rooting, opening of the mouth, and touching the roof of the mouth.*

The rooting reflex is elicited by a light touch of the cheek or area around the outside edge of the mouth and is sometimes referred to as the cardinal point reflex, because the areas of sensitivity occur in a pattern around the mouth like the points on a cardinal's hat. The reflex signifies the beginning of a transformation from a crude withdrawal reaction to tactile stimuli (the embryo's first reaction to touch around

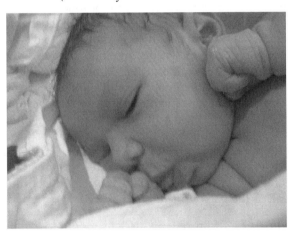

Figure 4.5 Infant rooting reflex leading into suck reflex. Stimulation of the side of the mouth with the neonate's fist has resulted in opening of the mouth on the same side and tongue protrusion. Palmar reflex can also be seen in both hands.
Source: Author's collection.

the mouth). Ultrasound has shown babies touching the side of their face, opening the mouth, and sucking the thumb while inside the womb.[17]

Primarily a 'searching', the rooting reflex leads into suckling if rooting is rewarded by insertion of the nipple or the teat into the baby's mouth. If, for any reason, the baby does not immediately find the breast or the bottle, it may continue to stimulate the reflex by 'nuzzling' and rooting against whatever it can find. Odent[19] described how the rooting reflex is strongest in the first few hours after birth, when the newborn is primed to find the breast. If, for any reason, the neonate is separated from the mother, it will continue to root for a couple of days, but if it does not receive gratification for its 'rooting' attempts, the reflex will start to weaken, making it more difficult to establish feeding later on. This can be a problem in cases of sick or premature babies who are separated from the mother at birth in order to receive essential medical treatment. The relative strength of the reflex will fluctuate according to hunger. A healthy, hungry baby will root voraciously, but the reflex may be difficult to elicit in the same baby shortly after a feed, only for it to return a little later.

Both the palmar and the rooting reflexes provide examples of how reflexes elicited by the sense of touch can lead into the training of other sensory systems. Clinging behaviour in other mammals is seen not only in connection to the acquisition of food but also in serving an emotional need. Peiper[16] described how, in the case of the rooting reflex, 'when we touch the region of the infant's mouth, reflexes are elicited that turn the head and move the lips so that the touching object is drawn into the mouth. This life preserving function is innate, but the ability to turn to the nipple or the bottle when it appears in the field of vision is not. This is rapidly learned. From the rooting reflex there develops a conditioned reflex that at the sight of the breast or the bottle turns the head to the correct position in space.'

In the first year of life, a baby uses its mouth to explore the outside world. Beginning with the instinct to feed, the mouth later becomes an important receptor for understanding and for testing the world around him – through taste, texture, and later picking up of objects and placing them in the mouth, learning about size by matching the oral experience of an object with how it looks (vision) and with how it feels (touch).

'The first region of the neocortex to develop in the foetus is the part that will become the representation of the mouth and tongue in the somatosensory and motor cortex. The neocortex then develops in concentric zones extending from this outer core region.'[20] Activities seen on ultrasound such as thumb sucking probably stimulate the formation of cortical maps of the mouth and the hand, which continue through nursing and feeding practices after birth.

Feeding practices are also a source of comfort and social communication through the taking of turns. Wolff[21] described two patterns of sucking: nutritive sucking, which is found in all animals and involves continuous and simultaneous coordination of sucking, swallowing, and breathing; and non-nutritive sucking, which is unique to humans and is different in nature from nutritive sucking in that it is characterized by alternating bursts and pauses. Kaye[22] suggested that suckling sets up a dialogue between mother and child. 'Baby sucks while mother remains passive; baby pauses and mother becomes active; baby resumes sucking, mother stops movement.'[23] This pattern is similar to normal conversation. Non-nutritive sucking enables the baby to passively observe its surroundings while comforted by oral stimulation. This is a type of self-regulation (Figure 4.6).

In societies where an infant is in constant physical contact with the mother, carried on her hip or in a sling, it does not have to wait and cry in order to be fed. The babies of mothers who are kept in close physical contact cry less and the mothers are more closely attuned to their baby's needs. Mothers are able to anticipate hunger in their baby through increased restlessness and changes in breathing, so that the mother offers the breast before the baby has to signal discomfort through fussing and crying. Within a few months, the infant can reach for the breast and suckle by itself, being able to regulate its own needs and to find comfort.[i] Just as Peiper suggested, touch and smell lead into visually seeking,

---

[i] This has implications for emotional regulation. Links between early physical and later emotional regulation are explored in more detail in the book *What Babies and Children Really Need. How Mothers and Fathers Can Nurture Children's Growth for Health and Well Being.* Goddard Blythe SA. 2008. Hawthorn Press, Stroud.

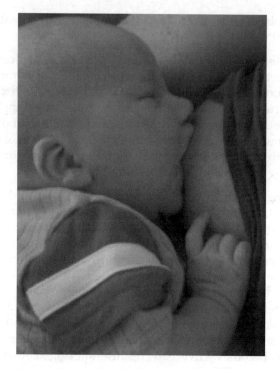

Figure 4.6   Suck reflex
Source: Alami Images/Peter Widman.

reaching, and suckling, supported by increasing postural control and eye–hand–oral coordination. Rooting and suckling are just the beginning of this process.

Functions of the Rooting Reflex

- Initiates searching (rooting), suck, and swallowing (suck reflex);
- Response to touch that results in transferring touch reaction to *visual* response to breast or bottle;
- May help to develop the facial muscles involved in smiling.

The rooting reflex persists slightly longer in breastfed babies.

What happens if the rooting reflex is not inhibited at three to four months of post-natal life?

The rooting reflex is associated with increased sensitivity of the area around the mouth often combined with immature control of the fine muscles around the mouth that are necessary not only for feeding, but also for speech. Rooting and suck reflexes influence the position of the tongue in the mouth, with the tongue remaining further forward, which affects the development of a more mature swallow pattern. This can interfere with the ability to chew and to grind when solid foods are introduced, so that the older baby pushes food out with its tongue or 'pouches' food in the corner of the mouth and is reluctant to swallow. Later on, this can result in a 'faddy' or fussy eater who insists on a narrow range of foods that require minimal chewing and are easily swallowed.

Retained rooting and suck reflexes can also affect the ability to close the mouth fully (lip seal) so that saliva builds up and 'pools' at the front of the mouth. This, combined with an immature swallow pattern, results in dribbling – sometimes so copious and continuous that the child has a constant wet patch on his chin and on the front of his clothing.

When there are retained oral reflexes, they are often present in combination with other tactile reflexes such as the palmar reflex and the Babkin response. This neurological loop means that there can be problems in the development of independent hand and mouth movements resulting in 'overflow' as in Figure 4.2. This continued immature sensory-motor connection can be observed when a child tries to write, draw, or use the hand for a skilled activity. Hand movements are accompanied by involuntary mouth movements such as chewing, sucking, or biting the tongue; when speaking or eating, the child may have difficulty in keeping the hands still.

Effects of a Residual or Retained Rooting Reflex

- Hypersensitivity to tactile stimuli around the lips and the mouth;
- Tongue may remain forward in the mouth, making the chewing and swallowing of certain foods difficult;
- Dribbling;
- Immature control of the muscles of the lips, tongue, and jaw, resulting in articulation problems;
- Continued hand/mouth connection affecting independent hand and mouth movements.

SUCKLING AND SUCKING REFLEXES

Taste buds are evident at seven weeks' gestation and mature taste receptors at 12 weeks. The earliest coordinated behaviour a foetus demonstrates is related to sucking,[24] and sucking movements have been observed in utero from around the 18th to the 24th week of pregnancy. Frequency of sucking movements is influenced by taste, as the foetus can detect tastes derived from the mother's diet in the surrounding amniotic fluid. The use of serial ultrasound[18] has shown that sucking movements increase in frequency in the later months of pregnancy, although coordination of suck *and* swallow is not present until 23–34 weeks. A premature infant born at 34 weeks has the sucking and swallowing ability to feed orally from 34 weeks, but may not be able to feed efficiently from the nipple until 36 weeks. Sucking and swallowing movements in utero are usually preceded by oral-facial stimulation (rooting).

There is a difference between suckling and sucking, although the latter term is often used as a general term to describe both. *Suckling* describes feeding movements in the early months of life when the newborn uses a rhythmic up and down movement of the jaw combined with a protraction/ retraction stripping action of the tongue, although there are differences in the way that this mechanism is used depending on whether the baby is breast or bottle-fed.

Breastfed babies take a surprisingly large portion of the nipple into the mouth so that the nipple sits near the back of the throat. The baby's tongue then squeezes milk from the breast by massaging with the tongue against the ridges on the roof of its mouth. The ridges of the inside of the mouth help to keep the breast in place. Rather than simply squeezing milk out by sucking, milk is extracted using rhythmic pressure, which strips milk from the ducts.

Bottle-feeding uses a different mechanism. Sucking takes place nearer the front of the mouth with pressure applied to the frontal portion of the palate. It has been suggested that this can affect subsequent development of the palate and the position of the teeth, as well as the swallow mechanism. Breastfed babies have to work harder to extract milk, which helps to strengthen the jaw and associated muscles and to encourage the growth of straight, healthy teeth. Development of the jaw and muscles at the front of the mouth will influence the later feeding patterns of chewing and grinding when solid foods are introduced. The mechanisms involved in feeding also provide practice for the actions of many of the fine muscles needed for clear speech and articulation later on.[25]

Sucking involves more mature actions and generally develops circa six to eight months of post-natal life.[26] This more mature suck involves less jaw movement, more independent up and down movement of the tongue, and a tighter seal with the lips, creating more negative pressure within the oral cavity.[27]

Arvedson[24] states that 'oral feeding that requires suckling, swallowing, and breathing coordination is the most complex sensori-motor process the newborn infant undertakes.' She goes on to point out that 'the development of independent, socially acceptable feeding processes begins at birth and progresses throughout the first few years of childhood. Oral sensori-motor skills improve within general neurodevelopment, acquisition of muscle control that includes posture and tone, cognition and language, and psychosocial skills.' 'Successful pleasurable feeding experiences foster efficient nipple control, reaching, smiling, and social play. Thus, feeding gradually becomes a social event.' Crutchfield and Barnes[28] described feeding as 'the single necessary point of engagement between the infant and the environment for the child's biological survival.'

Ashley Montagu[29] explained how 'sucking is the major activity of the baby during the first year of life, and its lips presenting the externally furled extension of mucous membrane that lines its mouth, constitute instruments with which he makes his first sensitive contacts, and incorporates so much that is vital to him of the external world. Lips, tongue, the sense of smell, vision and hearing, are all intimately bound up with each other and the experience of sucking.'

Suckling also has an inhibitory effect on the asymmetrical tonic neck reflex (ATNR) irrespective of head position,[30] enabling the infant to feed while still under the influence of the ATNR even when the head is turned to one side.

Delacato[31] suggested that the *process* of nutritive suckling during breastfeeding provides training for monocular vision. 'As the infant suckles from the left breast his right eye is occluded by the breast and his right hand is restricted by the breast feeding position. While suckling the left breast he is biased toward left sided function.' This orientation is reversed when suckling from the right breast. 'When we change this natural situation and bottle-feed the child, we invariably see the right handed mother hold the baby in her left arm and hold the bottle in her right hand.'

Delacato went on to suggest that a regular bias to one side when feeding may affect the infant's neurological organization in terms of eye and hand preference. When an infant suckles, the eyes tend to converge, an important mechanism in the development of stereoscopic vision. Until recently, there has been little research to support Delacato's theory, but in 2007, a study found that young children who had been breastfed had better stereoscopic vision.[32]

Functions of the Suckling Reflex

- Facilitates suckling and feeding;
- Inhibits the ATNR while suckling is taking place;
- Exercises and strengthens the jaw muscles and tongue movements necessary for speech later on;
- Action of suckling may be connected to the ability to converge the eyes at near distance – necessary for visual fusion later on.

Effects of a Retained or Residual Suck Reflex

- Dislike or avoidance of foods that require chewing;
- Continued desire for oral stimulation, e.g. sucking fingers or clothes;
- Poor lip seal;
- Immature swallow pattern, which can lead to formation of arched palate;
- Poor control of the muscles at the front of the mouth involved in speech; can sometimes affect articulation;
- If present with palmar or Babkin reflexes, continued link between hand and mouth movements.

THE SPINAL GALANT REFLEX

In 1904, Bertolotti[33] described a 'réflexe dorsolombaire', which occurred in the newborn when stimulation was applied to the *dorsal* skin of the lumbar region on one side. Stimulation resulted in outward rotation of the hip to 45° on the same side. In 1912, the reflex was noted again by Noica,[34] who gave it the term 'réflexe de la masse musculaire sacrolombaire', observing that it was present in babies but not in adults. Five years later, Veraguth[35] described the same response which he found to be present in healthy infants and in sick adults. Galant[36] described the response as 'When the dorsal skin near along the vertebral column is stroked, the infant forms an arch with his body; the concavity of the arch is directed toward the stimulated area, and by arching in the opposite direction the infant evades the stimulus.'

Dorsal – *of or on the back.*

The spinal Galant reflex is a defence or avoidance reaction, and sensitivity can extend beyond the lumbar area to include the chest and the abdomen.[16] Isbert and Peiper[37] found that 'on application of the stimulus the pelvis is flexed backward and the ipsilateral leg is extended at the knee and hip joints and the other is flexed.' They also found that the position of the head could be changed by the stimulation of the anterior surface of the trunk. When one side was stimulated, it resulted in turning of the face to the stimulated side. Alteration of the head position indicated that the spinal Galant reflex may form the beginning of a chain reaction which extends into an asymmetrical tonic neck reaction (Figure 4.7).

The spinal Galant reflex is believed to be a spinal reflex.[7] In infancy, it begins to be inhibited during the first two to three months of life, but can remain physiologically present until about the sixth month. If present at higher ages, it is always considered pathological.

If both sides of the spine are stroked simultaneously *upwards* from the pelvis to the neck, the Perez del Pulgar Marx reflex is elicited. This reaction involves both sides of the body eliciting 'flexion of both legs, lordosis of the spine, elevation of the pelvis, flexion of the arms, lifting of the head, loud crying culminating in apnea and cyanosis, emptying of the bladder, and relaxation and bulging of the rectum with bowel movement; after the reflex has fully developed there is general hypotonia lasting for a few seconds.'[38] You may have observed a similar reaction when stroking firmly down both sides of a cat's spine. Not all

Figure 4.7   Spinal Galant reflex
Source: Dan Chen. Reproduced by permission of Fern Ridge Press, Eugene, OR.

features of the response are present each time it is activated. It should be inhibited in the first two to three months of post-natal life. Carbonell and Perez[39] described how, in a percentage of cases, stroking both sides of the spine upwards causes reflex urination.

Hz – hertz – unit of frequency. The SI unit of frequency equal to one cycle per second. Low frequency such as 100 Hz is detected as low-pitch sound; high frequency such as 12,000 is perceived as high pitch.

For details of Frequency Range of Vocals and Musical Instruments, see Appendix 2.

The functions of the spinal Galant reflex when it is physiologically present are not fully understood, although a number of suggestions have been made: firstly, that the spinal Galant reflex may act as a primitive conductor of sound in the womb. We know that the foetus responds to certain sounds from the fourth month of pregnancy, but due to the enclosed and aqueous environment of the womb, the foetus is only able to hear sounds transmitted as a result of bone conduction. After birth, we rely primarily on air conduction transmitted from the outer to the inner ear to hear a range of sound frequencies from circa 20 to 20,000 *Hz* in the first weeks of life. Over the course of the first three years of life, the young child will learn to 'tune in' to the sounds of his or her mother, gradually narrowing down the spectrum of frequencies to which it is sensitive, thereby losing the ability to detect irrelevant sounds and becoming more sensitive or attuned to the specific sounds of speech. The majority of speech sounds for most languages falls within a much narrower range of 125–8,000 Hz. The range of the human voice and *most* musical instruments falls between 80 and 4,000 Hz (the range of the organ and xylophone are higher) – this is roughly the same range of frequencies to which the foetus responds in the second half of pregnancy (200–4,000 Hz).

'Sound is not sound.'[40] Sound occurs as a result of vibration and is detected by receptors sensitive to specific speeds or frequencies of vibration. These are mostly located in the cochlea of the inner ear, but we also have vibration receptors located in the skin and proprioceptors. Hence, we can 'feel' a very low-pitched sound as vibration and can detect extremely high-pitched sound in the hairs of the skin. One hypothesis is that during the latter part of uterine life, vibration stimulates the skin, and the combination of Galant and Pulgar Marx reflexes helps to transmit vibration from the skin to the ear through a combination of skin and bone conduction.[41]

Secondly, it has been suggested that the spinal Galant and related reflexes may work together during the process of birth to give flexibility to the hips as well as to the shoulders as the baby works its way down the birth canal. This may be important for internal rotation during the second stage of labour, restitution at birth, and lordosis of the spine which assists in the final foetal ejection reflex at the moment of delivery. Pressure exerted on the lumbar region during each contraction may also prime the kidneys in preparation for urination after birth.

Third, after birth, the spinal Galant reflex facilitates mobility of the trunk, helping to initiate the later amphibian reflex necessary for commando crawling, creeping on hands and knees, and hip rotation needed for walking.

This reflex is thought to be a vestige of a more ancient form of behaviour found in amphibians and in reptiles, in whom it was originally a tonic skin reflex of the spine. In quadrupeds, the dorsal skin acts as an important sensory organ involved in the regulation of movements of the vertebral column necessary for locomotion. Dorsal sensory organs become less important in locomotion when the transition to the erect posture takes place (when the infant learns to stand on two feet), and the dominant sensory organs involved in posture and locomotion shift to the front of the body.

The involvement of the Galant and related spinal reflexes in the early stages of locomotion in the human infant, and in other species, is probably linked to the presence of a tail in swimming and quadrupedal species. In aquatic creatures, for example, oscillations of the tail generate propulsive power for swimming and act as a rudder, but in semiaquatic *tetrapods*, the tail tends to compromise speed of movement on land. However, the tail has other functions on land because it acts as a counterbalance to the elevated trunk of a biped, helping to regulate stride frequency, *except* in humans, where the arms take over the function formerly carried out by the tail. For land-based animals, the tail is important for balance, and in mice, for example, patterns of balance and locomotion change if the tail is removed. Cats use their tails for balance by moving the tail in the opposite direction to displacement from a supporting surface,[42] and adjustment of the tail contributes to realignment of the hips over the supporting surface. Primates have long tails for balance and prehensile tails for grasping when they swing through trees, but when the human infant learns to stand unsupported, it is the first time that the arms and hands become free from the task of providing *support* for posture and locomotion, becoming instead an integral part of posture and locomotion.

Tetrapod – *any four-limbed animal.*

While in the womb, many of the movements of the foetus are piscean in character, ideally adapted to the aquatic and relatively weightless environment of the womb. Towards the middle to the second half of the first year of post-natal life, the infant attempts to creep on its belly, then learns to push itself up off the floor to crawl on hands and knees. Through each of these stages of motor development, the spinal Galant reflex remains active as if contributing to the function of a tail. Once the upright posture is achieved, the arms are free and control of balance is mastered; the spinal Galant reflex becomes redundant as control of posture should shift to the front of the body; head righting reflexes lead adjustments of posture, and the arms and legs carry out integral functions in locomotion. Retention of the spinal Galant beyond one year of age may therefore be a feature of immaturity in mechanisms involved in postural control and/or may contribute to it.

Functions of the Spinal Galant Reflex

- Facilitates mobility of the trunk initiating amphibian reflex necessary for commando crawling, creeping on hands and knees, and hip rotation when walking;
- Develops asymmetry of movement;
- Probably assists in the birth process;
- May help to prime the kidneys for urination after birth;
- May act as a primitive conductor of sound in utero.

Effects of a Residual or Retained Spinal Galant Reflex

The spinal Galant reflex should be inhibited between three and nine months of post-natal life. Persistence beyond the first year is considered to be a sign of pathology, but assessment of many thousands of children at the INPP over the last 30 years has revealed that it can persist in the general population in the absence of *identified* pathology.

If the spinal Galant reflex is not inhibited in the first year of life, it can be elicited by a stimulus making contact with the lumbar region of the spine. This may go beyond the direct stimulus of stroking down one side of the spine to contact with clothing, pressure from the waistband of trousers or a skirt, leaning against the back of a chair, or shifting position when lying on the back during sleep. The response of flexion of the hip can make it difficult to sit still. These are the children who wriggle, squirm, and fidget in their chairs, and who find it almost impossible to sit quietly. If they are able to sublimate the motor reaction in order to sit still, they need to get rid of the energy in other ways, usually by making a noise. I describe these children as being like bluebottles in the house – they are constantly buzzing – and are unable to be still within their own bodies.

Inability to contain unwanted motor activity and to ignore body sensations can make it difficult to focus attention on external events. In addition to the problems created by having poor postural control when sitting, children who have a strongly retained spinal Galant reflex often present with symptoms of poor attention and concentration. They sometimes prefer to do their homework or to watch television lying on the floor because this avoids aggravating the reflex.

Children with a retained spinal Galant reflex are usually hypersensitive to touch, particularly in the lumbar area, to the extent that the reflex can sometimes be observed in *anticipation* of touch before a direct stimulus has been applied. It is sometimes associated with rigid refusal to wear certain types of clothing, texture of fabric, or clothes with labels which irritate the skin.

The spinal Galant reflex has also been associated with a higher incidence of nocturnal enuresis (bed-wetting) in the school-aged child. However, not all children who have a retained spinal Galant reflex continue to wet the bed into later childhood, and neither do all children who wet the bed have a spinal Galant reflex, but where both a retained spinal Galant reflex and bed-wetting persist, inhibition of the spinal Galant reflex is often accompanied by cessation or decrease in bed-wetting events.

Nocturnal Enuresis

Thirty per cent of children still wet the bed occasionally at four years of age. The incidence of bed-wetting declines as maturation takes place, decreasing from 10 per cent at 6 years of age to 3 per cent at 12 years and to 1 per cent at 18 years. It is more common in boys than in girls, and tends to run in families. It is sometimes associated with sleep disorders such as sleepwalking and night terrors. Organic aetiology is presently found in only 1–2 per cent of cases. Possible causes may include urinary tract infection, sacral nerve disorders, diabetes insipidus or mellitus, pelvic mass, psychological or emotional disturbances, and middle ear problems.[43]

The link between the spinal Galant reflex and a higher incidence of nocturnal enuresis may be connected to the Perez del Pulgar Marx reflex, the activation of which causes micturition in the neonate, and urination and defecation in certain mammals.[16] Maturation of cortical pathways and conditioning result in the inhibition of both reflexes during the course of normal development. Retention of these reflexes into later childhood is indicative of delay in the maturation of these pathways, and bed-wetting may occur as a result of immature cortical control during sleep, or of activation of the reflexes through tactile stimulation of the lumbar area when sleeping on the back or when changing position during sleep.

A link between middle ear problems and the spinal Galant reflex was implicated in a study carried out by Butler Hall and Hadley.[44] They investigated the reflex profile of a group of children who had speech and language impairment. The children then undertook a course of auditory integrative training (AIT). AIT is a specific method of sound therapy devised by French ear, nose, and throat surgeon Guy Berard to treat auditory hyper- and hyposensitivity and to improve auditory processing. The reflex profile of the children was reassessed following completion of the AIT programme. The only reflex which showed consistent modification following AIT was the spinal Galant reflex.

Otitis media (middle ear infection) is common in young children and occurs as a result of infection spreading up into the Eustachian tubes from the nose, throat, or sinuses. It usually develops as a secondary consequence of a cold, enlarged tonsils (which are the first line of defence for germs entering the upper respiratory tract), sinusitis, or enlarged and infected adenoids. Inflammation and enlargement of these structures can develop for a number of reasons: particles of food entering the nasopharyngeal cavity are a common cause in the first year of life and may occur as a result of an immature swallow pattern, poor position when feeding, or reflux. Bottle-fed babies tend to be more prone to middle ear infections. This may be due to the altered sucking technique needed for bottle-feeding and/or a tendency for cow's milk to stimulate increased mucus production. This is particularly true of the allergic child. Later on, retained rooting and infant suck reflexes can affect the development of chewing and swallowing movements and lip seal. The middle ear is normally ventilated three to four times per minute by swallowing, thereby maintaining a normal state of pressure. Nasal congestion or inflammation can interfere with equalization of pressure, while tongue position can interfere with swallowing.

A retained rooting reflex, for example, is often associated with persistent dribbling in the older child.

The reason for the connection between ear and nasal congestion and bed-wetting is believed to be partly due to the effect on breathing. Past studies have shown that when children have their adenoids or tonsils removed, their bed-wetting ceases. Dr Derek Mahoney,[45] an orthodontist at the Prince of Wales Hospital in Sydney, Australia, said that 8 out of 10 children referred to him for bed-wetting problems have a narrow palate. If the roof of the mouth is particularly narrow, the tongue is pushed back and can partially block the airway during sleep. Children can be given a device, similar to a brace, to widen the palate. In a previous Swedish study, 7 out of 10 children who had not responded to any other treatment saw improvements after using braces.

Dr Dudley Weider of the Dartmouth-Hitchcock Medical Center in Hanover, New Hampshire, followed over 300 children with bed-wetting problems who had surgery for airway obstruction: bed-wetting ceased in 25 per cent soon after the surgery, and 50 per cent stopped within six months. In a case series report by Weider et al.,[46] 115 children between the ages of 3 and 19 with symptoms of upper airway obstruction, who were night-time 'mouth breathers' and bed-wetters, were evaluated. Prior to surgery, children in the study had 5.6 enuretic nights each week. All children in the study underwent surgery to relieve upper airway obstruction; 111 out of 115 had tonsillectomy/adenoidectomy. The children were followed for 12 months after surgery. After one month, there was a 66 per cent reduction in the number of bed-wetting episodes each week; at six months, there was a 77 per cent reduction, and this figure remained constant through the 12-month follow-up period. Twelve children with secondary enuresis (onset of bed-wetting coincided with the development of upper airway obstruction) had all stopped bed-wetting at six months, and progress was maintained at 12 months.[25]

Biologically, an association between airway obstruction and nocturnal enuresis could exist for several reasons. Obstructive sleep apnoea interrupts sleep and may limit normal arousal and self-alerting mechanisms. Hormonal change [obstructive sleep apnoea and lower levels of antidiuretic hormone (ADH)] and increased intra-abdominal pressure have all been suggested as possible factors.

Finally, if the spinal Galant persists on one side only, it can lead to the development of scoliosis (curvature) of the spine.

Effects of a Retained or Residual Spinal Galant Reflex

- Difficulty sitting still;
- General restlessness;
- Attention and concentration;
- Bed-wetting;
- Can contribute to the development of scoliosis of the spine.

REFERENCES

1 Robinson R. 1891. The nineteenth century. 30:831. Cited in Peiper A. 1963. *Cerebral Function in Infancy and Childhood.* Consultants Bureau, New York.

2 Prechtl HFR. 1953. Über die Koppelung von Saugen und Greifreflex beim Säugling. *Naturwissenschaften* 12:347.

3 Halverson HM. 1927. Studies of the grasp response in early infancy. *The Journal of Genetic Psychology* 51:371–449.

4 Giordano GG. 1953. *Acta Neurologica* (Neapel) Feb. 1953, III. Quaderno. p. 313.

5 Richter CP. 1931. *Archives of Neurology and Psychiatry* 26:748.

6 Hooker D. 1938. *Proceedings of the American Philosophical Society* 79:597; *Psychol. Somat. Medicine* 4:199.

7 Fiorentino MR. 1981. *A Basis for Sensorimotor Development – Normal and Abnormal.* Charles C. Thomas, Springfield, IL.

8 Thomas A et al. 1954. *La Presse Médicale* 146:885.

9 Yakoylev A, Lecours AR. 1967. Myelogenetic cycles of regional maturation in the brain. In: Minowski A (Ed.). *Regional Development of the Brain in Early Life.* Davis FA, Philadelphia, PA, pp. 3–70.

10 Holle B, 1981. *Motor Development in Children. Normal and Retarded.* Blackwell Scientific Publications, Oxford.

11 Van Woerkom W. 1912. *Revue Neurologique* 20,II:285.

12 Gallahue DL, Ozmun JC. 1998. *Understanding Motor Development.* McGraw-Hill Book Company, Singapore.

13 Members of the Department of Neurology and the Department of Physiology and Biophysics, Mayo Clinic and Mayo Foundation for Medical Education and Research, Graduate School, University of Minnesota, Rochester, Minnesota. 1976. *Clinical Examinations in Neurology.* WB Saunders Company, Philadelphia, PA.

14 Babinski I. 1915. *Revue Neurologique* 28/2:145; 1922:1049.

15 Wartenberg R. 1952. *Die Untersuchung der reflexe (The Examination of Reflexes).* p. 163 of German translation. Thieme, Stuttgart.

16 Peiper A. 1963. *Cerebral Function in Infancy and Childhood*. The International Behavioral Sciences Series. Consultants Bureau, New York.

17 Devries JIP et al. 1985. The emergence of fetal behavior: II. Quantitative aspects. *Early Human Development* 12:99–120.

18 Miller JL et al. 2003. Emergence of oropharyngeal, laryngeal and swallowing activity in the developing fetal upper aerodigestive tract: an ultrasound evaluation. *Early Human Development* 71/1:61–87.

19 Odent M. 1991. The early expression of the rooting reflex. Paper presented at the European Conference of Neuro-Developmental Delay in Children with Specific Learning Difficulties, Chester, UK.

20 Allman J. 2000. *Evolving Brains*. Scientific American Library, New York.

21 Wolff P. 1968. Sucking patterns of infant mammals. *Brain, Behavior and Evolution* 1:354–367.

22 Kaye K. 1977. Toward the origin of dialogue. In: HR Schaffer (Ed.). *Studies in Mother-Infant Interaction*. Academic Press, London.

23 Trevathan WR. 1987. *Human Birth. An Evolutionary Perspective*. Aldine de Gruyter, New York.

24 Arvedson JC. 2006. Swallowing and feeding in infants and young children. GI Motility online. www.bioinfo.pl/.

25 Goddard Blythe SA. 2008. *What Babies and Children Really Need. How Mothers and Fathers Can Nurture Children's Growth for Health and Well Being*. Hawthorn Press, Stroud.

26 Morris SE. 1978. Oral motor development: normal and abnormal. In: Wilson JM (Ed.). *Oral Motor Function and Dysfunction in Children*. Proceedings of a conference on oral-motor dysfunction in children. University of North Carolina, Department of Medical Allied Health Professionals, Division of Physical Therapy, Chapel Hill, NC, pp. 114–206.

27 Allen AC. 1991. Preterm development. In: Capute AJ, Accardo PJ (Eds). *Developmental Disabilities in Infancy and Childhood*. Paul H Brookes Publishing Co., Baltimore, MD.

28 Crutchfield CA, Barnes MR. 1993. *Motor Control and Motor Learning in Rehabilitation*. Stokesville Publishing Company, Atlanta, GA.

29 Montagu A. 1971. *Touching. The Human Significance of Skin*. Columbia University Press, New York.

30 McPhillips M. 2006. The role of movement in early development and long-term implications for educational progress. Paper presented at the Vision, Basic Skills Development and Bridging the Skills Gap Conference, BABO, University of London, November 2006.

31 Delacato C. 1970. *The Diagnosis and Treatment of Speech and Reading Problems*. Charles C Thomas, Springfield, IL.

32 Singhal A et al. 2007. Infant nutrition and stereoacuity at age 4–6 years. *American Journal of Clinical Nutrition* 85/1:152–159.

33 Bertolotti M. 1904. *Revue Neurologique* 12:1160.

34 Noica. 1912. *Revue Neurologique* 20/1:134.

35 Veraguth. 1918. *Neurologisches Zentralblatt* 7.

36 Galant S. 1917. Der Rückgratreflex: ein neuer Reflex im Säuglingsalter mit besonderer Berücksichtigung der anderen Reflexvorgänge bei den Säuglingen. Doctoral Dissertation. Basler, Basel.

37 Isbert H, Peiper A. 1963. Cited in: Peiper A. 1963. See note 16.

38 Pulgar Marx I. 1955. *Revista Espanola de Pediatra* 11:317; also see *Zentralbl. Kinderheilk* 58:220, 1957.

39 Carbonell J, Perez JPM. Cited in: O' Doherty N. 1986. *Neurological Examination of the Newborn*. MTP Press Limited, Lancaster.

40 Steinbach I. 1994. How does sound therapy work? Paper presented at the 6th European Conference of Neuro-Developmental Delay in Children with Specific Learning Difficulties, Chester, UK.

41 Dickson V. 1989. Personal communication. Chester.

42 Walker C et al. 1998. Balance in the cat: role of the tail and effects of sacrocaudal transaction. *Behavioral Brain Research* 91(1–2):41–47.

43 *The Merck Manual of Diagnosis and Therapy*. 1999. Merck Research Laboratories, Whitehouse Station, NJ.

44 Butler Hall B. 1998. Discovering the hidden treasures in the ear. Paper presented at the 10th European Conference of Neuro-Developmental Delay in Children with Specific Learning Difficulties, Chester, March 1998.

45 Mahoney D. 2003. Cited in: *Pediatric News*. 31.7.03

46 Weider D et al. 1991. Nocturnal enuresis with upper airway obstruction. *Otolaryngology Head and Neck Surgery* 105:427–432.

CHAPTER 5

POSTURAL REFLEXES

Whereas individual reflexes can affect posture and behaviour in many different ways, postural control and coordination is the product of *all* reflexes working together. Collectively, the postural reflexes provide the basis for automatic (below the level of consciousness) control of posture, balance, and coordination in a gravity-based environment. Put another way, they enable man to be master of his own movements in space by providing the postural framework for adaptive, voluntary, and skilled movements.

The transition from primitive to postural reflex, which takes place in the first years of life, does not take place in a rigid step-by-step fashion but develops through the dual processes of maturation within the central nervous system and interaction with the environment. While there are developmental stages at which it is expected that the primitive reflexes will be inhibited and the postural reflexes take their place, during transitional periods, both primitive and postural reactions can coexist for a time. Retained primitive reflexes in an older child persist for a reason. In cases of brain injury, this is because damage to higher centres prevents the higher centres from successfully exerting inhibitory control, but the primitive reflexes can also persist if postural reflexes fail to develop. This is because the primitive reaction only becomes suppressed when the succeeding postural reaction is strong enough to provide support for the development of a wider range of voluntary patterns. In other words, at every stage of development, motor competency is linked to and dependent upon postural control.

Control of posture and movement is organized at three different hierarchical levels: the highest of these comprises the *association cortex* with major inputs from the *limbic cortex*. Different regions of the cortex mature at different rates. The first area to mature is the *motor area* followed by the *sensory area*, but the *association areas* are the last to mature, continuing their growth into the 20s and 30s.[1] Motivation to move is combined with perception and motor planning, and input from the limbic system assists the association cortex in translating needs into goals.[2] 'Plans and strategy are synthesized by the highest level, assisted by inter-connections with the caudate nucleus to accomplish goal-directed behaviour.'[3] Strategy is converted into tactics at the middle level. This is where the 'what' of intention is converted into the mechanics of 'how' the intended movements will be carried out. This level involves the *sensori-motor cortex*, the *cerebellum*, the *basal ganglia*, and the *brainstem structures*, and it is at this level that the postural reflexes support a wider range of volitional movements.

In this sense, posture and motor control perform rather like an orchestra with the cerebral cortex acting as the conductor. The conductor knows how the music should sound, and also has a clear idea of exactly how he wants the orchestra to interpret the sounds; the middle level comprises the players, who can produce any number of notes, rhythms, tones, and interpretations; the lowest level is the instruments which can produce a limited range of sounds, and then only in the hands of the individual master who knows how to play each one. The instruments are like the spinal level, where the intentions and repertoire of higher levels are played out in the execution of movement and posture. At this point, the analogy of an orchestra ends because the spinal cord can function autonomously through spinal reflexes and automatic movements, but in skilled movement, it is influenced by higher centres and should match motor output to cortical intent.

These three phases of movement have been described as the 'visualization', 'ideation', and 'execution' of controlled action.[4,5] Fiorentino[6] categorized movement control according to levels of postural control – apedal, quadrupedal, and bipedal, and their corresponding levels of mediation in the brain – brainstem, midbrain, and cortex (Table 5.1)

Fay[7] linked different levels of brain involvement to evolutionary development, mapping the locus of pathology to specific symptoms, types of movement disorder, and cerebral palsy as in Table 5.2.

Sensory integration *(SI)* therapy is a theory developed more than 30 years ago by occupational therapist, A. Jean Ayres. Ayres defined SI as 'the neurological process that organizes sensation from one's own body and from the environment and makes it possible to use the body effectively within the environment'.

Table 5.1   Levels of development

Levels of development	Characteristics	Reflexes	Level of movement
0. Spinal Reflexes	Active in the womb and increasingly controlled by higher centres in a gravity-based environment after birth	Mass cutaneous reflexes Flexor withdrawal response Cross extensor reflex	Piscean
1. Apedal	Predominance of primitive *brainstem* and *spinal* reflexes; motor development is at the level of a prone or supine lying creature	Moro reflex Tonic labyrinthine reflex Asymmetrical tonic neck reflex Oral reflexes – rooting, suck and Babkin and Grasping reflexes – palmar and plantar, spinal Galant reflex	Reptilian
2. Quadruped	Predominance of *midbrain* structures involving the development of righting reactions; motor development is at the level of child who can turn over and assume crawling and sitting positions	LHRR's Neck righting reflexes Amphibian reflex SRR's Parachute response Spinal galant reflex Symmetrical tonic neck reflex Landau reflex Babinski reflex	Mammalian
	Postural development ia at the level of a child who can pull itself into the upright position but sitll needs to use the arms and hands to support balance – "cruising" using objects for support	Symmetrical tonic neck reflex	Simian
3. Bipedal	Initiated at the level of the *cortex* involving many other centres including the basal ganglia and cerebellum: equilibrium reactions develop when muscle tone is normal to facilitate body adaptation in response to change in the centre of gravity	OHRR's Adult Babinski response	Human

Source: Originally published in *Reflexes, Learning and Behavior*, 2002, Fern Ridge Press, Eugene, OR.[8]

Table 5.2 Correlation of developmental and nerve structural levels with pattern movements

Motor level	Developmental/ characteristic movements	Ontogenous	Nerve pattern/ brain level	Paralytic	Irritative	Cerebral palsy
1	Piscean (nerve, trunk, and tail)	Embryonal (wriggle)	Spinal	Poliomyelitis Cord trauma	Spinal epilepsy Reactions of defence Myoclonus multiplex Fibrillation	High spinal
2	Amphibian (neck, trunk, tail, and extremities)	Pre- and post-natal (free swimming)	Bulbo-vestibular		Ménière's syndrome Basilar meningitis	Friedreich's ataxia Athetoid (from Greek word, meaning 'without place')
3	Mammalian (trunk and four feet)	Infant (creeping on hands and knees)	Ganglio-cerebellar	Athetosis Dyskinesia	Chorea (from Greek word, meaning 'to dance') Myoclonus electrica Parkinsonian syndrome	Chorioathetoid
4	Anthropoid Two hands and feet Man – two feet	Child (walking) Adult (walking)	Cortico-striatal Psychomotor	Stroke Mental defect Lethargy Stupor	Convulsions Manian response Toxic psychosis Hyper-aggressive behaviour	Cortical Spastic Mental retardation Speech defects

Source: Adapted from Fay T. 1948. Neuromuscular reflex therapy for spastic disorders. *The Journal of the Florida Medical Association* 44:1234–1240.

Both models illustrate the links between hierarchical development in the brain and types of locomotion.

From the above, it can be seen that the processes of development at every level in the brain and control of movement are inextricably linked. Brain maturation and increased hierarchical control facilitate the release of more advanced movement capabilities, but movement *experience* is also necessary to lay down efficient neural pathways. 'Practice and repetition of movement patterns result in them being absorbed into the individual's repertoire of skills, probably also resulting in physical changes taking place in the neurons concerned, so that the flow of impulses along a specific pathway is facilitated. Repetition enhances facilitation and adeptness.'[9]

HEAD RIGHTING REFLEXES

One of the first tasks a child must master in the first weeks of life is the development of muscle tone against gravity. Development of tone and posture follow a top-to-tail (cephalocaudal) and centre-outwards (proximo-distal) sequence *beginning* with the development of head control. Head control develops in the prone position slightly ahead of the supine position, but each time the infant achieves a new postural milestone such as sitting, four-point kneeling, standing, cruising, and walking, head position and adaptation must be re-calibrated to adapt to the new relationship with gravity.

Although this is the general principle, development also proceeds from the caudal end upwards as well.

From the moment of birth, the one constant source of stimulation to the brain is the stimulus provided by gravity. Gravity provides continuous stimulation to the muscles, joints, vestibular system, and all associated brain regions; even when asleep, movement or force against gravity provides ongoing stimulation. Additional stimulation results from the postural (spinal and antigravity) muscles and the joints. This unconscious form of touch, known as proprioception, is also the direct result of antigravity activity.[10]

Labyrinthine head righting reflexes (LHRRs) start to develop just a few weeks after birth (circa 2 months) as the infant learns to lift its head up in line with its body. The LHRR is elicited if the baby is held and the body is tilted forward,

Otolith – *a component of the vestibular apparatus. The vestibular system, or balance system, is the main gravity sensor. It provides the dominant input about an individual's movement and orientation in space. Together with the cochlea, the auditory organ, it is situated in the vestibulum in the inner ear. The vestibular system comprises two components:*

1. The semicircular canals, which detect rotational movements;
2. The otoliths, which detect linear translations.

There are two otolithic organs on each side:

1. The utricle;
2. The saccule.

The otoconia crystals in the otoconia layer rest on a viscous gel layer and are heavier than their surroundings. During linear acceleration, they are displaced, which in turn deflects the hair cells, thereby

backward or to one side, or by stimulation of the *otoliths*. As this reflex develops, the child will respond by trying to bring the head to the centre by adjusting the head position in equal proportion and in the opposite direction to the displacement of the body. The reflex comprises compensatory contraction of the neck muscles to keep the head level and in the correct relationship with the body. As a result of this automatic adjustment of head position, the reflex provides the vestibular system with a stable reference point from which other postural adjustments can be made.

The LHRR responds to impulses that arise from the otolith of the labyrinth, combined with other centres in the *midbrain* enabling the infant to maintain proper head alignment with the environment in the absence of other sensory channels.

Development of the LHRR can be observed during the first six months of post-natal life when the infant is pulled up to a sitting position from lying supine. At birth, there is virtually no head control, and the head lags behind the shoulders as the baby is gently pulled up. As the neck flexor muscles strengthen, the degree of head lag decreases so that by two months of age, there is a small amount of head lag; by three to four months, the head tends to follow the trunk, and by six to seven months, the baby anticipates being pulled by lifting his head himself.

Each new postural milestone, such as sitting, brings with it a new set of challenges, and there is often a short period when primitive reflexes become active again, until the postural reflex has adapted to the new challenge. This can sometimes be seen when a child first learns to sit up. Sitting should be accompanied by the development of a parachute response so that if sitting balance is lost in a forward or sideways direction, one or both arms extend in a protective reaction. If, however, head righting reflexes are not fully developed in the sitting position, because the parachute response is dependent on righting reactions being in place, and if balance is lost backwards, the parachute response cannot protect the baby from falling. The Moro response may be elicited temporarily because 'higher' postural mechanisms are not available (Figure 5.1).

Activation of the Moro reflex in specific situations relating to balance is sometimes seen in the normal school-aged child who has traces of a tonic labyrinthine reflex or

producing a sensory signal.

Most of the utricular signals elicit eye movements, while the majority of the saccular signals projects to muscles that control our posture.

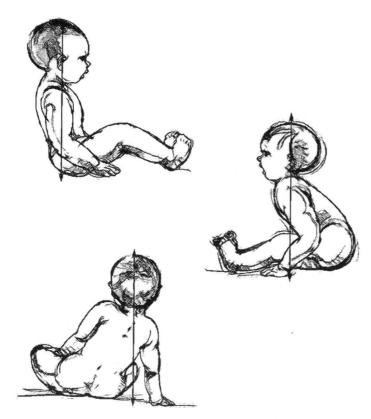

Figure 5.1 Head righting reflexes present in the sitting position
Source: Dan Chen. Reproduced by permission of Fern Ridge Press, Eugene, OR.

underdeveloped head righting reflexes. When the head is extended, there is a momentary loss of postural control and the 'lower' reflex is accessed. This may be seen when a child is playing games which involve extension of the head, such as serving overarm at tennis or putting the head back to catch a ball from high up in the air.

Some adults who suffer from anxiety and panic disorder also show a similar profile on assessment. Underdeveloped righting reactions affect control of balance and the associated eye movements. When a person goes into an environment where there is a lot of fast-moving visual stimuli, he or she cannot process the visual information quickly enough to filter out irrelevant information and to orient themselves in space. During the period of disorientation, the cortex is unable to 'make sense' of the plethora of sensory stimuli;

during the period of cortical confusion, lower brain centres including the limbic system alert the autonomic nervous system and stimulate biochemical reactions in response to perceived threat.

The vestibular system and associated pathways are particularly sensitive to inappropriate stimulation or overstimulation, or to any disturbance in the *timing* and *synchrony* of messages passing between balance centres in the body, the vestibular system, the eyes, and the regulatory influence of the cerebellum. When there is a lack of integration in signals passing from the body, the vestibular system, or the eyes up to the brain, we start to experience not only altered perception but also associated physiological changes. In this respect, we have all experienced temporary examples of what happens when this disassociation takes place.

Consider, for example, what happens if you spin round very fast a number of times. When you stop, for a few seconds your visual world appears to be moving and the image that you see is blurred. This is because you have overstimulated the vestibular system with body rotation. Fluid in the inner ear continues to be in motion for a few moments after the body has stopped turning, and the visual system cannot operate efficiently until the fluid in the vestibular system has also stabilized. During the period of 'dizziness' (the word meaning scatterbrained), you may also experience physical symptoms such as nausea, increased heart rate, sweating, and wobbly legs. These are the same *physical* sensations that are experienced in situations of extreme anxiety. In this way, the physical sensations associated with anxiety can be produced by overstimulation or inappropriate stimulation of the vestibular system and associated pathways. Motion sickness also occurs as a result of a similar process, when movement in a particular plane or combination of planes of movement upsets the normal relationship between body, balance, and vision.

The head righting reflexes are necessary to maintain congruence between body position, vestibular functioning, and the eye movements involved in gaze control. If the head does not make the appropriate compensatory adjustment in response to displacement of the body or the environment, the vector from which eye movements take their cue is off-centre, affecting the position of the image on the fovea and also potentially affecting the angle and direction of eye movements.

Dancers learn how to spin without getting dizzy by using a technique called 'spotting'. When spinning, the body starts to turn before the head while the eyes remain focused on a single spot. When it is no longer possible to keep the head in the same place, the head turns as quickly as possible to refocus on the same spot. The maintenance of a visual fixation point with delayed movement of the head allows the cortex with the help of vision to maintain a visual reference point despite rotational movements of the body. Target fixation allows visual suppression of the vestibular stimulation – discus throwers use the same principle when throwing. Under normal conditions of movement, body, balance, and eyes operate in an integrated fashion, and the head righting reflexes enable the correct relationship to be maintained through (preconscious) postural adjustment even when visual cues are not present, e.g. in the dark, when moving backwards, or when blindfolded.

The *oculo-head righting reflex* (OHRR), on the other hand, responds to *visual* cues and is dependent on the functioning of the *cerebral cortex*. It maintains the head in a stable position and the eyes fixed on visual targets despite other movements of the body. This is necessary to focus the image on the fovea, for visual fixation and for maintaining visual attention when the body is moving, and occurs as a result of neural connections between the eyes and the vestibular system.

The vestibular system also sends signals to the neural structures that control eye movements as well as to the muscles that keep us upright. Projections to centres involved in the control of eye movements provide the anatomical basis for the *vestibular-ocular reflex* (VOR), which is required for stable vision. The VOR provides a mechanism whereby when the head moves in one direction, the eyes rotate in the direction opposite to the movement of the head. The timing of the opposing movement is essential for the target to remain fixated on the fovea, enabling vision to be sharp and clear. Children who have underdeveloped head righting reflexes in combination with retained tonic neck and tonic labyrinthine reflexes have difficulty shifting gaze without the head also having to move. This affects clarity and the stability of the visual image seen by the brain and can interfere with reading. If the child additionally has an active asymmetrical tonic neck reflex, he or she cannot separate hand, head, and eye movements, which can affect coordination when writing.

The significance of the VOR for reading and writing cannot be overstated. Schmidt and Lee explained how 'a similar relationship among the eyes, head and hand appears to exist when a manual action is required. Biguer, Jeannerod and Prablanc (1982)[11] found that the onset of eye movements occurs almost simultaneously with the initiation activity of electromyogram signals in the arms and neck. This temporal coordination among the eye, hand, head and limb movements is quite flexible . . . In addition to the temporal relationship among eye, head and limb movements, there is also a spatial facilitation when these degrees of freedom interact. Manual aiming accuracy is better when the head is free to move than when the head position is fixed.'[12]

If the tonic neck and labyrinthine reflexes are retained in the school-aged child and the head righting reflexes are underdeveloped, a 'mismatch' occurs between intended movements and the action that takes place. This is because head righting reflexes help to provide a stable platform from which centres involved in the control of eye movements operate using head position as the point of reference. If head righting reflexes are absent or underdeveloped, the eyes do not have a stable point from which to gauge the *speed* and the *degree* of compensatory movements required. The eyes then find it difficult to converge, fixate, not to overshoot the target, and to move within the parameters required for the task in hand. The results of this are often seen when fixation, convergence, eye tracking, and hand–eye tracking tests are carried out on children who have reading and writing difficulties which have not responded to normal remedial intervention in the past.

Berthoz[13] described the combination of eye movement adjustments necessary to a coherent visual image to the brain as 'gaze control'. In a speech intended for an American Academy of Human Development (AAHD) conference, Svea Gold explained why gaze control is so important for academic learning and social interaction:

> Gaze control is the magic that happens when a baseball player runs across the field, chasing a ball that is swooping above him in a beautiful arc and then actually catching it. He is always changing his body position in relationship to the ground and to the ball, and yet that ball stays in constant focus in his field of vision.

Gaze control is what lets you see the image on the television set right side up, when you get up from the couch to answer the phone. Even though you are slightly bent over in the process crossing the room, you can still see the actors on the screen as standing up, and not at an angle.

Many, many of the children we see, especially children on the autism spectrum have problems with their gaze. For them seeing is as if they were looking through binoculars on a moving car. We have known it. Now we have a name for such a problem.[14]

In the book *The Dreaming Brain*, J. Allan Hobson says:

The term oculo motor movement is commanded by brainstem neurons that send their axons directly to the eye muscles. The latter's highly complex activity which we call gaze, is coordinated via interactions between three paired nuclei, the oculomotor nucleus (or third cranial nerve) which commands primarily vertical eye movements; the trochlear nucleus (or fourth cranial nerve) which commands primarily oblique movements, and the abducens nucleus (or sixth cranial nerve) which commands primarily lateral movements.

The vestibular system of the brain stem is specifically concerned with the complexities of head and eye control. Ask anyone with dizziness or vertigo about the important functions of this system. Vestibular neurons receive information about head position from the inner ear and relay that information to the oculomotor neurons. When the connections between the vestibular and the oculomotor systems are cut, as may occur in multiple sclerosis, paralysis of gaze will result.

A brilliant Indian autistic, Tito Mukhopadhyaya, explained it himself: 'I can look at you, or I can hear you. I can't do both!' This is the condition of a newborn baby – the baby stares at sound. It will take more neural development until the baby can listen and look at you at the same time.

Hobson goes on to say that 'head and eye position are related in turn, to the spinal control of posture by the reticular formation. Without the constant and precise operation of these three systems, we could neither walk and see nor sit still and read. None of the three functions described is exclusive to any one neuronal group, all three systems being in some way concerned with all three functions. Together with the cerebellum the integrated activity of these brainstem systems is responsible for giving sighted animals complex control of their acts.'

Pellionisz[15] attempts to explain the connections of the various areas in the brain that control 'gaze' by expressing the impact of each system in mathematical terms.

What is a vector? What is a tensor, and what is an eigenvector? And most of all, what does it mean to our children?

A vector is a different concept from the math you first learned in school: namely that 8 and 2 make 10. That is a sum. Nothing in the brain ever works that simply.

A vector is the symbol used by mathematicians and physicists for what happens when two forces interact. The arc that the baseball follows across the sky can be expressed as a vector. The arc results from the interaction between two forces: the power with which the ball is tossed, which would keep it going straight into the atmosphere, and the pull of gravity that would make the ball fall straight down.

A tensor is the mathematical symbol for the interaction when two or more vectors are involved. You can see this kind of interaction when you watch a sailboat being moored skillfully by an experienced captain. He is controlling the power of the wind by changing the angle of the sails; he makes allowance for currents of the water by using the angle of the rudder as counter force; he calculates the inertia of the forward movement of the boat, and in balancing all these different components he guides the boat to settle gently against the pier.

What is an eigenvector? The eigenvector seems to be the mathematical locus of all the points at which all the forces interact to keep the boat in balance.

Pellionisz tries to figure out what the forces are that, if kept in balance, will allow the eye to take the image that hits the retina and will then control the eye muscles to react in such a way that the child can keep that image in focus and allow the rest of the body to keep him or her steady.

What is important to us is not so much that we understand the mathematics of the situation, but that Pellionisz goes beyond the simplistic images that have been used to illustrate the brain and tries explaining the importance of the interactions of all the different systems. This is a rare contribution, because even today, neurologists split children's problems into separate areas. They call it 'co-morbidity' and make a list of whatever the symptoms are, instead of looking at the condition as a whole. That is what Pellionisz tries to do. That is what Delacato[i] means when he says do the whole thing or nothing.

The forces – the vectors Pellionisz talks about in explaining visual functions – depict the connections to and from three main systems: the vestibular, the visual, and the proprioceptive. Each system has a vector system of its own. Just think of it: the eyes take a sensory input – light that strikes the retina that actually turns an electric impulse into a chemical – and forward the impulse to various parts of the brain that then turn them into a motor expression. Motor expression can mean commanding the muscles that move the eyes and even controlling the muscles that keep the body upright.

The vestibular system takes a sensory input – gravity exerted on the fluid that then passes tiny particles along the hairs inside the semicircular canals – and interprets these via the cortex as to both position and speed of movement of the head in relation to movement of the body. In turn, this information is used to put in motion another set of complicated interactions: stimulating one set of muscles and inhibiting others so that the child can balance and will not fall down.

There is an example of a tensor system right there – interaction of several vectors.

How muscles react is also included into Pellionisz's calculations: input to the motor cortex includes the proprioceptive, which measures the outlines of the body, and the kinaesthetic, which measures the movement of the muscles. Each, again, takes sensory input: the pressure of the chair against your bottom, the pressure of the weight of a bowl against your fingers to tell the muscles of your arm how much effort it will take to lift it – these are all vector functions.

Now, since each of these systems has to work with the others, it makes it, mathematically speaking, a tensor system: more than one vector creating an impact.

The eigenvectors are the symbols of each set of systems – all the combined inputs – that make the functioning of the body possible.

Pellionisz measures the functions of a normal brain. As clinicians, we see children only when something is not working for them. So to get back to the image of the sailboat: if any of the forces that allow a sailboat to be controlled by the captain – the wind, the waves, the wheel that controls the

---

[i]Delacato C. 1981. *A New Start for the Child with Reading Problems*. David McKay, New York.

rudder – become unpredictable, the boat capsizes, falls over, or crashes into the pier.

Reticular formation – *a network of nerves extending from the medulla oblongata in the brainstem to the midbrain. It receives information from all over the body.*

The ascending reticular activating system connects to areas in the thalamus, hypothalamus, and cortex, while the descending reticular activating system connects to the cerebellum and sensory nerves.

Functions:

The reticular formation is involved in the control of physical behaviours such as sleep and wakefulness. It has also has been shown to play a major role in alertness, fatigue, and the ability to focus by excluding background information and 'filtering out' distractions while being able to become alert when the nature of sensory stimulation changes.

How does that relate to our children? If a child is blind, he may keep himself from falling over by rocking back and forth. He cannot use his eyes to know that when the walls are up and down and the ceiling is at a 90 degree angle he is sitting up straight. He uses gravity to tell him at what point he has to rock back so that he does not fall down.[14]

The function of the VOR is to generate compensatory eye movements which are equal in amplitude but are opposite in direction to the head movements that cause them. Gaze direction is the direction of the visual axis in space (eye in head + head in space), and the VOR is a system that stabilizes gaze during head movements. 'The performance of the VOR is most commonly defined in terms of its gain: (eye velocity)/(head velocity). Thus, for the reflex to be compensatory and to stabilize images on the retina during head movements, the gain must be close to unity.'[16]

In other words, postural head righting reflexes which ensure correct head alignment with the body in response to head or body displacement (and which operate below the level of consciousness) support the interaction of various systems involved in gaze control. They also provide functional support for the main *pathway* between the balance mechanism located in the inner ear and the body in a gravity-based environment – *the neck* – thereby ensuring congruence in the relationship between the vestibular system and the body which supports centres involved in the control of eye movements and visual-motor integration. Figure 3.3 provides a model to illustrate how these different systems work together.

Vestibular neurons in the brainstem (the vestibular nuclei) receive information concerning head position from the inner ear and from proprioceptors in the neck (vestibular-spinal system), from where this information is relayed to the oculomotor neurons (vestibular-oculo loop). Head and eye positions are related to the spinal control of posture by the reticular formation, but all three systems also depend on the modulatory function of the cerebellum (vestibular-cerebellar loop) for regulating actual control of posture, eye movements, and coordination (integration). 'Without the constant and precise operation of these three systems, we could neither walk and see nor sit still and read.'[17] Proper head alignment provides the framework for synchronous operation of these three systems.

RIGHTING, PLACING, AND EQUILIBRIUM REACTIONS

There are three types of postural reflex:

1. Righting reactions;
2. Placing reactions;
3. Equilibrium reactions (cortical).

Righting Reactions

Righting reactions describe responses to gravity which result from somatosensory, visual, and proprioceptive influences acting *together*, when all three inputs are available and are functioning appropriately. They describe the infant's ability to maintain the head and body in relation to space and the relationship of various parts of the body to each other. If the position of one section of the body is altered, other parts will be adjusted as in the action of OHRRs and LHRRs. Another example of a righting reaction is the *Landau reflex*.[ii]

The *Landau reflex* emerges between three and four months of post-natal life, following the emergence of head righting in the prone position. While the OHRRs and LHRRs right the head, the Landau reflex develops extensor tone through musculature in the neck down through the trunk, hips, knees, and ankles. If the baby is held in *ventral suspension*, the baby will respond by extending the head and the trunk. Over the next six months, the extensor tone works its way down the body to include the legs. If the tester depresses (flexes) the head, the trunk and legs will also flex until the head is released. The normal response to release of pressure on the head is extension of the head, trunk, and legs (Figure 5.2).

The reticular formation has also been traced as one of the sources for the introversion and extroversion character traits. Introverted people have been found to have a more easily stimulated reticular formation, resulting in a diminished desire to seek out stimulus. Extroverted people, however, have a less easily stimulated reticular formation, resulting in the need for more stimulation to maintain brain activity.

Ventral suspension – supported under the belly.

[ii] Described by Landau in 1917 as the radiopronator superius reflex. Landau E. 1960. *Anatomischer Anzeiger* 108:10–130,208–220.

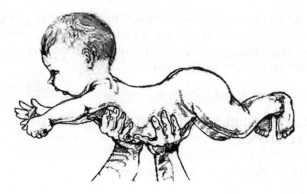

Figure 5.2   The Landau reflex
Source: Dan Chen. Reproduced by permission of Fern Ridge Press, Eugene, OR.

Increased extensor tone in the back and in the upper limbs facilitates improved weight bearing in the prone position at around four months of age (half arm extension), the ability to support the trunk with only one arm by five months, and increases extensor tone in the lower back for rolling, and also supports sitting between six and eight months, leading to later unsupported sitting.

The Landau reflex remains active in normal development up to three to three and a half years of age when it becomes integrated into more advanced patterns of postural control. It also acts as a 'bridging' reflex helping to develop extensor muscle tone and exerting an inhibitory influence on the tonic labyrinthine reflex (TLR) in flexion. Peiper[18] described the Landau reflex as a 'symmetrical chain reaction in the abdominal position' starting at the head and influencing the neck, trunk, arms, and legs down to the tips of the toes. 'This chain reaction is important for the development of normal rolling in cooperation with head righting and derotative righting reactions. Primitive head/neck reactions are suppressed with the evolution of the voluntary head righting reaction into vertebral righting (Landau reaction) and later axial (centrifugal) extension (the derotative righting response noted just prior to rolling over at 4–5 months of age).'[19] In other words, once developed, postural righting reactions operate together in a sequential fashion in the execution of coordinated movements.

The amphibian reflex develops at four to six months of post-natal life, first in the prone position and later in the supine position. If placed in water, a generalized amphibian

Figure 5.3   Amphibian reflex in prone position
Source: Dan Chen. Reproduced by permission of Fern Ridge Press, Eugene, OR.

reaction can be seen in rhythmic flexion and extension movements of the arms and legs at just four months of age. This reaction should appear on land by six months of age, when gentle elevation of the pelvis on one side results in automatic flexion of the arm, hip, and knee on the same side. This flexion response is a precursor to crawling on the tummy like a commando because it enables the baby to bend the leg on one side without affecting the other side. Children who have not developed an amphibian reflex in the prone position usually crawl in a homologous fashion (Figure 5.3).

Derotative righting reactions

Derotative righting reactions occur in two ways when placed in the supine position:

1. starting from the head and working down the body (head-on-body righting);
2. starting from the lower part of the body in response to crossing the midline (body-on-body righting).

Head-on-body righting occurs if the infant turns its head to one side, initiating a derotative response or a spiral uncoiling, which progresses from the neck to the shoulders, hips, and lower extremities.

Body-on-body righting occurs if the infant takes one side of the lower body across the midline, eliciting a derotative roll, beginning at the lower extremities and working upwards in a spiral to the hips, trunk, shoulders, and neck. These derotative righting reactions are precursors to more advanced *segmental rolling reflexes* (SRRs).

Figure 5.4   SRR from the supine position to the prone position
Source: Dan Chen. Reproduced by permission of Fern Ridge Press, Eugene, OR.

SRRs are a later modification of the head-on-body and body-on-body righting reactions. Whereas in the former, head and trunk are aligned when either is rotated or turned, the SRRs are strictly rotational reflexes. These reflexes will be needed later in development for the smooth execution of many gross motor activities including walking, running, athletics, downhill skiing, etc. as they facilitate sequential movements, that is, movement initiated in one part of the body to follow through to another section in a fluent coordinated manner, to achieve maximum performance with minimum energy output (Figure 5.4).

SRRs develop from two key positions – the shoulders and the hips – so that partial rotation of either upper or lower body can elicit a sequential/segmental roll.

Placing Reactions

There are a number of placing reactions. Crutchfield and Barnes[20] listed them as being visual, tactile, and proprioceptive: 'In response to certain stimuli the infant will flex his proximal joints and place his hands or feet on to a supporting surface. Developmentally, proprioceptive placing in the feet is correlated with spontaneous stepping' and 'is considered a residual form of foetal locomotor patterns modified by gravity.'[21] When the neonate's foot touches the floor, it activates the innate 'stepping' movement which many parents see as their child trying to walk, although the ability to walk is not achieved until many months later, when sufficient muscle tone to support body weight against gravity has developed (Figure 5.5).

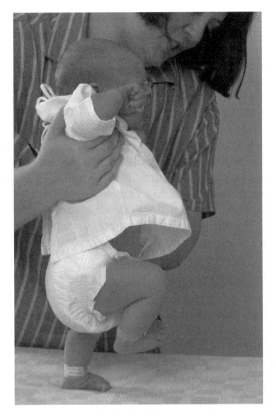

Figure 5.5   Infant stepping reflex
Source: Corbis/Jennie Woodcock/Reflections.

Visual placing develops later and is associated with independent walking. Visual and tactile placing are exhibited in the older infant, appearing between three and five months of age, and should remain for life.[21]

Equilibrium Reactions

Equilibrium reactions are contingent upon the presence of the righting reactions and only start to emerge in the second half of post-natal life. Equilibrium reactions are also elicited by stimulation of the labyrinths, but are compensatory in nature. They respond to changes in the centre of gravity, are primarily protective in nature, and work to modify the patterns of righting reactions. They are also dependent on having a visual reference point.

Equilibrium reactions occur in response to a sudden alteration in position or when balance is lost and they can be tested in prone, supine, sitting, and standing positions. In order to test in prone and supine positions, a balance board or tilting table needs to be used. When the surface is tilted slowly to one side, the child will react by flexing the trunk and head sideways in opposition to the pull of gravity, and the arm and leg will abduct. When testing the equilibrium reactions in sitting and standing positions, the body is tilted to each side, and forwards and backwards. As control of balance is lost, the child will use protective movements of the trunk and the limbs. Developmentally, the equilibrium reactions develop in prone and supine positions at 6 months, in sitting at 9 months, and in standing at approximately 14 months.[22] The parachute reflex is an example of an equilibrium reaction.

PARACHUTE REFLEX

The parachute reflex is the last of the postural reflexes to develop, usually emerging at eight to nine months of age. If the baby is turned face down towards the ground, the arms will extend to protect the head and trunk from the full force of impact, and it looks as if the infant is trying to catch himself. Prior to developing this reflex, the baby will actually bring the arms back to the plane of the body and away from the ground. If the infant is held upright and dropped towards the ground, the lower limbs first extend, then abduct. It is another example of defensive reaction. (If, for any reason, it is absent, instead of using the limbs to protect against a fall when control of position is momentarily lost, a Moro reflex may be elicited.) (Figure 5.6).

There are four 'pillars' on which later motor skills are built:

1. Head control;
2. Sufficient extensor tone to maintain posture against gravity;
3. Ability to rotate within the body axis;
4. Equilibrium reactions which support balance once the child attains semi-upright (sitting) and upright standing and moving.

Figure 5.6   Example of parachute reflex

Having looked at various individual reflexes and groups of reflexes in some detail, the next step is to examine the role of early development and the interaction of the developing child with its environment in integrating reflexes to support balance, posture, coordination, and learning for the remainder of life.

REFERENCES

1 Philip Rice F. 1992. *Human Development. A Life Span Approach.* Prentice-Hall International, London.
2 Brooks VB. 1986. *The Neural Bases of Motor Control.* Oxford University Press, New York.
3 Christiansen C, Baum C (Eds). 1991. *Occupational Therapy. Overcoming Human Performance Deficits.* Slack Incorporated, Thorofare, NJ.
4 Ayres AJ. 1973. *Sensory Integration and Learning Disorders.* Western Psychological Services, Los Angeles, CA.
5 Ayres AJ. 1989. *Sensory Integration and Praxis Tests.* Western Psychological Services, Los Angeles, CA.
6 Fiorentino MR. 1981. *Reflex Testing Methods for Evaluating CNS Development.* Charles C Thomas, Springfield, IL.

7   Fay T. 1948. Neuromuscular reflex therapy for spastic disorders. *The Journal of the Florida Medical Association* 44:1234–1240.

8   Goddard SA, 2002. *Reflexes, Learning and Behavior*. Fern Ridge Press, Eugene, OR.

9   Draper IT. 1993. *Lecture Notes on Neurology*. Blackwell Scientific Publications, Oxford.

10   Melillo R, Leisman G. 2004. *Neurobehavioral Disorders of Childhood. An Evolutionary Perspective*. Kluwer Academic/Plenum Publishers, New York.

11   Biguer B et al. 1982. The coordination of eye, head and arm movements during reaching at a single target. *Experimental Brain Research* 46:301–304.

12   Schmidt RA, Lee TD. 1999. *Motor Control and Learning. A Behavioural Emphasis*. Human Kinetics, Champagne, IL.

13   Berthoz A. 2007. Development and function of the balance system in the early years. *The 19th European Conference of Neuro-Developmental Delay in Children with Specific Learning Difficulties*. Pisa, September 2007.

14   Gold SJ. 2006. Using the head righting reflex to check for warning symptoms that something is wrong with the child's 'gaze control' and how to proceed from there. Svea Gold. Speech for AAHD conference October 2006: sjgold22@comcast.net.

15   Pellionisz A. 1985. Tensorial aspects of the multidimensional approach to the vestibule-oculo-motor reflex and gaze. In: Berthoz A, Jones M (Eds). *Adaptive Mechanisms in Gaze Control. Facts and Theories*. Elsevier Science Publishers BV, Amsterdam.

16   Tomlinson DR. 1988. Gaze shifts and vestibular-ocular reflex. In: Barber HO, Sharpe JA (Eds). *Vestibular Disorders*. Year Book Medical Publishers Inc., Chicago, IL.

17   Hobson AJ. 1988. *The Dreaming Brain*. Basic Books, New York.

18   Peiper A. 1963. *Cerebral Function in Infancy and Childhood*. The International Behavioral Sciences Series. Consultants Bureau, New York.

19   Capute A, Accardo PJ. 1991. *Developmental Disabilities in Infancy and Childhood*. Paul Brookes Publishing Co., Baltimore, MD.

20   Crutchfield CA, Barnes MR. 1993. *Motor Control and Motor Learning in Rehabilitation*. Stokesville Publishing Company, Atlanta, GA.

21   Milani-Comparetti A. 1981. The neurophysiological and clinical implications of studies on fetal motor behaviour. *Seminars in Perinatology* 5:183–189.

22   Shepherd R. 1980. *Physiotherapy in Paediatrics*. Butterworth Heinemann, Oxford.

CHAPTER 6

USE OF THE INPP SCREENING QUESTIONNAIRE

Specific learning difficulties and behavioural and emotional problems occur for many different reasons: mental retardation, sensory deficits, trauma, lack of environmental stimulation, frequent changes of school or change of teacher, frequent school absences, poor teaching, and emotional problems in the home or bullying at school, to name but a few. In 1976, Peter Blythe and David McGlown developed a series of screening questionnaires in an attempt to identify children and adults for whom neurological and developmental factors were a primary source of secondary educational, emotional, or behavioural symptoms.

The Blythe–McGlown Screening Questionnaire for Children has been in use for more than 30 years as an initial screening device to detect children who may be 'at risk' of developing later problems, and to identify underlying physical factors (immature primitive and postural reflexes) in children, and in adults already experiencing difficulties.

The Blythe–McGlown Screening Questionnaire for Children was originally published in 1979[1] and was re-published as part of a study investigating the reliability of the children's questionnaire in 1998.[2] It also forms the basis for three chapters of an earlier book, *What Babies and Children Really Need – How Mothers and Fathers Can Nurture Children's Growth for Health and Well Being*,[3] which examines the effects of the environment on a child's physical, emotional, and social development.[i]

These questionnaires were only intended to be used as initial screening devices to identify individuals for whom further developmental assessment is indicated. They should not be used for diagnostic purposes.

[i] Some of the contents of the next two chapters are reproduced with the permission of Hawthorn Press, Stroud.

The child questionnaire comprises a series of questions about early development, beginning with family history and following the development of the individual from conception through pregnancy, birth, infancy, pre-school, and school to the present day. Specific developmental criteria were selected for inclusion in the questionnaire, following an extensive search of medical and other relevant literature for factors which might either *cause* later developmental problems or might already be *symptomatic* of developmental deviation.

Although certain factors in development carry more weight in terms of their potential impact on later development, rarely is a single factor viewed in isolation sufficient to predict later problems. The questionnaire is intended to gather information and to compile a profile of risk factors linked to developmental problems in the individual.

Over the many years that the INPP Questionnaire has been in use, it has been found that if a child scores more than seven 'yes' answers on each numbered question (not including the sub-questions), it is highly probable that further investigations would reveal immaturity in the functioning of the central nervous system, which can be traced back to an earlier stage in development. In other words, few people escape without experiencing one or two minor problems or episodes at some stage in the early years, but unless a single event has been severe, or has occurred at a particularly vulnerable stage in development, it is unlikely to result in the emergence of related problems later on. If, however, there is a profile of factors in early development (seven or more), then the ability to compensate starts to be compromised. The higher the score, the more likely later difficulties are to emerge.

Congenital abnormalities, severe trauma or oxygen deprivation at birth would be exceptions to the single-factor trend.

Use of the questionnaires indicates that sequelae to factors early in development do not necessarily show up as major abnormalities at birth or even in the first few years of life, but can emerge in more subtle form as cognitive, emotional, or behavioural problems later on. The following two chapters cover some of the events before, surrounding, and following birth that can influence the later development of the child. It also explains how to use and interpret the INPP Questionnaire instrument.

THE INPP SCREENING QUESTIONNAIRE
FOR CHILDREN

Adapted from the original Blythe–McGlown Child Questionnaire (1979).
Devised by Blythe and McGlown. ©1979, 1998.
Amended by Goddard Blythe 2006.

Part 1 – Neurological

Historical Infancy
What are the presenting symptoms?
Has a diagnosis been given at any time ie. Dyslexia, Dyspraxia, ADHD, ADD? If so, please state:

a) Diagnosis
b) Diagnosis given by (name of profession)
c) Date of diagnosis
d) Treatment or interventions to date:

Numbered Questions:

1. Is there any history of learning difficulties in either parent or their families?
2. Was your child conceived as a result of IVF?
3. When you were pregnant, did you have any medical problems? eg. High blood pressure, excessive vomiting, threatened miscarriage, severe viral infection, severe emotional stress, please state:
    a) Were you under severe emotional stress (particularly between 25–27th week) of your pregnancy?
    b) Did you have a bad viral infection in the first 13 weeks of your pregnancy?
    c) Did you smoke during pregnancy?
    d) Did you drink alcohol during pregnancy?
4. Was your child born approximately at term, early for term or late for term? Please give details.
5. Was the birth process unusual or difficult in any way? If yes, please give details.

6. When your child was born, was he/she small for term? Please give birth weight, if known.

7. When he/she was born, was there anything unusual about him/her ie. the skull distorted, heavy bruising, definitely blue, heavily jaundiced, covered with a calcium-type coating or requiring intensive care?
   If yes, please give details.

8. In the first 13 weeks of your child's life, did he/she have difficulty in sucking, feeding problems, keeping food down or colic?

9. In the first 6 months of your child's life, was he/she a very still baby, so still that at times you wondered if it was a cot death?

10. Between 6 months and 18 months, was your child very active and demanding, requiring minimal sleep accompanied by continual screaming?

11. When your child was old enough to sit up in the pram and stand up in the cot, did he/she develop a violent rocking motion, so violent that either the pram or cot was actually moved?

12. Did your child become a 'head-banger' ie. bang his/her head deliberately into solid objects?

13. Was your child early (before 10 months) or late (later than 16 months) at learning to walk?

14. Did he/she omit a motor stage of:
    a) crawling on the stomach, and
    b) creeping on the hands and knees or was he/she a 'bottom-hopper' or 'roller' who one day stood up?

15. Was your child late at learning to talk? (2–3 word phrases by 2 years)

16. In the first 18 months of life, did your child experience any illness involving high temperatures and/or convulsions?
    If yes, please give details:

17. Was there any sign of infant eczema or asthma?
    Yes/No
    Was there any sign of other allergic responses?
    Yes/No

18. Was there adverse reaction to any of
    the childhood innoculations?   Yes/No

19. Did your child have difficulty learning to dress him/herself?

20. Did your child suck his/her thumb through to 5 years or more?
    If so, which thumb? Right/Left
21. Did your child wet the bed, albeit occasionally, above the age of 5 years?
22. Does your child suffer from travel sickness?

SCHOOLING

23. When your child went to the first formal school, ie. infant school, in the first 2 years of schooling, did he/she have problems learning to read?
24. In the first 2 years of formal schooling did he/she have problems learning to write?
    Did he/she have problems learning to do 'joined up' or cursive writing?
25. Did he/she have difficulty learning to tell the time from a traditional clock face as opposed to a digital clock?
26. Did he/she have difficulty learning to ride a two-wheeled bicycle?
27. Was or is he/she an Ear, Nose and Throat (ENT) child, ie. suffer numerous ear infections, is a 'chesty' child or suffer from sinus problems?
28. Did/does your child have difficulty in catching a ball, ie. eye-hand coordination problems?
29. Is your child one who cannot sit still, ie. has 'ants-in-the-pants' and is continually being criticized by the teachers for not sitting still?
30. Does your child make numerous mistakes when copying from a book?
31. When your child is writing an essay or news item at school, does he/she occasionally put letters back to front or miss letters or words out?
32. If there is a sudden, unexpected noise or movement, does your child over-react?

HOW TO USE THE INPP QUESTIONNAIRE

Looking behind the questions:

Question 1. Family History

It is recognized that up to 50 per cent of specific learning difficulties for which no external cause (social-environmental factors) has been identified carry a hereditary tendency. Tendency does not mean certainty. Patterns of genetic inheritance can be traced back to at least four generations, so a genetic predisposition to a specific disorder or syndrome can exist within a family and can remain silent for two or three generations with its negative effects being either suppressed or expressed as a result of environmental influences.

The role of specific genes in the development of illnesses such as Huntington's chorea and certain types of breast cancer are well known, but not everyone carrying the rogue gene will succumb to the illness. Dr Ursula Anderson, in her book *The Psalms of Children*, explains that 'certain genes contain memories that penetrate consciousness to varying degrees. Indeed, in genetic parlance we talk about the degree of penetrance of a gene. In some cases the penetrance – its expression, is total and immutable – particularly those that determine morphology, which is what pertains to appearance, form and shape (physical characteristics, family likenesses, etc.). But genes also mutate, altering their expression and effect.' These she describes as 'susceptibility genes with a complex mode of inheritance whose expression in my opinion would include and depend on quality of life of the individual having these genes. Mutable genes relate to the degree to which the environment and experience from conception through adolescence either facilitates, diminishes or cancels their expression.'[4,5] Mediating factors would include the combination of genes received from both parents at birth, health of both parents prior to and at the time of conception, the course of pregnancy, birth and development in the first years of life, as well as the degree of stress experienced at different stages of life and the resources available to deal with stress. In this way, the road map for the expression of genetic inheritance is set out in advance, but the route we take may alter if, how, and when that expression takes place.

Hereditary characteristics associated with hypersensitivity of the nervous system can appear as superficially separate disorders, although many share fundamental weaknesses in immaturity in the functioning of the central nervous system.

This range of disorders includes specific learning disabilities, allergies, emotional hypersensitivity, and psychosomatic disorders. This syndrome of hereditary susceptibility was highlighted in a study carried out by Richard Eustis in 1947,[6] in which he reported that 48 per cent of children over six years of age who were part of a family tree covering four generations shared one or more of the following conditions: left handedness, ambidexterity, and body clumsiness in addition to specific speech and reading disabilities. He suggested that these conditions were manifestations of a syndrome, hereditary in origin, which is characterized by a slow rate of neuromuscular maturation, which probably implies slow myelination of the motor and association nerve tracts.[3]

An example of hereditary predisposition for certain learning problems can be seen in a specific type of dyslexia, which is characterized by deficit in phonological processing and primarily affects males. In a series of published papers in the 1970s and 1980s, Annett[7,8] proposed a 'right-shift theory of handedness' in which it was suggested that, 'the prevalence of right-handedness and left hemisphere specialization for speech is due to a single factor which induces the typical pattern of cerebral specialization.' It was suggested that factor could be the presence of a single gene (rs+). People who do not carry this gene are at risk for the development of speech and speech-dependent language processes. People with specific deficits of phonological processing have reduced right hand/left hemisphere bias if they do not have the rs+ gene.[9] The reason it affects males more than females may be due to two factors: first, males have only one phonological gene; females have two. If males have not inherited the rs+ gene, they do not have a secondary 'back-up' to support phonological processing when problems exist. Second, the *corpus callosum* of the female brain has up to 40 per cent more neural connections between the two cerebral hemispheres, facilitating increased left/right brain communication so that if there is a problem in language decoding on one side of the brain, there is greater flexibility in accessing language centres on the other side to support language skills. It is probable that boys whose fathers have this specific type of dyslexia and who do not inherit the rs+ gene are more likely to suffer from a type of dyslexia involving difficulty with phonological processing.

Corpus callosum – the band of nerve fibres joining the two cerebral hemispheres through which the two hemispheres communicate.

A family history of learning or emotional problems does not condemn a child to developing them, but it does increase the probability that they might occur, depending on the cause and the nature of the familial problem.

Question 2. Was Your Child Conceived as a Result of In Vitro Fertilization (IVF)?

In August 2005, figures were released revealing that 1:100 babies born in the UK are now born as a result of IVF. At the time of writing, IVF accounts for 1.4 per cent of all UK births, 10,242 of them in 2004. As techniques to improve the outcome of IVF improve, there is a danger that it comes to be viewed in the public perception as a safe alternative to natural conception and that couples undergoing IVF are not fully aware of the potential longer-term risks involved.

Fertility is the product of a healthy ovum and sperm, two healthy reproductive tracts, and a mother's body and hormonal system able to support and to sustain a pregnancy to term. Infertility occurs when one or more of these factors are compromised. During the process of natural conception, nature tests the strength and viability of the sperm through a process of ruthless competition where only one strong sperm among millions will win the race and will have the strength and endurance to penetrate the protective outer coating of a ripe, healthy ovum. After conception has taken place, the immune system of the mother's body must override its natural reaction to reject the growing zygote as a foreign, invading body, thereby testing compatibility between mother, father, and child.

The natural conception of every child is an example of survival of the fittest, but the process of IVF is not as rigorous as nature in the selection of egg and sperm. In order to sustain the pregnancy following implantation, additional hormones have to be taken by the mother, and these hormones can have subtle effects on the process of neural development. There are, therefore, a number of additional risk factors present before, during, and after IVF.

A group of Dutch and Australian researchers published findings in the *British Medical Journal* in 2004 showing that babies born as a result of fertility treatment are more likely to be born prematurely and to have a lower birth weight than those conceived naturally. Single IVF babies are more likely to face birth problems than naturally conceived singletons, but the risks faced by twins are higher than for either group.

Previous studies have indicated that the increased risk of low birth weight and premature birth associated with IVF is partly because IVF is more likely to result in a multiple pregnancy. Twins and triplets, whether conceived naturally or using assisted reproduction techniques, are known to face a higher rate of birth problems than single babies. The authors of a study based at the Leiden University Medical Center in the Netherlands and at Flinders University in Adelaide, Australia[10] combined the results of 25 previous studies on the health of IVF babies, and looked at the outcomes of singleton and twin pregnancies separately.

Policy is now changing on this in favour of single implantation.

Their findings suggest that compared to naturally conceived singletons, even single IVF babies are twice as likely to be born before 37 weeks' gestation, and are three times more likely to be born before 32 weeks. The implications of premature birth and low birth weight on subsequent development are explored later in this chapter. The researchers also found that single IVF babies were three times more likely to have a very low birth weight and were slightly more likely to encounter other birth complications.

The study does not prove that it is the IVF itself that is causing the increased risk, although it is a mediating factor. It is probable that the fertility problems which have led to the need for assisted conception may also interfere with the course of pregnancy and successful outcome in some cases, and that the underlying health of women who need IVF also has an impact on their ability to carry a baby to full term.

Jerome Burne, a freelance journalist writing in the *Daily Mail* on 12 December 2006, wrote that while the UK pioneered the technology, it has contributed little to the long-term studies needed to establish just what is safe.[11] He quoted American researchers who, in November 2006, revealed that 'by the time children born of parents with infertility problems were six, they had four times the risk of developing autism. They also had nearly three times the risk of serious disorders such as cerebral palsy and cancer.'

Results of a study presented at the Society for Maternal-Fetal Medicine Conference in San Francisco on 9 February 2007[12] show an increased risk of birth defects in children born as a result of fertility treatment. Although the number of children affected was still relatively small, among a sample of 61,208 births, the incidence of a child born as a result of assisted conception having a birth defect increased from 2 to 3 per cent. Not surprisingly, the chances of a defect increased with the complexity of the intervention with IVF carrying the highest risk. The biggest difference was seen in the rate of gastrointestinal problems, such as defects in the abdominal wall or organs not in the right place. Babies conceived through reproductive technology were nearly nine times more likely to have such problems – one in 200 births versus six per 10,000 for the others.

Effects on future fertility are not confined to women who undergo IVF. A team of scientists from Rigshospitalet in Copenhagan compared the fertility of 1,925 Danish men whose mothers had needed help to conceive with those whose mothers had conceived naturally. They found that 50 per cent of men conceived as a result of fertility treatment were more likely to be infertile compared with men conceived naturally. Men born as a result of hormone-based fertility drugs had the poorest sperm of all.[13] While these results might be the result of genetics with infertile couples passing problems on to their offspring, they also raise questions about the effects of drugs containing female hormones on the development of male sexual organs in the womb. Risk factors for children born as a result of IVF are increased.

Question 3. When You Were Pregnant, Did You Have Any Medical Problems?

e.g. High blood pressure, excessive vomiting, threatened miscarriage, severe viral infection, severe emotional stress; please state:

a) Did you have a bad viral infection in the first 13 weeks of your pregnancy?
b) Were you under severe emotional stress between 25 and 27th week of your pregnancy?
c) Did you smoke during pregnancy?
d) Did you drink alcohol during pregnancy?

Please note that complications of pregnancy are not limited to the above list.

High blood pressure

High blood pressure during pregnancy is important because it tends to reduce the blood supply to the uterus, also reducing the amount of oxygen and nutrients to the placenta and the foetus. This can result in a small, dysmature baby. Small and immature babies are less likely to survive the first weeks of life, have difficulty with temperature control, and are more liable to infection, jaundice, and anaemia. Immature babies are also at risk of respiratory problems due to immaturity of the lungs.

Maternal high blood pressure leads to alterations in many maternal organ functions. Renal functioning in the mother is impaired, which, if it is allowed to progress, results in protein being excreted in the urine. Changes also occur in the functioning of the central nervous system of the mother such as a build-up of fluid in the brain (cerebral oedema), which can cause headaches and visual disturbances. If blood pressure continues to rise, liver functioning can be affected and may ultimately lead to pre-eclampsia.

Pre-eclampsia and eclampsia are conditions which only occur in pregnancy. Both are serious and life-threatening for mother and baby, if they are allowed to develop unchecked. Pre-eclampsia seldom occurs before the 20th week of pregnancy. Its development can be slow and insidious, with clinical signs becoming evident before symptoms are felt. Blood pressure rises and, as a result of the rise in blood pressure, protein is shed from the kidneys into the urine. The kidneys are unable to excrete fluid from the body effectively, resulting in a build-up of fluid, weight gain, and swelling. Premature labour is more likely, or the baby will need to be induced early for the safety of both mother and child.

The causes of pre-eclampsia are still not fully understood. A recent study[14] has found that women who go on to develop pre-eclampsia have high levels of two key proteins in their blood. The proteins, which disrupt blood vessel formation, also suggest potential targets for treatment, but the reasons why these particular protein levels are raised are not yet known.

Excessive vomiting (hyperemesis)

There are many old wives' tales associated with pregnancy; some have no scientific evidence to support them, while others are based on observations handed down from one generation to the next. It used to be thought that early morning sickness was a good sign, indicating a 'safe' pregnancy that was likely to proceed to term. In this context, one explanation for the occurrence of morning sickness was that the levels of hormones needed to sustain the pregnancy (particularly progesterone) must be high, and that nausea was due to the mother's sensitivity to elevated levels of specific hormones in her system associated with the pregnancy. Nausea usually decreases after the first 12 weeks, and it was believed that this was due to the mother adapting to altered levels of hormones in her system.

More recently, it has been suggested that the nausea, morning sickness, vomiting, and food aversions that often accompany early pregnancy evolved to protect the developing foetus from toxins which are potentially harmful to the developing baby.[15] These symptoms should decrease as the major organs are formed and the placental barrier is established (12 weeks' gestation), making the foetus less vulnerable. This hypothesis suggests that nausea fulfils a useful function by leading to avoidance of foods that contain substances likely to interfere with embryonic and foetal development,[16] or in the case of vomiting, by helping to rid the body of potentially teratogenic substances. Teratogens are chemicals that interfere with normal tissue development and can result in birth defects.

Nausea and excessive vomiting may also occasionally occur when dietary deficiencies or sensitivities are present in the mother. Empirical evidence obtained from long-term use of the INPP Questionnaire indicates that a history of persistent nausea and vomiting throughout pregnancy is more likely to have occurred in allergic families, particularly in those families where the mother had a history of wheat, gluten, or dairy intolerance, and may herself be deficient in minerals and trace elements.

Minerals and trace elements have a dual influence upon the biochemistry of the body. On the one hand, minute quantities of trace elements support certain functions and act as cofactors in the synthesis of hormones; on the other hand, they help to maintain a balance in the levels of other substances in the body. Zinc, for example, helps to minimize the build-up of aluminium and to maintain a healthy ratio of zinc to copper; calcium acts as an antagonist to lead. In theory, a mother who is deficient in zinc or calcium at the time of conception may also have elevated levels of aluminium, copper, or lead in her system. Continued vomiting in the early weeks may be one way whereby her body attempts to protect the developing embryo from the harmful effects of these potentially toxic substances in the first weeks of pregnancy, before the placenta matures sufficiently to act as a barrier to potentially harmful substances affecting the foetus.

The suggestion that nausea and food aversions have evolved to impose dietary restrictions on the mother in order to protect the developing embryo is not new.[17] In an ideal world, dietary deficiencies or excesses could be corrected prior to conception, helping to minimize prolonged nausea through pregnancy and making pregnancy a more enjoyable experience for both mother and child. This is where organizations such as Foresight in the UK[18] – the organization for preconceptual care – aim to educate couples before conception to correct any dietary deficiencies, to balance hormonal status (particularly in women who have been on the contraceptive pill for a number of years), and to screen for sexually transmitted diseases (STDs) or other diseases of the reproductive tracts.

Prolonged and excessive vomiting is another matter, because it depletes the mother not only of nutrients but also of hydration, and upsets the electrolyte balance of her body. Electrolytes are substances that yield ions in solutions so that the solutions conduct electricity; they are dependent on the correct balance of salt to fluid in the solution, and electrolyte imbalance can impair functioning of the heart and the nervous system. Prolonged and excessive vomiting (hyperemesis) can be harmful to both mother and child, and usually requires medical treatment. It may also predispose the baby to be born with mild deficiencies which, in theory, could affect the child's digestive system's ability to process certain food types after birth. This may show up in the early weeks of post-natal life as colic, vomiting, unusual bowel patterns, or skin disorders (skin reactions such as eczema that are not a reaction to direct skin contact often indicate a problem with the gut in processing certain types of food). Too often, such problems are treated as isolated symptoms instead of being investigated as part of a continuum, which might have had its origins in either family history and/or uterine life.

Threatened miscarriage

Only a fraction of eggs present in a woman's ovaries when she is born will be fertilized, and a smaller number still will go on to produce healthy babies. The ratio of natural 'wastage' is even greater for the sperm. Nature is ruthless in the process of natural selection and will tend to reject a zygote that does not precisely replicate the blueprint for healthy reproduction. Although nature also makes mistakes, miscarriage is one way in which she attempts to discard an imperfect embryo, an embryo developing in a hostile environment or a pregnancy in which there are compatibility issues between host and visitor (mother and child). Studies carried out in the 1940s and 1950s investigating prenatal loss in mammals other than man presented evidence supporting a peak rate of loss around the time of implantation.[19] In the late 1950s, Hertig et al.[20] examined a small group of human ova and estimated a loss of some 40 per cent before and during implantation.

In 1954, a team of paediatricians, psychologists, and public health workers began a 10-year longitudinal study on the island of Kauai, in which they followed the course of over 3,000 pregnancies and studied over 1,000 of the live-born children. They found that 'of the pregnancies reaching four weeks gestation, an estimated 239 per 1000 ended in death of the conceptus, with the monthly rates of loss forming a decreasing curve from a high of 108 per 1000 women under observation in the 4–7 weeks period, 70 for 8–11 weeks and 45 for 12–15 weeks, to a low of 3 losses between 32 and 35 weeks.'[21] If these figures are representative of the general population today, they indicate that the most vulnerable period for the embryo following implantation is the first four to seven weeks, and this figure does not account for losses that occurred in women who did not know they had conceived, i.e. before the first missed menstrual period.

A study carried out on several hundred pregnant women by Dr Euan Wallace[22] of Monash Institute of Medical

Research in Victoria found that those who miscarried had significantly lower levels of a protein, macrophage inhibitory cytokine 1 (MIC1), which regulates the growth and development of the placenta. Very early in pregnancy, the placenta invades the lining of the uterus and establishes a connection between the mother and the baby for the transfer of oxygen and nutrients to the baby and the excretion of waste products back through the mother's system. Placental functioning is crucial to the continued success of the pregnancy, to supply oxygen and nutrients to the foetus, and to protect the foetus from harmful substances.

In many cases, threatened miscarriage can be treated effectively if medical help is sought, and the mother goes on to give birth to a perfectly healthy baby, but the process/event gives rise to the question, 'why?' Why did the mother's body attempt to reject the foetus? Were problems already present in the developing baby or in the maternal environment in which the baby was growing? In using the INPP Questionnaire, details of any medical treatment received to sustain the pregnancy should also be listed together with the time in pregnancy when they were given.

Periods of prolonged bed rest during pregnancy can be significant because they deprive the foetus of vestibular stimulation. This may be important because the vestibular system is the first of the sensory systems to mature, being in place just eight weeks after conception and functioning at 16 weeks post-conception, and it is the only one of the sensory systems to be fully myelinated at birth in the full-term infant. It is believed that movement experience in the womb helps to prepare the vestibular system to carry out its tasks in response to motion after birth. Movements made by the mother stimulate alteration of position and movements in the foetus. As early as the first trimester, regular exercise patterns have been observed with ultrasound, which have shown rolling, flexing, turning, etc.[23] The movements appear as graceful somersaults, flexing of the back and neck, turning the head, waving arms, kicking legs – all self-initiated and expressive in nature. When the baby moves in utero, the heartbeat accelerates. DeMause[24] summarized reactions seen during the second trimester when 'the fetus now floats peacefully, kicks, turns, sighs, grabs its umbilicus, gets excited at sudden noises, calms down when the mother talks quietly, and gets rocked back to sleep as she walks about.'

Viral infection

The developing embryo and foetus is at its most vulnerable to teratogens in the first 12 weeks of pregnancy during the time when the major organs are being formed, before the placental barrier is established, and at times of rapid growth, proliferation, and cell migration. Certain illnesses such as German measles, toxoplasmosis, and syphilis are known to interfere with development, with the effect being influenced by the time in pregnancy when the disease is contracted.

The thalidomide tragedy provides an example of how it is not only the agent that can cause defects, but also the *time* in development when the embryo or foetus is exposed to the agent. Thalidomide was a drug given to pregnant women to treat the symptoms of nausea and morning sickness. Some women took thalidomide and gave birth to healthy babies; others took the drug at the time when the limbs were being formed, and gave birth to babies with severely stunted growth of the arms and/or legs. Whether the drug had a teratogenic effect depended on the exact time in pregnancy when the drug was taken. Luckett[25] noted that although thalidomide caused several foetal deformities when administered to humans, rhesus macaques and baboons, all species with haemochoral placentas, and animals such as galalgos, which have epitheliochoral placentas, are apparently unaffected by the drug. Epitheliochoral placentas have a greater number of layers to prevent the passage of harmful substances into the foetal system.[26] It may be that the human placenta has evolved to protect the foetus from ancient enemies, but has not evolved sufficiently to protect the unborn child from the more recent chemical creations of man.

If the mother develops rubella (German measles) in the first 12 weeks of pregnancy, it can affect the growth of foetal organs resulting in deafness, blindness, heart defects, and other abnormalities. Toxoplasmosis, a relatively rare disease in pregnancy, contracted through contact with cat faeces, can affect the baby's eyesight. As the age of motherhood increases, there is also a risk that the woman may have had a greater number of sexual partners with increased risk of exposure to STDs such as chlamydia (bacterial) and syphilis. Syphilis, which is caused by a thin motile spirochete, can be transmitted to the foetus if it is still present in the mother's body after the 20th week of pregnancy. Adequate treatment before the 20th week will prevent it from being passed on to the developing baby.

Which Viruses Can Harm an Unborn Baby?

Although there are a number of viruses that are potentially harmful to an unborn baby, the great majority of pregnancies are unaffected and proceed normally. Vaccination programmes such as measles, mumps, and rubella (MMR) have also helped to prevent the spread of some of the viruses that can harm an unborn baby. The following viruses are listed by the National Library of Health as posing a potential risk to the unborn child.[27]

Chickenpox is caused by the varicella zoster virus. If chickenpox is caught in the first 13 weeks of pregnancy, there is a very small risk (about 1 per cent) that the baby will develop eye problems, underdeveloped limbs, or brain damage. If chickenpox is caught in weeks 13–20 of pregnancy, the risk rises to about 2 per cent.

If chickenpox is caught after 20 weeks, there does not appear to be any risk of abnormality to the baby. However, if chickenpox is caught within seven days before birth, the newborn baby may develop a severe form of chickenpox.

Most pregnant women (about 90 per cent) are already immune to the chickenpox virus because they had it as a child.

Measles is now rare in the UK as it is routinely vaccinated against in childhood. However, if a pregnant woman does contract the measles virus, especially towards the end of her pregnancy, her baby will be at increased risk of being born premature. Measles caught earlier in the pregnancy increases the risk of miscarriage and stillbirth.

Cytomegalovirus (CMV) is caused by a virus from the herpes family of viruses. About 1 in 100 babies will catch this infection, but only 1 in 10 of these will develop any problems as a result. Potential problems can include learning difficulties, swollen liver or spleen, jaundice, or visual impairments.

Mumps in pregnancy is not known to cause problems for the unborn baby, but it can increase the risk of miscarriage during the first 12–16 weeks of pregnancy. Like measles and German measles, mumps is now rare in the UK as it is routinely vaccinated against in childhood.

Colds and flu viruses should not have an effect on an unborn baby, unless a secondary infection develops requiring treatment with antibiotics, or the mother develops a very high temperature or other complications. Antibiotics should be used cautiously by mothers-to-be. Streptomycin (used to treat tuberculosis), for example, can cause hearing loss in the baby, and tetracyclines (including minocycline, oxytetracycline, and doxycycline), used to treat acne and respiratory infections, if taken in the second or third trimester, can discolour the developing baby's teeth. A study reported in the *American Journal of Respiratory and Critical Care Medicine*[28] revealed that when a mother is exposed to high doses of antibiotics while pregnant, the chances of her baby developing asthma, allergies, or eczema dramatically increase. If the mother develops a very high temperature, it can increase the risk of miscarriage, and the relative risks of using or not using medication need to be weighed up on an individual basis.

Severe emotional stress

It used to be said that a stressful pregnancy would result in a fretful baby. As the process of motherhood was taken under the wing of medicine, such 'old wives' tales' have tended to be dismissed. However, scientific observation now indicates that psychological stress experienced by the mother in pregnancy can affect foetal brain development and birth weight, and can lead to depression in later life.[29]

The physiological components of stress were initially proposed by Hans Selye in 1956.[30] In the preface to his book *The Stress of Life*, he said, 'no one can live without experiencing some degree of stress all the time. Stress is not necessarily bad for you; it is also the spice of life, for any emotion, any activity causes stress. But, your system must be prepared to take it. The same stress which makes one person sick can be an invigorating experience for another.'

Resilience to stress is dependent on the function of a general adaptation syndrome (GAS). 'It is through the general adaptation syndrome that our various internal organs –

especially the endocrine glands and the nervous system – help to adjust to the constant changes which occur.'[29]

The GAS consists of three stages:

1. the alarm reaction;
2. the stage of resistance;
3. the stage of exhaustion.

Initially, stress triggers an alarm reaction, which causes autonomic processes such as heart rate and adrenaline secretion to speed up. The resistance stage begins with some automatic mechanism for coping with the stressor as the body attempts to make appropriate adjustments to restore equilibrium. If equilibrium is successfully restored, then relaxation can occur. If, however, attempts to maintain equilibrium are extended or prolonged, exhaustion begins to set in with effects upon general health. The primary indicants of the exhaustion stage are the development of illnesses such as ulcers, adrenal enlargement, and shrinkage of lymph and other glands that confer resistance to disease.

Stress results in a change in biochemistry, resulting not only in heightened secretion of corticosteroids during the alarm phase, but also altered levels of *catecholamines* including dopamine, epinephrine (adrenaline), and norepinephrine. Increased catecholamine and corticosteroid secretion affects a wide range of physiological processes such as heart rate, blood pressure, breathing, inflammation, and other functions including hormonal secretion and activity in emotional centres in the brain such as the amygdala. The amygdala is involved in the making of memories, particularly those of an emotional nature. Increased activity in the amygdala has been found to be associated with decreased activity in the attention-focusing, organizing, and planning activities of the frontal lobes of the brain.

Why Should Stress-related Changes in the Mother Also Affect the Developing Baby?

Studies carried out on rats have shown that high stress levels in the mother lower the level of the male hormone testosterone in the womb. Levels of testosterone at key stages in embryonic development can influence how the brain develops. Further studies on rodents reported by

Catecholamines – *a group of physiologically important substances including adrenaline, noradrenaline, and dopamine, which have various different roles (mainly as neurotransmitters) in the functioning of the sympathetic and central nervous system.*

Neurotransmitter *– a chemical substance released from nerve endings to other nerves and across synapses, to other nerves and across minute gaps between the nerves and muscles or glands that they supply.*

Synapse *– the minute gap at the end of a nerve fibre across which nerve impulses pass from one neuron to the next.*

Anne Moir and David Jessel in the book *Brain Sex*[31] showed that by manipulating hormones at critical times in gestation, behaviour could be changed from male to female and vice versa. They also found that by manipulating hormones, they could alter the structure of the brain itself.

The word 'hormone' comes from the Greek word *hormao*, meaning to excite. Biochemistry, the chemical messenger system for the nervous system, has a powerful effect on behaviour, perceptions, and emotions. Hormones are mind as well as body chemicals. Acting on the brain, they direct the body at key stages in the lifespan, such as puberty, pregnancy, and menopause, to make changes in the body. Before birth, hormones influence how the brain develops, and all through life, their chemical influence can change interconnections and communication within the nervous system.[32]

One example of hormonal impact on the nervous system has been observed when gonadal steroids have been given for the treatment of menopausal symptoms in hysterectomized women. Effects have been observed on axonal outgrowth, connectivity, and function, affecting performance on perceptual-spatial skills, learning and memory.

One biological system involved in stress is the hypothalamic-pituitary-adrenal (HPA) axis. When the mother's HPA axis is in 'overdrive', it increases levels of cortisol. High levels of cortisol inhibit intrauterine growth, may, in some cases, lead to premature birth, and could, in theory, alter cortisol receptors in the brain of the developing foetus. High cortisol levels are present in people with major depressive disorder. O'Keane and Scott[29] suggested that exposure to high levels of cortisol in the womb could permanently increase the 'set point' in relevant brain areas, resulting in stress response and behavioural alterations consistent with the later onset of depressive illness.

Adrenaline circulating in the mother's system also passes to the baby. Chemically, the baby feels what the mother is feeling. While on the positive side such symbiosis could be described as one factor in the origin of sympathy, on the negative side, sudden, excess, or continuous exposure to elevated levels of adrenaline while in the womb could, in theory, 'set' the baby's stress response for later life. The effects will depend on timing, extent, and duration of exposure to stress. In this way, a baby born to a mother who has suffered extreme stress during pregnancy could behave like a miniature stressed adult after birth – being more prone to crying, fretting, sleep disturbances, feeding problems, and hypersensitivity – 'the womb in a very real sense, establishes the child's expectations. Maternal, foetal communication is endocrine (hormonal) during pregnancy rather than neural

– the foetus experiences the emotions of its mother through the biochemical changes that take place in her body and therefore also in his/hers.'[33]

A four-year follow-up of the offspring from the Avon Longitudinal Study of Parents and Children found increased emotional and behavioural problems in the male offspring of women with high anxiety scores during pregnancy. 'An association between low birth weight and the development of adult metabolic diseases has often been shown. It is thought that exposure of the foetus to an adverse intrauterine environment may lead to permanent programming of tissue function.'[34]

The potential impact of maternal stress in 'setting' the foetus' neurohormonal clock for later life is not a new observation. In the 1940s, Dr Lester W. Sontag[35] published a paper following his wartime observations of the effects of stress on the expectant mother. He suggested that maternal stress heightened a child's biological susceptibility to emotional distress, and that this was a primary physical mechanism of which emotional hypersensitivity was a secondary outcome. The theory of a heightened physical susceptibility to stress was independently investigated some years later by Dr Peter Blythe in a paper *A Somatogenic Basis for Neuroses*.[36] Both authors, starting from different clinical and theoretical backgrounds, came to the conclusion that just as emotions can affect the body (psychosomatics), so biochemical and neuro-developmental factors can affect the mind (somatopsychics).

Subsequent research supports this theory. For example, one study, published in the *Journal of Clinical Endocrinology*,[37] was carried out after separate research on animals showed that high levels of stress in a mother during pregnancy could affect brain function and behaviour in her offspring, and other evidence suggested that maternal stress in humans can affect the developing child, including lowering its IQ. Researchers measured levels of the stress hormone cortisol in 267 pregnant women. Blood samples were taken from the mother and amniotic fluid from around the foetus in the womb from 17 weeks' gestation. Higher cortisol levels in the mother's blood were reflected in higher levels in the amniotic fluid. Amniotic fluid is mainly produced by the foetus and is a good indicator of its exposure to a range of substances, including hormones. Cortisol, which is pumped into the blood when we become anxious, is good in the short term because it helps the body to deal with a stressful situation, but long-term stress can cause tiredness and depression, and can make an individual more prone to illness or allergic reactions, because cortisol is re-directed from its many key roles in the regulation of almost every physiological system: blood pressure, cardiovascular function, carbohydrate metabolism, and immune function are among the best known functions of cortisol.

Here it should be noted that there are major differences between stress and trauma. At the extreme end of the stress scale are traumatic events that cause sudden unexpected shock. Whereas stress activates the sympathetic division of the autonomic nervous system (fight or flight), neurophysiological studies in animal experimentation have demonstrated that physiological shock occurs during a traumatic event. This shock produces a sharp and immediate biochemical reaction in the animal, causing the secretion of protective hormones[38] which are accompanied by a high energetic charge in the musculature of the body. This provides the organism with the ability to create a fight/flight (sympathetic) or freeze (parasympathetic) response. Although shock usually occurs as a result of a physical event such as resistance to blood flow, pooling or loss of blood, heat, or sepsis, animals and humans are also susceptible to *psychogenic* shock.

Shock is characterized by systemic arterial hypotension (arterial blood pressure less than 80 mm of mercury), sweating, and signs of vasoconstriction including pallor, cyanosis, a cold, clammy skin, and a low-volume pulse inducing a state of circulatory failure associated with low cardiac output and inadequate perfusion of viscera, in order to preserve circulation to the brain and coronary vessels. During shock, perfusion is insufficient to meet the metabolic demands of the tissues; consequently, cellular hypoxia and end-organ damage ensue. Such a dramatic change in the circulatory system of the mother will also affect blood supply to the baby. I know of three cases where the mother experienced a major trauma while pregnant (paternal suicide, murder of the father, and armed robbery where the mother was tied and gagged for 24 hours before being found) wherein the children were born with brain damage or developed autism after birth. While there is no proof that the traumatic events were the direct cause of damage to the child, psychogenic trauma would have resulted in physiological changes in the mother and in the developing baby. Foetal exposure to an adverse uterine environment may lead to permanent changes of tissue function and/or may affect the process of *neural migration* influencing whether cells reach their target addresses in the developing brain, die off, or alter their course of direction.

Change of direction in the process of neural migration, while acting as a defence mechanism against the re-experience of pain in the future, can also affect how the system reacts to positive as well as negative events in the future.

Potential effects of drugs

Certain drugs used either for medical or for recreational purposes are also known to affect embryonic and foetal development.

Alcohol

Even small quantities of alcohol can affect foetal growth; larger quantities are associated with foetal alcohol syndrome (FAS), intrauterine growth retardation, and mental retardation.

When a pregnant woman drinks alcohol, so does her baby, and in the early weeks of pregnancy, alcohol passes directly from mother to embryo. This is the most vulnerable period for organ development. Later in pregnancy, alcohol passes swiftly through the placenta to the baby. Alcohol in the body is broken down much more slowly by the immature foetus with the result that the alcohol level in the baby's blood remains elevated for longer. This, combined with the small size of the developing baby, means that the ratio of alcohol in the foetal bloodstream is significantly higher than in the mother. In common with other teratogens, timing of alcohol consumption can affect specific systems with birth defects, such as heart defects, being more likely to result from drinking in the first trimester, while growth problems are more likely to result from drinking in the third trimester. Drinking at any stage of pregnancy can affect brain development, and no level of drinking can be considered entirely safe.

FAS is one of the most common known causes of mental retardation. Classic features of FAS include babies who are abnormally small at birth and whose growth fails to catch up later in development; distinctive facial features such as small eyes, short or upturned nose, and small, flat cheeks.

Certain organs, particularly the heart and brain, may not form properly; the brain is affected not only in size but also formation, with fewer convolutions resulting in a smooth appearance. Many children born with FAS suffer coordination, attention, and behavioural problems, which continue into later life. These may include problems with learning, memory, and problem solving. Adolescents and adults have varying degrees of psychological and behavioural problems, making it difficult for them to hold down a job and to sustain meaningful relationships.

The most obvious signs of FAS usually occur in women who are heavy drinkers (more than five units per day), but it can also occur in women who have drunk moderately small amounts. Research carried out at the University of Washington in Seattle (2001) on a group of middle-class children up to age 14 years found that children whose mothers were social drinkers (one to two drinks per day) scored lower on intelligence tests at seven years of age than the average for all children in the study. At 14 years of age, these children were more likely to have learning problems, particularly with mathematics, and to have memory and attention problems.[39]

The teratogenic effect of alcohol is both structural in terms of brain development and functional. 'The infant is born not only with a brain smaller in size but with a reduced number of brain neurons, as well as altered distribution resulting in mental deficiency in varying degrees from milder behavioural problems to obvious mental handicaps.'[40]

Animal studies have shown that while many areas of the brain are affected by maternal alcohol exposure, its effect seems to be particularly detrimental on the hippocampus,[41] a part of the brain involved in memory. It has therefore been speculated that both the intellectual decrements and the behavioural deficits seen in infants born to mothers using alcohol during pregnancy may result directly from the specific hippocampal structural alterations.[42]

In the same article, reproduced for Foresight – the association for the promotion of preconceptual care – the author goes on to cite research which has shown that the more mothers had reported drinking during pregnancy, the poorer the overall performance of the newborn and the pre-school child.

On the second day of life they had a longer latency to begin sucking and had a weaker suck. They also suffered from disrupted sleep patterns, low level of arousal, unusual body orientation, abnormal reflexes, hypotonia and excessive mouthing. By 8 months and onwards, these infants continue suffering from disrupted sleep-wake patterns, poorer balance and motor control, longer latency to respond, poorer attention, visual recognition and memory, decrements in mental development, spoken language and verbal comprehension including lower IQ scores.[42]

Smoking and Recreational Drugs

In much the same way that babies born to mothers who drink alcohol during pregnancy are exposed to levels of alcohol, so pregnant women who smoke impose second-hand or passive smoking on their unborn child. The most common outcomes of smoking in pregnancy are reduced length of gestation, low birth weight, and a slightly elevated incidence of deficiency in physical growth and in intellectual and behavioural development. The effects are thought to be a result of exposure to carbon monoxide and to nicotine. Carbon monoxide probably has the effect of reducing oxygen supply to body tissues, while nicotine stimulates hormones that constrict the vessels supplying blood to the uterus and the placenta, resulting in less oxygen and fewer nutrients reaching the foetus.

Studies on both animal and human subjects have shown that both nicotine and the inhalation effects of tobacco affect the immune system, possibly contributing to a greater susceptibility to miscarry among women who smoke as well as a greater incidence of respiratory problems such as bronchial asthma in children born to mothers who smoke.

Cocaine

Cocaine, once the recreational drug of the rich, has at the time of writing become increasingly available to all levels of society. In addition to cocaine's highly addictive properties and its effect on the primary user, cocaine readily crosses the placenta affecting the foetus. It constricts blood vessels, thereby reducing blood and oxygen supply to the foetus, affecting general growth, and particularly growth of the bones and the intestine.

Approximately 31 per cent of women who use cocaine during pregnancy give birth before term, and 15 per cent have premature detachment of the placenta – a potentially lethal event for the foetus. About 19 per cent give birth to small babies,[43] but the most devastating consequence for the baby is that it is born an addict. Newborns suffer withdrawal symptoms; they may be hyperactive, tremble uncontrollably, interact less with other people, and have difficulty learning.

Apgar score – a method of assessing the general status of the newborn immediately after birth.

Characteristics of infants exposed to cocaine in the womb include prematurity, low birth weight, smaller head circumference, and low *Apgar score* at birth. The addicted newborn usually has a piercing cry, is irritable and hypersensitive, and switches from sleep to screaming for no apparent reason. They are often inconsolable. Feeding is affected, and physiologically they have high respiratory and heart rates. Startle responses are overreactive, and they are easily overstimulated. They are unable to interact with caregivers and therefore miss out on physical and social interactions in the early weeks which are essential ingredients of the normal bonding process between child and caregiver. Chasnoff et al.[44,45] observed that they were unable to respond to the human voice and face, and that there was a higher incidence of cerebral infarction (stroke) and sudden infant death syndrome (SIDS). The latter may be a result of sleep pattern abnormalities associated with apnoea and deep sleep resulting in increased susceptibility to primitive startle reactions.[46,47]

Mary Bellis-Waller[48] found that adolescents with social and behavioural problems who had been born to mothers who used crack cocaine (smoking) during pregnancy were unable to empathize with others, and that part of the frontal lobe of the brain normally involved in empathy simply had not developed. Their antisocial behaviour at a later age is not immoral – they had no understanding of the effect of their behaviour on other people – they seemed to be unable to 'feel as someone else' and were therefore unable to understand the implications and consequences of their behaviour either for themselves or for others. Intrauterine exposure to crack cocaine can therefore have long-term effects on behaviour.

> What I learned in my work was that crack-affected children don't bond and don't have empathy because they are overwhelmed by normal stimuli and so instead of being attracted to touch and gaze, turn away from it. That means they never form the habit of watching a face and learning to pick up moods, information, etc. from the face of another.[49]

As with any form of addiction, receptors can retain an appetite for the substance for life. If the child is exposed to the substance again later in life, the chances of becoming addicted are slightly increased.

Marijuana

Often erroneously viewed as a 'soft' drug, implying it is somehow safer than other 'hard' options, the effects of maternal marijuana use on the unborn child are controversial. Animal studies suggest that it does place the developing child at risk. Offspring of pregnant rats given a low dose of cannabinoids were found to perform poorly in learning tests throughout their lives compared to non-exposed offspring. The Italian research team[50] found that exposure to cannabinoids during gestation had an irreversible effect on chemical and electrical processes, resulting in hyperactivity during infancy and adolescence. In adult life, the offspring showed lower levels of glutamate in the hippocampus, a part of the brain involved in memory, visual ability, and learning.

Question 4. Was Your Child Born Approximately at Term, Early for Term, or Late for Term?

The normal length of pregnancy is 37 to 41 weeks. Babies are described as premature if they are born before 37 weeks' gestation or post-mature if they are born after 42 weeks or 294 days from the first day of the mother's last menstrual period. While the risks associated with prematurity are well recognized and are the direct result of immaturity in the functioning of vital systems, particularly the lungs, long-term factors associated with *prolonged* pregnancy are less well recognized outside of the world of obstetrics.

Prolonged pregnancy can occur for a number of reasons: uncertain menstrual data, if fertilization has taken place at a late stage in the woman's cycle, or if the woman has an unusually long menstrual cycle; failure of the cervix to soften, lack of stimulatory factors such as oxytocin and prostaglandin; or if there is placental insufficiency and labour fails to begin.

The placenta is a unique organ, being the only organ to be shared by two people, mother and baby (other than in errors of nature such as conjoined twins). The placenta has many functions: providing oxygen and nutrients to the baby, processing nutrients from the mother to make them suitable for the baby, and acting as a waste disposal unit and a barrier against many (but not all) substances that are harmful to the baby. In effect, the placenta acts as the lungs, kidneys, gut, and regulator of many hormonal functions including foetal growth.

The capacity of the placenta to support the needs of the growing foetus starts to decline towards the end of pregnancy. (If conception has occurred late in the cycle, then the placental function will usually be sufficient to support the foetus beyond 40 weeks.) When the baby is born, typical features of post-maturity will be evident such as large size, well-calcified skeleton, long nails, well-developed ear cartilage and genitalia, etc. If placental function has *not* been sustained, characteristic changes of growth retardation will be present (small-for-dates baby): amniotic fluid is diminished and may be stained by meconium (the first stool passed by the baby), there is absence of subcutaneous fat, and the skin is dry and peeling. The baby is usually of normal length but is underweight, and levels of blood sugar and blood clotting factors are often low.

Babies who have been subject to placental insufficiency are also at greater risk during the birth process from low glycogen stores; meconium aspiration syndrome, when the baby breathes in fluid containing the first stool; and limp cord syndrome, where the umbilical cord has lost some of its protective coating rendering it more prone to entanglement, tightening and shutting down of blood vessels providing vital oxygen and nutrients to the brain, and trauma-induced haemorrhage as a result of poor blood clotting factors. The need for operative delivery is therefore increased.

Post-mature babies for whom the placenta has continued to function well face potential problems at birth due to their increased size, particularly their larger and less mouldable skull (resulting from increased calcification in the final two weeks of pregnancy).

The onset of labour is naturally initiated not by the mother's body or by medical intervention but by the foetus, which signals its readiness to be born by increased activity in the adrenal axis affecting hormone levels in the placenta, which in turn stimulate the uterus to contract. Post-maturity may be an early indication that the foetus is 'not ready' to be born. This can occur as a result of decline in placental function, when the placenta does not respond to the signals from the baby.

In the last 10 years, use of the INPP Questionnaire on older children (7 years of age and upwards) who are experiencing problems with reading, writing, coordination, and/or behaviour has revealed an increasing incidence of children who were post-mature at birth. Further examination reveals generalized immaturity in the functioning of the central nervous system, confirmed by the presence of aberrant primitive and postural reflexes in the older child. Whether post-maturity is already a sign of neurological immaturity or whether the risks associated with post-maturity predispose the infant to being more vulnerable to subsequent developmental delays is not known. Nor can it be said that all children who were post-mature at birth are likely to have later difficulties. However, post-maturity does appear to be one significant factor in a profile of early developmental factors which might place a child at greater risk of having subsequent developmentally related problems.

Preterm birth

Prematurity is defined as childbirth occurring earlier than 37 weeks of gestation. The earlier the baby is born, the greater are the risks of complications, likelihood of needing prolonged special care, need for invasive medical interventions, periods of physical separation from the mother, and impoverished sensory stimulation in terms of movement experience, feeding, and touch. Infants born prematurely have an increased risk of death in the first year of life. They are also at a greater risk for developing serious health problems as a direct result of immaturity in vital organs (such as the lungs), fragility of developing organs and systems (such as the circulatory and nervous systems), and injury during birth. Health problems associated with prematurity include cerebral palsy, chronic lung disease, gastrointestinal problems, mental retardation, and vision and hearing loss.

Children who are born more than eight weeks early are also potentially at a disadvantage when they enter the educational system, which uses entry criteria based on

A baby born at 32 weeks is likely to need to spend some time in an incubator linked up to a ventilator and being tube fed. This is a very different sensory environment from the womb, where the baby is able to move around by itself as well as receive vestibular stimulation from its mother's movements.

chronological age calculated from birth date rather than on gestational age. Although premature babies do make up for lost time in achieving developmental milestones once they are fit and healthy, biological development proceeds from the time of *conception*. A child who is born at 32 weeks in July or August is not only going to be one of the youngest children in the school year based on birth date, but if school entry were to be based on *expected* date of birth, the child would be placed in the *next* school year allowing a margin of a further 10 months to make up for time lost in the womb, and for time spent fighting for life in the first weeks after birth. In the first five years of life when neurological development takes place at a rapid rate, the difference of a month in development can be the equivalent of a year, two decades later. The educational system in the UK, at the time of writing, does not take these developmental differences into account.

Researchers at Lucile Packard Children's Hospital and the School of Medicine found that 'babies born moderately early – eight to four weeks premature – are more likely than their full-term peers to struggle in kindergarten and grade school. Results from a study of a national database of young children are at odds with conventional wisdom that holds these "late preterm infants" are unlikely to suffer long-term effects from their early births. The findings also highlight the importance of regular developmental screening for this group to identify problems early.'[51]

> "These kids appear to require more support in school," said paediatric developmental specialist Trenna Sutcliffe a developmental paediatrician at the Mary L Johnson Developmental and Behavioral Unit. "They are about twice as likely at all grade levels studied to require special education or individual education programs, and teachers often indicate that their skills in math and reading are below average."[52]

More than 80 per cent of the 500,000 preterm infants born annually in the USA are born within this window of 32 and 36 weeks' gestation.

A collaborative study between Stanford, Yale, and Brown medical schools compared the cerebral grey matter (GM) and white matter (WM) volumes of healthy eight-year-olds born at full term and children born prematurely using magnetic resonance imaging (MRI). Both GM and WM were significantly reduced in the preterm group compared to those born at term, but only the males who were born preterm had significantly reduced WM compared to other males born at full term. Volumes of WM were equivalent in the female groups. The researchers found significant, lingering reductions in the areas of the cerebral cortex responsible for reading, language, emotion, and behaviour. They concluded that 'preterm birth has a significant impact on brain development with increased risk for smaller GM and WM cerebral volumes. Males appear particularly vulnerable to adverse effects of preterm birth on WM development. However, girls with preterm birth show stronger correlation between neuro-anatomical variables and both neonatal risk factors and cognitive outcome compared with boys.'[53]

'It's fascinating,' said Allan Reiss, MD, the Howard C. Robbins Professor of Psychiatry and Behavioural Sciences. 'It's as though we're seeing echoes of the "big bang" of preterm birth at 8 years of age.' The differences persist even after the early medical hurdles have been cleared: preterm boys struggle more than preterm girls with speech and language, and have a harder time in academic and social situations as they grow older.[54]

The results of a long-term study involving more than one million men and women published in 2008 found that preterm birth is linked to lifelong health issues. The population studied spanned a 20-year period from 1967 to 1988, and the post-natal outcomes of babies born after 22 weeks and before 37 weeks' gestation were examined. The study found that boys born between 22 and 27 weeks had the highest rate of early childhood death, had lower educational achievement, and reproduction rates were considerably lower for men and women born premature when compared to those born at term. Reproduction increased in direct proportion to higher gestational age. Women born preterm were more likely to have offspring of their own born prematurely and with complications. The lower the gestational age, the greater the risk of having less education.[55] 'When a baby is born preterm, we tend to focus on the short-term risk of complications. While it is true that the risk of complications is highest in the immediate time period including hospitalization and the first year of life, that risk continues into adolescence. And the earlier you're born, the higher the risk. Those who are born extremely prematurely are likely to have complications throughout their lives.'[56] These findings raise ethical issues not only in relation to the long-term outcomes of extremely premature babies (babies born at 23 and 24 weeks), but also to risk factors associated with IVF, wherein a higher percentage of babies born as a result of IVF are twice as likely to be born before 37 weeks' gestation, and are three times more likely to be born before 32 weeks.[10]

Question 5. Was the Birth Process Unusual or Difficult in Any Way?

Much of the discomfort experienced by the mother during labour is a direct result of the unique human combination of bipedalism (upright posture) and the growth of the size of the cranium. 'It is the price we pay for our large brains and intelligence: humans have exceptionally big heads relative to the size of their bodies and the opening in the human pelvis through which the baby must pass is limited in size by our upright posture.'[57]

A normal vaginal delivery provides many benefits to the baby: while on the one hand, birth is often said to be a hazardous journey, on the other, it helps to prepare the baby to meet the demands of the world outside the womb. Maternal contractions provide the deepest tissue massage a child will ever experience at any time again in life, helping to rid the lungs of fluid in preparation for breathing, priming the kidneys for effective urination after birth, and awakening the sensors of the skin and proprioceptors located in the muscles, tendons, and joints for control of movement in a gravity-based environment later on.

Pressure applied to the head as a result of squeezing from uterine contractions stimulates the foetus to release thyroid hormones and adrenaline, which will help the baby to regulate temperature after birth. The same squeezing of the head inhibits inhalation until after the head has been born, which is important to prevent the baby from inhaling fluid or other substances present in the birth canal until the airway is clear. Vaginal delivery is also thought to 'prime' the immune system as the baby is exposed to bacteria normally present in the maternal vaginal and anal tracts, which help to confer a natural resistance to exposure to the same or similar bacteria in life. Various primitive reflexes such as the asymmetrical tonic neck reflex (ATNR) and the spinal Galant probably assist birth and are also reinforced by the process.

Babies born by elective caesarean section (CS) miss out on some of the benefits of a vaginal delivery. Babies born by emergency CS experience some of the advantages of a vaginal delivery but are then exposed to the negative consequences of the events necessitating emergency CS. Either situation has potential consequences for later development.

Medical indications for an elective CS include:

- head-to-pelvic incompatibility (cephalopelvic disproportion);
- placenta praevia;
- multiple pregnancy with three or more foetuses.

Possible indications for an elective CS include:

- breech presentation;
- moderate to severe pregnancy-induced hypertension;
- diabetes;
- intrauterine growth retardation;
- antepartum haemorrhage.

Indications for an emergency CS include:

- cord prolapse;
- uterine rupture;
- eclampsia;
- failure of labour – ineffective contractions which do not improve following administration of oxytocin;
- foetal distress, if delivery is not imminent. Signs of foetal distress can be meconium in the water, changes in the foetal heart rate, and excessive movements of the baby. If these occur before the first stage of labour is completed, a CS may be the only safe option.

Effects of caesarean section on the baby

The major risk for the baby is breathing difficulties after birth, which are four times more likely in a baby born by caesarean.[58] The first task a baby must accomplish at birth is learning how to breathe by itself. This involves replacing the shallow episodic breathing movements practised before birth with regular rhythmic respirations following lung expansion. 'At term, approximately 110ml of lung fluid is present within the respiratory tract. During delivery compression of the chest wall assists in the expulsion of some of this fluid, the remainder of which is absorbed by the pulmonary circulation and lymphatic system after birth. Infants delivered by Caesarean section are denied the benefits of chest compression and therefore expression of lung fluid.'[59] The authors go on to explain that 'compression and decompression of the baby's head during delivery is thought to stimulate the respiratory centre in the brain which in turn maintains the stimulus to respiratory effort. Carotid baroreceptors, sensitive to changes in pressure, may also contribute to respiratory stimulus by their response to the circulatory change which takes place when the placental circulation ceases,' i.e. when the umbilical cord is cut.

Further reading on the effects of different types of birth on the baby and mother–baby interaction may be found in Gentle Birth, Gentle Mothering, *Sarah Buckley*[ii]

Various studies have indicated that children born by CS experience a higher incidence of immune-related problems including an increase in the incidence of allergies. A study carried out at the Norwegian Institute of Public Health in Oslo in 2005 found that out of 2,656 babies, those born by CS were twice as likely to develop an allergy to cow's milk compared to those delivered naturally. None of the children who grew out of intolerance to cow's milk by their second year had been born surgically. The same team had previously discovered a link between caesarean birth and egg, fish, and nut allergy.[60]

Forceps

Before the development of anaesthetics, use of antiseptics, and modern surgical techniques, delivery by CS was not a safe option and forceps were used to help extract a baby stuck in the birth canal. Forceps are designed to cradle the baby's head so that traction (pulling) on the handles helps the baby to be born. Forceps can only be used when the first stage of labour is complete and the cervix is fully dilated.

Indications for forceps to be used are the following:

- if the baby's head has descended but contractions have stopped or are not effective;

[ii]Buckley SJ. 2005. *Gentle Birth, Gentle Mothering.* One Moon Press, Brisbane.

- prolonged labour with a delay due to unfavourable position of the baby. Forceps can be used to rotate the baby's
  head;
- foetal distress;
- to protect the baby's head in premature births or in breech
  delivery;
- maternal fatigue or if the mother has a medical condition
  when prolonging pushing is contraindicated;
- administration of epidural analgesics has rendered the
  mother unable to push effectively.

Effects on the Baby

Forceps delivery can be distressing for both the mother and
the baby. A local anaesthetic is usually administered to the
mother before the forceps are used. The forceps may leave
temporary marks or bruising to the baby where the forceps
have been applied. If the mother has been given increased
analgesia immediately before forceps are used, the baby
may be born suffering from the effects of analgesia, and may
be slower to breathe and to feed. There is always some
degree of force when forceps are used. In rare cases, this can
result in damage to the baby's head, neck, or spine.

Occasionally, a degree of torsion may occur resulting in
slight misalignment of the cervical area. Cranial osteopaths
and chiropractors often see these babies when they are a few
weeks old suffering from poor sleeping patterns and difficulties associated with feeding. In Europe, a particular type
of misalignment has been identified called kinetic imbalance
of suboccipital strain (KISS) syndrome. Fortunately, if identified early enough, KISS syndrome can be effectively treated
by a doctor trained in the special techniques of manual
medicine. If KISS or related syndromes persist, they can
show up as postural, feeding, sleep, learning, or behavioural
disorders later on. Not all babies who have undergone a
forceps delivery will suffer from related problems, but there
is a greater degree of risk when intervention or force of any
kind has to be applied.

Vacuum extraction

Vacuum extraction is a slightly gentler method of assisting
delivery than use of forceps when a baby has got into
difficulties. A vacuum extractor (ventouse) or a suction cup

is applied to the lowest part of the baby's head. The cone-shaped cup is attached to a pump, which creates a vacuum, which serves as an external handle with which to gently rotate the baby's head and to apply traction.

Effects on the Baby

- Babies sometimes have cone-shaped heads for a couple of days when they have been with the assistance of ventouse. A cephalhaematoma, or blood blister, may form on top of the baby's head, but this usually disappears in a week, or the baby's head may be slightly grazed or bruised. Very occasionally, the baby can suffer a degree of cerebral trauma.

Prolonged or precipitate labour

Labour takes place in three stages: the first describes the period when uterine contractions facilitate dilatation (opening) of the cervix. This is the longest stage of labour, usually taking up to 12 hours for a mother giving birth to her first child and less for subsequent children. The second stage describes the time from full dilatation of the cervix to the baby being born. This is the active stage of labour for the mother and may take up to two hours with a first baby or as little as five minutes for a mother who has already given birth. The third stage describes separation and expulsion of the placenta and membranes. The third stage can last from five minutes up to one hour. The above times are only approximate and there is considerable variation in the 'normal' duration of labour. Labour is usually considered prolonged if it exceeds 24 hours in a mother delivering her first baby and 12 hours for a woman who has had a prior delivery. It used to be said that for the benefit of mother and baby the sun should not rise and set on the same labour.[61]

Causes of Prolonged Labour

Factors causing delayed progress of labour are:

- inadequate intensity and frequency of uterine contractions;
- over-distention of the uterus (in cases like twins or large babies);
- unfavourable position of the baby;

- pelvis is too small for the passage of the baby's head;
- medications given for pain relief (epidural anaesthesia) have reduced the mother's ability to push.

Effects of prolonged labour are:

- increased chances of operative deliveries – forceps, vacuum, CS;
- decreased supply of oxygen to the baby.

Prolonged head compression, instrumental delivery, or hypoxia may lead to intracranial haemorrhage. Lack of oxygen to the foetus can lead to stillbirth or to permanent brain damage.

Precipitate Labour

A precipitate labour is defined as a labour which lasts for an hour or less and usually occurs in mothers having their second or subsequent baby. The frequency and strength of contractions may cause foetal hypoxia. Rapid moulding and alteration in intracranial pressure during delivery increases the risk of intracranial haemorrhage. The lack of resistance in the pelvis or soft parts means the baby does not experience the gentler compression, sensory stimulation, and reflex involvement of a slower delivery.

Other factors during the birth process

Other factors prior to birth, such as foetal position, will affect the process of birth. Position of the baby's head prior to and during the birth process has been described in relation to the tonic labyrinthine reflex (TLR) and ATNR in Chapter 3.

Breech presentation is worthy of mention because it can both be the cause of birth complications or may be indicative of an existing problem prior to birth. Difficulties arise in delivery of breech presentation due to a tendency for early rupture of the membranes and a long first stage of labour, because the buttocks, knees, or feet are poor dilators of the cervix, and the largest, hardest, and most vulnerable part of the baby is born last. Risks to the baby include stillbirth, umbilical hernia due to traction of the cord, premature separation of the placenta, premature inspiration due to cooling of the lower part of the body being born first, stoppage of placental circulation, injuries such as fractures or dislocations to the limbs, depression or fractures of the skull, sternomastoid haematoma due to pulling on the child's neck, blue asphyxia due to pressure on the cord or placenta, white asphyxia due to pressure on the head or spine, and cranial injuries. In view of the risks involved, it is not surprising that the preferred mode of delivery for breech presentation is often, but not exclusively, CS.

Innate behaviour is programmed by the genes, is passed from one generation to the next, and is carried out without learning or prior experience. Innate behaviour falls into four categories:

1. Kineses – *the organism changes the* speed *of its movements in response to an environmental stimulus.*
2. Taxes – *directed movement towards or away from a stimulus.*
3. Reflexes – *stereotyped movement of a body part in response to a stimulus.*
4. Fixed action patterns – *stereotyped and often complex series of movements in response to a stimulus.*

When a breech is detected during pregnancy, an attempt may be made to turn the baby (external cephalic version) at about 35 weeks, but if the baby is small it may revert to a breech position. Unless there are obvious causes such as multiple pregnancy or other medical conditions, it has been suggested that persistent breech presentation may be an indication of immaturity in vestibular functioning.[62]

Remember that the vestibular system is formed early in development. The vestibular system is the primary source of orientation in space and is especially important in utero from where the external orientation senses of vision and hearing cannot help the baby know its position in space. Berthoz[63] described the semicircular canals of the vestibular apparatus as 'essentially inertial receptors. They function without a base and, consequently are as advantageous to the bird flying as to the lion capturing its prey or the monkey jumping from branch to branch' – also to water-dwelling species. Suspended in water with the effects of gravity reduced, the semicircular canals act as a primary sensor of position in space before birth.

Breech presentations also occur in non-human primates and in other mammals, but in species such as chickens the unborn chick instinctively knows that in order to break out of the shell safely, it must peck in an upward direction. If it tries to peck down, it will not be able to get out. This is an example of innate behaviour. The role of the vestibular system in mediating innate behaviour can be seen in moths when they show a positive *taxis* to light, or in fish, which swim by orienting the dorsal surface away from the force of gravity and towards the light. If the gravity-detecting organs of a fish are removed or if the light enters the side of a fish tank, the fish becomes disorientated. If the gravity detector is removed, fish become 'lost in space', swimming vertically or upside down as they orient to the light alone.[64] Breech presentation that persists in the absence of other medical causes may be an early indication of immature vestibular functioning. In 2008, a study was published showing that men and women who were delivered in breech presentation at full term had more than twice the risk of breech delivery in their own first pregnancies compared with men and women who had been cephalic presentations.[65] Although the primary interpretation of these findings is that in these cases breech presentation is a heritable characteristic, the findings are also consistent with the 'baby doesn't know which way is up' theory of breech delivery. 'I suspect the inherited part is the vestibular-gravitational orientation immaturity.'[66]

Foetal distress

Foetal distress occurs when the foetus is deprived of oxygen and becomes hypoxic. Severe prenatal hypoxia is a major cause of brain damage. Studies which have tested the behavioural outcomes of hypoxia on rodents have found delayed development of sensory and motor reflexes during the first post-natal month of rodent life, impairment of motor function, learning, and memory in adult animals, and an increase in cell death and cell loss in brain tissue in the first days after birth.[67] Generally speaking, the more complex the brain, the more vulnerable it is to the effects of oxygen deprivation.

REFERENCES

1 Blythe P, McGlown DJ. 1979. *An Organic Basis for Neuroses and Educational Difficulties*. Insight Publications, Chester.
2 Goddard SA, Hyland D. 1998. Screening for neurological dysfunction in the specific learning difficulty child. *The British Journal of Occupational Therapy* 10:459–464.
3 Goddard Blythe SA. 2008. *What Babies and Children Really Need. How Mothers and Fathers Can Nurture Children's Growth for Health and Well Being*. Hawthorn Press, Stroud.
4 Anderson UM. 1996. *The Psalms of Children*. She-Bear Publications, Ellicottville, NY.
5 Anderson UM. 2004. www.andersonbeyondgenome.com
6 Eustis RS. 1947. The primary origin of the specific language disabilities. *Journal of Pediatrics*. XXXI:488–455.

7 Annett M. 1972. The distribution of manual symmetry. *British Journal of Psychology* 63:343–358.

8 Annett M. 1985. *Left, Right, Hand and Brain. The Right Shift Theory.* Lawrence Erlbaum, London.

9 Annett M. 1995. The right shift theory of a genetic balanced polymorphism for cerebral dominance and cognitive processing. *Cahiers de Psychologie Cognitive* 14/5:427–623.

10 Helmerhorst FM et al. 2004. Perinatal outcome of singletons and twins after assisted conception: a systematic review of controlled studies. *BMJ* 328:261.

11 Burne J. 2006. IVF: why we must be told the truth over birth defects. *Good Health Daily Mail*, 12 December 2006.

12 El-Chaar D. 2007. Fertility treatment raises birth defect risk. Presented at conference hosted by The Society for Maternal-Fetal Medicine, San Francisco, 9 February.

13 Jensen TK et al. 2007. Fertility treatment and reproductive health of male offspring: a study of 1925 young men from the general population. *American Journal of Epidemiology* 165/5:583–590.

14 *The New England Journal of Medicine* 355:992–1005. Cited in: New Scientist.com.news service, 22 September 2006.

15 Profet M. 1995. *Protecting Your Baby-to-Be: Preventing Birth Defects in the First Trimester.* Addison-Wesley, Reading.

16 Horrobin D. 2001. *The Madness of Adam and Eve. How Schizophrenia Shaped Humanity.* Corgi Books, London.

17 Profet M. 1992. Cited in: *The Adapted Mind.* Barkow JH et al. (Ed.). Oxford University Press, New York.

18 Foresight. http://www.foresight-preconception.org.uk/

19 Brambell FWR. 1948. Prenatal mortality in mammals. *Biological Review* 23:379–407.

20 Hertig AT et al. 1959. Thirty-four fertilised human ova, good, bad and indifferent, recovered from women of known fertility. A study of biologic wastage in early human pregnancy. *Pediatrics* 23:202–211.

21 Werner EE et al. 1971. *The Children of Kauai. A Longitudinal Study from the Prenatal Period to Age Ten.* University of Hawaii Press, Honolulu.

22 Tong S et al. 2004. Serum concentrations of macrophage inhibitory cytokine 1 (MIC 1) as a predictor of miscarriage. *Lancet* 363:129–130.

23 Van Dongen GR, Goudie EG. 1980. Fetal movements in the first trimester of pregnancy. *British Journal of Obstetrics and Gynecology* 87:191–193.

24 DeMause L. 1982. *Foundations of Psychohistory.* Creative Roots, New York.

25 Luckett PW. 1974. Reproductive development and evolution of the placenta in primates. *Contributions of Primatology* 3:142–234.

26 Trevathen WR. 1987. *Human Birth. An Evolutionary Perspective.* Aldine de Gruyter, New York.

27 National Library for Health. 1982. http://www.cks.library.nhs.uk

28 McKeever TM et al. 2002. A birth cohort study using the West Midlands General Practice Database. *American Journal of Respiratory and Critical Care Medicine* 166:827–832.

29 O'Keane V, Scott J. 2005. From obstetric complications to a maternal-foetal origin hypothesis of mood disorder. *British Journal of Psychiatry* 18:367–368.

30 Selye H. 1956. *The Stress of Life.* McGraw-Hill Book Co., New York.

31 Moir A, Jessel D. 1991. *Brain Sex. The Real Difference Between Men and Women.* Mandarin, London.

32 Gibbs RB. 1994. Estrogen and nerve growth factor-related systems in the brain. Effects on basal forebrain cholinergic neurons and implications for learning and memory processes and aging. In: Luine VN, Harding CF (Eds). *Hormonal Restructuring of the Adult Brain. Basic and Clinical Perspectives,* Annals of The New York Academy of Sciences, New York, Vol. 743, pp. 165–199.

33 Verny T. 1982. *The Secret Life of the Unborn Child.* Sphere Books Ltd., London.

34 O'Connor TG et al. 2002. Maternal antenatal anxiety and children's behavioural/emotional problems at 4 years: report from the Avon Longitudinal Study of Parents and Children. *British Journal of Psychiatry* 180:502–508.

35 Sontag LW. 1944. War and the foetal maternal relationship. *Marriage and Family Living* 6:1–5.

36 Blythe P. 1974. *A Somatogenic Basis for Neurosis and the Effect Upon Health.* The Institute for Psychosomatic Therapy, Chester.

37 Sarkar P et al. 2007. Ontogeny of foetal exposure to maternal cortisol using midtrimester amniotic fluid as a biomarker. *Clinical Endocrinology* 66/5:636.

38 Deuschl G et al. 2001. The pathophysiology of tremor. *Muscles and Nerves* 24/6:716–735.

39 Cited in: *Medical References: Drinking Alchohol During Pregnancy.* http://www.marchofdimes.com/

40 Barnes DE, Walker DW. 1981. Prenatal ethanol exposure permanently alters the rat hippocampus. Cited in: *Mechanisms of alcohol damage in utero.* CIBA Foundation Symposium, 105, Pitman, London.

41 West JR et al. 1984. Prenatal and early postnatal exposure to ethanol permanently alters the rat hippocampus. Cited in: *Mechanisms of Alcohol Damage in Utero.* CIBA Foundation Symposium, 105, Pitman, London.

42 Tuormaa TE. 1994 The adverse effects of alcohol on reproduction. *International Journal of Biosocial and Medical Research* 14/2.

Reproduced for Foresight, The Association for the Promotion of Preconceptual Care.

43 http://www.merck.com/

44 Chasnoff IJ et al. 1985. Cocaine use in pregnancy. *New England Journal of Medicine* 313:666–669.

45 Chasnoff IJ et al. 1986. Prenatal drug exposure: effects of neonatal and infant growth development. *Neurobehavioral Toxicology and Teratology* 8:357–362.

46 Kaada B. 1986. *Sudden Infant Death Syndrome. The Possible Role of the Fear Paralysis Reflex*. Scandinavian University Press, Oslo.

47 Goddard SA. 2002. *Reflexes, Learning and Behavior*. Fern Ridge Press, Eugene, OR.

48 Bellis Waller M. 1993. *Crack Affected Children. A Teacher's Guide*. Corwin Press, Inc., Newbury Park, CA.

49 Bellis Waller M. 2006. Personal communication.

50 Mereu G et al. 2003. Prenatal exposure to a cannabinoid agonist produces memory deficits linked to dysfunction in hippocampal long-term potentiation and glutamate release. *Proceedings of the National Academy of Sciences of the United States of America* 100/8:4915–4920.

51 Chyi LJ et al. 2007. Cognitive school outcomes of infants born at 32 to 36 weeks gestation. *Pediatric Academies Society's Annual Meeting*, Toronto, Canada. May 2007.

52 Conger K. 2007. Slightly early birth may still spell trouble later in school. Stanford Report. Stanford News Service. 9 May 2007. www.news-service.stanford.edu/news/2007/may9/med-premature

53 Reiss A et al. 2004. Sex differences in cerebral volumes of 8-year-olds born preterm. *The Journal of Pediatrics*. 145/2:242–249.

54 Portions of brain are smaller in children born prematurely. Genetics, hormones may shield girls' brains from adverse effects of early birth. *Stanford Report*. 18 August 2004.

55 Swamy GK. et al. 2008. Association of preterm birth with long-term survival, reproduction, and next-generation preterm birth. *JAMA* 299:1429–1436.

56 Swamy G. 2008. Cited in: Preterm birth linked to lifelong health issues. *Science Daily*. www.sciencedaily.com/releases/2008/03.

57 Rosenberg K, Trevathen WR. 2001. The evolution of human birth. *Scientific American*, November 2001, pp. 77–81.

58 Statistic quoted on Birth Choice UK website. www.BirthChoiceUK.com

59 Bennett RV, Brown LK. 1989. *Myles Textbook for Midwives*. Churchill Livingstone, Edinburgh.

60 Eggesbø M et al. 2005. Cesarean delivery and cow milk allergy/intolerance. *Allergy* 60/9:1172.

61 Quoted by Bull J. 2005. The possible role of primitive reflexes in the birth process. Midwifery Lecture delivered to students

attending The Institute for Neuro-Physiological Psychology Training Course in Identification, Assessment and Treatment of Neuro-Developmental Delay, Chester, November 2005.

62 Odent M. 1991. The early expression of the rooting reflex. Paper presented at the European Conference of Neuro-Developmental Delay in Children with Specific Learning Difficulties, Chester, UK.

63 Berthoz A. 2000. *The Brain's Sense of Movement*. Harvard University Press, Cambridge, MA.

64 Audesirk T, Audesirk G. 1996. *Biology. Life on Earth*. Prentice Hall, Upper Saddle River, NJ.

65 Nordtveit TI et al. 2008. Maternal and paternal contribution to intergenerational recurrence of breech delivery: population based cohort study. *BMJ* doi: 10.1136/bmj.39505.436539.BE.

66 Beuret L. 2008. Personal communication.

67 Golan H, Huleihel M. 2006. The effect of prenatal hypoxia on brain development: short- and long-term consequences demonstrated in rodent models. *Developmental Science* 9/4:338–349.

CHAPTER 7

POST-NATAL FACTORS USING THE INPP QUESTIONNAIRE

Question 6. When Your Child Was Born, Was He/She Small For Term? Please Give Birth Weight, If Known

Studies carried out in the Netherlands in the 1980s (the Gröningen studies) found that several neonatal neurological deviations, particularly low birth weight in relation to the length of gestation, were significant background factors for minor neurological dysfunction later on.[1,2] An association between low birth weight and the development of adult medical and metabolic diseases, such as cardiovascular diseases and diabetes, was also repeatedly demonstrated. In addition to the physical effects of low birth weight on health in later life, one study found that low birth weight for gestational age, particularly at term, was also associated with adult psychological distress, which was not mediated by childhood factors, suggesting a direct link between early life factors and adult mental health. The researchers concluded that a neurodevelopmental pathway was probably involved.[3]

Early life experiences such as birth weight can have an influence on cognition[3] and behaviour[4] in childhood, and may be the result of a number of other factors: premature birth with all the risks that accompany the immature infant; impaired foetal growth resulting from placental insufficiency leading to a reduced oxygen and nutrition supply to the developing brain; and structural changes to biological mechanisms such as the hypothalamic-pituitary axis[5] (with its powerful influence on hormones, emotional and cognitive responses), the growth hormone axis, and thyroid function. Low birth weight is not an absolute determinant of health, neurological dysfunction in childhood, or the development of adult psychological problems, but as with many events in early life, it carries slightly increased risks.[6]

Question 7. When He/She Was Born, Was There Anything Unusual About Him/Her?

i.e. the skull distorted, heavy bruising, definitely blue, heavily jaundiced, covered with a calcium-type coating or requiring intensive care. If yes, please give details

The medical condition of the child is assessed immediately after birth using the Apgar score, based on five parameters: heart rate, respiration, muscle tone, skin colour, and response to stimuli. Apgar scores are typically assessed at both one and five minutes after birth. A normal infant in good condition will score between 7 and 10. A score of below 7 indicates a degree of asphyxia and requires resuscitation. The need for resuscitation is significant because shortage of oxygen to the brain can result in cell death and damage – the longer the period of oxygen deprivation, the greater the risk of subsequent problems.

In addition to criteria using the Apgar score, other physical observations provide information about the condition of the baby: misshapen skull, swelling, haematoma, or bruising indicate that the baby may have had a 'rough ride' while being born. Stress or strain placed on the region of the neck and on the back of the head (atlanto-occipital region) can result in structural misalignment of the spine at the base of the skull. This can affect not only posture and muscle tone as the child grows up, but may show up earlier as a baby who is a poor sleeper, does not like being placed on either its back or its tummy, suffers from colic in the first 12 weeks of life, and, if uncorrected, may have postural-related learning problems later on.

Jaundice

Jaundice is common in the first week of life and occurs as a result of an increase in the level of bile pigments (bilirubin) in the blood and tissues. Before birth, the foetus needs a high level of haemoglobin in order to attract sufficient oxygen across the placenta. After birth, this high level is no longer required, and the excess needs to be broken down and removed. This, combined with the fact that the red blood cells of the newborn also have a short lifespan, results in an increased need for haemolysis (breaking down of blood corpuscles) and in a higher production of bilirubin, which is normally conjugated in the liver and is converted to a harmless substance by bacteria in the gut. Early feeding of the baby helps to stimulate motility in the gut and provides glucose for the manufacture of liver enzymes, which help the infant to metabolize bilirubin.

Most babies develop a slight degree of jaundice in the first few days of life (physiological jaundice, which is regarded as normal). Approximately 50 per cent of infants become clinically jaundiced, but only in 20 per cent of these (10 per cent of all infants) does the level of bilirubin contained in the blood reach potentially dangerous levels.

Mild physiological jaundice is common and is due to a temporary inability to deal with the normal metabolism of bilirubin. In full-term babies, physiological jaundice appears after the first 24 hours of life and reaches a peak on the fourth or fifth day. In preterm infants, it usually begins within 48 hours after birth and may last up to two weeks. Mild symptoms of jaundice are not a cause for concern provided that

- it does not appear in the first 24 hours;
- the serum level of bilirubin does not exceed a safe limit;
- the highest level does not occur on the third or fourth day of life;
- jaundice fades by the seventh day and the baby is otherwise well.

If signs of jaundice *exceed* the limits listed above, it ceases to be physiological and is considered pathological. Pathological jaundice should be treated at the earliest possible stage to prevent damage to the *basal ganglia*, which are particularly sensitive to the toxic effects of elevated bilirubin levels. The most effective form of treatment is exposure of the infant to blue light, which converts bilirubin into the harmless blue pigment known as biliverdin. More serious causes of jaundice such as blood group incompatibility or hypothyroidism require special treatment.

Disorders of the basal ganglia do not cause weakness or reflex changes. They cause problems in the control of voluntary movement, resulting in either increased or decreased movement and in changes in muscle tone and posture.

Question 8. In The First 13 Weeks of Your Child's Life, Did He/She Have Difficulty in Sucking, Feeding Problems, Keeping Food Down or Colic?

Feeding problems can arise for a number of reasons. In premature babies, feeding problems are a direct result of complications associated with premature birth, including underdeveloped rooting and suck reflexes.

Problems with sucking and/or chewing can be connected to underdeveloped infant rooting and suck reflexes even in the full-term baby, particularly if mother and baby have been separated for a time at birth.[i] If, on the other hand, the rooting and infant suck reflexes are retained a few months later when the child must learn how to chew and to grind food, they can interfere with the development of more mature feeding movements. Chewing is important not only because it breaks down food and begins the process of digestion in the mouth, but it also stimulates movement of the gut further down the digestive tract. It is in the gut that the majority of absorption takes place.

Odent noted that babies who are born early or unwell, when placed in an incubator, can be seen 'rooting' in the first hours after birth. When their rooting attempts do not receive a reward (breast or bottle), the rooting activity, occurring as a vacuum activity, starts to decline. In other words, the rooting reflex is particularly responsive in the first hours after birth, but becomes less reactive if not used at this sensitive time.

Skeletal torsion or misalignment resulting from trauma at birth can also affect sucking, swallowing, and chewing, and development of the bite because the movements involved in successful suckling are dependent on the alignment of the jaw and the palate. Babies who experienced increased pressure, torsion, or use of force at birth on the neck region (e.g. abnormal presentation or forceps) may also find certain feeding positions uncomfortable and may have difficulty or may be unwilling to feed unless a number of different positions are tried. Early difficulties with feeding in the first weeks of life can affect subsequent development of oral muscle tone, swallow pattern, and the resting position of the tongue in the mouth, with subsequent effect not only on feeding but also potentially on speech.

Some babies develop colic in the first 12 weeks of post-natal life. Colic is generally thought to be an attack of spasmodic pain in the abdomen arising from the presence of some

[i] Odent M. 1991. The early expression of the rooting reflex. Paper presented at The European Conference of Neuro-Developmental Delay in Children with Specific Learning Difficulties, Chester, March 1991.

indigestible matter in the lower part of the gut, which excites spasmodic contraction of the intestine.

Empirical evidence from analysis of families where the INPP Questionnaire has been used indicates a trend whereby babies born to mothers who suffered from severe nausea and vomiting during pregnancy or who have a history of food intolerances are more likely to have feeding-related problems (including colic) in the first 12 months of life. Allergic reactions of the skin such as infantile eczema, which are not a direct result of skin contact with a known allergen (washing powder, for example), are sometimes indicative of problems with the gut in processing certain foods.

Some babies vomit up a significant proportion of the feed on a regular basis. If this occurs in a bottle-fed baby without any other obvious cause being present, or develops for the first time when formula feed or cow's milk is introduced, it *might* indicate an inability to break down additional proteins and fats which are present in cow's milk but are not contained in breast milk. There can also be other reasons.

On the other hand, *regular* or persistent projectile vomiting is a serious matter. There are a number of medical conditions which cause projectile vomiting and which require treatment. Additionally, regular projectile vomiting can result in dehydration, electrolyte imbalance, and malabsorption syndrome, where the baby becomes depleted of vital nutrients. This can affect not only weight gain, growth, and immune functioning, but also sleep patterns, activity levels, and mood disturbances, and may render the child more prone to allergies and related difficulties later on.

Problems experienced by the baby can sometimes arise as a secondary result of micronutrient deficiency which has occurred during pregnancy. Foresight noticed that mothers who were zinc deficient were more prone to severe nausea and vomiting during pregnancy. Vitamin and mineral analysis of older children frequently finds those who suffer from allergies also tend to have low-zinc status and essential fatty acid (EFA) deficiency. In adults, a particular type of colic can develop known as lead or 'painter's' colic, which is directly due to the absorption of lead into the system.

Although no connection has been made to infantile colic, it seems plausible that even slightly elevated levels of lead in the infant could lead to 'colicky' spasms.

Independent vitamin and mineral analysis of school-aged children seen at INPP who have a history of feeding problems in infancy and in early childhood has found that a high percentage have a low calcium level and an elevated level of lead in the hair. This may be important because calcium and lead are antagonists – calcium helps to keep lead levels in the body normal. In these cases, it is not known whether the children have been exposed to polluting levels of lead, which have then affected calcium status, whether low levels of calcium have enabled lead level to build up, or whether there is a problem in the absorption of calcium arising either as a result of an inability to handle dairy products or a shortage of vitamin D.

Vitamin D is necessary for the body to absorb calcium. Vitamin D is obtained primarily through exposure to sunlight, and in cool temperate climates it is known that there is insufficient sunlight to provide for all the body's needs during the winter months unless it is supplemented through dietary sources (e.g. fish). In the post-war years, mothers and children were advised to supplement the diet with cod liver oil, a rich source of vitamin D. In recent years, doctors in the UK and in the USA[7] have reported a return of rickets, a disease thought to have been eradicated in the 1930s with improved nutrition (the term rickets is said to have been derived from the ancient English word *wricken*, which means 'to bend'). In several European countries, rickets is also called the 'English disease', a term that probably stems from the fact that at the turn of the 19th century, rickets was endemic in larger British cities. If the mother has a low vitamin D level, the child can be born with a relative vitamin D deficiency as a result of decreased maternal transfer. Breastfeeding, usually regarded as the best source of nutrition for babies, can also lead to vitamin D deficiency in the child if the mother is deficient, and as rickets has started to return, it has led to the advice to supplement vitamin D when breastfeeding.

Whatever the reason, where there is biochemical evidence of abnormality on vitamin and mineral analysis in the older child, it provides an indication that further specialist investigation should be recommended. Digestive problems, irrespective of the source, can affect the availability of neurotransmitters, the chemical messengers of the nervous system.

Gershon[8] described the gut as being a 'second brain' with 'a mind of its own'. He said that the gut contains an intrinsic nervous system that is able to mediate reflexes in the absence of input from the brain and the spinal cord. There are more nerve cells in the gut than in the remainder of the peripheral nervous system, and it is also a chemical warehouse containing every neurotransmitter (chemical substances through which cells communicate) found in the brain. Problems in the functioning of any part of the digestive tract have the potential, via their effect on the chemical messenger system, to affect the functioning of the central nervous system.

Question 9. In the First 6 Months of Your Child's Life, Was He/She a Very Still Baby, So Still That at Times You Wondered If It Was a Cot Death?

Babies who exhibit little movement in the cot or crib, or when they are left to play freely when awake, may be exhibiting early signs of hypotonia (poor muscle tone) or under-arousal.

Question 10. Between 6 Months and 18 Months, Was Your Child Very Active and Demanding, Requiring Minimal Sleep Accompanied by Continual Screaming?

There is a vast range of 'normal' as regards the amount of crying and sleeping a baby does across different cultures, and there can be many reasons for a demanding baby. Babies who consistently cry *excessively* through the day and night and who will not be consoled are signalling discomfort of some kind. At the other extreme, babies who are listless, rarely cry, demand attention, or engage with the people around them may be exhibiting early indications of neurological dysfunction.

Babies often cry and become restless before a feed, and some will do so frequently (every 2–3 hours) in the early weeks of life. This is normal and is more common in small babies and in preterm babies who need a high milk intake to catch up growth and weight, and who take in less food at each feed. Breastfed babies tend to want to feed more often than bottle-fed babies. It can take several weeks to establish a routine which works for mother and baby, and babies who are fed 'by the clock' tend to cry more than babies who are fed on demand. This is all perfectly normal and should not be a cause for concern.

Babies who have had a traumatic birth requiring forceps, ventouse extraction, or other complications affecting the atlanto-occipital area of the spine (the uppermost portion of the spine where it enters the base of the skull), such as the cord around the neck at birth, sometimes suffer from neck discomfort or headache when laid down. Practitioners of manual medicine such as cranial osteopaths and chiropractors can often do much to relieve the discomfort if treated early.

Babies who have congestion of the upper respiratory tract (blocked nose, mouth breathers, and snorers) tend to suffer from more disturbed sleep. Pressure in the middle ear arising from an immature swallow pattern can result in pain, similar to the discomfort we experience when an aircraft descends too quickly – this type of middle ear pressure does not necessarily develop into a middle ear infection (otitis media) but can result in a miserable baby who does not like being put down.

Children who are later diagnosed with attention deficit hyperactivity disorder (ADHD) often have a history of being poor sleepers and of having sleep-related problems which persist well into childhood.

Question 11. When Your Child Was Old Enough to Sit up in the Pram and Stand up in the Cot Did He/She Develop a Violent Rocking Motion, So Violent that Either the Buggy or Cot Was Actually Moved?

Rocking can be a normal part of development and often increases for a short time prior to learning a new motor skill such as just before learning to creep on hands and knees. At these times, the action of rocking helps to facilitate the transition from one stage of motor development to the next. On the other hand, occasionally children develop a persistent and at times violent rocking action, which they resume even when interrupted. Similar behaviour is sometimes seen in institutionalized individuals, for instance patients in mental hospitals, children in orphanages where they receive little sensory or social attention, in autistic spectrum disorders, and under conditions of extreme emotional distress. While in these cases a persistent rocking habit is often interpreted as being part of the 'condition', there is also some evidence to suggest that babies and children who develop a persistent rocking habit may have a hypoactive vestibular system and the action of rocking provides additional vestibular stimulation, helping them to feel good. In other words, in these cases, the rocking action is fulfilling a function, and may provide pointers as to what type(s) of intervention and sensory stimulation would be helpful.

Question 12. Did Your Child Become a 'Head-Banger', i.e. Bang His/Her Head Deliberately Into Solid Objects?

Head banging is sometimes seen among children who are hyposensitive to *external* sensory stimuli, but who have a high degree of *internal* excitation. Similar to the examples mentioned in relation to persistent rocking in the previous question, head banging may be an attempt at self-stimulation. It may also be seen under conditions of *extreme* frustration.

Question 13. Was Your Child Early (Before 10 Months) or Late (Later Than 16 Months) at Learning to Walk?

Most babies learn to walk some time around the time of their first birthday, although the age range at which a child may learn to walk can vary from 9 to 18 months. Any time from 10 to 16 months is considered normal.

Walking represents an important landmark in motor development because it signifies acquisition of postural reflexes, substantial inhibition of primitive reflexes, mastery of balance, and development of muscle tone sufficient to support the weight of the body. A child who is late at learning to walk (16 months or later) may be exhibiting early signs of delay in motor or postural development and/or vestibular functioning.

Despite parents' desire to see their infant walking as soon as possible, walking early is not always in the child's long-term interests either, if it reduces the time that the infant spends in crawling and in creeping first. As discussed in earlier chapters, crawling and creeping are integrating activities which combine vestibular, visual, proprioceptive, and inter-hemispheric training through action. Early walkers can sometimes miss out on aspects of sensory-motor integration normally entrained through the experience of crawling and creeping.

Question 14. Did He/She Go Through a Motor Stage of:
A) Crawling on the Stomach, and
B) Creeping on the Hands and Knees or Was He/She a 'Bottom-Hopper' or 'Roller' Who One Day Stood up?

In the USA, crawling refers to commando-style crawling with the tummy in contact with the ground; creeping refers to creeping on hands and knees. In the UK, the term crawling is more often used to describe crawling on hands and knees, and the term creeping is rarely used. In this context, we have used the definition of the terms used in the USA.

There is often confusion between the terms crawling and creeping. Crawling precedes creeping and describes forward movement carried out with the tummy in contact with the floor (commando crawl). Creeping usually begins sometime between seven and nine months of age, and describes movement carried out on hands and knees with the tummy off the ground. Both crawling and creeping develop in stages, and not all children pass through all the stages.

There are many children who do not crawl or creep in the first year of life and who do not develop later problems. However, among children who *do* have specific learning difficulties, the incidence of children who did *not* crawl and creep is higher. Crawling and creeping are landmarks of motor development, and of interest in the context of the child's developmental history *as a whole*.

Question 15. Was Your Child Late at Learning to Talk? (2–3 Word Phrases by 2 Years)

Children's language develops through a series of identifiable stages. Language in its broadest term describes the ability to communicate. Children go through many phases of pre-speech in the first year of life, but the emergence of recognizable words used in a meaningful sequence is a milestone in a child's development.

By 12 months, most children have one or two words that they say with meaning, and are able to comply with simple commands. By 18 months, one or two words are used to convey a more complex meaning such as 'cup', meaning 'I want a drink', or baby words such as 'tractor' to say, 'there is a tractor in the field'. Intonation is often used to compensate for lack of vocabulary. By two to three years of age, a child should be able to use two or three words together, to talk about and to ask for things using short phrases such as 'Daddy home now', 'socks off', 'want drink'. They may also start to use single-word questions such as 'where?' or 'when?'

Development of speech depends on many factors: normal brain functioning, adequate hearing, fine motor control of the lips, tongue, and swallow mechanism combined with breathing; and adequate exposure to the sounds of language on a daily basis and also, just as important, receiving a positive response for their own attempts at vocalization. Development of speech can therefore be delayed for a number of reasons.

If a child has not started to put two words together by the end of the second year (24 months), and two to three word phrases by three years, it can be an indication of an existing problem with either hearing, motor skills, a more generalized language problem, or lack of environmental linguistic stimulation.

Question 16. In The First 18 Months of Life, Did Your Child Experience Any Serious Illness Involving High Temperatures and/or Convulsions? If Yes, Please Give Details

Most children suffer from a variety of minor illnesses in the first years of life. This is important in helping the developing immune system to recognize past enemies and to launch a future defence. However, serious illnesses involving very high temperature and/or accompanied by febrile convulsions in the young child can, in some cases, result in lasting damage or may compromise the developing central nervous system. Illnesses that might fall into this category include pertussis (whooping cough), scarlet fever, septicaemia, meningitis, encephalitis, and bronchiolitis.

A normal temperature is between 36.0 and 36.8°C (96.8–98.24°F). In children, any temperature of 38°C (100.4°F) or above is considered high and is classed as a fever. Conditions that can cause fevers are flu, ear infections, roseola (a virus causing a temperature and rash), tonsillitis, kidney or urinary infections, or any of the common childhood diseases such as measles, mumps, chickenpox, and whooping cough. Occasionally, a high temperature can occur if a young child (especially newborn) is overdressed. This is because young babies are less able to regulate their own body temperature. Other causes of fever may be teething or reaction within 48 hours to immunization.

Why does fever occur?

A successful immune response attacks one type of microbe, overcomes it, and provides future protection against that microbe, but no other. If exposed to the microbe again, it recognizes it, remembers, and overcomes it. The human body has three lines of defence against microbial attack (infection):

1. External barriers that prevent microbes from penetrating the body such as the skin.
2. Mucous membranes of the digestive and respiratory tracts, which secrete mucus containing antibacterial enzymes which destroy bacterial cell walls. Mucus in the nose or in the mouth traps microbes at the point of entry, preventing them from entering the body. If microbes are swallowed, they are killed by a combination of acid in the stomach and protein-digesting enzymes. If they survive further into the digestive tract, the intestine is inhabited by bacteria that are harmless to the human body but which secrete substances that destroy invading bacteria or fungi.

3. If microbes penetrate both the primary and the secondary defence systems, and if the natural killer cells that destroy cells of the body that have been infected by viruses fail to stop the virus proliferating, the body responds by producing a fever. Fever slows down microbial reproduction and increases the body's fighting abilities.

A fever is the body's natural assault on invading microbes. Body temperature is regulated by the hypothalamus, a part of the brain containing temperature-sensitive nerve cells which act as the body's thermostat. The thermostat is normally set at 37°C (98.6°F), but when foreign organisms invade, the thermostat is turned up. Raised body temperature increases the activity of white blood cells which attack bacteria and reduce the iron concentration in the blood. Many bacteria require more iron to reproduce at temperatures above 38°C, so the fever acts to increase the body's defences against microbes and to create unfavourable conditions for microbe reproduction. A child who has experienced a *series* of serious illnesses involving very high temperature may be showing signs of an immune system under stress and of immaturity in the ability to regulate body temperature under stress, and/or may suffer assault to the immature nervous system *as a result* of the high temperature. High temperatures can cause problems and can also be symptomatic of existing problems.

Febrile convulsions are seizures which occur when a child develops a high fever of over 39°C (102.2°F). They typically occur during the early stages of a viral infection such as a respiratory infection, while the temperature is rising rapidly. They are the result of immaturity in electrical systems in the brain not yet sufficiently mature or resilient to cope with the stress of a high temperature. They are most common between the ages of six months and three years, but can occur up to six years of age. Three per cent of children have at least one febrile convulsion in infancy or in early childhood. Onset before the age of one and a family history of febrile convulsion increase the risk by up to 20 per cent. The majority of children grow out of febrile convulsions without long-term adverse effects, but about one per cent of children do subsequently develop epilepsy. This is more likely if the child has a longer than normal convulsion, or has recurrent seizures in the same illness.[9] An individual *and* family history of febrile convulsions may be significant in children who later exhibit problems of attention and in adults who suffer from panic disorder.

Question 17. Was There Any Sign of Infant Eczema or Asthma?   Yes/No
Was There Any Sign of Allergic Responses?   Yes/No

An allergic reaction occurs when the immune system identifies a normally harmless substance as a potential threat and reacts by producing antibodies. When an allergen (an irritant which stimulates the immune system to react) comes into contact with its antibody, it leads to the release of substances such as histamine, which are responsible for the allergic reaction such as asthma, hay fever, eczema, or dermatitis.

In inhaled allergic reactions such asthma and hay fever, the individual produces large amounts of reagin antibodies, which stick to mast cells in the mucosa so that when the antigen is inhaled, histamine is released from the mast cell. There are a vast number of potential inhaled allergens from pollen to dust mites, feathers to pesticides, and in some children, asthma only occurs when they have an infection or when they take vigorous exercise. Children who suffer from allergies also seem to be more prone to infection. Allergies are caused by a combination of genes and environment, and may well be a throwback to a time when we lived in closer proximity to creatures or substances that posed a real threat to life. Generations later, the immune system continues to react to relatively innocuous substances as if the danger is real.

Allergic reactions affecting the skin can either occur as a result of direct contact with an allergen such as washing powder, or can be symptomatic of problems in the gut. Inability of the gut to handle specific substances, gluten for example, can result in damage to the hair cells (villi), which line the gut and which normally help to move food down through the system. Damage to the lining of the gut wall can then result in a 'leaky' gut when substances seep through the damaged lining and leak into the blood stream from where they act as toxins and stimulate the immune system to react. Problems with the gut can develop for a variety of reasons from enzyme deficiency, inability to break down certain proteins (such as gluten or casein), and absence of 'friendly' bacteria in the gut, to name but a few. Babies who are breastfed are less likely to develop allergies even when there is a strong allergic tendency within the family.

Fitzgibbon[10] and others who specialize in the area of nutritional medicine also refer to the effect of biochemical problems on mood, energy, and behaviour. Overproduction of histamine results in the release of opiate-like substances into the blood stream, which have an effect on mental processes as well as in producing physical symptoms. The effect of this potent cocktail on the child can be similar to an adult who is under the influence of alcohol or who is 'stoned', and may go some way to explaining why many children suffering from allergies are tired, irritable, and 'below par' much of the time, in addition to sleep being affected by itching skin, snuffles, or wheezing. Poor sleep can also affect growth because growth hormone is secreted during sleep.

Stress is also known to increase allergic reactions. Children who have a retained Moro reflex tend to be more prone to allergies. This is thought to be the result of heightened sensitivity and reaction to stress which is typical of the child with a retained Moro reflex[11] and which is accompanied by biochemical changes in response to stress. Cottrell[12] noticed that the frequency and intensity of asthma attacks was reduced in a small sample of patients after the Moro reflex was inhibited.

Allergic skin reactions that cannot be explained by direct skin contact with a known allergen can be symptomatic of biochemical imbalance. Vitamin and mineral analysis can help to identify whether low levels of minerals, trace elements, and EFAs are one source of the problem, and appropriate supplementation can often help to reduce the incidence of inflammatory reactions (zinc, for example, is often used in skin creams and in topical applications for eczema, and EFAs have anti-inflammatory properties). Analysis and supplementation should only be carried out under professional supervision, but can be a useful avenue of investigation for children who suffer not only the misery of dry, inflamed, and infuriatingly itchy skin but also the secondary effects on concentration, sleep, and mood.

Question 18. Was There Adverse Reaction to Any of the Childhood Inoculations? Yes/No

The childhood vaccination programme has virtually eliminated some of the most feared diseases of childhood from the past. As we have lost first-hand experience of those diseases, it is easy to become complacent about the very real risks they still pose if vaccination is not maintained. In the UK, all children start their immunization programme at two months of age (Table 7.1).

The majority of children receive their vaccinations with little or no side effects. Occasionally, children may become ill following one of their vaccinations, and in rare cases may exhibit marked change in behaviour and/or may regress

Table 7.1 Childhood immunization schedule (September 2006)

Age	Vaccine	Method of administration
2 months	Diphtheria, tetanus, pertussis (whooping cough), polio, haemophilus influenzae type b (DTaP/IPV/Hib)	One injection
3 months	Pneumococcal conjugate vaccine (PCV)	One injection
4 months	DTaP/IPV/Hib	One injection
	PCV	One injection
	Meningitis C (MenC)	One injection
Around 12 months	Hib/MenC	One injection
Around 13 months	Measles, mumps, and rubella (MMR)	One injection
	PCV	One injection
3 years, 4 months to 5 years	DtaP/IPV	One injection
	MMR	One injection
13–18 years old	Tetanus, diphtheria, and polio (Td/IPV)	One injection

developmentally. Whether vaccination acts as a trigger for developmental regression in these cases is controversial, but some authors maintain that 'an autistic spectrum disorder (ASD) phenotype has recently been described that is associated with developmental/behavioural regression, enterocolitis and immune abnormalities.[13,14] Parental reports from the UK and the US and elsewhere frequently cite exposure to the measles-mumps-rubella (MMR) vaccine as the trigger for their child's physical and behavioural deterioration.'[15] The reasons why MMR is a suspected cause of bowel problems in a very small number of children and not in others are not yet known, although various factors have been identified as potential risk factors. These include 'familial autoimmunity, pre-existing dietary allergy/intolerance, vaccination with *MCV* while unwell (including current or recent antibiotic administration), and receipt of multiple simultaneous vaccine antigens with the associated potential for immunological interference, particularly for mumps and measles.'[15] The increasing number and concentration of vaccinations that a child receives in the first 18 months of life at a time in development when both the central nervous and immune systems are developing at a rapid rate may be 'one shot too far' for children with an immature central nervous system or a sensitive autoimmune response. Further research is needed to identify common factors within the family and the developmental histories of the very small number of children who it is suspected have been adversely affected by vaccination to see if it is possible to identify susceptible children and to avoid suspected vaccine damage in the future.

MCV refers to measles containing vaccine.

Question 19. Did Your Child Have Difficulty Learning to Dress Him/Herself?

Learning to dress is a complex task requiring both gross and fine motor skills including balance, the ability to use one limb independently of the other, a sense of direction, and in the case of items such as shoes and socks, the ability to tell the difference between left and right. Added to this are fine motor skills of handling fasteners such as buttons and zips (involving visual near-point convergence), and eventually learning to tie shoelaces and a school tie (crossing the midline, bilateral integration, and the ability to follow sequential procedures).

Children learn to dress themselves in different stages and may initially start with the easier items, such as pulling on a tee shirt while sitting down. Dressing while standing up, for example, putting on a pair of trousers or a skirt, involves standing on one leg, while lifting the other one and stepping into the item of clothing while holding the trousers or skirt with both hands – this requires sufficient ability to maintain balance on one side of the body without the need to use the upper body to help support balance, a surprisingly complex task. Very young children still use their arms to support balance. This process can be seen in reverse in the elderly when balance starts to deteriorate and they revert to sitting or using one hand to support themselves when getting dressed or undressed. Children who have immature balance often have difficulty with these everyday tasks.

Putting clothes on the right way round involves directional awareness – another spatial skill – and tying of shoelaces requires the two sides of the body to be able to carry out separate manipulations, cross over and reverse the final manoeuvre – in terms of brain functioning, this is a highly complex task involving bilateral integration, sequencing, and reversal. Tying of shoelaces becomes possible from about seven years of age (assuming the child has had instruction and practice).

Children with immature balance and motor skills are often later at learning to dress themselves and continue to experience difficulties with tying shoelaces, putting clothes on the right way round, etc. This is a separate issue from the increasing number of children who are late at learning to dress themselves because busy working parents have not had the time to let their child go through the slower process of learning to dress by themselves, rather than doing it for them.

Question 20. Did Your Child Suck His/Her Thumb Through to 5 Years or More? If So, Which Thumb?   Right/Left

Many children continue to suck a thumb or fingers beyond the first two years of life, and non-nutritive sucking, whether it is on a dummy or the thumb or fingers, is developmentally normal in the early years. The question was originally inserted to establish *which* thumb the child chooses to suck. Children will usually select the thumb or fingers of the dominant hand[16] and at the time the questionnaire was devised, it was thought that if the asymmetrical tonic neck reflex (ATNR) was retained on the dominant side, a child might select the non-dominant thumb/fingers to suck as the ATNR would prevent bending the arm and bringing the hand to the mouth. However, the ATNR is normally present in the first four to six months of life on both sides and does not interfere with thumb sucking at that time. The action of sucking also has an inhibitory effect on the ATNR when the head is turned to one side and may therefore serve a useful purpose.

Some children continue to suck their thumb or fingers into later childhood (beyond 5 years). In some cases, retention of the infant rooting and suck reflexes can result in a continued need for oral stimulation and therefore prolonged sucking, which then becomes a habit. Sucking is both comforting and calming, and some children are unable to break the habit because the action of sucking provides an additional 'feel good' factor. According to some cranial osteopaths, this can be true for children who have had a difficult birth, which has resulted in a degree of intracranial pressure. By exerting pressure with the thumb on the roof of the mouth using a cantilever action, the pressure of the thumb and sucking movements help to relieve cranial discomfort. The child is treating itself!

The action of sucking is also associated with increased visual convergence, drawing near objects into focus and blurring or distancing the greater world outside. This point was illustrated by a teacher who became exasperated by a 13-year-old boy in her class who continued to suck his thumb noisily all through her lessons. During one recreation period, she put her coffee on one side and went down to the bottom of the school garden, where she found a secluded spot and sat down to suck her thumb for five minutes. She described how the noise and bustle of the school playground in the distance receded; she felt more 'centred' and could focus on objects at near distance more easily; most of all, she felt calm. Just as sucking is comforting in infancy, it is possible that it continues to fulfil a function in children who are visually stimulus bound or who have poorly developed near-point convergence at a later age.

Question 21. Did Your Child Wet the Bed, Albeit Occasionally, Above the Age of 5 Years?

Developmental and neurological reasons for continued bed-wetting can be linked to a retained spinal Galant reflex in the older child. Stimulation of the lumbar region when shifting position at night or the pressure from the waistband of pyjamas can be sufficient to stimulate the Galant and/or associated Pulgar Marx reflexes, which in turn stimulate micturition, which is under reduced cortical control during deep sleep. However, as mentioned in earlier chapters, the spinal Galant is not present in all children who experience nocturnal enuresis, and not all children who have a retained spinal Galant continue to wet the bed, but when bed-wetting and a retained spinal Galant reflex coexist, inhibition of the reflex through a reflex integration programme is often followed by cessation of bed-wetting.

The sleep phases of young children also follow a different sequence and rhythm from the sleep phases of adults. Normal sleep consists of two types of sleep: rapid eye movement (REM) and non-REM (NREM) sleep. NREM comprises four electroencephalograph (EEG) (brainwave patterns) stages associated with increasingly deeper stages of sleep and reduced arousal. Newborn babies spend more time in REM sleep, and the transition from NREM sleep is less well defined. Sleep disorders including recurrent night terrors, sleepwalking, and some cases of nocturnal enuresis are thought to be connected to brainwave variations and differences in the way that the immature brain makes the transition from one sleep phase to another. In the waking state, brainwave variants affect attention and short-term memory.

Mature patterns of sleep normally start to develop over the first two to three years of post-natal life. Nightmares are particularly common from three to four years following scary stories, television, or computer games, because this age group does not easily differentiate between fantasy and reality. Overexcitement, fear, stress, and changing routine are all factors that can affect sleep cycles in young children at various times and are quite normal if linked to specific events.

However, recurring sleep disorders such as regular night terrors, sleepwalking, and bed-wetting can occur when normal sleep cycles become disturbed, if brainwave activity is immature in the older child, or at times of stress.

Links between middle ear infections (otitis media) and bed-wetting among children are often overlooked as the two are viewed as separate disorders. Otitis media is common in young children and can occur as a secondary product of infection, resulting from inflammation of nasopharyngeal cavities (nose and soft palate), allergy, unusually small ear canals, or enlarged adenoids. Normally, the middle ear is ventilated at least three to four times a minute by swallowing, which maintains a normal state of pressure in the Eustachian tube (the tube between the nose and the ear). If a child has an immature swallow pattern (possibly as a result of retained rooting or infant suck reflexes), small particles of food or liquid can enter the nasopharyngeal cavity, increasing the susceptibility to infection.

Biologically, an association between upper airway obstruction and nocturnal enuresis could exist for several reasons. Obstructive sleep apnoea interrupts sleep and may limit normal arousal and self-alerting mechanisms. Hormonal change [obstructive sleep apnoea and lower levels of anti-diuretic hormone (ADH)] and increased intra-abdominal pressure have been suggested as possible factors.

Children who suffer from frequent ear and sinus infections, enlarged adenoids, and/or who snore are more likely to wet the bed. One theory is that breathing problems create a physical pressure in the abdomen, which stimulates urination. Another is that the breathing problems can lead to low blood oxygen concentrations, which can then affect the levels of hormones involved in urine production. There is an increased incidence of bed-wetting among children who snore,[17] and studies have shown that when children had their adenoids or tonsils removed, bed-wetting ceased in 25 per cent of the cases following surgery and in 50 per cent within six months of surgery. Twelve children with secondary enuresis (onset of bed-wetting coincided with the development of upper airway obstruction) had all stopped bed-wetting at six months, and progress was maintained at 12 months.[18]

Question 22. Does Your Child Suffer From Travel Sickness?

Motion sickness does not usually occur until the second year of life, after the child has learned to stand and walk. Susceptibility increases with age, tending to peak between 4 and 10 years of age and gradually decreasing thereafter.[19] Females tend to be more prone to motion sickness than males regardless of age and are more susceptible when taking oral contraceptives,[20] during menses or pregnancy.

Many theories have been suggested as to the cause of motion sickness, but it is generally accepted that it occurs when there is a discrepancy in the timing and synchronicity of messages passing from different sensors involved in the perception of motion to the brain.

Three primary systems are involved in the perception of motion:

1. the balance mechanism in the inner ear (vestibular system);
2. feedback from the body via the muscles, tendons, and joints (proprioception);
3. visual input.

Messages sent to the brain by these different systems inform the brain about the plane, direction, and degree of motion. When all three systems are in agreement, perception under conditions of motion remains relatively stable.

Motion sickness is caused if there is conflict between signals being received from the visual and vestibular systems, or between the two components of the vestibular system (semicircular canals and otoliths), and comparison of those inputs with the individual's expectations derived from previous experience.[21] Mismatch in the timing of information being sent to the brain by the different motion receptors results in the onset of the physical sensations of motion sickness – dizziness, disorientation, initially warmth followed by cold sweats, nausea, and eventually vomiting. Nausea is thought to occur as a result of stimulation of axons of the vestibular nuclei which go to an area of the brainstem called the area postrema, which is an emetic (vomiting) centre.[22] Symptoms can occur without the stimulus of actual bodily movement. For example, the visual stimuli alone provided by video games, simulators, and widescreen films can be sufficient to produce physical symptoms of motion sickness. When the British Broadcasting Corporation (BBC) changed its weather map to simulate movement around the map of the UK in 2006, a number of viewers wrote complaining of nausea simply as a result of watching the weather forecast! Symptoms of motion sickness are not confined to nausea and vomiting but can include drowsiness, headache, apathy, depression, and generalized discomfort.[23]

Dr Lawrence Beuret, who has specialized in the assessment and treatment of adolescents and young adults with neuro-developmental problems, has observed that a history of motion sickness and/or regular headaches and drowsiness in response to motion, if it persists beyond puberty, is often a reliable indicator of immature postural mechanisms acting as causal factors in problems with higher-order learning processes and anxiety. The link to anxiety is significant because many of the physical sensations associated with anxiety are the same as those produced by motion sickness in response to desynchronization of messages received by the vestibular, visual, and proprioceptive systems. The significance of the overlap in both symptoms and trigger mechanisms will be explained further in Chapter 9 when we examine the effects of neuro-developmental delay in adults.

Physical sensations associated with anxiety include increased heart rate (racing pulse), increased rate of breathing, sometimes leading to hyperventilation, sweating, and increased acid production in the stomach, leading to feelings of nausea and 'jelly legs'.

There can be many reasons for lack of integration in the functioning of motion sensory receptors in response to movement, which can stem directly from defects in specific receptors such as poor vision or disease of the labyrinth. People can be sensitive to movement in one plane of gravity only, being excellent travellers on land but as sick as a cat when they step onto a boat. This is because travel on water (and to a lesser degree by air) markedly increases stimulation of tilting motion. Modern high-speed trains also involve increased side-to-side tilting motion. Some people experience a mild degree of motion sickness when travelling in the back of a car but have no problem when they are front-seat passengers. This is because when seated at the back, there is increased stimulation to peripheral vision but reduced frontal vision. Frontal vision is normally used to match visual signals to the stimulation received by the vestibular and proprioceptive receptors. Others are only free from symptoms of motion sickness when they are driving. This is because the driver receives additional proprioceptive input, which is matched to cortical intent (anticipation and motor planning). Increased stimulation to one type of receptor can increase or decrease the experience of motion sickness.

Many children experience mild degrees of motion sickness at some stage in middle childhood, which settles down following major periods of myelinization that occur between six and a half and eight years of age, and again around the time of puberty. If motion sickness has been severe and persistent in early childhood in the absence of other causal factors or continues beyond puberty, then it can be indicative of underlying postural problems and lack of vestibular-proprioceptive-visual integration.

SCHOOLING

Question 23. When Your Child Went to the First Formal School, i.e. Infant School, in the First 2 Years of Schooling, Did He/She Have Problems Learning to Read?

There is a big variation in the age at which children learn to read. Some children are able to make sense of words before their fifth birthday, while others may be approaching seven before reading starts to take off. The National Curriculum in some parts of the UK insists that all children are taught to read at the same age, and much of subsequent teaching and educational assessment is built upon the premise that chronological age is consistent with reading level. This policy condemns some children to underachievement from the moment they enter school.

Rudolf Steiner, Maria Montessori, Louise Bates Ames, and other experts in child development and education, all recognized that chronological age is not the only deciding factor in reading readiness. Neurological and physiological development are of equal importance, and a number of people have suggested that true readiness for reading coincides with the timing of the shedding of the first milk teeth, which usually occurs at about six years of age. Children seen at the INPP with neuro-developmental issues are often late in shedding their first milk teeth, suggesting that developmental delay affects more than simply the functioning of the nervous system.

Delay in motor development also affects far more than the coordination needed for catching a ball. Motor skills extend from control of posture and balance through to the eye control needed to maintain focus on one part of a page (fixation), for the two eyes to fuse the two separate images seen by each eye into one clear image (convergence), for the eyes to follow along a line of print without jumping ahead to the line below or the line above (saccades), and the ability to adjust focusing distance at speed (accommodation). The visual system depends on postural mechanisms and motor skills to support the visual skills needed for reading. Children who have immature postural control frequently exhibit immaturity in the oculomotor skills necessary for reading.

Reading is also connected to hearing. The English language, in particular, requires the ability to match visual recognition of a symbol to the sounds that the symbol represents (phonological awareness). Unless a child can *hear* the difference between *b* and *d*, *m*, and *n*, the rules of spelling in the English language are meaningless. Symbols such as *b* and *d*, *p*, and *q* only face in different directions on the basis of the fact of the individual letter *sounds* that they represent. Children who have difficulty with auditory discrimination (being able to hear the difference between similar sounds such as *d* and *t*, *s* and *f*, and *f* and *th*) will often substitute the wrong letter for a similar sound. No amount of teaching will help them to understand the mistake, unless they can hear the difference themselves.

Reading is also a directional skill. You will remember that a cognitive sense of direction is linked to secure knowledge of where the body is in space (vertical orientation). Children with poor balance and body control also often have poorly developed cognitive directional skills. The *b* or *d* dilemma can arise from directional as well as, or as a result of, hearing discrimination problems.

Finally, learning to read is closely linked to developmental readiness in terms of physical abilities. If a child is still struggling to learn to read by the age of 7, physical factors should always be investigated. Ideally, these should include eliminating any problems with eyesight (optometrist), oculo-*motor* functioning and postural control (neuro-developmental practitioner), and hearing including *auditory discrimination*.

Standard audiometric tests will identify hearing deficit, but more detailed tests are needed to identify problems with auditory discrimination and auditory processing.

Question 24. In the First 2 Years of Formal Schooling Did He/She Have Problems Learning to Write? Did He/She Have Problems Learning to Do 'Joined Up' or Cursive Writing?

All of the developmental factors listed under reading also apply to writing: posture, balance, fine motor skills, visual functioning, and hearing. However, there is an additional component added to writing – the need to use the hands *and* the eyes together. Some children can control the eye movements necessary for reading through the process of conscious compensation as long as they only have to use their eyes. When control of the hand is added to the task, they cannot get eyes and hand to work together (visual-motor integration), resulting in a discrepancy between verbal performance (oral), reading age, and written performance.

Question 25. Did He/She Have Difficulty Learning to Tell the Time from a Traditional Clock Face as Opposed to a Digital Clock?

Most children learn to tell the time using an analogue (as opposed to a digital) clock at some time between their seventh and ninth birthdays. Learning to tell the time using a traditional clock is a spatial skill – a child needs to be able to see the difference between up and down, left and right, before and after, big and little – as well as to recognize the numbers on the clock face. Spatial skills, like directional skills, are supported by secure knowledge of one's own position in space (postural control). Children who have immature balance and posture are often delayed in learning to tell the time.

Question 26. Did He/She Have Difficulty Learning to Ride a Two-wheeled Bicycle?

Children usually master riding a bicycle without stabilizers sometime between their sixth and eighth birthdays. Riding a bicycle combines a number of physical skills: children must find their centre of balance and must be able to control it over a narrow base of support. They must be able to keep their upper body in one position, while getting their two legs to move from opposing positions. They must also be able to turn their arms in either direction without losing their balance and to look at where they are going. In the early stages of learning to ride, balance is easier to control once the child starts to move, but wobble sets in when he or she stops, sets off, or slows down. This is because speed helps to compensate for insecure balance, and children with poor balance control will often use speed at the expense of accuracy in other situations such as sports, or when writing, to compensate for the underlying dysfunction.

In the Netherlands and in some other parts of Europe, children learn earlier as bicycles are more widely used for transport.

Being late at learning to ride a bicycle (assuming the opportunity to learn has been available) may be an indication of immature balance, postural control, and motor skills including difficulty in getting the two sides of the body to carry out separate tasks (bilateral integration). Several retained primitive and underdeveloped postural reflexes are implicated in the difficulty of learning to ride a bicycle.

Question 27. Was or Is He/She an Ear, Nose and Throat (ENT) Child, i.e. Suffer Numerous Ear Infections, Is a 'Chesty' Child or Suffer from Sinus Problems?

Most children will suffer from colds, coughs, and the occasional chest or ear infection in the first seven years of life. Minor illnesses are probably quite important in exposing the immune system to a range of germs and in building up resistance so that when we meet the same or similar enemies later in life, the immune system can launch an effective defence. *Frequent* ear, nose, and throat infections, on the other hand, can have an effect not only on hearing at the time, but also on the child's auditory processing later on.

Otitis media or infection of the middle ear usually occurs as a result of infection spreading up into the Eustachian tubes from the nose, throat, or one of the sinuses. In other words, it usually develops as a secondary consequence of a cold, enlarged tonsils (which are the first line of defence for germs entering the upper respiratory tract), sinusitis, or enlarged and infected adenoids. Ear infections are usually accompanied by throbbing or acute pain, deafness, and tinnitus, which either occur during the acute phase of the infection or during the recovery phase. Treatment is usually with antibiotics, but persistent and recurring infections may require more radical treatment such as minor surgery to perforate the ear drum, to relieve pressure, and to drain fluid; insertion of grommets to improve ventilation of the middle ear and to prevent future build-up of fluid; or, in cases where infected, inflamed, or enlarged adenoids are thought to be contributing, adenoidectomy and/or tonsillectomy.

While treatment with antibiotics or surgery may solve the problem in the short term, the longer-term effects of repeated ear, nose, or throat infections can be more widespread. Hearing can be impaired for up to eight weeks after the acute period of infection has cleared up. It is in the first three years of life that children learn to 'tune in' to the sounds that are specific to their mother tongue. This is one of the 'sensitive periods' or developmental windows for learning and for practising the sounds of speech. Frequent or prolonged periods of intermittent deafness resulting from congestion or infection can have an effect on the child's ability to discriminate between similar sounds later on. When tested on a standard hearing test, hearing levels may be found to be within the normal range, but the *brain's* ability to hear the fine-tuning differences can be impaired, particularly to sounds in the higher frequencies such as *s* and *f*, *sh*, and *ch*.

It is also during the early years that children learn to orient to sound (localization), to 'switch off' attention to unwanted sounds, and to focus attention on specific sounds. Paradoxically, some children who have had frequent ear, nose, and throat infections in the early years appear to be *hyper*sensitive to certain sounds at an older age, presumably because they could not hear them during periods of infection or post-infection and did not develop an adequate mechanism to shut them out or to dampen them down at the time. Both hearing impairment and hypersensitivity (hyperacusis) can cause problems with effective listening, attention, and also potentially speech and language later on. French ear, nose, and throat surgeon Guy Berard, who developed the method of sound therapy known as auditory integration training (AIT), said that 'hearing equals behaviour'.[24]

Why might a history of repeated ear, nose, and throat infections have an impact on balance and behaviour?

Physiologically, balance and hearing have a number of pathways in common: both the vestibular apparatus (balance) and the cochlea (hearing) are located in the bony labyrinth of the inner ear; sensory information from both vestibular and hearing systems is transmitted to other centres using the same cranial nerve – the eighth – or vestibular-acoustic cranial nerve; both share the same fluid – the endolymph – which is set into motion by movements of the head (vestibular stimulation and low-frequency vibration[25]) or vibrations which fall within the frequency range of the cochlea (hearing).

Both systems are involved in orientation. The vestibular system informs the brain about *internal* equilibrium based upon position and movements of the head, while the auditory system detects and locates external acoustic stimuli. Balance functions in cooperation with vision in response to external stimuli that fall within the range of vision (to the front and the periphery); hearing supports balance in alerting us to external stimuli that occur outside of the range of vision, particularly behind and beyond peripheral vision. The location of external auditory stimuli depends upon the difference in timing in the reception of auditory stimuli in each ear. Hearing impairment in *one* ear can therefore affect the ability to locate accurately the source of sound. Hearing impairment in both ears can affect awareness of events outside of the field of vision, particularly behind the self. This can clearly be seen when hearing becomes impaired in old age and the elderly person is unaware of the presence of people behind them or trying to walk past them in a busy street. Posture and gait can also become affected by hearing impairment or loss of external auditory stimuli. The latter can be observed in people using personal stereos or iPods when walking down the street. Head position, rhythm of movements, and the part of the foot placed on the supporting surface alter, affecting the walk.

Pressure resulting from middle ear infection, glue ear, or Eustachian tube congestion alters the flexibility and response of the ear drum, reducing hearing sensitivity, and also causing pain, discomfort, reduced sensitivity to external acoustic stimuli, and increased sensitivity to internal sensation. This can result in a child who feels generally miserable, out of sorts, and who has difficulty in understanding what is being said.

Otitis media can affect taste and smell (affecting eating habits), breathing (mouth breathers), quality of sleep, and speech development as well as hearing. Children with impaired hearing do not hear instructions clearly the first time and often respond adversely to the raised tone of voice used when the instruction has to be repeated. This can make for a child who appears to be slow at following instructions and who is overreactive and argumentative when the instruction is given a second time.

Continuous nasal congestion affects sleep and over a long period of time can have an impact on growth, because growth hormone is secreted at night and during sleep. Use of steroids and stimulants (Ventolin) for the treatment of upper respiratory tract infections and asthma can increase heart rate and can result in generalized over-arousal in susceptible children.

Question 28. Does/Did Your Child Have Difficulty Catching a Ball?

To catch a ball, the eyes need to be able to track a moving object approaching at speed. This involves the combined visual skills of convergence, divergence, and accommodation. When the eyes focus on an object at near distance, both eyes must converge on the object – this 'fuses' the two single objects seen by each eye into one, so that the brain can see one clear, single image. When focus must be adjusted to further away, the eyes have to break out of convergence (diverge) to take in a wider visual field before converging again at the new focal distance. The ability of the eyes to converge/diverge/converge at speed is called accommodation and is necessary to adjust visual focusing at speed. This ability is needed for many activities such as driving, copying from a blackboard or from a book, or tracking an object approaching at speed.

For those children who have difficulty tracking a fast approaching object, by the time focus has been readjusted, it is too late to bring the hands together to catch the ball and they either miss the ball entirely, drop it, or let it fly past them. In some cases, the child is startled when it finally manages to visually 'place' the ball at the split second before it hits them, and instead of bringing the hands together to catch it, the hands are used in a defensive action, repelling the ball, or if the Moro reflex is retained, the arms abduct. The same child may have no difficulty in throwing a ball accurately, because the target can be visually placed *before* the ball leaves the hand.

For slightly different reasons, kicking a ball can be a problem. Kicking involves standing on one leg and swinging the other one without falling over. This only becomes possible when a child has developed sufficient control of static balance to be able to stand on one leg combined with independent use of either side of the body. As with all the other questions above, difficulty in catching or kicking a ball might provide one indication that control of eye movements and/or balance are not commensurate with chronological age.

Question 29. Is Your Child One Who Cannot Sit Still, i.e. Has 'Ants-in-the-pants' and Is Continually Being Criticized by the Teachers?

The most advanced level of movement control is the ability to stay totally still.[26] Stillness requires control of static balance, posture, and freedom from the need to use movement or other parts of the body to support posture. Children who cannot sit still may be fidgety for a variety of reasons: boredom, difficulty maintaining attention, distractibility, or immature control of static balance and of the postural mechanisms that support balance.

Question 30. Does Your Child Make Numerous Mistakes When Copying from a Book?

The most common causes of mistakes when copying are lack of attention or immature eye movements. As discussed in the sections above relating to reading and writing, convergence, tracking, and *accommodation* are necessary to adjust focusing and to maintain visual attention.

Question 31. When Your Child Is Writing an Essay or News Item at School, Does He/She Occasionally Put Letters Back to Front or Miss Letters or Words Out?

Letter and word reversals and/or omissions

Many children reverse letters and numbers in the early stages of learning to write, and the problem seems to be more prevalent among left-handed children, probably because the direction of western script (right to left) favours the right-handed child from a purely mechanical point of view. As children become more fluent at both the recognition and forming of letters, reversals and omissions decrease, so that the direction and sequence of letters should be stable by about eight years of age. If letter, number or word reversals, omissions, or mirror writing persist beyond eight years of age, they are usually a sign of a dyslexic-type specific learning difficulty and further assessment by an educational psychologist should be sought.

Although reversals and omissions can point to a specific learning difficulty at an earlier age, there is a neurological reason why they are not considered a definitive sign before eight years of age. The nervous system of the child goes through periods of increased myelinization at key stages in development. These are the first year of life, years one to three, six and a half to eight years, puberty, and again in the early to mid-20s. At the same time that myelinization is taking place, the brain also goes through a period of neural 'spring cleaning', when pathways and cells that are not commonly used are allowed to die off while connections between others are strengthened. This pruning or clearing of neural clutter is similar to the neurological equivalent of tidying your bedroom – the less you have, the easier it is to find what you need.

If children are still showing signs of difficulty above eight years of age, it may suggest a number of unresolved problems which require further investigation:

1. *Directionality* – this is a spatial skill partly dependent on the efficient functioning of the vestibular-cerebellar loop and its related pathways.
2. *Immaturity* in the development of eye movements necessary for reading and writing. This can be the result of a specific oculomotor problem but is often connected to

existing problems with balance and coordination, because balance provides the platform on which stability of eye movements depends.

3. *Phonological processing* problems. The child may have difficulty with auditory *discrimination* (hearing the difference between similar letter sounds) or *speed of auditory processing,* which is a factor in being able to hear individual sounds within a word, particularly vowel sounds. Timing is also important because the difference between the brain hearing a sound as *d* or as *t* is a difference of just 40–60 milliseconds in the timing of the onset and offset of the first and second bursts of sound. Children can also have problems with *locating* sounds (orientation), filtering out background noise, and *hyperacusis* (hypersensitivity). Any one or a combination of these can cause difficulty in the accurate decoding of auditory information or the translation of sounds into the correct visual symbol.

Question 32. If There Is a Sudden, Unexpected Noise or Movement, Does Your Child Over-react?

Some children are hypersensitive to sound or to specific sound frequencies. There can be many reasons for hypersensitivity, and hyperacusis is particularly prevalent in children diagnosed with autistic spectrum disorder. As with many other questions on the INPP Questionnaire, hyperreactivity to sound can be both a cause of other learning and behavioural problems and/or symptomatic of an existing underlying disorder.

Children who have a history of intermittent conductive hearing loss due to middle ear infections are sometimes hypersensitive to the frequencies that have been impaired as a result of a period of infection. This is thought to be because the normal protective mechanisms against loud or unwanted sounds which develop in the first months of life (acoustic stapedius reflex) are not required at the same level of sensitivity when hearing is impaired. When hearing is restored, the protective mechanism is underdeveloped and the child has reduced tolerance for certain sounds.

Individuals who have a retained Moro reflex tend to have increased sensitivity to sudden loud noises. Auditory sensitivity resulting from a retained Moro reflex can be helped in

Hyperacusis is defined as an inability to tolerate everyday sounds. People with hyperacusis may find that certain sounds are more difficult to listen to than others, and some sounds may cause pain in the ears, even when those sounds do not bother others. Often, the most disturbing or painful sounds can be sudden high-pitched noises like alarms, bus brakes, silverware and dishes, children's screams, and clapping. Sometimes, hyperacusis can be so severe that people avoid public or social settings.

Source: http://health.groups.yahoo.com/group/Hyperacusis Support/

two ways: (1) a reflex stimulation and inhibition programme, which helps to reduce overreaction to sounds and increases cortical involvement in the perception of sensory stimuli; (2) an auditory training programme, which can help to reduce sensitivity to specific frequencies and to improve the functioning of the acoustic stapedius reflex.

SCORING THE INPP QUESTIONNAIRE

Each numbered question on the questionnaire is given a score of 0 or 1.

0 = negative response to the question (*no*)
1 = positive response to the question (*yes*)
Maximum possible score = 32/32.
Minimum score = 0/32.

Although there are a number of sub-questions included under the main numbered questions, a score is only assigned for each *numbered question*. No additional score is given for the sub-questions, irrespective of the number of additional factors/sub-questions present within each numbered question.

The total number of positive answers is then added up. If a child scores 7 or more positive answers, it indicates that it is highly probable that further investigations/assessment of neuro-developmental status will provide evidence of neuro-developmental delay. The questionnaire should *not* be used in isolation as a diagnostic device. It should *only* be used as *an initial screening tool* to ascertain whether further investigations or referral should be carried out.

RESEARCH INTO THE RELIABILITY OF THE INPP QUESTIONNAIRE

An abridged version of a study carried out in 1997 is included in Appendix 1. This study (reproduced with the permission of the *British Journal of Occupational Therapy*[27]) compared the early developmental profiles of 70 children age 8–10 years who had developed problems with reading, writing, and/or copying with 70 children of the same age who had no problems with reading, writing, or copying using the INPP Screening Questionnaire. The study showed clear differences in the developmental history of children who had later developed reading, writing, or copying problems compared to children of the same age who had no specific learning difficulties.

Differences were present, not only in the total number of positive answers obtained for the group with specific learning difficulties – all total scores for this group were greater than 6, with some children scoring more than 12, whereas none of the comparison group scored more than 4 – but also differences on individual questions. The results of the differences on individual criteria between the two groups can be seen in Tables A1 and A2 in Appendix 1. Certain criteria, such as being late at learning to walk and being late at learning to talk, were present in more than 40 per cent of the sample with educational difficulties, but were not present in *any* of the comparison group.

In an earlier analysis of developmental factors using the INPP Questionnaire, Beuret found that the time of emergence of specific learning difficulties or symptoms of an emotional nature varied according to whether adverse events had occurred in pregnancy or during the birth process. He noticed that children who had a difficult birth were more likely to show up as having specific learning difficulties in the first 10 years of life. Children whose mothers had had medical problems during the pregnancy but had given birth without difficulty were less likely to show signs of specific learning difficulties in the childhood years, but were more likely to develop problems in late secondary school or higher education, and were more prone to suffer the effects of stress.[28] While differences on individual criteria on the questionnaire suggest various trends, they should not be used in isolation for predictive or diagnostic purposes. The *total* score on the questionnaire provides the most accurate indication of underlying neuro-developmental problems.

Before turning our attention to the problems that can emerge in adolescence and in adult life as a result of neurodevelopmental issues, it is necessary to examine the role of the vestibular-cerebellar system in further detail. Because this system is so closely connected to the functioning of balance, posture, coordination, and emotional functioning, and has been the subject of a number of discoveries, theories, and approaches over the last 200 years, the next chapter focuses on the history of the development of a vestibular-cerebellar theory and its implications for treatment.

REFERENCES

1 Hadders Algra M et al. 1986. Neurologically deviant newborn: neurological and behavioural developments at the age of six years. *Developmental Medicine and Child Neurology* 28:569–578.

2 Hadders Algra M et al. 1988. Perinatal correlates of major and minor neurological dysfunction at school-age – a multivariate analysis. *Developmental Medicine and Child Neurology* 30:482–491.

3 Wiles NJ et al. 2005. Birth weight and psychological distress at 45–51 years. *British Journal of Psychiatry* 187:21–28.

4 Kelly YJ et al. 2001. Birth weight and behavioural problems in children: a modifiable effect? *International Journal of Epidemiology* 30:88–94.

5 Thompson C et al. 2001. Birth weight and the risk of depressive disorder in late life. *British Journal of Psychiatry* 179:450–455.

6 Gale CR, Martyn CN. 2004. Birth weight and later risk of depression in a national birth cohort. *British Journal of Psychiatry* 184:28–33.

7 Cited in: *Lack of vitamin D made worse in winter*. Tuesday, October 28, 2003. http://www.CNN.com./HEALTH

8 Gershon MD. 1998. *The Second Brain*. Harper Collins, New York.

9 Macnair T. 2006. Febrile convulsions. http://www.bbc.co.uk/health/

10 Fitzgibbon J. 2002. *Feeling Tired All the Time*. Gill & Macmillan, Dublin.

11 Goddard SA. 2002. *Reflexes, Learning and Behavior*. Fern Ridge Press, Eugene, OR.

12 Cottrell S. 1988. Aetiology, diagnosis and treatment of asthma through primitive reflex inhibition. Paper presented at the 2nd International Conference of Neurological Dysfunction, Stockholm.

13 Wakefield AJ et al. 1998. Ileal-lymphoid hyperplasia non-specific colitis, and pervasive developmental disorder in children. *Lancet* 28:351/9103:637–41.

14 Horvath K et al. 1999. Gastrointestinal abnormalities in children with autistic disorder. *Journal of Pediatrics* 135/5:559–563.

15 Wakefield AJ et al. 2006. Gastrointestinal comorbidity, autistic regression and measles-containing vaccines: positive rechallenge and biological gradient. *Medical Veritas* 3:796–802.

16 Delacato CH. 1959. *The Treatment and Prevention of Reading Problems*. Charles C Thomas, Springfield, IL.

17 Alexopoulos EI et al. 2006. Association between primary nocturnal enuresis and habitual snoring in children. *Urology.* 68/2:406–409.

18 Weider D et al. 1991. Nocturnal enuresis with upper airway obstruction. *Otolaryngology Head and Neck Surgery* 105:427–432.

19 Benson AJ. 1998. Motion sickness. In: Stellman JM et al. (Eds). *Encyclopaedia of Occupational Health and Safety*, 4th ed., Vol. 50. International Labour Office, Geneva, pp. 12–14.

20 Gahlinger PM. 1999. How to help your patients avoid travel travail. Postgraduate Medicine online. 106/4. 1 October. http://www.postgraduate.com/issues

21 Eyeson-Annan M et al. 1996. Visual and vestibular components of motion sickness. *Aviation, Space, and Environmental Medicine* 67/10:955–962.

22 Webster DB. 1995. *Neuroscience of Communication*. Singular Publishing Group Inc., San Diego, CA.

23 Gordon CR et al. 1994. Seasickness susceptibility, personality factors and salivation. *Aviation, Space, and Environmental Medicine* 65/7:610–614.

24 Berard G. 1993. *Hearing Equals Behaviour*. Keats Publishing Inc., New Canaan, CT.

25 De Quirós JL, Schrager OL. 1978. *Neurological Fundamentals in Learning Disabilities*. Academic Therapy Publications Inc., Novato, CA.

26 Rowe N. Personal communication.

27 Goddard Blythe SA, Hyland D. 1998. Screening for neurological dysfunction in the specific learning difficulty child. *British Journal of Occupational Therapy* 61/10:459–464.

28 Beuret L 1992. The role of neurological dysfunction in advanced academic failure. The Fourth International Conference of Neuro-Developmental Delay in Children with Specific Learning Difficulties. Chester, March 1992.

CHAPTER 8

THE DEVELOPMENT OF THE VESTIBULAR-CEREBELLAR THEORY

The vestibular system is the only one of the sensory systems that has no special sensation of its own. Awareness of vestibular functioning only reaches consciousness when it has to perform a task beyond its normal range of functioning or when something goes wrong. In other words, vestibular dysfunction 'speaks' through the other senses by heightening sensitivity, altering perception, and triggering physiological changes in the body.

Interest in the vestibular system has grown as technology has developed forms of transport that increasingly challenge the human body's ability to adapt to different modes and speed of travel. One symptom of problems in tolerating motion is the development of motion sickness, which has long been recognized as a problem for people travelling by one of the oldest methods of man-made transport, by boat. Over 2,000 years ago, the Greek physician Hippocrates noticed that 'sailing on the sea proves that motion disorders the body'[1] (nausea is derived from the Greek root word *naus*, hence 'nautical', meaning ship). 'Nowadays there is a potential to cause motion sickness in a wide range of situations – in cars, tilting trains, funfair rides, aircraft, weightlessness in outer-space, virtual reality and simulators.'[2] The symptoms of motion sickness are thought to occur when the body is subjected to an unfamiliar external form of motion or to visual stimuli which are not in agreement with the position of the body, as, for example, occurs in a simulator. However, similar symptoms result from specific diseases of the inner ear such as labyrinthitis, vestibular neuritis, and Ménière's disease.

ORIGINS

It is a paradox that the most ancient of senses – the sense of balance – is one of the last to receive recognition for the role that it plays in education and in emotions in the modern world, but it was not always so.

As early as the second century AD, the Greek physician Galen made a study of the skull and investigated the inner ear. Its tunnel-like passages reminded him of the Cretan *labyrinthos*, leading him to describe them as labyrinths. Subsequent renaissance anatomists described and drew the vestibular apparatus, but it was not until the 19th century that the functional properties of the organs of balance received serious investigation.

In 1804, Joseph Mason Cox published a book, *Practical Observations on Insanity*, in which he described the use of new techniques using twisting, swinging, and rotation of patients in a specially designed chair for the treatment of patients in the Fishponds Private Lunatic Asylum, near Bristol. 'One of the most constant effects of swinging is a greater or less degree of vertigo, attended by pallor, nausea and vomiting, and frequently by the evacuation of the contents of the bladder.'[3] He went on to say that 'One of its most valuable properties is its proving a mechanical anodyne. After a few circumvolutions, I have witnessed the soothing lulling effects, when the mind has become tranquillized, and the body quiescent; a degree of vertigo has often followed and this been succeeded by the most refreshing slumbers.'[3]

Lunacy – *a form of insanity once believed to come with changes of the moon.*

William Saunders Hallaran (circa 1765–1825) was superintendent of the Lunatic Asylum in Cork, where he adapted and used Cox's chair for the treatment of patients. He wrote that 'Since the commencement of its use, I have never been at a loss for a direct mode of establishing a supreme authority over the most turbulent and unruly.'[4] One of the most useful effects of the chair at the time appears to have been the calming effect it had upon manic patients.

Cox's book was translated into German and was used for the treatment of the mentally disturbed in hospitals in Europe. One of these chairs was used by a Czech physiologist, Jan Evangelista Purkyne (sometimes spelled Purkínje or Purkiné) for experiments on vertigo. His primary interest was in investigating the subjective experience of visual motion after body rotation. He used rotating devices as opposed to simply rotating the body and observed that 'visual vertigo is a consequence of the conflict between unconscious involuntary muscular actions and voluntary conscious ones in the opposite direction.'[5]

In the 1820s, Flourens, a French neurophysiologist, carried out a series of experiments on pigeons and rabbits in which he removed various portions of the brain. He not only determined the functional significance of the cerebral hemispheres, cerebellum, and medulla,[6] but he also described the effects on posture and behaviour on pigeons when the semicircular canals were cut. Hitherto, it had been assumed that the semicircular canals were formed as part of the hearing apparatus, but Flourens'[7] experiments showed that 'the loss of each duct affected postural equilibrium, flight and movement but had no effect upon hearing. When stimulated, each canal caused eye movements (nystagmus) in its own plane.'[8]

In 1838, Prosper Ménière, a French physician, was appointed as director of the Institut des Sourds-Muets in Paris. This was an institute for the treatment of deaf mutes. In 1861, Ménière presented a paper before the French Academy of Medicine in which he suggested that the symptoms of a complaint known as 'apoplectiform cerebral congestion' accompanied by symptoms of hearing loss, vertigo, and tinnitus were related to and probably caused by disease of the labyrinth of the inner ear and not of the brain.[9] Despite Flourens' earlier experiments on pigeons, the functions of the ear in relation to balance had not yet become an accepted part of mainstream medicine. It was still believed that vertigo was related to epileptic seizures and strokes, and probably resulted from an abnormally high level of blood in the vessels of the brain. Standard practices used for the treatment of vertigo at the time involved bleeding and leeching.

Observations of human subjects were followed a few years later by physiological studies on animals. Goltz, following Flourens' lead, used pigeons as his experimental subjects. His findings confirmed that the semicircular canals have an important function in the maintenance of equilibrium, particularly of the head, but also of the rest of the body,[10] but Goltz believed that the mechanisms involved operated as a result of hydrostatic pressure of the endolymph on the membranous semicircular canals.

Josef Breuer,[11,12] better known for his work with Sigmund Freud on hysteria, carried out experiments on the vestibular organs of fish, frogs, and birds, and deduced that it was not variation in hydrostatic pressure in the semicircular canals that was responsible for equilibrium, but changes in directional currents in the endolymph in response to head movements. He later recognized the role of the otoliths, suggesting that it was the displacement of weight of these tiny stones in response to head movements which altered position/traction of the hair cells.[13,14] At much the same time, but independently of Breuer, Mach[15] carried out similar experiments on birds and fish, publishing his papers in 1873 and 1874. Both pioneers reached almost identical conclusions at the same time. Their collective findings became known as the Mach–Breuer hypothesis. 'Overall, Breuer developed a simple basic concept to explain how the inner-ear vestibular receptors work. All receptors respond to a shear force associated with acceleration, angular in the case of the semi-circular canals and linear in the case of the macules. This shearing force results in a bending of the tiny hairs projecting into the cupula of the otolithic membrane, which in turn results in a change in firing rate of the afferent nerves supplying these sensory organs.'[16]

William James was the brother of Henry James the writer. It has been said that William James was the psychologist who wrote like a novelist, while Henry James was the writer who wrote novels like a psychologist.

William James, a doctor and psychologist, observed that while deaf mutes often had general problems with balance and coordination, they did not seem to be as susceptible to dizziness as 'normal' subjects when exposed to rapid rotation or to motion sickness when travelling on the sea. In a study of 519 deaf mutes tested using rapid whirling with the head placed in a variety of positions, he found that 186 experienced no dizziness at all, in contrast to 200 students from Harvard College who all suffered vertigo as a result of vestibular stimulation. In a paper, 'The Sense of Dizziness in Deaf Mutes',[17] he wrote, 'The modern theory, that the semi-circular canals are unconnected with the sense of hearing, but serve to convey to us the feeling of movement of our head through space, a feeling which, when very intensely excited, passes into that of vertigo or dizziness, is well known. It occurred to me that deaf-mute asylums ought to offer some corroboration of the theory in question, if a true one. Among their inmates must certainly be a considerable number in whom either the labyrinths or the auditory nerves in their totality have been destroyed.' However, although deaf mutes were less susceptible to dizziness as a result of rotation, when James carried out further experiments in which they were placed underwater, depriving them of their normal tactile and proprioceptive sensations, they completely lost their sense of spatial orientation and became distressed. A similar phenomenon occurs in fish, if the gravity-detecting organ is removed – unable to orient to gravity, they orient towards the light, pointing in any direction to which the other senses direct them, even swimming upside down as they become 'lost' in space.[18]

This phenomenon is referred to as taxis. Taxis is a direct movement either towards or away from a stimulus. Moths, for example, show a positive taxis towards light. Fish usually swim upright by orienting their back surface away from the source of gravity and towards the light. When the gravity sensor is removed, orientation becomes stimulus-bound to light.

One of the treatments for patients with Ménière's disease in the early 1900s was to irrigate the external auditory canal. Austrian otologist Robert Bárány observed that nystagmus developed not only as a result of rotation, but also when the water used for irrigation was either too warm or too cold, and that temperature variations induced vertiginous spinning sensations in the patient. He deduced that if the water used for external irrigation was different from body temperature, the endolymph would flow in the opposite direction, eliciting compensatory *nystagmus*. By observing the rotary reaction of the vestibular system, he was able to define the sensation of dizziness in terms of objective signs such as nystagmus and muscular reactions. In 1906, he devised two tests to measure vestibular function. The first was a caloric test that produced nystagmus by the injection of warm or cold water into the external auditory meatus based on his earlier observations; the second test involved the use of a rotating chair to produce nystagmus. The degree of nystagmus provided a measure of vestibular functioning in response to movement. The chair used to administer the test is now known as the Bárány chair, and in 1914, Bárány was awarded the Nobel Prize for Physiology or Medicine for his work on the balance mechanism.[19]

Nystagmus – involuntary, rhythmic, oscillatory movements of the eyes.

In 1933, a neurologist, Paul H. Schilder wrote an article, 'The Vestibular Apparatus in Neurosis and Psychosis',[20] in which he said that 'The vestibular apparatus is not only an organ for perception, it is an organ which gives rise to important reflexes. These are reflexes to turning and progressive movement. But there are also reflexes which act according to the position of the labyrinth in space. These are reflexes of posture and are probably related to the function of the otoliths. The labyrinth is therefore an organ which influences the muscle tone of the body. Certainly it is only one of the many organs which are responsible for tone, attitude and posture. But the vestibular apparatus is the means for bringing to clearest focus, the sensory impulses which influence our system of attitude and tone.'

He went on to note that 'Hoffman and Fruboese have shown that the optic perception of the vertical direction is dependent on the static organ' (otolith) and he observes that in patients with vestibular dysfunction, 'the perception of space is changed in a characteristic way. Parallel lines very often appear instead of crosses and angles. Also a triangle is seen as two parallel lines.' He accepted that the vestibular apparatus is only *one* of the many apparatuses for orientation in space but suggested that it 'influences the perception of directions and it is more than probable that the parietal lobes give the final shape to directions.'

Schilder described the relationship between vestibular functioning and normal body image, explaining how 'vestibular tone and the tone of the postural reflexes, let us feel the part of the body on which the tone is acting, transposed into a direction which is opposite to the direction of the pull of the tone. Or in other words, the vestibular influence distorts the postural model of the body, the knowledge and perception of our bodily ego.' Centrifugal forces acting on the body change the perception of body weight (semicircular canals) but also, 'irritation of the otoliths dissociates the postural model of the body'. 'A normal function of the labyrinth in all its parts is necessary for a unified postural model of the body.'

Schilder also linked abnormal vestibular functioning to vegetative symptoms such as nausea, dizziness, and abnormal perception of heat and cold. He showed that vestibular-cerebellar deviation and past pointing could be influenced by suggestion under hypnosis,[21] and noted Bauer's findings that certain cases of neurosis were accompanied by abnormal vestibular-cerebellar signs.[22] He concluded that 'probably the psyche can act on the vestibular system in a double way. Either affecting the nervous regulation directly or affecting it via the vasomotor innervation of the labyrinth.'

Leidler and Loewy[23] found spontaneous nystagmus was present in 64 out of 78 cases of patients diagnosed with neurosis together with turning perceptions in the head and visual illusions of objects turning. They noted that the direction of perceived movement was different in cases of neuroses from organic vestibular disease and suggested that vestibular phenomena in the neurosis are a part of the vegetative vasomotor disturbances in the neurosis, which may have a special influence on the vestibular apparatus, which is especially sensitive to general vasomotor disturbances. Either way, the vegetative *symptoms* experienced by the *patient* were the same.

Von Weizsäcker[24] observed that every organic disease brings with it a pattern of psychic reactions – or that every organ has a corresponding psychic representation – that organic disease neurotizes the individual. Goldstein[25] was of the opinion that there are motor tendencies throughout the body which can disrupt the unity of the body unless they are united under the influence of cerebellar function. He believed that the postural and righting reactions are *the starting point* for postural and motor unity, and that the vestibular apparatus acts as the head organ of kinaesthetic function, which has its representatives all over the body. Schilder concluded that 'vestibular changes disrupt the unity of the postural model of the body.'

In the 1940s, three papers were written by doctors Hallpike, Cawthorne, and a young research fellow, Dr Gerald Fitzgerald. The first paper explained the standardized techniques and described observations in the clinical setting of cerebral lesions. The second addressed the neuro-otology of peripheral and brainstem connections of the vestibular system and offered a fresh analysis of the functional neuroanatomy of their circuits. The third revisited the problem of Ménière's disease in the light of these discoveries, based on meticulous analysis of 50 cases attending the National Hospital, Queen Square, London.[26] One of the first 'general' interventions for vestibular problems was the Cawthorne–Cooksey exercises.[27-29] These are a one-page handout of activities that progress from simple head movement to complex activities, such as throwing a ball. These exercises are still used for vestibular rehabilitation and have been adapted for use in other programmes which claimed to provide a 'cure' for dyslexia.

In 1968, Ray Barsch,[30] director of teacher preparation in the Department of Special Education at the University of

Wisconsin, wrote that from the beginning of time, man has been a space-oriented being, and that man is designed to move. Every infant is a space pioneer learning a system of thrusting and counter-thrusting against gravity in order to achieve balance. Achieving spatial proficiency provides a framework on which to build a lifetime of progressive complexity. Self-sufficiency depends upon the origin and development of patterns of movement and the relationship of these movements to learning.

Barsch described *rotation* and *revolution* as the two basic forms of movement: rotation on an axis and revolution around another body. Man, he explained, is continuously exposed to the force of gravity as a result of the earth's rotation on an axis – if it were not for the counterbalancing mechanics of antagonistic muscles, every movement would follow a full rotation. A constant state of readiness is therefore necessary, prepared to alter, modify, and redirect activity as necessary. This, he said, is the beginning of *attention*. Orientation in space involves both arousal and attention. Effective orientation in space begins with head control, because it is the head which gives direction throughout life and becomes the principal reference point for balance.

Movement efficiency comprises and facilitates many other functions: muscular strength, dynamic balance, body awareness, spatial awareness, and temporal (time) awareness. The latter develops as a result of experiencing how long it takes to move from one point to another; in other words, temporal awareness is dependent on physical interaction in space. When movement efficiency is acquired, degrees of freedom become possible: bilaterality, rhythm, flexibility, motor planning, and motor control. Postural control and balance are crucial for the development of these higher skills but also for language. Language, he said, is not only an aural/oral ability but also a visuospatial phenomenon. Human development begins with extensive movement and only limited cognitive efficiency; gradually, that pattern is reversed so that the individual moves less and acquires more on a cognitive level. What was once only known physically can eventually be appreciated within the graphic symbols on the page.

Barsch described balance as being a state of stability produced by the equal distribution of weight on each side of a vertical axis. All of the first year of life prepares the infant for this in the biped position. Good balance achieves this with a minimum amount of energy and fatigue between any particular muscle or muscle group.

The vertical axis necessary for the definition of balance is the line of gravity. Balance requires that a *centre* of gravity is located at the point where the vectors of force converge. This centre is located within the region of the midpoint between the hips (pelvic girdle) – the point of unity between the upper and lower halves. This is located at slightly different points in the body depending on gender and age. The centre for males is circa 56 per cent height above the floor; for females, circa 55 per cent; and for children, slightly higher. The lower the centre of gravity, the more stable the body; feet form the weight-bearing base. Ideally, weight should be evenly distributed between the heels and the fore part of the foot – uneven distribution increases the demand on each foot.

DEVELOPMENT OF BALANCE

In the first year of life, organization of movement progresses from the head downwards, from homologous to homolateral, allowing equal use of the sides to be developed. In the second half of the first year, crawling results in cross pattern or diagonal patterning – interweaving of both sides across both midlines. Crawling also develops dynamic balance around a midline with the centre of gravity lowered and the base established at the knee tucked under the pelvis. This can later be translated into walking. Failure to crawl can result in poorly coordinated movements in the later walking pattern.

CEREBELLUM AND BALANCE

The cerebellum works *together* with the vestibular system, antigravity muscles, and the eyes, and it is the coordination between these systems which results in good balance, adaptability, and flexibility of movement. Balance in man is a bilateral equation, and alignment of body parts must be correctly placed over the supporting base. Proprioception of

Labyrinthine and tonic neck reflexes *are* crucial in providing proprioceptive feedback through the neck at different stages in development. Retention of the asymmetrical tonic neck reflex (ATNR) and the symmetrical tonic neck reflex (STNR), or lack of head righting reflexes in the older child will affect proprioceptive-vestibular matching.

Abnormal plantar and Babinski reflexes can affect balance and proprioception from the base upwards.

the neck is important for vestibular organs to maintain balance (as are the feet in providing a stable supporting base as well as vision).

How do these earlier discoveries and observations of how the vestibular apparatus functions link to problems of reading, writing, and spelling?

Also during the 1960s, Frank Belgau, a former flight engineer, changed career to become an elementary school teacher in Texas. He noticed that reading difficulties were often present in bright children, and that the walking pattern of children who had reading problems was different from other children's. His earlier experience as a flight engineer coupled with a long-term interest in the motion properties of pendulums provided him with clues as to how to develop activities that could make an immediate observable improvement in children's reading and academic performance.

He developed a parent training programme in which parents spent one to one and a half hours per week with their children using a sensory-motor programme. Many of the parents were also scientists associated with the NASA space programme. Their insights helped to direct his attention to the role of balance and the vestibular system in learning processes and to the development of the Belgau balance boards. One board sits atop two rotating rockers providing an unstable surface (tilting) on which to practise various coordination activities such as throwing and catching a bean bag. The board demands increased proprioceptive involvement in all activities; the second board sits atop two swivel plates providing vestibular stimulation (rotation) in a variety of positions allowing the user to increase the level of difficulty. A grid on the top of the board provides a mechanism for keeping the body centred, allowing both sides of the brain to be equally involved. Activities on the board are designed to improve the integration and timing of both hemispheres of the brain, as well as integration of the vestibular, visual, kinaesthetic, and tactile senses.[19] Belgau's

Soft signs – with the help of a standardized and age-adequate neurological examination technique, various forms of minor neurological

practical methods have provided the basis for later assessment and intervention programmes used by others for the remediation of dyslexia, dyspraxia, and attention deficit-related problems.

In 1973, Jan Frank and Harold Levinson (a psychiatrist) carried out a study in which they examined children who had been referred for psychiatric evaluation on the basis of poor response to reading instruction. They examined the children for '*soft signs*' of neurological dysfunction using a range of tests for static and dynamic balance, proprioception, tonus, and cerebellar signs including the fingertip approximation test, finger-to-nose test, heel to toe, dysdiadochokinesis, plus writing, drawing, and ocular fixation and scanning. In a sample of 115 children, 112 children (97 per cent) showed evidence of vestibular-cerebellar dysfunction. The drawing tests using the Goodenough[31] and *Bender–Gestalt* designs (1938) revealed disturbances in spatial orientation in all cases. Spatial signs included rotation of the Bender–Gestalt cards, copying paper and/or figures, rotation of the head and body, and tilting of the original figures from their intended horizontal and vertical axes. The authors speculated that these spatial adjustments of the figures and/or the self, tilting of the figures, and problems with angle formation 'suggested that the automatic co-pilot or the inner ear spatial steering and equilibrium mechanism of the vestibular apparatus and cerebellar-vestibular circuits was impaired'.[32]

In the discussion section of the same study, Frank and Levinson described the reading disturbance in *dysmetric* dyslexia as being similar to the difficulty experienced by normal readers when trying to read a sign from the window of a moving train. 'The ensuing fixation nystagmus interferes with intentional fixation on the one hand and sequential scanning on the other, and results in letter and word scrambling.' They acknowledged that correlation between vestibular-cerebellar disturbances and reading difficulties does not indicate causation but suggested that these signs 'may be indicative of a general central nervous system difficulty'. As a result of their findings, they formulated the following hypotheses:

1. The cerebellar-vestibular circuits provide a harmonious well-integrated and stable motor background for visual perception.
2. This motor background or motor Gestalt is nothing more than the subliminal, automatic, integrated motor activity of the eye muscles, head, and neck so that ocular fixation and sequential scanning of letters and words can take place.

dysfunction (MND), such as mild dysfunctions in muscle tone regulation, choreiform dyskinesia, or fine manipulative disability, can be diagnosed. Soft signs provide evidence of MND but do not necessarily point to the cause of the dysfunction.

Bender–Gestalt test[i] – a neurological test designed to help in the diagnosis of loss of function and organic brain damage in children and in adults, consisting of nine geometrical figures that are copied, the drawings being evaluated according to the overall quality of the reproductions, their organization in relation to Gestalt grouping laws, and the errors made.

Dysmetria (Greek: 'difficult to measure') is a symptom exhibited by patients after cerebellar injury or injury to proprioceptive nerves (nerves that carry information about

[i]Bender L. 1938. *A Visual Motor Gestalt Test and its Clinical Uses.* American Orthopsychiatric Association, New York.

the position of joints and extremities) resulting in an inability to fix the range of movement in muscular activity. Rapid and brisk movements are made with more force than necessary.

3. In the presence of a cerebellar-vestibular dysfunction and subclinical nystagmus, ocular fixation and sequential scanning of letters and words are disordered, and letter and word scrambling results.

4. This scrambling and resulting dysmetric visual perception lead to deficient comprehension or dyslexia.

5. A primary cerebellar-vestibular dysfunction in children, together with its resulting dysmetric visual perception and accompanying anxiety, can lead to maturational lag.

6. The use of cerebellar-vestibular harmonizing agents such as cyclizine alone or in combination with reticular activating and alerting agents such as methylphenidate (Ritalin) is suggested for the prevention and treatment of dysmetric dyslexia in cerebellar-vestibular-positive pre-school and school children, respectively.

Electronystagmography – electrical recording of eye movements.

Finally, they advocated the use of *electronystagmography* for the detection of subclinical nystagmus in children suspected of having dysmetric dyslexia.

Over the next 25 years, Levinson[33-39] published a series of books which explored the basis of his hypothesis, the functions of the cerebellum in relation to learning and phobic disorders, and the use of anti-motion sickness and anti-histamine preparations prescribed as 'cerebellar-vestibular harmonizing agents' to re-calibrate the functioning of the vestibular-cerebellar loop and associated circuits, thereby affecting eye movements and postural stability. While his definition of dyslexia has broadened to include general disorders of the cerebellar-vestibular loop which affect learning and behaviour, he does not claim that *all* forms of dyslexia are the result of vestibular-cerebellar dysfunction, saying that 'I am keenly aware that all solutions are incomplete and that multiple solutions may exist.' What Levinson offers in diagnosis and treatment through medication is *a* solution to the riddle dyslexia when clinical evidence of vestibular-cerebellar dysfunction is present; he does not offer a global solution.

His theory has also been misrepresented under the popular title of 'space dyslexia'. In his book *A Scientific Watergate*, Levinson cites an example described by Lestienne of the effects of reduced gravity on Russian and French cosmonauts when they were placed in a gravity-free environment. He states that '"Temporal information processing in the

nervous system: Special Reference to Dyslexia and Dysphasia" was the topic selected for discussion (without reference)
at the Rodin Society Conference in September 1992 . . .
Francis Lestienne also reported to the Rodin Society that the
French-Russian cosmonauts began reading upside-down
and backwards at zero gravity – an inner ear determined
condition I call "space dyslexia".[40] In other words, Levinson was describing the cognitive effects of disassociation
between vestibular-proprioceptive and visual functioning,
which arise when the vestibular system is unable to act
as the primary reference point for position in space. Under
conditions of zero gravity, astronauts and cosmonauts
can adapt to altered stimulation by using other sensory
systems to compensate, but during periods of reorganiza-
tion and adjustment, temporary visual-perceptual disturbances occur. Levinson has never suggested that astronauts
or cosmonauts were dyslexic, rather, that a temporary
dyslexia-type phenomenon can appear when the vestibular
system loses the primary physical stimulus – gravity.

This has been misinterpreted by some to mean that cosmonauts who could mirror read under conditions of zero gravity had dyslexia. This is not the case. What was being described was a temporary alteration in sense of direction, which can occur under conditions of zero gravity.

Change in the gravitational reference point results in a temporary alteration of perception of direction and other visual-
perceptual disturbances. Levinson later went on to write in
personal communication that 'my definition of space dyslexia includes the whole gamut of dysfunctions associated
with dyslexia, i.e., reading, writing, spelling, math, coordination, balance, etc',[41] but his use of the term space dyslexia
is broader than simply the description of the effects of zero
gravity on cosmonauts. Like Barsch, he sees specific learning difficulties, with identifiable features of cerebellar-
vestibular dysfunction, as being part of a general disordered
sense of space and use of the body in space.

In 2008 (personal communication), Levinson wrote,

> After examining many more thousands of patients (since
> 1973) and their diverse and often completely unexpected
> favourable responses to CV enhancing medication, I was
> forced to recognise that:
>
> 1. The manifest symptoms of dyslexics are resultants of
>   a dynamic interplay of a CV **dysfunctioning** versus
>   **compensatory** factors.
> 2. The CV system fine-tunes and affect the **entire** sensory-motor
>   and related anxiety, mood, concentration, activity, cognitive
>   etc. – and not just the visual system.

In November 1994, The International Dyslexia Association's Committee of Members defined dyslexia as 'A neurologically-based, often familial, disorder which interferes with the acquisition and processing of language. Varying in degrees of severity, it is manifested by difficulties in receptive and expressive language, including phonological processing, in reading, writing, spelling, handwriting, and sometimes in arithmetic. Dyslexia is not a result of lack of motivation, sensory impairment, inadequate instructional or environmental opportunities, or other limiting conditions, but may occur together with these conditions. Although dyslexia is life-long, individuals with dyslexia frequently respond successfully to timely and appropriate intervention.'

3. Since the degree of CV dysfunction varies from patient to patient as the favourable responses to developmental and therapeutic modalities varies dramatically from patient to patient, it also became clear that one could not define dyslexia and its many related CV-determined disorders on the basis of severity, since compensation and even over-compensation may often mask sub-clinical dysfunctioning symptoms.[42]

In view of the above, Levinson has modified his definition of dyslexia, describing it as 'a primary CV-induced dysmetric sensory-motor and Spatial-Temporal Sequencing Disorder in dynamic equilibrium with compensatory forces – resulting in a diverse spectrum of symptoms.'[41] This is very different from the classical definitions of dyslexia, which, generally speaking, rule out specific sensory impairments as primary causal factors.

The links between posture, balance, motor skills, and learning disabilities were the subject of a book, *Neurological Fundamentals in Learning Disabilities*.[43] The authors, de Quirós and Schrager, pointed out that there are important differences between the disciplines of neurology and neuropsychology. Whereas the former seeks to identify and to treat the symptoms of abnormalities caused by disease or damage, neuropsychology seeks to understand disturbances that interfere with human achievement (dysfunction). Many of the problems experienced by children with specific learning disabilities often fall between these two professional domains.

They maintained that knowledge (or the acquisition of knowledge) starts with intentional coordinated motor activities, that learning depends on coordinated motor activities of purposeful movement which involves the matching of action to intention. Motor activities are based upon posture and equilibrium; posture is made possible through the reflex activity of the body in relation to space, and in the developing child, new afferents are generated through contact – some intentional, much accidental – which allows him or her to imagine (visualize) action.

In the same book, the authors explain why experience of movement is important in order to develop body schema, image, and concept. 'To think with language requires more than purposeful *equilibrium* – it needs non-interference at the conscious level of efferent from the body.' 'At the beginning of life, motor activity anticipates mental action; then both factors are coincident; later, they coexist; finally, mental action subordinates motor activity.' They go on to say that 'the higher the level of the central nervous system employed to maintain the service of the body, the greater will be the difficulty in concentrating on higher skills on learning processes.'[42]

Learning a new motor activity requires a disruption of pre-existing functional units and selective choice of new motor combinations assembled into a new working unit. Primary integration of the postural system takes place in the first three years of life before a child is ready to start school. Simple tests for balance and proprioception can show whether a child has achieved the postural and motor skills commensurate with chronological age. For example, by three and a half years of age, a child should be able to perform the Romberg test without needing to use external reference points provided by vision. Finger opposition movements (necessary for writing), which should be present from five years of age, reveal that one side of the body is able to move without involvement of the other side – postural stability is a precursor to this. If simple tests provide evidence of postural problems, more extensive assessments can be carried out, also employing posturography analysis if indicated.

Schrager later went on to carry out evaluations of language-impaired and normal subjects using the one-leg stand test with older subjects. He video-recorded subjects standing on one (right) leg then digitalized the images at a rate of one frame per three seconds, to obtain 10 'still' images of postural adjustment over a total period of 30 seconds in each subject. He found that postural adjustments were significantly greater in the language-impaired subjects compared with the subjects with normal language ability, and suggested that further research should be carried out in this area.[44]

Reuven Kohen-Raz, former Chairman, Department of Special Education, Hebrew University, Jerusalem, and an internationally respected authority on postural control and childhood learning disorders, followed a similar path, eventually developing a piece of equipment – the interactive

Equilibrium – *the interplay between forces enabling the maintenance and control of postures and attitutudes.*

Attitude *is the result of reflexes that lead to the return to a species-specific position.*

balance system – which could provide evidence of a relationship between reading ability and postural control.[45] He
described posture as being the result of the operation of
'a neurophysiological apparatus which ensures the physical
stability and mobility of the organism against the pull
of gravity . . . a central neurophysiological system which
embraces a wide range of functional levels from spinal
reflexes to higher mental processes.' Postural control, he
said, was 'the precondition of all differentiated and complex
mental activities' – the beginning of the ability to differentiate between the inner and outer world, and the awareness
of the autonomous self in a universe of objects, 'rooted in
the human ability to assume an erect and flexible posture,
a stance, a standpoint which serves as a point of reference
for understanding the environment.' Ocular-motor mechanisms, which are controlled by the vestibular sense, are
linked to postural stability and are involved in the experience of subjectivity and objectivity. This is in part because
postural control is linked to three systems:

1. the visual system – external;
2. the vestibular system – internal;
3. the proprioceptive system – modulatory.

The vestibular and postural systems mature early and are
essential for the higher processes of sensory integration.
Dysfunction tends to upset all higher and later processes of
intermodal interaction necessary for the acquisition of higher
academic skills. Kohen-Raz pointed out that important
milestones in mental development coincide with phases of
developmental progress in postural control. Crawling on
hands and knees, for example, coincides with an infant's
awareness of depth perception (the visual cliff experiment);
when a young child learns to stand unsupported, speech
development accelerates; when a child becomes able to
stand alone with eyes closed (circa 4–5 years of age), the
threshold for mastering Piaget's concrete operation stage is
usually reached. This is the time when a child begins to be
able to internalize complex actions and to understand
without always needing to see. Kohen-Raz listed difficulties
with certain common features that arise from postural
immaturity including visual and acoustic sequence processing, inadequate perception, graphic reproduction of
geometrical forms (see Figures 8.1–8.3), confused spatial

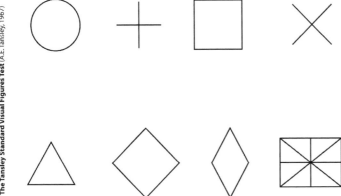

Figure 8.1 Tansley standard figures[ii]

Figure 8.2 Example of problems with graphic reproduction of geo-metrical forms. Reproduced with permission of INPP, Chester.

[ii]Tansley AE. 1967. *Reading and Remedial Reading*. Routledge and Kegan Paul Ltd., London.

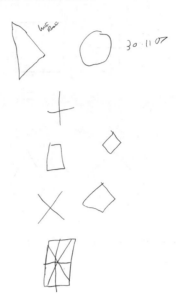

Figure 8.3   Example of confused spatial organization when reproducing geometrical forms. Reproduced with permission of INPP, Chester

organization, poor short-term memory, clumsiness, and deficits in surface and deep structure language.

Kohen-Raz advocated the use of simple pass/fail tests, such as the Romberg and Mann Tests to assess balance, as well as instruments for the measurement of postural control. One such instrument was the interactive balance system based on the concept that bipedal man still stands on four balance points (formerly four feet), which are relocated as one weight-bearing centre on each forefoot and on each heel, with the cerebellum acting as the intermediary between the four points, in the four nuclei. The machine has two foot plates, with sensors at the front and at the back, which detect weight distribution and variations between front and back and left and right. Posture can be assessed on solid platforms with the eyes open and closed, and then on soft foam pads with the eyes open and closed. The device measures general stability, synchronization, weight percentages, and weight distribution. His studies have shown different patterns of measurement in different populations: autistic children appear to perform better when standing on foam pads with the eyes closed (increased proprioceptive feedback);

deaf children are better with the eyes open (vestibular inad-
equacy?); in children diagnosed with dyslexia, the postural
system, which should normally be able to compensate, is
weaker; the lower the frequency of continuous sway, the
more mature is the postural control, which is reflected in
improved learning ability.

Having obtained all these data, Kohen-Raz went on to use
a programme of integrative balance and motor exercises
with first-grade school children. Exercises were given in
open space and were loosely structured, and the children
were given the freedom to improvise. During the activities,
the children were taught:

- To perceive the difference and the boundaries between
  personal and *general* space.
- Within the personal space, movements were free and
  unlimited.
- Within the general space, the personal space of other
  children must be conceived and respected.
- Exercises were carried out in pairs.
- Body awareness was trained.
- The body had to be moved between static and moving
  objects involving oculomotor stimulation and postural
  stress.
- Emphasis was on bimanual coordination, execution of
  synergetic movements, and the suppression of synkinetic
  responses.
- Execution of exercises with monocular and bi-ocular
  occlusion.
- Children were asked to describe verbally the intended
  and executed motor act.

At the end of the programme, the first-grade children who
had taken part in the exercises showed statistically significant greater progress in reading and in arithmetic than the
controls [experimentals (n = 469) and controls (n = 535)
recruited from 14 different schools for culturally disadvan-
taged populations].[45]

Use of the interactive balance system was extended to incorporate balance training as well as for assessment purposes.
The Tetrax Biofeedback device enables the subject to view
gravity displacements of his body, and he can be trained to
improve abnormal postural control by propelling his body

to targets as prescribed by a therapist or through the use of computer games linked to the Tetrax device. The Tetrax machine has foot plates comprising sensors which can operate like the accelerator, brake, or reverse gear on a car; the device also has a computer screen attached so that the child can play a computer game with the feet such as running a maze or 'cops and robbers' while standing up, simply by depressing or lifting the forefoot or heel of each foot. In this way, control of balance and posture can be modified by increasing proprioceptive-vestibular interaction in the service of achieving a visual-cortical goal.

Vestibular and cerebellar functioning are also tested as part of The INPP Method as developed by Peter Blythe and David McGlown in the 1970s (see Chapter 10). The INPP Method uses the assessment of primitive and postural reflexes and standardized neurological tests for cerebellar involvement to provide evidence of vestibular, postural, and cerebellar problems in children and in adults. While individual aberrant reflexes will interfere with posture, motor coordination, and vestibular-cerebellar functioning, the *presence* of aberrant reflexes also *reveals* dysfunction in the operation of these systems. Assessment of primitive and postural reflexes in the older school child can help to identify those children who would benefit from a physical programme of intervention, as well as to provide clinical criteria from which to select the most suitable type and appropriate developmental level of physical intervention for each child.

In the 1980s and 1990s, Henrietta and Alan Leiner, together with Robert Dow, published the results of a series of investigations into the functioning of the cerebellum based on the theory that the cerebellum is involved in more than simply the coordination of motor activities. They based their investigations on the premise that during the course of human evolution, 'the cerebellum enlarged more dramatically than any other part of the brain except the cerebral cortex;[46,47] and the phylogenetically new parts of the cerebellum developed in parallel not with the cerebral cortex as a whole but specifically in parallel with cerebral association areas.'[48,49] The number of nerve cells in the enlarged human cerebellum exceeds the number in the cerebral cortex[50] and 'this cerebellar mechanism in the hindbrain is connected by millions of nerve fibres to many parts of the brainstem and forebrain, including all the lobes of the cerebral cortex'.[50] In other words, the cerebellum may act as a coordinator between the brainstem, the midbrain, and the cortex, between the body and the forebrain.

In 1986, Leiner et al.[48] argued that it is the unique enlargement of particular areas of the newest part of the cerebellum in man – the neodentate – that has enabled him to improve the performance of any other part of the brain to which it is linked as a result of two-way neural connections, and that the cerebellum contributes to mental skills. Using *positron emission tomography (PET)* scans, they were able to show that the dentate nucleus was actively involved in cognitive operations such as word association tasks, mental imagery of movement sequences, error detection, etc., and that these mental tasks were carried out in the absence of motor activity, although the main function of the cerebellum had always been assumed to be the modulation of motor activities.

In order to understand why vestibular and postural problems may have an effect on some of the 'higher' functions of the cerebellum, it is necessary to look at the hierarchical organization of the cerebellum in greater detail.

While it is the cerebral cortex that enables us to perform the higher functions which are unique to mankind, it is the cerebellum which regulates man's every movement. Although it can initiate nothing by itself, the cerebellum monitors impulses from the motor centres in the brain and the nerve endings in the muscles. While the incoming impulses outnumber efferent impulses by at least 3:1, it is the cerebellum's task to eliminate and to inhibit extraneous movement in order to fine-tune motor output. Impulses from the cerebellum are directed to the vestibular system, the eyes, the muscles, and joints of the lower limbs and the trunk. Ultimately, the cerebellum is responsible for regulating the postural reflexes and muscle tone[51] and was described by Sherrington as the head ganglion of the proprioceptive system.[52]

Similar to the structure of the brain as a whole, the cerebellum is organized in three phylogenetic layers: at the base is the archicerebellum. This is an evolutionary outgrowth of the vestibular system from where certain fibres pass directly to the cerebellar cortex, with the majority relaying information via the vestibular nuclei and the reticular activating system in the brainstem. Situated above the archicerebellum

PET – a highly specialized imaging technique that uses short-lived radioactive substances to produce three-dimensional coloured images of those substances functioning within the body. These images are called PET scans.

PET scanning provides information about the body's chemistry not available through other procedures. PET studies metabolic activity or body function. PET has been used primarily in cardiology, neurology, and oncology.

Archi – meaning ancient. Paleo – meaning old. Neo – meaning new.

is the paleocerebellum, which receives action potentials from the skin, joints, and primary endings, the neuromuscular spindles (tactile and proprioceptive). The neocerebellum has developed together with the cerebral cortex in mammals, achieving its greatest size in primates with the most recent evolutionary development – the neodentate of the dentate nucleus – being a development unique to humans. The neocerebellum plays a major part in the regulation of hand and mouth movements influencing clarity and control of the motor aspects of speech production, finger and hand movements (Table 8.1).

The Leiners' findings lend credence to the hypothesis that the cerebellum acts in concert with other structures as part of a fronto-subcortical system devoted to the storage and organization of timed sequential behaviours,[53] associative learning,[49] word generation,[54] and rapid shifting of attention from one task to another.[55] Hallett and Grafman[53] suggested that 'The role of the cerebellum in timed sequential cognitive processing may be analogous to its role in motor pro-

Table 8.1 Organization and major functional connections in the human cerebellum

Phylogenetic	*Major connections*	*Type of function*
Archicerebellum	Vestibular	Posture (subconscious)
Paleocerebellum	Spinal cord Sensory	Progressive movement, e.g. walking, running, etc.
Neocerebellum	Cerebral cortex via pons	Fine muscle coordination, particularly of the hands and mouth (motor aspects of speech)
Dentate nucleus	Association cortex	• Word association • Mental imagery of movement sequences (ideation) • Practice-related learning • Error detection • Judging time intervals and velocity of moving stimuli • Rapidly shifting attention between sensory modalities • Cognitive operations in three-dimensional space

Based on results shown on PET scans, published in Leiner et al.[56]

cessing and suggest a mechanism by which cognitive events become sequenced and temporally labelled.'

In 1994, a group of researchers at Sheffield University devised an early screening test sometimes referred to as the 'wobble test' for dyslexia. This test was based upon the vestibular-cerebellar theory first mooted by Frank and Levinson in 1973, and it also utilized the concept of the Belgau balance board as part of the assessment procedure.

One of the researchers[57] had noticed, while working at a school for children with dyslexia, that the balancing ability of children with dyslexia was significantly different from other children when they had to perform balance tests using a blindfold. When she carried out additional tests for cerebellar functioning, the cerebellar tests revealed similar discrepancies between the two groups. 'The cerebellum could be described as an extremely complex auto-pilot system. As we learn new skills this system gradually becomes programmed so that when we need that skill again, the cerebellum takes over and the activity is performed automatically. If there is a problem and the cerebellum cannot be programmed, you have difficulty learning new skills. Then, even if you do learn to do it, you may still have to think about what you are doing each time. The US research and our own work certainly seem to suggest that this could be happening in dyslexia.'[58] The Sheffield test also includes tests for balancing, word rhyming, repeating a nonsense word, pressing a button on hearing a tone, and naming objects pictured on cards – all problems identified as being features of dyslexia. The idea was that the test could be used as an early screening device to detect children who were showing early signs of dyslexic tendencies.

In 2005, two members of the same team joined together with other scientists attempting to establish the neurobiological basis of dyslexia. They carried out a study with normal readers (n = 19) and children with developmental dyslexia (n = 16). Both groups were asked to perform various cognitive, literacy, and balancing tasks. 'Children balanced on the left or right foot, with eyes open or closed, for a period of 10 seconds during which their movements were recorded with a motion-tracking system. Dyslexic children were less stable than the control children in both eyes-open conditions (left foot $P = 0.02$, right foot $P = 0.012$). While there were no group differences during the eyes-closed conditions, the dyslexic children dropped a foot to correct balance significantly more often than control children ($P < 0.05$). Incidence analysis showed that 50% of the dyslexic group fell into the "impaired" category on the eyes-open balancing tasks; when the mean balancing scores and the foot drops were considered, only three of our dyslexic children showed no evidence of balancing difficulties. There were strong correlations between reading and spelling scores and the mean eyes-open balancing score ($r = 0.52$ and 0.44, respectively). Thus, while not all children with developmental dyslexia show impaired balancing skills, low-level motor dysfunction may be associated with impaired literacy development. This could be due to several factors, including the involvement of the cerebellum, the magnocellular system, or more general developmental immaturity.'[59]

In the same year, the first results from a modified version of the INPP clinical programme, adapted for use in schools, were published.[60] The INPP Schools' Programme consists of two developmentally appropriate test batteries to be used with

1. children aged four to six years;
2. children from seven and a half years.

The test batteries are designed to assess both static and dynamic balance, three reflexes which have been consistently shown to play a part in specific learning difficulties, and additional tests for visual discrimination and visual-motor integration. The INPP Schools' Programme also contains a programme of developmental exercises designed to be carried out for 10 minutes per day with a class of children over the course of one academic year. The programme has been used in many primary schools across the UK and in Germany since 1996. The published results provided a summary of findings from a series of independent studies in individual schools, involving more than 810 participants.

One of the studies contained within the summary was conducted across seven schools in Northern Ireland.[61] The aim of this research was to determine whether retained reflexes predict poor educational progress and to evaluate the effectiveness of the INPP Developmental Exercise Programme for Schools by measuring the educational progress associated with undertaking the prescribed exercises.

The programme was evaluated for children who had high levels of retained reflexes and who were underachieving educationally (the criteria for which the programme was designed), and also for all children, regardless of their reflex or educational scores.

Measures of retained reflexes, balance, educational ability, and concentration/coordination were made in a controlled study of P5 children (7- to 9-year-olds) at the start (September 2003) and at the end (June 2004) of the school year. In each school, one P5 class undertook the exercises and the other did not.

Two P2 classes (4- to 5-year-olds) in each school also participated in the research. All children in this sample were tested using the INPP test battery devised for four- to six-year-olds, and teachers also assessed the children's educational status using educational baseline assessment. None of the P2 classes undertook the exercises, but the children's reflex status at the beginning of the school year was compared to educational measures at the end of the year to investigate whether the presence of retained reflexes at the start of the school year could predict educational progress at the end of the year. A total of 672 P2 and P5 children participated in the research. The following conclusions were drawn:

- Thirty-five per cent of P5 children and 48 per cent of P2 children showed elevated levels of retained reflexes at the first assessment.
- Fifteen per cent (49) of P5 children had a reading age below their chronological age. Of these, 28 also had elevated levels of retained reflexes.
- Elevated levels of retained reflexes are correlated with poor educational achievement at baseline.
- Children who undertook the exercise programme showed a statistically significant greater decrease in retained reflexes than children who did not undertake the exercises.
- Children who undertook the exercise programme showed a highly significant improvement in balance and coordination, and a small but statistically significant increase in a measure of cognitive development over children who did not undertake the exercises.

- No difference was found in reading, handwriting, or spelling in those children who were already achieving at or near their chronological age.
- Children with high levels of retained reflexes *and* a reading age below their chronological age who undertook the exercise programme made greater progress.
- Retained reflexes are correlated with poor cognitive development, poor balance, and teacher assessment of poor concentration/coordination in the P2 children.
- Neurological scores and teacher assessment at baseline predicted poorer reading and literacy scores at the end of the study.

The aim of the research across all participating schools (including the Northern Ireland study) was to assess whether neurological dysfunction was a significant factor underlying academic achievement in a general school population. All children were tested using the age-appropriate INPP Developmental Test Battery together with additional standard educational measures to assess drawing (Goodenough-Harris[62]) and reading at the beginning and at the end of the programme.

A total of 440 children aged eight to ten years were assessed using the INPP Developmental Test Battery and additional educational measures. Two hundred and thirty-five children undertook the developmental exercises every day; the remaining 205 children did not take part in the exercise programme. Children who participated in the daily INPP exercises made significantly greater improvement on measures for signs of neurological dysfunction, balance, and coordination than the comparison group. Children who had scores of greater than 25 per cent on tests for neurological dysfunction and whose reading age was lower than the chronological age at the outset also showed small but significantly greater progress in reading than children who did not take part in the programme.

These findings suggest that problems with balance and coordination are not confined to dyslexia but may also play a part in educational underachievement in the general population in the absence of any diagnosis of specific learning disability. These are the children who are often not picked up as being in need of help because it is assumed that they are progressing well enough. In this respect, other researchers have also found evidence of the ATNR in the general school population and a correlation between retention of the ATNR and poorer reading performance.[63]

SIGNIFICANCE OF VESTIBULAR DYSFUNCTION

So far in this chapter, we have followed the course of various discoveries, theories, and methods for examining and treating vestibular disorders from a clinician's perspective. But what are some of the symptoms of vestibular dysfunction as experienced by the patient diagnosed with a vestibular disorder, or by the child who is struggling in the classroom? How and why do these subjective symptoms translate into specific learning and emotional problems?

SYMPTOMS OF VESTIBULAR PROBLEMS[64]

Sensations of dizziness can occur for a variety of reasons, but dizziness which occurs as a result of labyrinthine dysfunction can result in a host of symptoms. Patients with labyrinthine disease (as opposed to dysfunction) describe sensations of dizziness and 'the world looks very different from how it did'. Ear symptoms are commonly noted, as are others such as problems with memory and fatigue. Less severe symptoms can also occur if *vestibular reflexes* are abnormal and/or head righting reflexes have not developed. This is because primitive reflex interference can result in vestibular-proprioceptive mismatch, and/or lack of appropriate head righting reflexes results in inability to match body and head position to cortical intention.

Vestibular reflexes include tonic labyrinthine reflex, ATNR, STNR, and labyrinthine head righting reflexes.

Other symptoms of vestibular dysfunction commonly listed include sensations of spinning, imbalance, feeling constantly drunk, of being on board ship; light-headedness, feeling faint, and sensations of continuous internal movement with the external environment – nothing is stable; *vision can be affected so that the world appears as if looking through the wrong lenses*; the eyes will not focus correctly. Symptoms often get worse when the head is moved.

Proprioception can also be affected as signals from the ground upwards do not agree with signals from the balance system downwards. Symptoms increase with head movements, when suffering from a cold (nasal or Eustachian tube congestion), in the dark (reduced vision), in small rooms or in crowded environments (shops and supermarkets), or when using a computer. Tiredness and hormonal variations connected to menstruation can also make symptoms worse. Because the effects of vestibular dysfunction can only be experienced through the other sensory systems, it can result in heightened sensitivity in one or several senses such as increased sensitivity to light, smell, sound, and perceptual illusions.

Specific ear symptoms[64] may include feelings of fluid in both ears, tinnitus, momentary deafness, and increased sensitivity to sounds.

General symptoms include nausea, fatigue, and low stamina. This is common with inner ear problems because the brain has to put all of its energy into maintaining balance instead of balance being an automatic, subconscious process.

Cognitive symptoms can arise such as problems with memory and thinking, probably due to distorted sensory input and mental processing overload. Patients complain of feeling mentally clumsy, as if walking through a mental fog, spaced out and vacant.

Sleep patterns can be affected with sufferers complaining of vivid dreams and frequent waking.

Affective symptoms of depression and anxiety can also develop: the former as a result of feeling generally unwell and out of touch with the world; the latter because the emotional sense of security is partly based on physical stability. If vestibular dysfunction is extreme, it can lead to loss of self-reliance, self-confidence, and self-esteem. It is therefore hardly surprising that a child with undiagnosed vestibular dysfunction may struggle to achieve in the classroom and may also develop problems of a behavioural nature.

To summarize, the vestibular system is involved in the filtering and fine-tuning of all sensory information before it enters the brain – light, sound, motion, gravitational energy, air pressure, and temperature. It is responsible for controlling and for fine-tuning our vision; hearing; balance; sense of motion, altitude, and depth; sense of smell; sense of time; sense of direction; and anxiety/depression levels as mentioned above. Therefore, any one or a cluster of these processes can be affected when suffering from an inner ear dysfunction. Specific learning difficulties and perceptual problems are only a few of the possible symptoms that can arise from a dysfunction of the inner ear. Because the functioning of the vestibular system is so closely linked via the reticular activating system to the functioning of the autonomic nervous system, inner ear dysfunction can also have a significant impact on emotions and on behaviour at any time through the lifespan.

REFERENCES

1 Hippocrates. In: *Hippocrates VII*. 1994. Epidemics 2/4–7. *The Nature of Man*. Trans. Wesley D Smith. Loeb Classical Library, Harvard University Press, Cambridge, MA.

2 Golding J. 2007. Motion sickness: friend or foe? *The Inaugural Lecture of John Golding*. March 2007, London.

3 Cox JM. 1804. *Practical Observations in Insanity*, pp. 106. Baldwin and Murray, London.

4 Hallaran WS. 1810. *An Enquiry into the Causes Producing the Extraordinary Addition to the Number of Insane, Together with Extended Observations on the Care of Insanity: with Hints as to the Better Management of Public Asylums*. Edwards & Savage, Cork.

5 Purkinje J. 1820. Beiträge zur näheren Kenntniss des Schwindels aus heautognostischen Daten. *Medicinische Jahrbücher des Kaiserlich-königlichen Österreichischen Staates* 6:79–125.

6 Flourens MJP. 1824. *Recherches Experimentales sur les Propriétés et les Functions du Système Nerveux dans les Animaux Vertébrés*. Crevot, Paris.

7 Flourens MJP. 1830. Experiences sur les canaux semi circulaires de l'oreille. *Mémoire Académie Royale Sciences* (Paris) 9:455–477.

8 Hawkins JE, Schacht J. 2005. Sketches of otohistory. Part 7: The nineteenth-century rise of laryngology. *Audiology and Neurootology* 10/3:130–133.

9 Ménière P. 1861. Mémoire sur des lesions de l'oreille interne donnant lieu à des symptômes de congestion cérébrale apoplectiforme. *Gazette Médicale de Paris* 55:17–32.

10 Goltz F. 1870. Über der physiologische Bedeutung der Bogengänge des Ohrlabyrinthes. *Archives of Physiology* 3:172–192.

11 Breuer J. 1874. Über die funktion der bogengängen des ohrla-byrinthes. *Wiener Medizinisch Jahrbuch* 4:72–124.

12 Breuer J. 1875. Beitrage zur lehre vom statischen sinne (gleichgewichtsorgan,vestibularapparat des ohrlabyrinths). Zweite Mitteleilung. *Wiener Medizinische Jahrbuch* 5:87–156.

13 Breuer J. 1889. Neue Versuche an den ohrbogengängen. *Arch. ges. Physiol.* 44:135–152.

14 Breuer J. 1891. Über die Funktion der Otolithenapparate. *Plügers Archiv* 48:195–306.

15 Mach E. 1873. Physikalische Versuche uber den Gleichgewichts-sinn des Menschen, Sitzungsberickte der kaiserl. *Akademie der Wissenschaften* 68:124–140.

16 Wiest G, Baloh RW. 2002. The pioneering work of Josef Breuer on the vestibular system. *Archives of Neurology* 59:1647–1653.

17 James W. 1882. The sense of dizziness in deaf mutes. *American Journal of Otology* 4:239–254.

18 Audesirk T, Audesirk G. 1996. *Biology. Life on Earth.* Prentice-Hall Inc., Upper Saddle River, NJ.

19 http://www.balametrics.com

20 Schilder P. 1933. The vestibular apparatus in neurosis and psychosis. *The Journal of Nervous and Mental Disease* 78/1:1–23.

21 Schilder P. 1920. Uber hallucinationen. *Zeitschrift für Neurologie* 53:169–173.

22 Bauer J. 1916. Der Baranusche Zeigeveruch etc. bie traumatis-chen neurosen. *Wiener Klinisch Wochenschrift* 40.

23 Leidler R, Loewy K. 1923. Der Swindel der Neurosen. *Monatschrift für Ohrenheilkunde und Laryngo Rhinologie* 57/1.

24 von Weizsäcker V. Cited in: Schilder P. 1933. The vestibular apparatus in neurosis and psychosis. *The Journal of Nervous and Mental Disease* 78/1:1–23.

25 Goldstein K. Cited in: Schilder P. 1933. The vestibular appara-tus in neurosis and psychosis. *The Journal of Nervous and Mental Disease* 78/1:1–23.

26 Cited in: Compston A. 2007. From the archives. *Brain* 2005 128/7:1475–1477; doi:10.1093/brain/awh566

27 Cawthorne T. 1944. The physiological basis for head exercises. *The Journal of the Chartered Society of Physiotherapy* 30:106.

28 Cawthorne T. 1946. Vestibular injuries. *Proceedings of the Royal Society of Medicine* 39:270–272.

29 Cooksey FS. 1946. Rehabilitation in vestibular injuries. *Proceed-ings of the Royal Society of Medicine* 39:273–275.

30 Barsch RH. 1968. Achieving motor perceptual efficiency. A self-oriented approach to learning. Volume 1 of *A Perceptual Motor Curriculum.* Special Child Publications, Seattle, WA.

31 Goodenough F. 1926. *Measurement of Intelligence by Drawings.* World Book Co, New York.

32 Frank J, Levinson H. 1973. Dysmetric dyslexia and dyspraxia. Hypothesis and study. *Journal of The American Academy of Child Psychiatry* 12/4:690–701.

33 Levinson HN. 1980. *A Solution to the Riddle – Dyslexia.* Springer-Verlag, New York.

34 Levinson HN. 1984. *Smart but Feeling Dumb.* Warner Books Inc., New York.

35 Levinson HN. 1986. *Phobia Free.* M Evans and Company Inc., New York.

36 Levinson HN. 1990. *Total Concentration.* M Evans and Company Inc., New York.

37 Levinson HN, Sanders A. 1991. *The Upside Down Kids.* M Evans and Company Inc., New York.

38 Levinson HN. 1992. *Turning Around the Upside Down Kids.* M Evans and Company Inc., New York.

39 Levinson HN. 2000. *Feeling Smarter and Smarter.* Stonebridge Publishing Ltd., Lake Success, NY.

40 Levinson HN. 1994. *A Scientific Watergate.* Stonebridge Publishing Ltd., Lake Success, NY.

41 Levinson HN. 2007. Personal communication. August 2007.

42 Levinson HN. 2008. Personal communication. January 2008.

43 De Quirós JB, Schrager OL. 1978. *Neurological Fundamentals in Learning Disabilities.* Academic Therapy Publications Inc., Novato, CA.

44 Schrager OL. 2000. Balance, control, age and language development. Paper presented at the 12th European Conference on Neuro-Developmental Delay in Children with Specific Learning Difficulties, Chester, March 2000.

45 Kohen-Raz R. 2004. Postural correlates of learning and disabilities and communication disorders. *The European Conference of Neuro-developmental Delay in Children with Specific Learning Difficulties.* Chester, March 2004.

46 Passingham RE. 1975. Changes in the size and organisation of the brain in man and his ancestors. *Brain, Behavior and Evolution* 11:73–90.

47 Stephan H, Andy OJ. 1969. Quantitive comparative neuroanatomy of primates: an attempt at a phylogenetic interpretation. In Petras JM, Noback CR (Eds). *Comparative and Evolutionary Aspects of the Vertebrate Nervous System.* Annals 167. New York Academy of Sciences, New York, pp. 370–387.

48 Leiner HC et al. 1986. Does the cerebellum contribute to mental skills? *Behavioral Neuroscience* 100:443–454.

49 Leiner HC et al. 1991. The human cerebro-cerebellar system: its computing, cognitive and language skills. *Behavioral Brain Research* 44:113–128.

50 Zagon IS et al. 1977. Neural populations in the human cerebellum: estimations from isolated cell nuclei. *Brain Research* 127: 279–282.

51 Bloedal JR, Bracha V. 1997. Duality of the cerebellar motor and cognitive function. *International Review of Neurobiology* 41/6: 613–634.

52 Sherrington C. 1906. *The Integrative Function of the Nervous System*. Cambridge University Press, Cambridge.

53 Hallett M, Grafman J. 1997. Executive function and motor skill learning. *International Review of Neurobiology* 41:297–323.

54 Posner MI, Raichle ME. 1994. *Images of Mind*. Freeman, New York.

55 Courchesne E et al. 1994. Impairment in shifting attention in autistic and cerebellar patients. *Behavioral Neuroscience* 108:848–865.

56 Leiner HC et al. 1993. Cognitive and language functions of the human cerebellum. *Trends in Neuroscience* 16:444–447.

57 Fawcett AJ. 1994. Cited in: A wobble now means less work later. *The Independent*, 26 April 1994, London.

58 Dean P. 1994. Cited in: A wobble now means less work later. *The Independent*, 26 April 1994, London.

59 Stoodley CJ et al. 2005. Impaired balancing ability in dyslexic children. *Experimental Brain Research* 167/3:370–380.

60 Goddard Blythe SA. 2005. Releasing educational potential through movement: a summary of individual studies carried out using the INPP test battery and developmental exercises programme for use in schools with children with special needs. *Child Care in Practice* 11/4:415–432.

61 North Eastern Education and Library Board (NEELB). 2004. An evaluation of the pilot INPP movement programme in primary schools in the North Eastern Education and Library Board. Northern Ireland, Final Report. Prepared by Brainbox Research Ltd for the NEELB. http://www.neeelb.org.uk/

62 Harris DB. 1963. *Children's Drawings as Measures of Intellectual Maturity*. Harcourt Brace and World Inc., New York.

63 McPhillips M, Sheehy N. 2004. Prevalence of persistent primary reflex and motor problems in children with reading difficulties. *Dyslexia* 10:316–338.

64 http://www.vestibular.org/vestibular

CHAPTER 9

THE EFFECTS OF NEURO-DEVELOPMENTAL DELAY IN ADULTS AND IN ADOLESCENTS

The problems associated with neuro-developmental delay are not confined to the childhood years. As children grow up, the nervous system continues to develop and change, but if problems related to aberrant primitive reflexes are not corrected during childhood, the associated problems tend to grow up with them like threads or traits, which become woven into the fabric of the personality. Abnormal primitive and postural reflexes represent a structural weakness in the functioning of the central nervous system (CNS) and can continue to undermine performance and resilience to certain types of stress in later life. This can show itself in a number of ways: educational and/or emotional difficulties which emerge at or around the time when the transition is made from school to higher education; low tolerance threshold for stress; anxiety, agoraphobia, and panic disorder.

In a paper written by Peter Blythe and David McGlown in 1980, they described this as being 'an organic basis for neuroses' and fertile ground for the development of 'secondary neuroses'.[1] The authors began:

> It is of interest to note that when a person's ability to function adequately in everyday life is impaired, in the absence of any organic pathology, the terminology most commonly used to describe what has happened to the individual is that he or she has suffered a nervous breakdown. In Britain a frequently used medical description is that of nervous debility, which is suggestive of a 'feebleness' of the nerves, while in Sweden the same patient condition is designated nervkollaps. All three descriptions suggest that the central nervous system

> has malfunctioned, thereby permitting the emergence of a symptom or syndrome which has been, either singularly or collectively, classified as neuroses.
>
> In contrast to the viewpoint of central nervous system involvement there has been ample speculation over the years as to why some people suffer from emotional disorders – neuroses – while others appear to have an inherent immunity to life's stressors. The theories have ranged from specific to unspecific genetic weakness, intra-uterine endocrine experience, birth trauma, early emotional traumatic life experiences including the 'lack of bonding' and 'separation anxiety'; impaired love relationships in the family, incorrectly learned behavioural responses, through to constitutional inadequacy.
>
> This paper presents the results of 10 years of research (1969–1979) . . . which has shown that many patients, both children and adults, suffering from neurotic symptoms or syndromes, plus those who appear to be resistant to the therapy of choice, have a hitherto undetected cluster of central nervous system dysfunctions which should now be acknowledged as the primary causation, with the emotional symptoms being the secondary neurosis.[1]

In other words, a cluster of immature reflexes which persist into later life can predispose an individual to be more prone to stress. This is because increased cortical involvement is required to support the basic functions of posture, balance, control of movement, and perception, and to compensate, cover up, or 'override' the underlying weaknesses. The cortex, over-involved in the processing of information normally screened by lower centres, can become 'overloaded'. This can, in turn, affect cognitive processing, cognitive attribution, and somatic affect.

The effects of abnormal reflexes beyond the childhood years depend on the reflex profile of the individual (how many reflexes are involved, which reflexes, and the relative strength of each reflex), as well as many other environmental factors, which can act as mediators between the effects of immaturity in the functioning of the CNS and resilience or susceptibility to the development of emotional disorders. Positive environmental factors would include a happy and stable home environment, ability to succeed at something, and living in an environment that does not place continuous stress on the weakest systems.

In 1967, Holmes and Rahe[2] developed a social readjustment rating scale to investigate the relationship between social readjustment – stress – and susceptibility to illness. They listed life events according to the degree of adaptation required to adjust to the life change. This list begins with death of a spouse with a rating of 100, followed by divorce (72), marital separation (65), death of a close family member (63), personal injury, or illness (53). Marriage (50) and vacation (13), usually regarded as happy events, are also listed as stressful on the life readjustment scale. They found that a person with a score of 200 to 250 during a one-year period has a 50 per cent chance of developing illness or health change. With a score of 300 or more, a person's chances increase to 80 per cent. Individuals with immature reflexes are particularly prone to experience stress when readjustment is required in an area of weakness.

In line with Holmes and Rahe's findings, symptoms of immature reflexes tend to appear for the first time during or following times of significant change. Students who have performed well through school years can experience difficulty for the first time when they have to adapt to the requirements of higher education: the combination of leaving home, being responsible for themselves, learning to make new friends, and coping with large amounts of reading in a less-structured learning environment can bring to the surface difficulties that have been previously concealed by working hard, structured teaching, and a supportive family and school environment. Other major life events or changes include preparing for and sitting examinations, making formal presentations, cohabiting, adjusting to the rapid hormonal and lifestyle changes that accompany and follow the birth of a child, a new job, or change of circumstances or environment. The onset of puberty can be a trigger for the appearance of emotional problems, and although there can be many reasons for this, in some cases the hormonal changes that occur at puberty, which normally consolidate neurological development, reawaken problems left behind in the first three and a half years of life.

Adults who have unidentified issues related to vestibular dysfunction and/or aberrant reflexes tend to be the patients who do not seem to gain long-term benefit from pharmacological intervention or interventions aimed at changing behaviour. Those adults who seek out neuro-developmental therapy have often received a number of different therapies in the past over several years from which they have gained a good understanding of the *psychological* reasons behind their presenting problems, but are unable to change or benefit from these therapies, despite a desire to get well. This can be because no amount of change in thought patterns and/or behaviour alters the way that they *feel*. 'When feelings of anxiety or fear are stronger than logic, in the long term, feelings will win.'[3]

When underlying neuro-developmental problems are identified and treated at a neurological and physical level (sometimes with the addition of supportive cognitive therapy), adults are able to overcome their emotional problems and students become better equipped to succeed in their chosen careers.

PROBLEMS IN HIGHER EDUCATION

Whereas there is an increasing body of evidence to support the theory that retained primitive reflexes can underlie difficulties in the learning of basic skills such as reading and writing, the role of postural reflexes and the *relationship* between primitive and postural reflexes in supporting higher aspects of learning is often either ignored or misunderstood. Many motor training programmes operate by stimulating the development of postural reflexes through vestibular stimulation and general motor training. Some children make significant gains on these programmes, while for others, posture and coordination improve but there is little or no crossover into improved educational performance. This can be because the intervention is being aimed at a *higher* developmental and neurological level than the primary level of dysfunction.

Postural reflexes develop with primitive reflexes persisting underneath.

The key to success in any programme of intervention is to *begin* the intervention from the most basic level of ability (rather than disability) and to build on it – i.e. to meet the patient where he or she is – and use this as the *starting* point for the programme. *Postural reflexes* can be stimulated and trained through the use of exercises carried out in sitting and standing positions, but while strengthened postural reflexes will improve general coordination and balance, they do not necessarily inhibit underlying primitive reflexes. In these cases, the newly trained postural skills become functionally proficient when they are practised in the training environment but do not become permanently integrated functions. This means that when the newly trained skill has to be adapted to a new or different situation, it cannot be accessed and applied to solve new problems and to adapt to new or rapidly changing situations. Behavioural outcomes of this type of profile include a tendency to avoid novel situations, a desire to stay within a familiar 'comfort' zone, and an unwillingness to learn new skills or to tackle new problems for the first time.

A different profile can occur if primitive reflexes have been inhibited, but postural reflexes do not develop sufficiently. This profile can result in a functional 'no man's land' in which the individual is able to see the problem that needs to be solved but does not know 'how' to go about solving it. These are the grown-up equivalent of the children described by one head teacher as being 'the almost, nearly there children'[4] – individuals who have all the ingredients and potential for success, but who do not seem to be able to combine them together to make the transfer into consistent performance.

This lack of integration at a physical level is often reflected in learning styles and in behaviour. The adolescent or adult who has either underdeveloped or poorly integrated postural reflexes may have difficulty adapting to new situations, applying known concepts or methods for solving problems, linking and integrating known facts with new information, multiprocessing, sequencing, coping with large volumes of information (information overload), and flexible thinking.[5]

Advanced cognitive processing involves both hierarchical and bilateral integration in brain functioning. A weakness in bilateral integration can affect problem solving. Specific problems with maths provide examples of how both poor bilateral integration and/or hierachical organization can interfere with solving mathematical problems. This is illustrated in certain types of dyscalculia. In order to understand how postural and vestibular problems can interfere with higher brain functions in relation to maths, it is useful to examine some specific features of dyscalculia in more detail.

Dyscalculia

To find a solution to a mathematical problem requires both hemispheres of the brain to work together. Carrying out a simple arithmetic calculation can involve up to nine changes in hemispheric dominance, together with the ability to sequence operations (cerebellum), to hold number facts in working memory, and to articulate the answer using verbal language. Renee Lawton Brown[6] from the Hampstead Dyslexia Clinic used the example shown in Figure 9.1 to illustrate the minimum number of interchanges and procedures involved.

Figure 9.1 illustrates how lateral (inter-hemispheric) communication is need in *both* directions – from right to left and from left to right – in order to solve arithmetical problems.

The effect of weaknesses in the hierarchical structure on cognitive performance is less immediately obvious but may be better understood by re-examining the role of the vestibular system and the cerebellum, specifically in relation

$$58 \times 79 = ?$$

TASK	HEMISPHERE
1. Recognition of numbers and symbols	Right
2. Find meaning of the symbols	Left
3. Register necessary procedure and carry out sequential tasks	Left
4. Hold number facts in working memory	Left
5. Find a number pattern (multiplication table), and align numbers in correct columns	Right
6. Integrate result in working memory	Left
7. Recognition of number obtained	Right
8. Test plausibility of answer (estimation)	Right
9. Articulate the answer	Left

Figure 9.1 Inter-hemispheric cooperation and procedures in solving simple math problems. Based on an example originally developed by Renee Lawton Brown, Hampstead Dyslexia Clinic

to dyscalculia. *Dys* means 'difficulty' and *calculia* is derived from the Latin word *calculus*, meaning 'small stone'. In the original context, it refers to the ancient use of pebbles used for counting, which was later developed into the abacus. This earlier use of stones as 'mind tools' or as concrete representations of concepts suggests that physical interaction has been used as an aid to support and to precede conceptual understanding of numbers for generations.

Dyscalculia describes developmental lag of one year or more in the acquisition of numerical skills, including:

- inability to recognize number symbols;
- mirror writing (directional);
- failure to recognize mathematical operations involved in computation or problem solving (procedural sequencing and inter-hemispheric communication);
- inability to recall tables (sequencing);
- inability to maintain proper order of numbers in calculation (vestibular and/or visuospatial).

It has been found that dyscalculia is more prevalent in children of lower socio-economic status. Unlike dyslexia, it is equally distributed between the sexes, and there is an association between premature birth and later difficulties with number skills.[7] Badian[8] proposed three types of dyscalculia:

1. difficulty with computational procedures such as addition, subtraction, and multiplication;
2. attentional sequential dyscalculia affecting, for example, multiplication tables and sequencing of procedures;
3. spatial dyscalculia, describing difficulty handling multi-column arithmetic problems and place values.

Dysfunction in either hemisphere can impair acquisition of numerical skills but appears to be more profound if present in the left hemisphere.[9–11] *Left* hemisphere dysfunction has been found to be associated with construction dyspraxia and below-average performance on tasks such as the embedded figures test[12] (figure-ground effect), poor auditory and visual discrimination, and motor coordination abilities.

Right hemisphere dysfunction in a group of children who showed no signs of structural abnormality on brain scans

(MRI or CT) manifested itself as grapho-motor impairments and slow cognitive and motor performance, although reading development was normal.[13] Additional right hemisphere symptoms included emotional and interpersonal difficulties, difficulty adapting to new situations, difficulty maintaining friendships, tendency to be withdrawn and shy, poor eye contact, and difficulties with spatial perception and imagery. Some of this group also had features of attention deficit hyperactivity disorder (ADHD), which, it was suggested, might be a secondary effect of right hemisphere dysfunction and brainstem factors.[13] Many of these symptoms associated with right hemisphere dysfunction can also occur as a result of dysfunction in the vestibular system and associated pathways which support the processes of visual perception in the right hemisphere.

Vertigo – the physical characteristics of vertigo include disorientation and loss of postural and ocular control accompanied by ancillary autonomic symptoms such as cold, nausea, vomiting, and cold sweating stemming from a primary dysfunction in the balance system.

Risey and Briner[14] found a relationship between patients with central *vertigo* and dyscalculia. When asked to count backwards in two's, patients diagnosed with central vertigo consistently skipped and displaced decades. For example, when counting backwards, they would go, 98, 96, 94, 92 – 80 – 88, 86, 84, 82 – 70, – 78, 76 . . . , etc. The error appeared at each decade except when passing from 12 to 8. Repetition produced the same result even when the error was pointed out to them and they recognized the mistake. Vertigo patients also had difficulties with mental arithmetic and central auditory processing, lower scores for arithmetic, and digit span errors on the Wechsler Adult Intelligence Scale (WAIS), and difficulty with backward digit span recall compared with non-vertigo patients. This suggests that vestibular dysfunction can affect visual, auditory, and mental *sequencing* processes.

VESTIBULAR CONNECTIONS TO THE RETICULAR ACTIVATING SYSTEM (RAS)

We have already seen how the vestibular system acts independently of the cerebral motor cortex with its actions being reflexive in response to changes of head position. From the inner ear, primary neurons pass to the brain, where their cell bodies aggregate in the vestibular ganglion. Axons leave this ganglion and enter the brainstem, where they terminate in four vestibular nuclei from where they have a multiplicity

of connections to oculomotor centres, the reticular formation, the thalamus, and the spinal cord. Connections from
the vestibular system to other brain centres are probably
more widespread and diverse than any other sensory system.
The four vestibular nuclei have five major connections:

1. vestibulocerebellar connections – involved in the coordination of motor activity and equilibrium;
2. vestibulospinal tracts – involved in the maintenance of
   body equilibrium through reflexes;
3. vestibular-ocular connections – involved in the regulation of movements of the eyeballs and the maintenance of
   the stability of the image on the retina, despite movement
   of the head;
4. vestibulocortical connections – involved in the conscious
   experience of dizziness, disorientation, vertigo, etc.;
5. accessory pathway – linked to the descending reticular
   areas and nuclei of the brainstem, which then discharge
   to the lower motor neurons via the multi-synaptic
   reticulo-spinal tract.

As mentioned earlier, the RAS controls the overall degree
of cortical alertness and establishes *the sleep/wake cycle* (RAS).
Consciousness depends upon the cyclical interplay between
an arousal system (RAS), a slow wave-sleep centre, and a
paradoxical sleep centre, all located in the brainstem. The
cells controlling consciousness form a chain that extends
through the centre of the brainstem to the midbrain from
where its activity spreads out to both left and right hemispheres. Nerves carrying information branch off from the
main sensory and motor tracts into the RAS to keep it
constantly informed about the activity of other parts of
the nervous system. The RAS also has a *'gating' system*[15,16]
that regulates the amount of sensory stimuli which reach the
cortex by closing or opening the gate rather like a volume
control. Closing of the gate prevents further information
from reaching the cortex, trapping excitation within the
body; opening of the gate allows more information to reach
the cortex (Figure 9.2).

Links from the vestibular to the reticular system are particularly important in the somatic experience of disorientation,
levels of arousal, and associated anxiety. This is because the
descending reticular formation is concerned with relaying

The gate control theory of pain, proposed by Melzack and Wall in 1962, is the idea that the perception of physical pain does not occur as a direct result of activation of pain receptor neurons, but is modulated by interaction between different neurons, which are pain-transmitting and non-pain-transmitting. The theory asserts that activation of nerves that do not transmit pain signals can interfere with/ block signals from pain fibres and can inhibit an individual's perception of pain.

This is thought to be one contributing factor in ADHD, when levels of arousal are held within the body and are not dispersed higher up to the cortex. One of the effects of methylphenidate (Ritalin) – used to treat the symptoms of ADHD – is to open the gate in the RAS, thereby enabling the cortex to exercise increased control.

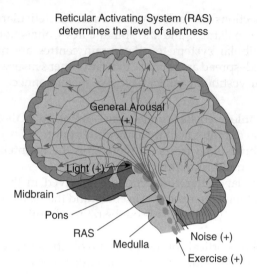

Reticular Activating System (RAS) determines the level of alertness

Figure 9.2 Ascending RAS

impulses from the hypothalamus to target organs of the autonomic nervous system affecting heart rate, blood pressure, breathing, production of acid in the stomach, etc., and these systems are innervated below the level of conscious control. Abnormal vestibular functioning has the potential, via the RAS, to overstimulate either the sympathetic or parasympathetic divisions of the autonomic nervous system, resulting in specific physiological changes which quickly become associated with the trigger event – a physiological pathway to the conscious experience of fear or anxiety.

Alain Berthoz, in his book *The Brain's Sense of Movement*,[17] described how thoughts are 'an internalised form of action', and in a later book, *Emotion and Reason*,[18] he explained emotion as being 'a simulation of action, an emulation of a hypothetical state or a reaction to a situation that may be pleasant or dreadful, and that circumvents the usual pathways of action.' Many years earlier, Darwin had observed that 'there is no thought without bodily action'.[19] If these models are correct, then it is hardly surprising that an impoverished or impaired vocabulary of movement and/or movement experience can affect and interfere with an individual's thought processes and emotions. In two of my earlier books, *The Well Balanced Child*[20] and *What Babies and Children Really Need*,[21] I described how all living things share the experience of motion in common and that motion, in the sense of physical movement, has long been associated with emotions. In Latin, the phrase *mōtus animā* was used to describe 'movement of the spirit', while the modern word emotion is a post-classical formation derived from vulgar Latin *ex-movēre*, meaning to 'move out' or to 'excite'. In French, this became *émoumoir*, which the English borrowed and used in the sense of 'moving, agitation'.[22]

Links between diseases of the vestibular apparatus, vertigo, and psychological symptoms have long been recognized but have usually been viewed from the perspective of the effect of the mind on the body. Freud[23] viewed vertigo as one of the major *symptoms* of anxiety neurosis, although he associated the cause of anxiety with frustration of the *libido*. French[24] believed that nausea and vertiginous sensations on a psychogenic level develop when a patient puts up an active defence against his/her passive tendencies. Bauer and Schilder[25] suggested that psychogenic vertigo is an expression of intransigence between two spheres of psychic experience – in other words, conflict – but later on, Schilder's clinical observations pointed to 'a broader role for the vestibular apparatus in neurological development and behaviour, and it was his contention that organic changes in the vestibular apparatus might be highly significant in the etiology of certain neuroses and psychoses.'[26,27] Peto[28] suggested that the vestibular system is the precursor of those mental functions which are grouped together as superego. These psychological models may well have their origins in the development and integration of the nervous system as well as in external life events.

Libido – *psychic energy*.

Freud's theory of personality was based on the concept of three forces at work – the *id* (unconscious), the *ego* (conscious), and the *superego* (conscience). Freud proposed that in the first months of life, the infant operates at the level of the id, the energy force or libido which comprises the instinctive aspect of the personality, which contains the primitive motivational drives for the basic physiological needs of survival and pleasure such as food, water, sex, and warmth. The id functions in the irrational and emotional part of the mind and is only concerned with instinctive drives and demands. It is the eternal child that says, 'I want and I want it now'. The ego begins its slow and gradual development towards the end of infancy and symbolizes the child's contact with its external environment, its purpose being to satisfy the needs and demands of the id within a framework that will be acceptable to both society and the superego. The ego develops out of a growing awareness that you cannot always have what you want, and it operates on a reality principle. The superego starts to develop at about five years of age and operates on the principle of perfection derived as a result of the internalization of the morals taught by the surrounding family, society, and codes of belief and religious practice (the parent within). In simple terms, when the needs and demands of the id can be met within an environmentally and socially acceptable way, the ego is healthy. If, on the other hand, feelings and motivational drives are stronger than the ego's ability to contain them, or to negotiate successfully between the demands of the id and the expectations of the superego, the ego experiences conflict.

Immaturity in the functioning of the CNS can disturb the balance between feelings and logic (the id and the superego), causing the ego to suffer conflict and stress – the feeling of being pulled in different directions – and ultimately, feelings of helplessness (Figure 9.3).

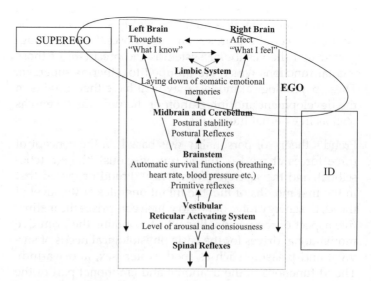

Figure 9.3 Interrelationship between different brain centres and emotional affect

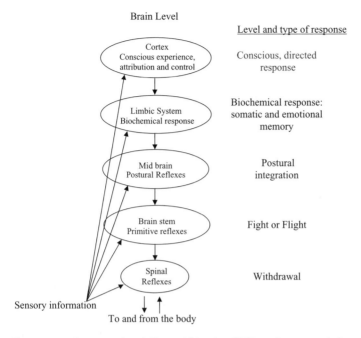

Figure 9.4   Structural stability within the CNS – a framework for emotional stability

Figure 9.4 shows another model which illustrates the different *levels* within the brain at which anxiety-provoking stimuli are mediated. Stages of development in the CNS start at the spinal level progressing up through primitive to postural reflexes, which act collectively as developmental building blocks to support higher centres involved in emotional regulation and in the integration of the three Freudian levels of consciousness, the id, the ego, and the superego.

Instability at any level of postural integration represents a structural weakness in the functioning of the nervous system, which can affect if, how, when, and where in the cortex information is relayed, potentially undermining the ability of the cortex to control lower functions.

As discussed in previous chapters, the physical symptoms of vestibular-proprioceptive-ocular disassociation are the same as those experienced under conditions of motion sickness and vertigo. The origin of the word vertigo means 'swimming in the head' and is now used to describe sensations of dizziness, unsteadiness, and visual disturbances that occur in response to head movements and which, in susceptible individuals, are enhanced in positions of height. Vertigo, dizziness, and motion sickness are linked to the senses of balance, vision, and spatial orientation under conditions of movement. The interaction of gravity and postural sensors tells the brain where the body is in space, in what direction it is pointing, direction of movement, and if it is turning or standing still. When there is conflict between the different sensors involved in balance and orientation, physical, perceptual, and emotional symptoms occur.

Different parts of the nervous system involved in the maintenance of balance and orientation:

* *inner ears – monitor the directions of motion (internal);*
* *eyes – monitor external signals in relation to body position in space;*
* *proprioceptors – muscles, tendons, and joints which inform which part of the body is down and touching the ground.*

Possible Symptoms of Vestibular Disorders

The type and severity of the symptoms associated with vestibular disorders can vary. They include vertigo and dizziness; balance and spatial orientation; visual, hearing, cognitive, and psychological disturbances. The word 'dizzy' originally meant 'scatterbrained' – a description of what occurs in the inner ear when vestibular reactions to movements of the head are slow to settle down after the movement has started or stops. Symptoms of dizziness can be spinning or whirling sensations of the self (subjective vertigo), or of the environment (objective vertigo). There may be additional feelings of floating or of being heavily weighted or pulled in one direction. One adult patient who had suffered from anxiety and hitherto undiagnosed balance problems most of her life reported how, as a child, she used to 'float down the stairs and scare (her) mother by tapping her on the shoulder while floating in the air!'

Command of balance can be affected in a variety of ways from general clumsiness, difficulty walking in a straight line, or turning movements such as turning a corner. Posture may be affected and the head is sometimes tilted to one side. Because balance is already unstable, there tends to be increased sensitivity to subtle alterations in walking surface.

Vision can be affected in a variety of ways from focusing to eye tracking. The latter is similar to visual problems present in some types of dyslexia where the letters on the page appear to move, float, or blur, or when there is double vision. Sensitivity to light is sometimes increased, particularly under fluorescent or flickering lights (similar to symptoms of scotopic sensitivity syndrome), and also similar to the example of the effect on fish described in the previous chapter when the gravity-detecting organ had been removed and they became stimulus bound to light in order to orient themselves in space.[29]

Visual disturbances can make busy visual environments extremely stressful so that crowded places such as large shops, city underground stations, or complex patterns on carpets or wallpapers can create physical feelings of discomfort such as nausea and headache, a visually induced form of motion sickness. When multisensory information is discrepant, it can interfere with cognitive processing. When an individual is unable to 'make sense' of his or her environment, it results in increased anxiety. Unless the physical nature of these sensations is identified, they tend to be interpreted as being of psychological origin.

Vestibular disorders can also affect hearing and auditory processing. There can be hearing loss, distortion and/or tinnitus (ringing or whooshing noises in the ear), difficulty in locating the source of sounds, which can affect sense of position in space, and in the ability to occlude or select certain sounds. It is also often associated with heightened sensitivity to loud noises. Vestibular disorders can alter sensitivity in one or several sensory channels. This is because having no specific sensation of its own – we only become consciously aware of the functioning of the vestibular system when it is disturbed in some way – the disturbance is experienced through the other senses.

Because vision and hearing are implicated, *perception* – the cognitive interpretation of external sensory stimuli – can also be affected. There can be problems with depth perception, or the figure-ground effect, and the patient becomes easily exhausted from trying to 'make sense' of a world in which perception is unstable and unreliable. This can affect concentration, sustained attention. and short-term memory. The patient can become easily confused or disorientated in certain environments or when carrying out specific tasks. The degree of stress generated in simply trying to function can have psychological repercussions such as loss of self-confidence, self-reliance, and self-esteem, and depression, anxiety, and panic disorder are often *secondary* outcomes of vestibular-related disorders. If vestibular-generated anxiety always occurs in specific situations, then the person may

This is thought to play a key role in many of the behaviours associated with autistic spectrum disorders. Unable to integrate sensory information, their cognitive understanding of the world is disintegrated. Hyper- or hyposensitivity in different sensory channels then results in the need for alternative defence mechanisms which may be characterized by withdrawal or overstimulation of another sensory system.

Phobia *means fear.*

develop avoidance behaviour, and if this becomes a fixed behavioural pattern it can result in the development of ago-raphobia or other *phobias*. Vestibular disorders can be of a primary or secondary nature, with aberrant reflexes being either symptomatic of a primary vestibular disorder or contributing to vestibular dysfunction as a result of immature postural development.

Identifying the aetiology of abnormal behaviour is crucial to the successful outcome of treatment. Anxiety can develop in response to exogenous and/or indigenous factors. Exogenous anxiety usually responds well to therapies that deal with existing life problems and psychological attitudes such as cognitive behavioural therapy (CBT) or pharmacological treatment. Indigenous anxiety that arises as a result of internal factors (and there can be many reasons for these as well), but those that develop specifically in relation to vestibular dysfunction, will respond better to methods aimed at the physical basis of the problem. These might include vestibular-cerebellar harmonizing medications such as those prescribed by Dr Levinson for the treatment of phobic disorders, or vestibular and reflex intervention programmes.

Agoraphobia

In 1982, Blythe and McGlown[30] published the results of a pilot study which had investigated the presence of neuro-developmental delay in a sample of 23 adult patients diagnosed with agoraphobia (19 female, 4 male: mean chronological age 41 years). Tests were carried out in three categories:

1. gross muscle coordination and balance;
2. presence of aberrant primitive and postural reflexes;
3. tests for oculomotor and visual-perceptual problems.

Results are shown in Figures 9.5 and 9.6.

Nystagmus *describes spontaneous, rapid, rhythmic movements of the eyes which occur during fixation or on ocular movements.*

Over 95 per cent of the sample showed problems with static balance on the Romberg test, and the same percentage showed signs of increased physiological *nystagmus*. Increased physiological nystagmus can occur for a number of reasons, but two types are specifically linked to either direct vestibular stimulation as a result of head rotation or indirect stimulation as a result of optical stimulation from the environment.

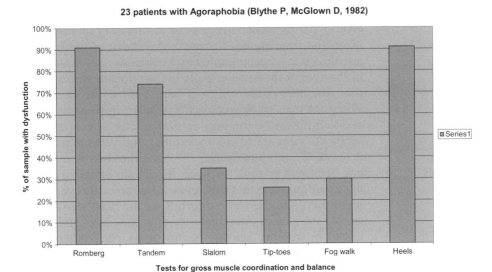

Figure 9.5   Percentage of patients with abnormal signs on tests for gross muscle coordination and balance

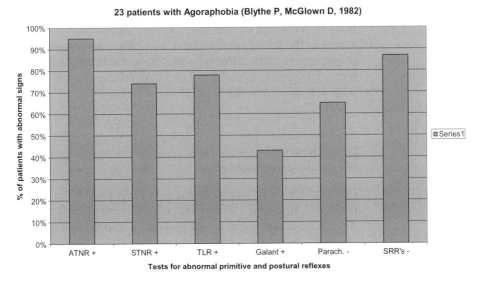

Figure 9.6   Percentage of patients with abnormal signs on tests for aberrant primitive and postural reflexes

Under normal conditions, the vestibular-ocular reflexes ensure that the visual image is kept stationary on the retina when the head moves (rotates). Movement of the head in any direction is accompanied by a compensatory movement of the eyes of the same velocity in the opposite direction. In this way, the visual image is kept centred on the retina. When the eyes track an object accurately, movement of the endolymph inside the semicircular canals is compensated for by the same speed of oppositional movement in the eyes; it is called *smooth pursuit*. If the head movement is larger, and it is not possible to keep the image stationary with maximum movement of the eyes, a fast saccadic eye movement occurs in the same direction as the head movement, so that the gaze is once again fixed on the object and is followed by another smooth pursuit movement. Alternation between smooth pursuit and saccadic eye movement is called *nystagmus*. Nystagmus which is induced as a result of stimulation of the semicircular canals (head movement) is called *vestibular nystagmus*. Nystagmus which is elicited by movement of the surroundings when the head is stationary is called *optokinetic nystagmus*. Increased nystagmus under either condition indicates poor integration of neural cell groups involved in vestibular information concerned with movements of the head, visual signals about movements of the image on the retina, and proprioceptive signals about movements of the eyes relative to the head. Abnormal tonic, labyrinthine, and head righting reflexes can interfere with integration at this level (Figure 9.7).

The findings were highly suggestive of an underlying CNS disorder with 82 per cent of the group having a sufficiently large cluster of dysfunctions to warrant the diagnosis of secondary agoraphobia.

In a smaller sample of eight subjects diagnosed with agoraphobia, Ljunggren[31] found that all subjects showed some degree of oculomotor weakness and a profile of aberrant reflexes – only one subject had less than five uninhibited or untransformed primitive and postural reflexes – consistent with the definition of neuro-developmental delay.

In a later study[32] which investigated the developmental history of 103 patients diagnosed with agoraphobia using the Blythe–McGlown Screening Questionnaire for adults, over 90 per cent described experiencing problems with oculomotor functioning; 90 per cent suffered from heightened

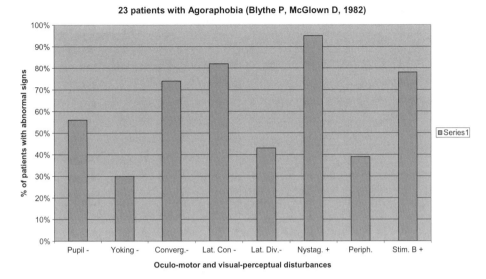

Figure 9.7   Percentage of patients with abnormal signs on tests for oculomotor and visual-perceptual disturbances

sensitivity to light; 88 per cent had problems with balance; and 87 per cent described problems with coordination. The full analysis of the developmental and symptomatic criteria examined in this group is shown in Figure 9.8.

Anxiety disorders

Anxiety disorders are classified by the *Diagnostic Statistical Manual of Mental Disorders IV* (DSM IV) as 'neurotic, stress related and *somatoform* disorders' with subtypes including general anxiety disorder.[33] Anxiety disorders include:

1. panic disorder without agoraphobia;
2. panic disorder with agoraphobia;
3. agoraphobia without a history of panic disorder;
4. specific phobia;
5. social phobia;
6. obsessive-compulsive disorder (OCD);
7. post-traumatic stress disorder (PTSD);
8. acute stress disorder.

Somatoform – *relating to a group of psychologically induced conditions that have the characteristics of physical disease but for which no organic cause can be found.*

Some anxiety disorders, such as post-traumatic stress disorder, are directly related to life events, while others can develop as a secondary outcome of hypersensitivity in the functioning of the nervous system.

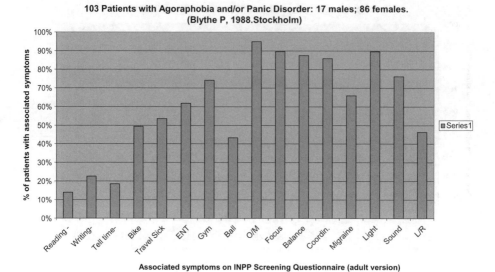

Figure 9.8 Analysis of developmental indicators in 103 patients diagnosed with agoraphobia and/or panic disorder

Anxiety can manifest itself in three ways:

1. cognitively: in thoughts;
2. somatically: in physiological and biological processes;
3. feelings: emotions.

Individual methods of treatment for anxiety disorders target different components of anxiety. CBT, for example, focuses on changing thought processes such as attribution and reaction patterns in response to anxiety-provoking situations (training thoughts to control behaviour). Unlike some of the other talking treatments, CBT focuses on the 'here and now' problems and difficulties. Instead of focusing on the causes of distress or on symptoms in the past, as psychoanalysis does, CBT looks for ways to improve state of mind now. Pharmacological treatment is aimed at altering physiological and biological processes. Neuro-developmental treatment investigates whether there are physical reasons for situational anxiety and sets out to identify and, if possible, to correct the underlying mechanisms at fault.

A clinical psychologist working at a hospital in Scotland carried out a study of 26 patients to investigate the incidence of abnormal reflexes in adults who had sought clinical treatment for anxiety disorder. Using tests selected from the INPP Test Battery, Forrest assessed 26 patients and 26 controls for the presence of the following reflexes:

- *Vestibular reflexes (primitive)*
  Moro reflex
  Tonic labyrinthine reflex
  Asymmetrical tonic neck reflex
  Symmetrical tonic neck reflex
  Landau reflex;
- *Tactile reflexes (primitive)*
  Palmar reflex
  Rooting reflex
  Suck reflex;
- *Postural reflexes*
  Oculo-head righting reflexes
  Labyrinthine head righting reflexes
  Amphibian reflexes
  Segmental rolling reflexes.

Forrest found a significant difference in the reflex test mean scores from patients with anxiety and from control participants, with the tonic labyrinthine reflex and underdeveloped labyrinthine head righting reflexes showing the highest scores in the anxiety patients compared with the control group. In her discussion of the findings, she suggested that 'These reflexes are regarded as exerting an influence over sensory processing, to the extent that the individual's relationship with gravity cannot function adaptively. A variety of problems result, and include dysfunction of balance, coordination and proprioception, all governed by the central nervous system.'[34]

Why Should a Retained TLR and Lack of Head Righting Reflexes Be Involved in the Experience of Anxiety?

Chapter 3 explained how, when normal righting reactions are present, postural stability and control of muscle tone can be maintained irrespective of head position. If the TLR is still present, movement of the head forwards or backwards through the mid-plane results in reflexive changes in either flexor or extensor muscle tone affecting the body's ability to maintain upright balance. These actions of the body do not then match the intentions of the vestibular system or the motor cortex, resulting in disassociation or vestibular-proprioceptive mismatch[35] and the onset of physical sensations similar to motion sickness and the experience of anxiety.

Risk factors among individuals who develop this type of anxiety may have been present for some time. Beuret[36] described how the development of this pattern prior to the onset of symptoms could be observed in a group of young adults who showed signs of academic failure for the first time during higher education.

In the early years of schooling, these students had exhibited no learning difficulties, readily learning to read and write, but

> By the ages of 9–12 they began to avoid unnecessary reading or writing. In some cases they reverted back to printing. However, academic achievement was consistent with ability. The one factor present in all cases was a history of motion sickness or more subtle variants such as headaches, nausea or drowsiness while reading in a moving vehicle.
>
> About ages 13–14, headaches appeared during prolonged reading, academic performance dropped below ability and markedly increased study time was required to maintain grades. At ages 14–18, headaches and fatigue began to appear on school days. Often they required naps after school. A noticeable gap appeared between ability and performance, further increases in study time were required to maintain grades and concentration began to drift when reading.
>
> At the college or university level, they were uniformly overwhelmed by the increased academic demands. They rapidly exhibited similar symptoms of stress and decompensation, including headaches (occasionally progressing to migraines); increased fatigue; disorganisation; difficulties with memory and concentration; and anxiety and/or depression. Grades dropped precipitously and they questioned their ability and intelligence.[37]

ADOLESCENT AND ADULT MANIFESTATIONS OF NDD – A CLINICAL PERSPECTIVE

By Lawrence J. Beuret, MD

Multiple factors converge in adolescents and adults with NDD to create elusive and diffuse symptomatology. Early reading and learning difficulties are generally absent; fine motor and writing problems are minimal; gross motor co-ordination is little affected; athletic ability may be above average, and early behaviour is within age-appropriate norms. Academically 'not working up to potential' and emotionally and/or behaviourally not responding to accepted therapeutic or pharmacological interventions are the hallmarks of NDD in this population. This differs sub-stantially from younger children whose symptoms closely correlate with the continued presence of primitive reflexes.

The underdevelopment or absence of postural reflexes has a much greater influence on symptom development and functional limitations in this older population. DeQuirós and Schrager[35] provide one of the most detailed insights into pathology created by incomplete development of this reflex system. In summary, they state that any deficiency in the critical systems of postural control must be compensated for by the intervention of the highest level (most recently evolved) areas of the CNS. This follows the dictates of Jackson's Law[38] – the most highly developed, most complex functions will be sacrificed to maintain functions earlier evolved, more primitive, and more critical to survival. In humans, these encompass high-level and complex cortical activities such as comprehension, executive function, ana-lytical, and synthetic abilities, as well as cognitive and pro-cessing competence.

Primitive reflexes have very specific and quite predictable symptoms and limitations associated with their presence. Postural reflexes, when absent or incompletely developed, manifest with diffuse, elusive signs and symptoms. Com-pensatory processes and such factors as personality, IQ, interests, learning styles, and stress levels further overlay, disguise, modify, and individualize these already vague manifestations.

If the sequences of normal primitive reflex inhibition and postural reflex appearance are viewed chronologically, the resulting pattern in Figure 9.9 suggests the postural reflex system does not develop until the inhibition of the primitive reflexes has actively begun or is nearly completed. Clinical evidence proves quite the contrary. Younger children ex-tensively treated through occupational therapy (OT) and sensory integration (SI) intervention commonly show highly

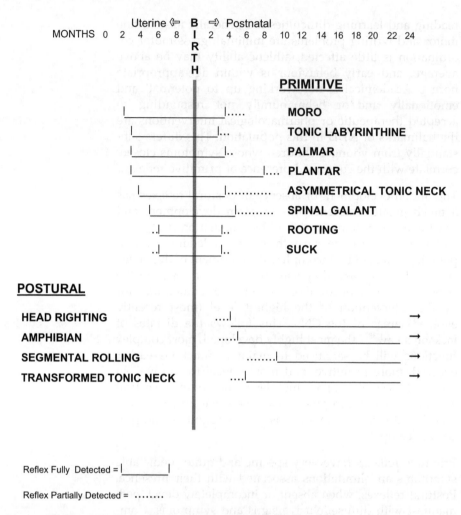

Figure 9.9   Chronological presence of primitive and postural reflexes

or completely developed postural reflexes (ocular and laby-rinthine head righting, amphibian, segmental rolling, trans-formed tonic neck). Those who have had no early OT or SI intervention show a more even distribution between retained primitive reflexes and incomplete or absent postural reflexes. These treatments incorporate various forms of vestibular stimulation which promote development of the postural reflex system, as well as improve balance and gross motor coordination. In the older population, it is common to see a reflex profile in which primitive reflex inhibition is virtually complete, but postural reflexes are incompletely developed or absent.

Treatment response further confirms the primitive and pos-tural reflex systems are, indeed, two independent systems and are not sequential. The development of postural reflexes is completely independent from the state of inhibition of the primitive reflexes. When treatment is initiated with a series of remedial exercises addressing vestibular and proprio-ceptive integration, postural reflexes rapidly develop, even though incompletely inhibited primitive reflexes remain at the same level or decrease at a much slower rate.

In four cases where patients prematurely stopped neuro-developmental treatment then resumed treatment 4–10 years later, primitive reflexes remained unchanged or further diminished, but initially developed postural reflexes regressed; vestibular-proprioceptive symptoms returned, and oculomotor function deteriorated. All four returned to treatment because reading difficulties had re-emerged in college.

In this older population, vestibular-proprioceptive mis-match becomes the common thread throughout an indi-vidual's history, testing, and treatment response. Motion sickness or some abnormal response to motion is present in all cases, although intensity and frequency is highly corre-lated with certain personality factors.[39] As detailed later in personality factors and their relationship to compensatory mechanisms, personality factors correlate especially well with past behavioural responses to manifestations of NDD, as well as with responses observed during treatment.

Motion sickness – nausea, vertigo, headache, and fatigue being the most frequently reported symptoms – occurs uniformly in response to attempting to read or to engage in some form of visual fixation (reading a map) while riding in a moving vehicle. Other abnormal motion responses may be present concurrently with, or independently from, motion sickness. These can involve adverse reactions to lateral, vertical, interrupted, and rotational forces such as those encountered on winding roads, hilly terrain, stop-and-start traffic, amusement rides, and elevators.

See final chapter for further details of tests contained with the diagnostic assessment.

When any of the above abnormal responses to motion are present, parallel findings in the initial diagnostic assessment further confirm the presence of vestibular-proprioceptive disturbance. Most frequently observed is the tendency to misestimate the degree of motion taking place in specific testing situations.

Romberg II is a standard neurology test for static balance used in the initial diagnostic assessment. It involves standing barefoot with the feet touching, arms at the sides, with eyes closed. The usual response to this test is a slight regular sway or deviation of 0.5–1.0 cm from a central axis. When subjects are asked to illustrate with the thumb and index finger how wide a range of movement they felt took place, the *perceived* distance they show will be 5–8 cm, several times the *actual* range. Less commonly, a range of sway may be 3–5 cm, but the perceived distance demonstrated will be markedly reduced or felt to be absent entirely.

Other areas of testing which document the role of this vestibular-proprioceptive malfunction include the ocular and labyrinthine head righting reflex tests, dynamic balance tests, and oculomotor testing. These malfunctions create extraneous responses during testing procedures and are useful in gauging the severity of vestibular-proprioceptive disturbance, as well as in providing an ongoing method of monitoring their correction during treatment.

A typical response during the lateral movements involved in testing the head righting reflexes is an exaggerated sensation of falling or loss of balance, a parallel of the exaggerated sense of movement in the Romberg II test.

In these tests, the subject is seated on the floor with legs straight forward and touching. For the ocular head righting reflex, vision is fixed on a point, 1.0–2.5 m forward, at eye level, with eyes open. For the labyrinthine head righting reflex, the eyes are closed, the subject imagining visual fixa-

tion on the eye-level point. The subject is tilted in 15° incre-
ments from vertical to 60°, to the left, then back to vertical,
then to the right and back to vertical.

The exaggerated sense of movement (from vestibular-
proprioceptive mismatch) prompts resistance to the lateral
movement, extension of the homolateral arm, or reflexive
extension of the contralateral leg in an attempt to limit or to
counterbalance the exaggerated sense of movement. These
responses are completely involuntary and are often surprising to the subjects themselves.

During dynamic balance testing, instinctively increasing
speed functions to offset balance instability. In the course of
oculomotor testing, vertigo, difficulty balancing, frontal and
temporal pressure or headache, sensations of ocular pressure, and nausea may accompany tests requiring rapid and
interrupted horizontal eye movements. Significantly, these
same symptoms develop when the individual attempts to
read in a moving vehicle.

As treatment corrects the mismatched sensory input, patients
report reduction and eventual elimination of motion sickness, improved balance, better reading comprehension, and
absence of eye discomfort. In direct parallel, there is a reduction and, finally, an elimination of extraneous responses
during testing.

In adolescent and adult populations, the initial NDD screen-
ing/consultation becomes a multifaceted tool for leading
the patient from various presenting complaints to appreciat-
ing the role underlying physical aspects of NDD have played
in undermining individual function. Patients typically arrive
by referral for academic underachievement or for behavioural and emotional problems that have not responded to
customary therapeutic or pharmacological treatment. Educators and therapists who become familiar with the effects
NDD can have on their particular disciplines find it revealing for the individual to complete an NDD checklist
(summary of the risk factors and common manifestations).
This introduces the concept of a physical or neurophysiological process underlying their disorder.

There is an additional Blythe–McGlown Questionnaire for adults. Depending on the age of the subject, one or both questionnaires may be used.

During the initial office visit, the Blythe–McGlown Screening Questionnaire provides the basis for the history taking
and interview process. A careful construction of a disorder's

past and present history will reveal for the patient (and parents) parallel patterns of physical, academic, behavioural, and emotional involvement.

Especially for adolescents, identifying a physically based process as underlying presenting problems can be a great relief for both patient and parents. This effectively places the source of a presenting problem in a more neutral physical arena, rather than being attributed to being 'someone's fault'. This can effectively reframe the source of the problem to a common underlying cause – NDD – over which no one had control. When this concept is clearly conveyed during the initial meeting, there is little difficulty in gaining the teenager's cooperation for subsequent testing and remediation.

Unfortunately, adequate or above-average academic performance in the early school years can deter identification of underlying NDD. A progressive drop in academic performance in a teenager most likely will be attributed to attitude or to motivational problems common to this age group.

Academic competence in the early school years, despite the presence of NDD, can be due to a number of factors. The NDD may be of a milder degree – a less severe trauma to the CNS – that only manifests when academic requirements exceed a certain threshold level. The individual may have highly developed compensatory abilities, routinely seen in children with higher IQs. The educational setting may have been especially supportive and not locked into a rigid schedule and demanding structure. Home schooling, Montessori, and Waldorf systems are familiar examples.

No matter what has supported early academic success, one consistent marker signals when the student has reached a critical threshold and has begun to decompensate – the approach to reading for pleasure. When interest in non-required, unassigned reading begins to diminish, change in subject matter or format, or is eliminated completely, this signals the beginning of a gradual deterioration in performance, resulting in the label 'not working up to potential'.

As the CNS, already weakened by the presence of NDD, is increasingly confronted with complex neuro-processing functions like reading, the first line defence for dealing with this stressor is avoidance. The final trigger for decompensation may come from a number of sources. Steadily increasing academic demands, especially the volume of reading, and increasing complexity of the material requiring comprehension is a prominent factor. Emotional stress – parental divorce, moving, changing schools, losing close friends – can provide 'the final straw'. In a carefully recorded history of reading development – early interest in reading, reading progress in the first grades of school, changes in the kind of reading materials, physical symptoms associated with prolonged reading – a change in reading pattern or subject matter will be the first indicator, *in retrospect*, of this decompensation point.

Some noted exceptions to this pattern actually support its validity. The student who is primarily an auditory learner may never have had interest in unrequired reading. High auditory retention permits this individual to exhibit adequate or even above-average academic performance well into the early years of high school, with little or no reading. Superior auditory retention, coupled with a high IQ and well-developed inferential skills, makes it possible for this student to acquire essential basic knowledge from lectures and discussion with classmates. Then, employing substantial inferential skills, this student can effectively 'fill in the blanks' and exhibit academic performance comparable to classmates who learn from reading. This approach eventually falters when supplemental reading is absolutely necessary to acquire essential course knowledge. The result is an abrupt deterioration in performance.

One student was referred by his therapist for NDD evaluation and treatment when he began to exhibit uncharacteristically disruptive and defiant classroom behaviour. The change began during his second year of high school and was accompanied by a precipitous drop in academic performance. After he had been progressing well in his remedial programme, I asked him what insight he had into the source of this behaviour. He stated he had found if he was sufficiently obnoxious, the teacher would never call on him to read.

A highly gifted student began to experience migraines in the third grade. These progressed with increasing intensity and frequency over the next two years. His reading history indicated he had never reduced the time he spent in unrequired reading, even when the migraines had become more frequent and were clearly associated with his constant reading. In his case, the drive for learning overrode any natural instinct to avoid and limit his reading, even though the migraines often resulted.

Changes in reading material and format can signal this point, even though reading time is not altered. Many boys stop reading books but continue to avidly read sports magazines and the sports sections of the newspaper. Here, combinations of highly interesting subject matter coupled with narrow columns of print reduce oculomotor stress sufficiently to allow reading to continue, apparently unchanged. A teenage girl reported that she continued to read as much as always, except, her mother noted, she had changed from biographical books to romance novels. The change to a less-demanding level of comprehension, accompanied by high interest, allowed her to maintain an unchanged reading volume.

The adolescent who begins to exhibit academic deterioration may be referred for testing to identify causal factors. Unfortunately, testing which is useful in identifying early learning disabilities in younger children may give inconclusive or inconsistent results when used to evaluate these older students. IQ testing relies on a statistically significant discrepancy between verbal and performance scores. In a learning disability, the performance score is significantly lowered by NDD-based factors such as fine motor disturbance, hand–eye coordination difficulties, oculomotor dysfunction, and spatial-perceptual problems. This discrepancy presents unequivocal evidence for a learning disability, and appropriate remedial intervention and support automatically follow.

The adolescent with emerging NDD-based difficulties presents with a far different picture. The verbal score will be high, but performance not reduced as significantly as in the classic learning disability. The testing psychologist may note some unusual scatter within various sub-test scores, but on the whole, the verbal performance differential is not as pronounced. This difference can be attributed to two factors. The NDD-related motor functions – fine motor, oculomotor – are not as severe as in a learning disability, or they may be better compensated for. Incomplete postural reflex development may underlie certain types of odd sub-test scatter by virtue of higher-level cortical impairments, but the ultimate effect is not sufficiently pronounced to definitively diagnose a learning disability. The end result – inconclusive – lends to attributing any pronounced change in academic performance to attitudinal or motivational issues of the adolescent years.

Gifted students, along with those having higher IQs, are notoriously excluded from any supportive services from educational systems, even though the deterioration or inconsistency in performance is observed by parents and teachers alike. In these situations, high IQ truly becomes a detriment. The high total IQ score exceeds the threshold defined as 'qualifying for services'.

A gifted adolescent with NDD can present a particular dilemma, both to himself and to teachers and parents. The high IQ confers an exceptional ability to compensate for, override, or alter symptoms which would typically be present in the average student with the same degree of NDD. Interest and desire for learning can effectively override or cancel out normal perception of these symptoms, distorting both the student's reading history and response to specific testing procedures for NDD.

This difference in the experiencing and perception of symptoms which typically accompany NDD can be illustrated by the following. If NDD is causing significant disturbance in oculomotor function, there are anticipated effects on the reading process. The expected responses would be:

'When you are reading, especially for an extended period of time, do you find that you often skip lines or reread the same line?' *Yes.*

'At the point where you begin to skip or reread lines, do you notice any physical symptoms such as pressure or discomfort around the eyes, headaches, or fatigue?' *Yes, I start to yawn a lot and if I keep trying to read, I get a headache on the sides of my head.*

'When you start to feel tired or have the headache, do you notice anything happening with the print on the page such as letters getting fuzzy or double, or do letters or words seem to be moving on the page?' *Yes, it will look like some letters are disappearing from the words.*

During the oculomotor testing component of a diagnostic assessment, this same individual will report symptoms paralleling those provoked by extended reading. Slow and rapid horizontal eye movements become erratic or difficult to sustain; a temporal headache appears, and yawning may occur. Testing for delayed recovery of binocularity (the mechanism behind the apparent movement or distortion of print) will be abnormally extended.

In the highly gifted adolescent, the answers and testing symptoms can be completely different. The answer will be *no* to all questions concerning physical or visual symptoms which should typically accompany extended reading. During oculomotor testing, no associated symptoms will be reported, even though horizontal eye movements are hideously disturbed and recovery of binocularity is abnormally prolonged.

This difference in symptom *experience* suggests several possible mechanisms. The motivation to read and learn, in the gifted adolescent, may completely override normally experienced accompanying symptoms. Inherent beliefs held by gifted students – 'I can do anything I put my mind to. I should be able to be able to do everything, perfectly. I am gifted, and by definition, can't be having any problem with reading or learning' – may lead to the construction of elaborate denial systems which completely erase any perception of symptoms. A further mechanism may be that the symptoms do not appear to be 'logical' and are thus dismissed, denied, or overridden by higher cortical mechanisms.

A gifted high school student's report of his motion sickness history illustrates a clear example of an ability to cognitively eliminate a physical symptom. In answer to the question 'Did you ever experience motion sickness in the past, or do you experience it presently?'

He responded, 'I had it for a long time when I was growing up, then three years ago decided I didn't need to have it anymore. I had to work on it for a while, but now I never have it.'

Gifted or high-IQ individuals, left to their own devices, will deny, not experience, or rationalize away many key symptomatic indicators of NDD. This can cause the final scoring obtained during the screening/consultation visit to be low or borderline in indicating NDD, even though prominent risk factors (difficult pregnancy, birth, or significant jaundice) have been reported. Here, the inclusion of brief tests for balance, fine motor coordination, and oculomotor function can reinforce that a problem does truly exist. This objective illustration of disturbed balance and oculomotor function for parents can more than make up for the low or borderline screening score.

Because emotional and behavioural disturbances frequently occur in the adolescent population, educators may naturally assume that academic performance deteriorates *because* of these problems. A careful examination of reading and academic histories shows the converse – the academic decline begins *before* the emotional and behavioural disturbances surface.

Faced with equivocal results from educational testing, many parents of underachieving adolescents seek IQ testing or neuropsychological evaluations from private sources. But clues as to the source of the problem may still be found within the educational system. Federal and state regulations in the USA now require standardized testing for all students. A pattern specific to NDD can appear in these testing results. The student will rate a high percentile ranking in verbal and language ability, but the ranking will drop significantly lower in reading comprehension. Most educators are at a loss to explain the significance of this difference.

From a neuro-developmental view, it follows logically. The student has adequate grounding in language and vocabulary *in isolation* but lacks the ability to apply it to reading comprehension, specifically because oculomotor dysfunction interferes with cognition and comprehension. Stated alternatively, the attention required to adequately control abnormal horizontal eye movements, so that text can be accurately read, ultimately reduces the cognitive capacity to comprehend *what* is being read.

Personality traits become a further factor in determining how NDD will eventually manifest in the adolescent and in the adult. The Jungian-described traits of introversion and extroversion have the most universal effect in colouring compensatory processes and symptom development. These traits may be ascertained in a formal manner from the Myers–Briggs Type Indicator,[40] from the social introversion scale of the Minnesota Multiphasic Personality Inventory (MMPI),[41] or simply from observation and historical information. They influence symptom development and manifestation in remarkably consistent ways.

Recent research documents that introverts and extroverts actually process information in differing manners.[42] In studies correlating personality traits and response to motion, Reason and Brand[39] describe how differently introverts and extroverts experience conditions that induce motion sickness. Their research, along with complementary findings in the psychopharmacological literature,[43] suggests there is both a cortical and vestibular component to motion sickness. The introvert is highly susceptible, and experiences and is able to describe the various symptoms common to motion sickness. The extrovert, on the other hand, is much less susceptible, and experiences and describes far fewer symptoms.

In the adolescent and the adult NDD population, a similar parallel holds true as far as the perception and reporting of symptoms by these two personality types. This difference in symptom perception is not limited exclusively to motion sickness, but extends to various oculomotor symptoms originating from the NDD.

For purposes of brevity, the introvert may be characterized as introspective, likes or needs to spend time alone, instinctively feels responsible for actions and their consequences, is internally motivated by what needs to be or should be done, has a high frustration tolerance, and is seen as responsible and persistent. The extrovert is socially and interactively oriented, requires continual interest and relevance for sustained task involvement, instinctively relegates responsibility to factors outside of self, presents as impatient and having a low frustration tolerance, and is liable to be viewed as irresponsible and scattered.

The introvert's answer concerning symptoms during reading might be

> If I read for more than three pages I notice my attention starting to drift and I have to go back and read it over once or twice to really understand it. This is where I begin to think about taking a break from the reading. When I keep pushing myself to finish the chapter, that's when I start feeling the pressure around my eyes and the headache over my eyes. At this point, what I'm reading no longer makes much sense.

The extrovert's answer is typically more oblique: 'I avoid reading as much as I can.' Why? 'Because it's boring.'

Do you feel anything around your eyes, or a headache, if you push yourself to read more? 'No, I don't read long enough for anything like that to happen'.

Both are equally affected by the oculomotor and comprehension disturbances created by NDD, but describe and respond very differently. In both cases, inherent responses arising out of personality differences can mask and delay recognition of the underlying academic problem created by NDD. The extrovert can easily appear as not serious about grades, more interested in socializing, having an 'attitude', not respectful, impulsive, and being too scattered – the classic attitude and behaviour problem.

The introvert's instinctive response to 'study harder' can, likewise, mask the emergence of academic decline from NDD. When problems with reading comprehension begin for the introvert, they may not be reflected in individual course grades because study time will have been extended to compensate for less efficient comprehension. Only by comparing an individual's time involved in study with that of peers who are making similar grades can any difficulty be detected. Lack of energy, depression, anxiety, and social withdrawal are frequent results of the introvert's struggle to maintain grades.

During the initial phases of treatment, vestibular-proprioceptive function normalizes and oculomotor disturbances resolve. Even before the physical function of these systems is fully corrected, there can be a marked improvement in both emotional and behaviour areas. These can be objectively documented with testing tools such as the MMPI.

Several areas can contribute to the emotional and behavioural changes during NDD remediation. The remediation programme definitely relieves the developmental stresses imposed on the CNS. Energy levels increase and avoidance behaviours diminish. Self-doubt and self-image issues created by academic deterioration lessen as reading becomes more efficient and comprehension improves. Parents consistently report that the treatment programme causes their children to feel 'more at ease with themselves'.

At the college level, students with NDD are most vulnerable during their first two years. A student with NDD with an academic record of sufficient quality to enter college is already experiencing a significant level of stress. The major changes unique to this phase of their educational lives impose a cumulative level of stress, as quantified by standard stress rating scales[2], equivalent to those encountered during divorce. These include moving away from home, increased academic demands, marked changes in schedule, and altered living and eating habits.

Unfortunately, when NDD goes undetected, these students simply become a statistical casualty – every institution expects to have a certain percentage of dropouts. In parallel with the ego-damaging effects of academic deterioration, these students manifest symptoms commonly labelled psychosomatic – migraines, difficulty concentrating, sleep disorders, anxiety, depression, or are assumed to be somehow sabotaging their prior academic potential and success. Increased alcohol consumption and recreational drug use start to appear as attempts to self-medicate and to relieve these symptoms. Here, again, prior academic success prevents an accurate diagnosis of the real problem, the underlying NDD.

Adults with NDD rarely appear for treatment of their own accord in the USA, but are referred by psychology and psychiatry professionals, or have seen results in their children's treatment and recognize some of the same issues existing within themselves. Most report they have always felt they never truly functioned at their true potential. Age does not appear to affect a patient's response to treatment. My oldest patients are presently 63 and 64. In both cases, their vestibular-proprioceptive and reflex inhibition/development changes in response to the treatment programme have occurred at the same rate as children and adolescents. The major difference with adults lies in the almost uniform need for parallel therapeutic support to deal with the changes that occur from the treatment programme and to gain insight into how the NDD has limited their lives in the past.

Before moving on to discuss the implications of neuro-developmental problems for educational policies in the future, it is helpful to examine the development of The INPP Method in the context of other theories and practices, from its beginnings in the late 1960s to the present day.

REFERENCES

1 Blythe P, McGlown DJ. 1980. *An Organic Basis for Neuroses and the Existence, Detection and Treatment of Secondary Neuroses.* Svenska Institutet för Neurofysiologisk Psykologi, Göteborg.
2 Holmes TH, Rahe RH. 1967. Social readjustment rating scale. *Journal of Psycho-somatic Research* 11:213–218.
3 Blythe P. 1987. Personal communication. Chester.
4 Griffin P. 2007. Personal communication. Chester.
5 Beuret LJ. 2000. The role of postural reflexes in learning. Part 2. Paper presented at the 12th European Conference of Neuro-developmental Delay in Children with Specific Learning Difficulties. Chester, UK, March 2000.
6 Lawton Brown R. 1990. Dyslexia and maths. Paper presented at the 2nd European Conference of Neuro-developmental Delay in Children with Specific Learning Difficulties. Chester, UK, March 1990.
7 O'Hare A. 1999. Dysgraphia and dyscalculia. In: Whitmore K, Hart H, Willems G (Eds). *A Neurodevelopmental Approach to Specific Learning Disorders.* MacKeith Press, London.
8 Badian NA. 1983. Developmental dyscalculia. In: Mykelbost HR (Ed.). *Progress in Learning Disabilities.* Grune and Stratton, New York.
9 Shalev RS et al. 1988. Developmental dyscalculia. *Cortex* 24:555–561.
10 Manor O et al. 1993. The acquisition of arithmetic in normal children: assessment by a cognitive model of dyscalculia. *Developmental Medicine and Child Neurology* 35:593–601.
11 Wertmanelad R, Gross-Tsur V. 1995. Developmental dyscalculia and brain laterality. *Cortex* 31:357–365.
12 Witkin HA et al. 1971. *Children's Embedded Figures Test.* Consulting Psychologists Press. Inc., Palo Alto, CA.
13 Manor O, Amir N. 1995. Developmental right hemisphere syndrome: clinical spectrum of the non-verbal learning disability. *Journal of Learning Disabilities* 28:80–86.
14 Risey J, Briner W. 1990. Dyscalculia in patients with vertigo. *Journal of Vestibular Research* 1:31–37.
15 Melzack R, Wall P. 1965. Pain mechanisms: a new theory. *Science* 150:171–179.
16 Wall PD, Melzack R. 1962. On nature of cutaneous sensory mechanisms. *Brain* 85:331.
17 Berthoz A, 2000. *The Brain's Sense of Movement.* Harvard University Press, Cambridge, MA.
18 Berthoz A. 2003. *Emotion and Reason. The Cognitive Science of Decision Making.* Oxford University Press, Oxford.
19 Cited in: Berthoz A. 2003. *Emotion and Reason. The Cognitive Science of Decision Making.* Oxford University Press, Oxford.

20 Goddard Blythe SA. 2004. *The Well Balanced Child*. Hawthorn Press, Stroud.

21 Goddard Blythe SA. 2008. *What Babies and Children Really Need. How Mothers and Fathers Can Nurture Children's Growth for Health and Well-being*. Hawthorn Press, Stroud.

22 Ayto J. 1990. *Dictionary of Word Origins*. Columbia Marketing, St Ives.

23 Freud S. Cited in: Brown JAC. 1991. *Freud and the Post Freudians*. Penguin Books, Harmondsworth.

24 French TM. 1930. Beziehungen des Unbewussten zur Funktion der Bogengaenge. *The International Journal of Psycho-analysis* 16:73–86.

25 Bauer J, Schilder P. 1919. Ubereinige psycholphysiologischen mechanismen funtioneller neurosen. *Zeitschrift für Nervenheilkunde* 164:279.

26 Shaskan DA, Roller WL. 1985. *Paul Schilder. Mind Explorer*. Human Sciences Press, New York.

27 Schilder P. 1933. The vestibular apparatus in neurosis and psychosis. *Journal of Nervous and Mental Disease* 78:1–23, 137–164.

28 Peto A. 1970. To cast away. *Pyschoanalytic Study of the Child* 25:401.

29 Audesirk T, Audesirk G. 1996. *Biology. Life on Earth*. Prentice Hall, Upper Saddle River, NJ.

30 Blythe P, McGlown D. 1982. Agoraphobia – is it organic? *World Medicine*, July 1982, pp. 57–59.

31 Ljunggren M. 1982. Agoraphobia – an organic basis? An explanatory neuropsychological approach. Unpublished Master's Thesis. Universitet Göteborg, Psychologiska Institutionen.

32 Blythe P. 1988. An analysis of the developmental history of 103 patients diagnosed with agoraphobia and/or panic disorder. *The 2nd International Conference of Neuro-Developmental Delay*. Stockholm, October 1988.

33 *Diagnostic and Statistical Manual of Mental Disorders IV (DSM IV)*. 1994. American Psychiatric Association, Washington, DC.

34 Forrest DS. 2002. Prevalence of primitive reflexes in patients with anxiety disorders. Thesis submitted to the University of Edinburgh in part fulfilment of Doctorate in Clinical Psychology.

35 De Quirós JL, Schrager OL. 1979. *Neuropsychological Fundamentals in Learning Disabilities*. Academic Therapy Publications, Novato, CA.

36 Beuret LJ. 1992. The role of neuro-developmental delays in advanced academic failure. *The 4th European Conference of Neuro-Developmental Delay in Children with Specific Learning Difficulties*. Chester, UK, March 1992.

37 Beuret LJ. 1994. Seminar paper delivered to The Institute for Neuro-Physiological Psychology Supervision, Chester.

38 Roeckelein JE. 1998. *Dictionary of Theories, Laws, and Concepts in Psychology*. Greenwood Press, Westport, CT.

39 Reason JT, Brand JJ. 1975. *Motion Sickness*. Academic Press, London.
40 Briggs Myers I. 1998. MBTI Manual (A guide to the development and use of the Myers Briggs type indicator), 3rd ed. Consulting Psychologists Press, Washington, DC.
41 Butcher JN, Williams CL. 2000. *Essentials of MMPI-2 and MMPI-A Interpretation*, 2nd ed. University of Minnesota Press, Minneapolis, MN.
42 Johnson DL et al. 1999. Cerebral blood flow and personality: a positron emission tomography study. *American Journal of Psychiatry* 156:252–257.
43 Croucher T, Hindmarch I. 1973. The spiral after effect (SAE) as a measure of motion sickness susceptibility and the effect on the SAE of an antimotion sickness drug and a central nervous system depressant. *Psychopharmacology* 32:2.

CHAPTER 10

DEVELOPMENT OF THE INPP METHOD – FROM THEORY TO FACT

Peter Blythe, PhD

The origins of neuro-developmental delay (NDD) as defined by The Institute for Neuro-Physiological Psychology (INPP) began to emerge amidst a maelstrom of theories, claims, and counterclaims as to the possible causes of specific learning difficulties (SpLD) – in the USA, 'specific learning disabilities' – dyscalculia, dysgraphia, reading problems, spelling difficulties, attention deficit disorder (ADD), attention deficit hyperactivity disorder (ADHD), specific dyslexia, and what is currently referred to as developmental coordination disorder (DCD). This was despite the fact that it had long been accepted by the majority of researchers that there was a neurological dysfunction underlying most of the SpLDs.

The first real evidence in support of a neurological causation came from Dr Rudolf Berlin of Stuttgart, a physician and eye surgeon who had a patient who lost the ability to read due to a brain lesion. When he wrote up this case in 1872, he described the condition as 'dyslexia'. A few years later, in 1877, a German neurologist, Professor Dr Adolf Kussmaul of Heidelberg University, studied an adult who had lost his ability to read, following a cerebral vascular injury, although he was still able to speak fluently. He called the condition 'alexia' or 'word blindness'.

From that time onwards, the names given to the neurological dysfunction proliferated, and by the 1960s, one had such diagnostic 'labels' as 'minor' or 'diffuse brain damage', 'cerebral dysfunction', plus at least 30 other odd labels. The net result of this was that in 1963 a special US task force was formed under the auspices of the Department of Health, Education and Welfare in Washington, DC, to investigate the various anomalies in terminology and to assist in the identification of SpLD, specific learning disabilities.

Under the leadership of Dr Samuel D. Clements, a psychologist from Chicago, the Task Force produced its first report in 1966, entitled *Task Force One: Minimal Brain Dysfunction in Children*.[1] In this document, it was suggested that the term 'minimal brain dysfunction' (MBD) should be used in future, rather than the earlier terms that were suggestive that the child's difficulties were as a result of some form of brain damage. Accordingly, Clements wrote 'minimal brain dysfunction' as referring '. . . to children of near average or above average intelligence with certain learning or behavioural disabilities, ranging from the mild to severe, which are associated with deviations of functions of the central nervous system. These deviations may manifest themselves in various combinations of impairment in perception, conceptualization, language, memory, and in control of attention, impulse or motor function.'[1]

The Task Force One Report further indicated that MBD could be the result of genetic variations, biochemical irregularities, perinatal brain insults, or other illnesses or trauma during the maturation and development of the central nervous system (CNS), or from unknown causes. It also stated that severe sensory deprivation could also be a causal factor, and finally concluded with the words, 'during the school years a variety of learning disabilities is the most prominent manifestation of the condition which has been designated by this term.'

Then, the Report undermined itself by listing as many as 99 signs or symptoms that could be found in children diagnosed as having MBD, with the 10 most commonly found symptoms being hyperactivity; perceptual-motor impairments; emotional lability; general coordination deficits; disorders of attention span; impulsivity; disorders of memory or thinking; specific learning disabilities in reading, writing spelling, and arithmetic; disorders of speech and hearing; equivocal neurological signs and electroencephalogical irregularities. If that was not enough to discredit the concept of MBD, many of the 'symptoms' of MBD were such observable behaviour patterns as coordination problems, hyperactivity, poor impulse control, memory disorders, etc., that explained nothing as to causation, and even the neurological signs that were recognized were considered to be 'soft signs', such as mixed laterality, poor muscle tone, evidence of poor balance, or lack of good finger movements (dysdiadochokinesia).

Following the publication of the Task Force Report, there were, for a time, a number of pieces of research trying to elicit the causal factor of MBD, and these were summed up by Underwood in 1976: 'The dysfunction may be a genetic, hereditary condition, or an insult to the central nervous system prior to birth (rubella, toxaemia, drug reaction, rh Factor, etc.) during the birth process (skull fracture, jaundice, anoxia, etc.) or in early childhood while the brain is still undergoing development (high fevers, febrile convulsions, measles, whooping cough, etc.'[2]

Despite all the research, no one had demonstrated, except for the detection of abnormal electroencephalogram (EEG) patterns of specific lesions, exactly how genetic transmission or various assaults on the CNS – some of them being mentioned by Underwood above – had affected CNS functioning, which meant that making a diagnosis of MBD could only be arrived at by a cluster of the symptoms mentioned in Task Force One. And it was that lack of a reliable and replicable ability to diagnose MBD that caused not only confusion, but led eminent members of the medical profession, such as the Scottish paediatric neurologist Tom Ingram, to state, 'MBD is not a diagnosis; it is an escape from making one.'[3]

To keep the record straight, this type of reaction had occurred four years before the Clements Report was published, when an international study group consisting of leading neurologists and psychologists met in Oxford in September 1962 to discuss what should be the correct term to identify those children who were manifesting educational and behavioural difficulties within the educational system. At that time, the term predominantly in use was 'minimal brain damage', and members of the study group thought this term was inaccurate because it suggested that there was an injury that caused anatomical changes, although there was no evidence or history of damage. The group therefore suggested that the diagnostic term 'minimal cerebral dysfunction' be adopted because there was evidence that the cerebral cortex was unable to perform certain tasks despite lack of evidence of damage or of evidence of a low IQ.[4]

The inability to produce clinical evidence of CNS malfunctioning led many others to be even more critical than Ingram. Becker[5] in 1974 described MBD in his paper, 'Minimal Cerebral (Brain) Dysfunction – Clinical Fact, Neurological Fiction?', as '. . . a jungle of woolly and unclear boundaries, blurred conceptions, and partly overlapping synonyms.'

Educators and teachers, on the whole, tended to either decry or to ignore the concept of MBD and its relationship to children in the classroom. The opposition was exemplified by Barbara D. Bateman of the Department of Special Education at the University of Oregon in Eugene when she wrote, 'I am not suggesting that central nervous systems do not differ from each other in ways, undoubtedly related to learning performance; I am, however, underscoring the fact that direct CNS manipulations are beyond the domain of the educator.' Later in the same paper, she added, 'Medical classifications such as MBD are as irrelevant to educational practice as educational classifications are to medical practice.'[6]

As it was widely accepted that if a child had MBD there was nothing that could be done to ameliorate the condition, it is little wonder that Barbara Bateman could state, 'Educators' willingness to attempt to use the MBD classification has had another result. It has provided a seemingly sophisticated and respectable excuse for both non-teaching and poor teaching. The teacher who is told that Mark has MBD may very understandably respond with some version of "No wonder I haven't been able to teach him" and stop trying. He has suddenly become something other than an ordinary child who needs more and better teaching than other children. He is now someone else's responsibility.'[6]

This attitude was even more bluntly expressed by Chalfant and Scheffelin in 1969 that, '(a) the Educator cannot fix the brain (b) he does not know what he would do differently if he knew the brain was damaged and (c) inferences about brain or problems which lie behind the brain tends to stop attempts at remedial work on the assumption that the damage and its behavioural consequences are permanent.'[7]

The above statements and attitude towards MBD and education were encapsulated by S. Alan Cohen from Yeshiva University in New York: 'The clinical labels "minimal brain dysfunction" and "dyslexia", as well as other perceptual or neurological designations, are not particularly helpful to remedial educators. Remedial education deals with children who do not perform school-related behaviours well. They may or may not have other symptoms but the reason for their referral to a special teacher is not their neurological condition but their inability to perform some series of tasks defined by the school as "reading".'[8]

To overcome all the objections that were made about MBD, such as those mentioned above, in March 1969, I started, with one of my applied psychology students, David McGlown, at a College of Education in Lancashire, to try to isolate what significant role physical, developmental factors appeared to play in specific learning difficulties (SpLD).[9,10] Within two years, three factors had been isolated, and these were:

1. aberrant patterns of motor development;
2. evidence of cross-laterality or marked ambiguity of lateral dominance of eye, hand, or leg; and
3. definite visual-perceptual problems, including difficulty in visual-motor integration (VMI) functioning,

while still acknowledging, and taking cognizance of the fact that there can be, and frequently is, other additional evidence of neurological involvement.

To prevent any misunderstanding of the original terminology, we felt it was necessary to clarify exactly what was meant by each of the above-mentioned three factors.

'Aberrant patterns of motor development' was meant to indicate the continued presence of the primitive, asymmetrical tonic neck reflex (ATNR), and the absence of what was referred to as being the 'transformed tonic neck reflex' (TTNR).

As a result of the research work that we had done, it appeared that the ATNR did not become inhibited at 24 weeks of neonate life, but had become transformed, and replaced by the opposite response to head movement, i.e. instead of getting extension of the jaw limbs and flexion of the occipital limbs, with the TTNR, one obtained flexion of the jaw limbs and extension of the occipital limbs. This meant that it was possible to determine, at any age, whether the ATNR was still present, therefore preventing the emergence of a full TTNR.

If the ATNR remains uninhibited beyond the accepted 24 weeks, or if it is 're-released' by physical trauma or pathological processes, it 'has a severe effect on a patient's motor behaviour.'[11]

In a group of children with SpLD, we had found that 84.21 per cent had a retained ATNR or a partially retained ATNR.

The importance of a retained or a strong residual ATNR is the effect it has upon later motor development; for example, it affects the infant's ability to subsequently crawl on the stomach like a commando or to creep on the hands and knees, and these hierarchical modes of mobility are not only precursors to obtaining the erect postural position and walking, but are vital stages that facilitate neuro-development and perceptual maturation.[12] In other words, we postulated that they are functions facilitating neural development, with neural development facilitating increased functional ability. This hypothesis was, to some degree, confirmed by Mrs J. Davies who was working with George Pavlidis, at that time a research fellow in the Department of Psychology at Manchester University. Unaware of the work that we were doing, Pavlidis and Davies were researching into the role of visual-perceptual problems – ocular-motor problems – in dyslexia. In addition to their finding that ocular/oculo-dysfunction was present in all the dyslexic children they examined, they also found a second 'universal' factor, that none of the dyslexic children had been through the motor stages of creeping and crawling.[13] This was later confirmed by Pavlidis[14] in 1981 when he wrote that a high percentage of children with reading difficulties and dyslexia had failed to go through the crawling and creeping stages of development.

In addition to ascertaining if the ATNR was still present, the term 'aberrant patterns of motor development' also included a child's failure to progress through the motor stages of creeping with the stomach in contact with the floor and then beginning to defy gravity by crawling on hands and knees. We were able to determine the answer to this by asking a child to lie on his/her stomach and then to crawl forward. The work that we had done had shown, at least to our satisfaction, that if a child had not completed this motor stage of development as an infant, due to an aberrant ATNR, the child would not be able to accomplish this at a later age, unless he or she had been specifically trained to do so.

'Evidence of cross-laterality or marked ambiguity of lateral dominance of eye, hand or leg' had long been associated with SpLD, in fact, since Orton in 1925, who found that children with SpLD were more ambidextrous than their peers who had no such problems, and later, Professor Oliver Zangwill wrote in 1960, '. . . our findings accord well within the view that the origin of these disorders is to be sought in an anomaly of cerebral dominance.'[15] To support his assertion, Zangwill quoted the naturalized French professor Julian de Ajuriaguerre, who had found a higher incidence of ambidexterity in dyslexics, and concluded that 'they are often badly lateralised.'

Finally, the term 'perceptual problems' was defined as the presence of increased physiological nystagmus and affected eye muscle movements that exhibited themselves as the lack of 'eyes yoking' or moving together, latent strabismus, the inability to ignore irrelevant visual stimuli within a given visual configuration, i.e. 'stimulus-bound' effect, and poor scanning–tracking ability. In addition, perceptual problems had to include 'VMI' difficulty – poor hand–eye coordination. Here it is worth noting that Clements et al. examined 84 children with MBD – SpLD – and compared them to 45 children who had exhibited no evidence of MBD as a control group. VMI was found to be present in 98 per cent of the MBD children, and no evidence of it was found in the control group.[16]

When all three of the above diagnostic categories were found to be present in the underachieving child, it was decided to call the overall problem 'organic brain dysfunction' (OBD). This diagnostic term was chosen as an attempt to alert educators and teachers to the fact that those children of average to above-average intelligence who were failing in the classroom may have a cluster of small, but detectable, physical dysfunctions that prevented them from demonstrating their intelligence in the normal and acceptable academic way, i.e. that the brain and the various parts of the body could never achieve automatic functioning (automaticity).

In a small study of 36 children with a variety of SpLDs, 27 boys and 9 girls, presented at the Symposium on Dyslexia: Its Diagnosis and Treatment held at Manchester University in February 1978, the following were demonstrated:

1. Absence or partial absence of the TTNR   88.88%
2. Presence of an ATNR   84.21%
3. Aberrant motor-developmental patterns of crawling and creeping   96.30%
4. Cross-laterality or marked ambiguity of laterality   96.30%
5. Increased physiological nystagmus   96.30%
6. Perceptual problems
   Lack of 'yoking'   48.15%
   Latent convergence or divergence   51.85%
   'Stimulus-bound' effect   74.07%
   Visual discrimination problems   62.96%
   VMI difficulties   100.00%

By 1971, we not only believed that we could detect and measure the degree of OBD affecting the learning-impaired child but we had also developed a remedial motor training programme to inhibit the ATNR, to stimulate the TTNR, to take the child through the developmental stages of crawling and creeping, to develop good gross and fine muscle coordination, and, finally, a series of oculomotor and hand–eye coordination exercises.

The OBD remediation programme required that it be done daily and needed 30–40 minutes to complete. Although it was arduous for both child and parents, it was successful with many children. This was demonstrated by a small piece of research completed by the Psychological Division of the Gothenburg Education Authority in 1983, when two teachers specializing in special education, who had also been trained in the OBD methods, were given a group of children with SpLD who had been resistant to all previous methods of intervention, thereby cancelling out any chance of the Hawthorne effect. Those children that remained in the treatment group all benefited from the OBD programme and were able to enter the regular educative process.[17]

In 1973, the book *Stress Disease* was published.[18] As a result of this, the writer came into contact with a large number of stress-prone individuals, whose symptoms persisted despite repeated attempts at medical or psychological intervention, and was able to examine them for the presence of OBD and to implement the INPP remedial programme.[19-23]

Following the formation of INPP in Chester, England in 1975, the research work continued, and it slowly became apparent that it was not sufficient to confine the OBD diagnostic assessment to examining for the presence or residual presence of an ATNR, and that it was necessary to examine for the presence of all the primitive reflexes that medical text books stated should not be present in 'normal' children. To our surprise, we found that many children with SpLD still had a cluster (three or more) of aberrant primitive reflexes present, together with the absence of the vital postural reflexes. Finding this was a major breakthrough, because it meant that from then onwards, we could examine the CNS for dysfunction with accuracy, rather than having to rely on 'soft signs', such as impaired balance and immature crawling and creeping patterns.

A number of small pieces of research that we did, or had instigated, had found that among the non-learning difficulty children, there could be evidence of only *one* residual primitive reflex, which had no affect on their academic performance. Although at the time this was news to us, we subsequently discovered that in 1900, Kennard had looked at two groups of young people, one group being hospitalized as 'organic' patients, and the second group, which was composed of 'above-average' performing high school students. Kennard's objective was to test for the prevalence of 18 'soft' or minor neurological signs in the two groups. He had found that 9 per cent of the high school students displayed evidence of the primitive Babinski reflex, which should not, in theory, be present above the age of 24 months.[24]

The next step, after examining for the presence of all primitive reflexes and the absence of the postural reflexes, was to create new reflex-inhibition movements to inhibit any of the primitive reflexes found to be present in the school aged child, thereby giving higher parts of the brain an opportunity to 'release' the appropriate postural reflexes.

In 1983, McGlown left INPP to continue the work of the BIRD Centre (The Centre for Brain Rehabilitation and Development) as a national charity that had been established by INPP some years earlier. Although it was not a significant part of the reason that McGlown decided to leave, we had begun to differ on what movements were necessary to implement a successful INPP remediation programme.

In view of the new knowledge we had gathered, I realized it was no longer necessary simply to get a child to crawl on the stomach and to creep on hands and knees, and then to do stylized walking in order to inhibit the aberrant reflexes. Rather, if one inhibited the aberrant primitive reflexes, it would be sufficient to permit the brain to release the missing postural reflexes, and as the transformation occurred, the child would begin to crawl and to creep correctly, without requiring further remedial intervention.

In the following year, 1984, it became clear that the diagnostic term OBD, as it had originally been defined in 1971, was no longer valid. This was because retention of the ATNR would prevent the child from commando crawling. In these cases, the failure to crawl was not a cause of the later emerging problems, but was a *symptom* of an existing delay in neurological maturation. Similarly, if a child had a persistent symmetrical tonic neck reflex (STNR), this would prevent the next developmental motor stage of creeping on hands and knees. So, just to use lack of crawling or creeping as a diagnostic criteria was, therefore, invalid. Equally, if there was a continued presence of an ATNR, this could result in cross-laterality or marked ambiguity of laterality. Finally, if the tonic labyrinthine reflex (TLR) is not inhibited, in its retained form, by 13 weeks of age, it could prevent the emergence of the vital postural head righting reflexes and subsequent visual-perceptual problems.[25–27]

To overcome the problem of definition, we started to use 'central nervous dysfunction' instead of OBD, but it soon became apparent that this also lacked in clinical objectivity, so, in 1987, INPP accepted the term 'neuro-developmental delay' (NDD). In the following year, Sally Goddard Blythe, the current Director of INPP and internationally acclaimed author, joined us and through her published research and her books and papers has developed the work much further, as this book will demonstrate.

To sum up the background to NDD, in 1980, I had asserted that 'the innate mechanistic processes involved in the inhibition, modification and transformation of the basic reflexes are observable, and more importantly are **replicable** at any age, to assist in the rehabilitation of neurological impairment', and that 'Every reflex has a purpose, and will not be fully suppressed unless it has successfully completed the job it was designed to do.'

Sally Goddard Blythe followed up the above statement in a paper she presented to The 2nd European Conference of Neuro-Developmental Delay in Children with SpLD held here in Chester in 1990 when she wrote that 'The remediation of aberrant reflexes is based on the primary concept of replication . . .', namely, that 'All human babies make certain stereotyped movements during the first year of life.'[28] These movements contain within them the natural antidote to the appropriate reflex at that stage in development, thus facilitating the inhibition of a primitive reflex on the one hand, and the subsequent release of a postural reflex on the other, together with continued CNS development.[27]

REFERENCES

1 Clements S. 1966. *Minimal Brain Dysfunction in Children: Terminology and Identification*. Task Force 1. U.S. Department of Health, Education and Welfare, Washington, DC.

2 Underwood R. 1976. Learning disability as a predisposing cause of criminality. *Canada's Mental Health* 24/4:11–16.

3 Ingram TTS. 1973. Soft signs. *Developmental Medicine and Child Neurology* 15:527.

4 Bax M, MacKeith R (Eds). 1962. *Minimal Cerebral Dysfunction*. The National Spastics Society, Education and Information Unit in Association with William Heinemann Medical Books, Ltd., London.

5 Becker RD. 1974. Minimal brain dysfunction – clinical fact, neurological fiction? *The Israel Annals of Psychiatry and Related Disciplines* 12:87.

6 Bateman BD. 1973. Educational implications of minimal brain dysfunction. *Annals of the New York Academy of Sciences* 205: 245–250.

7 Chalfant JC, Scheffelin M. 1969. *Central Processing Dysfunctions in Children*. National Institute of Neurological Disorders and Stroke, National Institute of Health, Bethesda, MD.

8 Cohen AS. 1973. Minimal brain dysfunction and practical matters such as teaching kids to read. *Annals of the New York Academy of Sciences* 205:251–261.

9 Blythe P, McGlown DJ. 1979. *An Organic Basis for Neuroses and Educational Difficulties*. Insight Publications, Chester.

10 Blythe P. 1990. *The History of the Institute for Neuro-Physiological Psychology (INPP)*. INPP, Chester.

11 Bobath B. 1971. *Abnormal Postural Reflex Activity Caused by Brain Lesions, 2nd ed.* William Heinemann Medical Books, Ltd., London.

12 Gesell A. 1954. The ontogenesis of infant behavior. In: Carmichael L (Ed.). *Manual of Child Psychology*. Wiley, New York, pp. 295–331.

13 Blythe P. 1977. Personal communication.

14 Pavlidis G, Miles T. 1981. *Dyslexia Research and its Application to Education*. John Wiley and Sons, Ltd., New York.

15 Zangwill OL. 1960. *Cerebral Dominance in its Relation to Psychological Function*. Oliver & Boyd, Edinburgh.

16 Quoted in Blythe P, McGlown DJ. 1979. *An Organic Basis for Neuroses and Educational Difficulties*. Insight Publications, Chester.

17 Bernhardsson K, Davidson K. 1983. *A Different Method of Helping Children with Learning Difficulties – The Dala Clinic Final Report* (written in Swedish). The Psychological Division of Gothenburg Education Authority, Gothenburg, Sweden.

18 Blythe P. 1973. *Stress Disease*. Arthur Barker, London. In paperback, 1976. *Stress the Modern Sickness*. Pan Books, London.

19 Blythe P. 1978. Minimal brain dysfunction and the treatment of psychoneuroses. *Journal of Psychosomatic Research* 22/4:247–255.

20 Blythe P, McGlown DJ. 1980. *An Organic Basis for Neuroses and the Existence, Detection and Treatment of Secondary Neuroses* (in English). Svenska Institutet for Neurofysiologisk Psykologi, Gothenburg, Sweden.

21 Vose RH. 1981. *Agoraphobia*. Faber & Faber, London.

22 Blythe P, McGlown DJ. 1981. MBD & OBD. *Swedish Medical Journal* 78/1,2:45–48.

23 Blythe P, McGlown DJ. 1982. Agoraphobia – is it organic? *World Medicine*, July, p. 10.

24 Kennard MA. 1966. Value of equivocal signs in neurologic diagnosis. *Neurology* 10:753–764. Quoted in Blythe P, McGlown DJ. *An Organic Basis for Neuroses and Educational Difficulties*. Insight Publications, Chester.

25 Blythe P. 1988. *A New Approach that Explains Specific Learning Difficulties and Provides an Effective Treatment*. INPP, Chester.

26 Blythe P. 1987. Oculo-motor dysfunctions and the effect on functioning. *Reflex Newsletter*, INPP, Chester.
27 Goddard S. 1990. The developmental basis for learning difficulties and language disorders. *INPP Monograph Series No.1*. INPP, Chester.
28 Thelan E. 1979. Rhythmical stereotypes in normal human infants. *Animal Behaviour* 27:699–715.

CHAPTER 11

OTHER FACTORS IN SPECIFIC LEARNING DIFFICULTIES

UNRAVELLING THE THREADS

The key to success for any remedial programme is in the identification of contributing underlying factors, thorough assessment, and matching intervention to the needs of the child. While problems with posture, balance, and motor control are often present in children with specific learning difficulties, they are not always the primary cause. Other factors of a physical (but not necessarily medical) nature that can contribute to problems with reading, writing, spelling, and concentration include auditory processing problems, structural problems affecting skeletal alignment, biochemical (including nutritional) factors, undetected problems with eyesight, and abnormal brain wave variants, affecting attention and concentration.

Auditory Processing Disorders

In Chapter 7, we explored how a history of frequent ear, nose, and throat infections, or periods of intermittent hearing loss in the early years, can contribute to learning and behavioural problems later on, even when normal hearing has been restored for several years. This is because the critical period for tuning in to the sounds of the mother tongue are in the first three years of life with a 'window' for continuing development up to approximately six years of age. Children who have suffered from periods of reduced hearing in the first six years of life can continue to experience problems with specific aspects of auditory processing for many years to come. Social and environmental factors, such as living in an environment with a lot of background noise, or where there has been little reciprocal linguistic interaction in the early years, can also play a part.

Auditory processing disorder (central) 'is a deficit in the perceptual (i.e. neural) processing of acoustic stimuli and the neurobiologic activity that underlies those processes and gives rise to the auditory evoked potentials.'[1] In other words, there is nothing wrong with the hearing apparatus, but neural pathways linking to the brain have 'switched off'.

Auditory discrimination describes the ability to detect the difference between different sound frequencies and specific speech sounds, particularly similar sounds in the English language, such as *s* and *f*, *f* and *th*, *th* and *sh*, *sh* and *ch* (all high-frequency sounds); and *p* and *b*, *b* and *d*, *m* and *n* (middle frequency).

If a child is unable to hear the difference between similar sounds, the rules of spelling (in English) have little relevance. The only reason that *b* faces in one direction and *d* in the opposite direction is because each letter symbolizes a *different* sound (Figure 11.1).

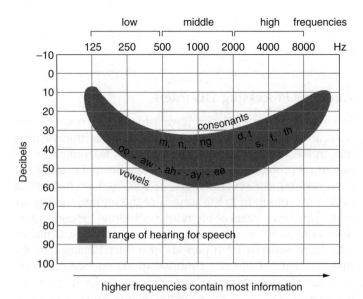

Figure 11.1   The sound sausage

The range of difference between medical diagnosis of hearing loss and the hearing acuity required to detect and use the sounds of language easily can be as wide as 40 decibels at certain frequencies. Children can pass the standard hearing tests but may still lack the acuity needed for discriminating between different sounds and being able to use the sounds of written language with accuracy and fluency.

Paul Madaule, Director of The Listening Centre in Toronto,[2,3] says that reading requires the translation of visual symbols on the page into an internal auditory image that is held in the mind (the mind's ear); writing requires the opposite process – translation of thoughts into internal speech, which is then transferred from auditory to visual through the motor system. A problem in any one of the components, auditory, visual, and in the case of writing – motor – can interfere with the ability to use written language. Poor auditory discrimination can result in difficulties matching visual symbols to the correct sounds. This can occur as a result of earlier hearing problems, when the brain does not 'hear' the fine-tuning differences, or if hearing levels are significantly different from the optimum hearing curve for the language that is being used.

Tomatis,[4] a French ear, nose, and throat surgeon, developed an interest in professional opera singers who started to lose the ability to pitch certain notes with accuracy. When he carried out a thorough examination of their vocal tracts and hearing, he noticed that in many cases, the problem was not with the voice, but with the ear. Years of singing high notes *fortissimo* had damaged the hearing apparatus, and as hearing started to decline, so the voice was unable to 'hit' the notes with its former clarity. He deduced that the voice can only produce what the ear can hear. The effects of hearing loss on speech development had long been known, but he wondered whether subtle differences in hearing could play a part in other language dysfunctions, particularly problems with written language such as dyslexia. Using frequency analysis, he determined that every language has its own range of sound frequencies, with variable levels of acuity required to hear and pronounce sounds, tonal variation, and accents that are unique to that language. Minor differences in an individual's hearing curve from the 'optimum' curve for that language could, in theory, result in difficulties hearing, saying, and 'seeing' what those sounds

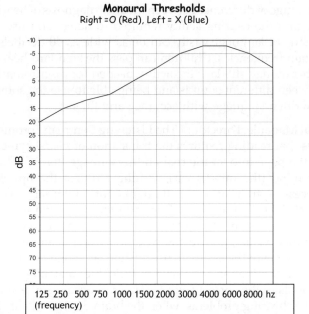

Monaural Thresholds
Right =O (Red), Left = X (Blue)

Figure 11.2   Optimum hearing curve (Tomatis)

mean (Figure 11.2). Figure 11.3 shows the differences in hearing in each ear in a child's audiometric curve compared to the 'optimum' curve identified by Tomatis. Figure 11.3 shows the results of an audiometric test carried out on a child who had passed all previous hearing tests and who had not been referred as a matter of routine for further investigations. Tomatis went on to develop a method of retraining the ear using specially filtered sounds.

Tomatis' theory also goes some way to explaining why it is increasingly difficult to learn a foreign language without betraying a trace of accent the older you are. When hearing has been well tuned in to the sounds of one language (native language) in the early years, it becomes more difficult to learn new sounds or variations which fall outside the native curve in later life. The sounds that lie within the English language (depending on dialect) fall within a relatively narrow band in terms of frequency sensitivity in the low and middle frequencies, but require excellent hearing in the high frequencies – these are the frequencies which are most often impaired during, and following bouts of otitis media (middle

Hearing can continue to be affected for up to eight weeks after the period of acute infection has cleared up.

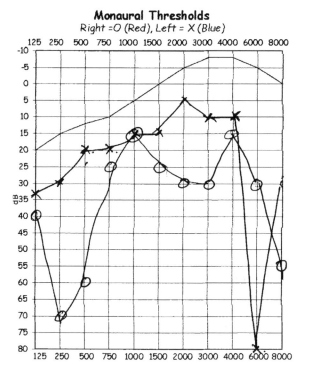

Monaural Thresholds

Right =O (Red), Left = X (Blue)

X = left ear;
0 = right ear.

Figure 11.3   Audiometric examination of child with reading and spelling problems. Child A: 9-year-old child with severe reading problems. In view of the 70-decibel loss at 250 Hz in the right ear and the 80-decibel loss at 6,000 Hz in the left ear, this child was referred for further ear, nose and throat (ENT) medical investigations before sound therapy could be recommended

ear infection), or the consequences of enlarged adenoids or tonsils, glue ear, or allergic rhinitis.

Auditory delay (lateral processing)

Tomatis also identified that the speed at which sounds are processed can vary according to the route used from the ears to the brain, and which ear is used as the leading ear.

The right ear provides the fastest route from the ear to the language decoding centre, which, for the majority of people (circa 96 per cent), is located in the left hemisphere of the cerebral cortex. Sounds processed by the left ear pass to a smaller language centre in the right hemisphere from where they have to cross over via the corpus callosum to the left hemisphere for decoding. The result is a small difference in the amount of time that it takes for sounds to reach the main language centre. The difference between the brain interpreting a sound as *d* or as *t* is a minute difference of some 40–60/1,000s of a second in the timing of the onset and offset of the first and second bursts of sound. Fractional delays in the timing of sounds reaching the brain can therefore play a part in the misperception of certain sounds, affecting auditory discrimination.

Auditory delay can also affect short-term auditory memory. One of the properties of sound is that it is transitory and must be remembered if it is to retain significance. Delay in processing sounds can make it harder to remember a sequence of individual sounds (necessary for word building) and following verbal instructions. The effect is similar to watching a newsreader in the television studio carry on a conversation with an overseas correspondent via satellite while on air. The viewer can see that there is a fractional delay from the newsroom asking the question and the journalist receiving it. In general terms, even a fractional delay in speed of processing can reduce the amount of auditory information that a child can process at one time and may be misinterpreted as being part of an attention/behaviour problem, rather than being symptomatic of dysfunction in a specific aspect of auditory processing. Auditory delay may show up on assessment using the Wechsler Intelligence Scale for Children (WISC) as poor performance on the digit span test.

Auditory confusion (orientation)

Auditory confusion is closely linked to *auditory stimulus-bound effect* (inability to filter out irrelevant auditory stimuli) and is usually the result of early problems with orienting to sound. In Chapter 8, we covered some of the work of Ray Barsch in relation to man being a space-oriented creature. Before a child can select salient sounds within an acoustic environment, he or she must first be able to locate the source of the sound. Orientation, according to Barsch, is the first step in paying attention to specific as opposed to multiple sensory stimuli. Voluntary as opposed to reflexive acoustic orientation to sounds starts to develop at about four months of age, around the same time as the Moro reflex is inhibited; the acoustic stapedius reflex develops and the infant also has sufficient control of eye movements to direct his/her vision towards the source of sound. The latter is connected to maturation of vestibular pathways involved in head control. Auditory confusion in the older child can be the result of a number of developmental factors: underdeveloped head righting reflexes, immature vestibular functioning, retained Moro reflex, underdeveloped acoustic stapedius reflex, unilateral hearing loss, and history of hearing loss or lack of ear preference (laterality). Any single factor or a combination of these factors can contribute to difficulties with orientation to sound, affecting attention, the ability to separate foreground from background noise (selective listening), and freedom from distractibility. The symptoms of auditory confusion can often be seen in behaviour.

Hyperacusis (hypersensitivity)

Hearing tests are carried out on all children in the early years to detect early signs of hearing impairment, but the effects of hypersensitivity do not form part of routine investigations. Hyperacusis can exist in deaf children, in children with a history of intermittent hearing impairment, as well as in children with hyperacute hearing. It can exist across all frequencies or only to specific frequencies, and it can have an impact on both learning and behaviour.

One of the first tasks in learning to listen is learning to occlude background noise. This is one of the functions of the acoustic stapedius reflex, to reduce the volume of sound admitted to the inner ear by as much as 20 decibels, not only in response to external noises, but also in response to internally generated sounds when a person uses their own voice. This protects the delicate inner ear from damage from general noise but also enables a person to speak without being distracted by the sound of his/her own voice. It is possible that for children who had a history of reduced hearing in the past, as a result of glue ear, congestion, or infection, the need for the acoustic stapedius reflex to operate at the time was reduced. Once the period of impairment has passed, the reflex is inadequately developed and does not protect against sounds at sensitive levels.

Guy Berard, another French ear, nose, and throat surgeon, based in Annecy in France, developed a hearing test to identify hyperacusis and found that it was particularly prevalent in some individuals diagnosed as being on the autistic spectrum. Some of their 'autisms' – specific types of stereotyped, avoidant and repetitive behaviours – could start to be understood in terms of defence mechanisms against intolerable or uncomfortable auditory environments. He said that 'hearing equals behaviour',[5] and he went on to develop a system of auditory integrative training (AIT) using filtered music, with sounds randomly switched between ears to desensitize the patient to certain sounds and to build up increased tolerance to all frequencies. AIT is still used effectively for the treatment of auditory hypersensitivity in specialist centres and clinics throughout the world.

Frequency and hemisphere-specific stimulation

There are now many different methods of sound therapy available, music therapy, and computer-based therapy programmes using animated video games and speech processing programmes that enable researchers and clinicians to alter the amplitude and *duration* of speech sounds.[6] The latter is based on observations that extending the duration of brief, rapidly changing transitional elements within the acoustic waveform of speech syllables results in significantly improved speech discrimination of those syllables in language-impaired children.[7]

The duration of speech sounds can also be altered simply by setting words to music. Empirical evidence on the power of regular singing to improve specific language problems is explored in The Well Balanced Child[i].

Another method, Johansen Individualised Auditory Stimulation (JIAS), tested on children in Denmark with dyslexia,[8] uses frequency-specific stimulation, and if appropriate, also hemisphere-specific stimulation to improve auditory discrimination and lateral processing in children identified as having problems in these areas. JIAS provides a clinical method for the identification, assessment, treatment, and subsequent evaluation of auditory discrimination and lateral processing disorders. A full hearing threshold test is carried out at the first assessment. This ascertains not only that the child does not have a hearing loss, but also plots the child's individual hearing curve, which can then be compared to the optimum (Tomatis) curve. A binaural hearing test and dichotic listening test is also carried out to identify if the child has developed a leading ear, and whether the leading ear is consistent with general lateral preference. If there are

[i]Goddard Blythe SA. 2004. *The Well Balanced Child*. Hawthorn Press, Stroud.

discrepancies between the individual hearing curve and the optimum curve, frequency-specific music is selected and the music adjusted through the use of specially developed software to compensate for the deficits and hypersensitivities in the individual curve. The music may also be biased towards one ear depending on the results of the binaural and dichotic listening tests. The child must listen to the music for 10 minutes per day, and tests are re-evaluated at six to eight weekly intervals. Adjustments will be made to the selected music according to changes that have taken place on audiometric evaluations in the preceding eight weeks. Examples of changes in audiometric curves before and after JIAS can be seen in Figure 11.4a–c.

Paul Madaule has developed a screening questionnaire to help identify children who are showing signs of auditory processing disorder. Similar to the INPP Questionnaires, this auditory questionnaire is intended to be used as an *initial screening device only*, to indicate which children should receive further (clinical) examination for auditory processing disorder. It should *not* be used as the basis for a diagnosis.

A listening checklist

Developed by Paul Madaule. The Listening Centre, Toronto, Canada. Reproduced with permission of Paul Madaule (all rights reserved)

> We cannot see listening. The only way to get at it is indirectly – through skills that are related to it in one way or another.
>
> This checklist offers a catalogue of skills and behaviors that will enable you to assess yourself, your child or your students with respect to listening.
>
> There is no score, simply check as many boxes as you feel appropriate.
>
> **Receptive Listening**
>
> This is listening which is directed outward. It keeps us attuned to the world around us, to what's going on at home, at work or in the classroom.
>
> - short attention span
> - distractibility
> - misinterpretation of questions
> - confusion of similar sounding words

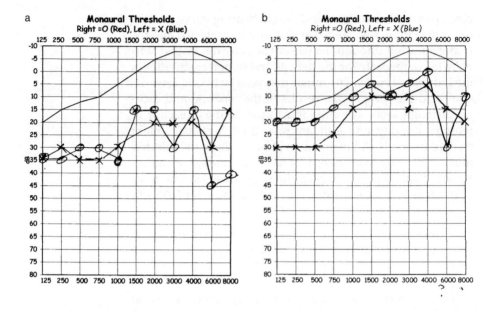

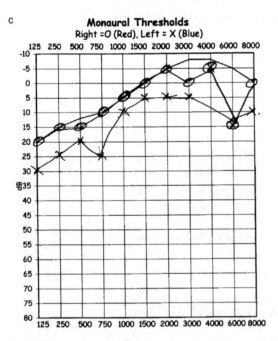

Figure 11.4 (a–c) Examples of audiometric examination of a child before and after 12 weeks of JIAS. (a) Child B before using JIAS. (b) Child B 12 weeks after starting JIAS. (c) Child B 18 weeks after starting JIAS. Child B will need a further 4+ months on sound therapy to improve the left ear in the low frequencies and both ears between 5,000 and 8,000 Hz

- frequent need for repetition
- inability to follow a series of instructions

Expressive Listening

This is listening that is directed within. We use it to control our voice when we speak and sing and our eyes when we read or write.

- flat and monotonous voice
- hesitant speech
- weak vocabulary
- poor sentence structure
- overuse of stereotyped expressions
- inability to sing in tune
- confusion or reversal of letters
- difficulty with reading
- poor spelling

Motor Skills

The ear of the body, which controls balance, co-ordination and body image, also needs close attention.

- poor posture
- fidgety behavior
- clumsy, uncoordinated movement
- poor sense of rhythm
- messy handwriting
- hard time with organization, structure
- confusion of left and right
- mixed dominance
- poor sport skills

Protection Issues

Listening is also the ability to leave out, or protect ourselves from 'noise', the information we don't need. Difficulty at that level is often related to behavioral and social adjustment issues.

- oversensitivity to sound
- low tolerance or frustration
- poor self-confidence
- poor self-image
- difficulty making friends
- tendency to withdraw, avoid others
- irritability
- immaturity
- negative attitude toward school/work

The Level of Energy

The sensory system, and the ear in particular, are most instrumental in providing and regulating the energy we need to lead harmonious and fulfilling lives.

- difficulty getting up
- tiredness at the end of the day
- habit of procrastinating
- hyperactivity
- tendency toward depression
- feeling overburdened with everyday tasks
- low motivation, lack of drive

Developmental History

This knowledge sheds light on the possible causes of a listening problem.

- stressful pregnancy
- difficult birth
- adoption
- early separation
- delay in motor development
- delay in language development
- recurring ear infections

Paul Madaule has developed a programme to improve listening – The Listening Fitness Trainer (LiFT)[9] – an electronic audio device which is used for sound stimulation *and* voice training. Children with auditory processing problems often have poor perception of their own voice. Although Tomatis had already maintained that the voice can only produce what the ear can hear, his pupil, Paul Madaule, recognized that the voice is also a *training instrument*, and that use of the voice can improve auditory processing by stimulating the audio-vocal feedback loop.

> The evanescent nature of sound means that it has to be remembered to be of use. One way of storing sounds is to repeat them. When the voice is activated the body acts as a resonator making it easier to hear. In young babies, where the head is small and the ears are closer together vocalisation helps to train the ear, while the ear refines what the voice can do. In the hearing impaired, it has been found they respond to much quieter sounds than would be expected if they make the sound themselves because use of the voice provides vibration through bone conduction, which by-passes the middle ear, while giving voice to sounds helps to improve the ability to pitch accurately and enhances discrimination. Use of the child's own voice is rather like a gymnastic session for the ear.[10]

Similar observations regarding the importance of voice work were made by Dr Colin Lane, who at one time specialized in teaching hearing-impaired students. One of the pieces of homework assigned to students was to listen to speech sounds on a tape recorder and to repeat them, one of the aims being to improve the clarity of articulation. One student made remarkable progress and when teachers tried to find out why this pupil had made more progress than others, they discovered that instead of listening to the sounds of someone else on tape, the student had recorded his own voice and was using his own speech as the 'model' from which to work. Despite the fact that the sounds he had recorded were unclear, his speech improved when he used his *own* voice as the model for 'sounding out'. Colin Lane was so fascinated by this that he returned to the University of Exeter for postgraduate studies and completed his PhD on the use of the child's *own* voice as being one of the most powerful teaching instruments. He has also developed a listening and voicing programme to improve concentration and literacy: Aural-Read-Response-Oral-Write (ARROW).[11]

Problems Related to Skeletal Structure

Misalignment of the skeleton can affect both structure (skeletal system) and functional development (nervous system), influencing posture, balance, coordination, and related functions. There are many types of structural abnormality that can occur for a variety of reasons, but one example sometimes seen in children with specific learning difficulties is *kinematic imbalance of sub-occipital strain* (KISS). KISS is primarily treated by therapists specializing in manual medicine. In Europe, practitioners of manual medicine are often medical doctors or chiropractors who have undergone specialist training in the diagnosis and treatment of KISS.

KISS affects the craniovertebral junction in newborn babies and in young children. According to Dr Heiner Biederman, who has worked with KISS for more than 20 years, problems affecting the craniovertebral junction can be regarded as one of the main reasons for asymmetry in posture and consequently asymmetry of the osseous structures of the cranium and the spine. In more than 35,000 small children and newborn babies seen by him and his colleagues for a variety of problems, 'we realized that the sub-occipital region – between the *occiput* and C3 (the *cranio-cervical* area) – plays a very important role in the senso-motor development,

Occiput – the lower and hinder part of the head where it merges into the neck.
Cranio – skull.
Cervical – pertaining to the neck.

exceeding the symptoms seen at that time and reaching far into adolescence and even adulthood. Cranial asymmetry, functional asymmetries and asymmetrical neurological patterns all contribute to this diagnosis.'

'The term KISS-syndrome is used to bring together a seemingly non-coherent group of symptoms and ailments found in newborn and small children, its dominant feature being the torticollis, often combined with an asymmetry of the head.' Risk factors for KISS include: intrauterine misalignment, mechanical intervention at birth, e.g. forceps, ventouse, etc., prolonged labour, and multiple birth.

Microsomy – general smallness.

Clinical signs of KISS may be torticollis, unilateral *microsomy*, C scoliosis and motoric asymmetries, unilaterally retarded maturation of the hip joints, and slowed motor development. Symptoms which may be observed during a neuro-developmental assessment or when taking a developmental history are: asymmetric posture; tilted posture of the head (torticollis); opisthotonus (head held in retroflection) – unable to lie on the back; uniform sleeping position – child will cry if moved; asymmetric motor patterns; asymmetric posture of trunk and extremities; and sometimes tilted head position similar to ATNR. There may also be a history of sleeping disorders: baby wakes every hour crying; extreme sensitivity of the neck; cranial scoliosis; swelling of one side of the facial soft tissues – asymmetry of facial features; blockages of iliosacral points; asymmetric development and range of movement of the hips; fever of unknown origin; loss of appetite and other symptoms of central nervous system (CNS) disorders.

Although the trigger is in the sub-occipital area, the entire spine is involved and can affect many other functions including the development of righting reactions, such as head righting reflexes, and the inhibition of primitive reflexes. 'Head stabilisation is a complex process involving the interaction of reflexes elicited by vestibular, visual and proprioceptive signals. Most of the afferent proprioceptive signals originate from the cranio-cervical junction. Any obstacle impeding these afferents will have much more extensive consequences in nervous system in formation which depends on appropriate stimuli (and feedback) to organise itself – cerebral organisation for the newborn begins at the head.'[12] In other words, problems with structure can 'block' development in other areas affecting posture, balance, integration and development of reflexes and dependent functions including the control of eye movements necessary for reading and writing.

Nutrition and Communication in the Nervous System

The nervous system operates through neurons. Neurons are specialized cells which are responsible for producing actions, thoughts, and feelings. Neurons are able to process, transmit, and store information as a result of two characteristics:

1. The ability to generate and conduct electrical signals;
2. The ability to secrete chemical substances that can alter the activity of other cells, particularly other neurons. These chemical substances are known as *neurotransmitters*.

Neurotransmitter – a substance made, stored, and released by neurons. Neurotransmitters are chemical messengers between neurons at chemical synapses.

Both types of communication result from the movement of ions across the nerve's membrane, and the efficiency of transmission is dependent on multiple factors. One factor that can affect how neurons communicate is nutritional status. This is because nutrition provides many of the chemical components for communication within the nervous system.

The subject of nutritional factors in specific learning difficulties warrants a specialist book running into several volumes. However, despite the importance of nutrition in influencing and regulating many important functions, the role of nutrition in formal education as a significant area for investigation when problems arise in concentration, behaviour, or other aspects of learning tends to receive very short shift. In the context of this book, a few examples may help to illustrate why, if a child is presenting with problems, nutritional status should not be overlooked.

In his book *The Second Brain*,[13] Dr Michael Gershon described how 'nerves talk with a chemical language' and that 'there is brain in the bowel. The ugly gut is more intellectual than the heart and may have a greater capacity for feeling. It is the only organ that contains an intrinsic nervous system that is able to mediate reflexes in the complete absence of input from the brain or spinal cord. When our predecessors emerged from the primeval ooze and acquired a backbone, they also developed a brain in the head and a gut with a mind of its own.' He went on to say that 'we have more nerve cells in our gut than in the remainder of our peripheral nervous system. The enteric nervous system is also a vast chemical warehouse within which is represented every one of the classes of neurotransmitter found in the brain, Neurotransmitters are the words nerve cells use for communicating with one another and with the cells under their control.'

The function of the gut at one end of the digestive system is influenced by nutritional input at the other end. In terms of the body's chemical status, we are what we eat. The body's needs from one day to the next are influenced by genes, climate, environment, and the demands of daily living. In the wealthy countries of the world, we do not tend to think of malnutrition, but the growing problems of obesity and food intolerance are also forms of malnutrition.

This subject is covered in more detail in one of my earlier books, *The Well Balanced Child*.[14] An extract from the chapter on feeding is included below.

Fads and fashions often turn a complete circle with the passage of time. At the beginning of the twenty-first century, we are just emerging from a period of being told that a low fat diet is good for the heart, but new findings are beginning to contradict this rather simplistic view. It is now being discovered that certain individuals who eat a diet with a relatively high fat content actually have lower cholesterol levels. The general consensus at the time of writing is that a healthy diet is not composed of 'good' and 'bad' foods, but rather depends on a balance between different food groups, different types of fat, climate, and life-style.

Protein and amino acids play a vital role in the expression of genes while fats provide a major constituent of nervous system tissue. Certain fats are important for the development of brain and body tissue. 'The building of brain tissue demands a one-to-one balance between Omega-3 and Omega-6 fatty acids. Omega-3 fatty acids are relatively scarce in the land food chain, but predominate in the marine food chain'[15]. The modern diet heavy in processed foods and animal fats is biased in favour of Omega-6 fatty acids with the typical American diet being estimated as comprising a 6:1 ration of Omega-6 to Omega-3 fatty acids. Essential fatty acids are necessary in helping to form the membrane barrier that surrounds the cells, the myelin sheath – the fatty coating that surrounds certain nerve pathways facilitating faster transmission of information along the nerve fibre – and preventing interference or 'cross chatter' from neighbouring pathways.

Micro-nutrients such as zinc, calcium, magnesium, manganese and selenium play a crucial part in how the body absorbs and uses nutrients and for the synthesis of essential fatty acids which also act as precursors to hormones. Deficiency in one area can result in a surfeit elsewhere. Calcium for example, helps to prevent lead levels building up; when calcium levels are low, lead levels tend to rise and vice-versa. Zinc helps to protect against raised levels of aluminium and is involved in maintaining the correct ratio of zinc to copper in the blood. Low zinc levels can affect wound healing, appetite, as in anorexia, and also taste, resulting in a child who will only eat a narrow range of bland foods, and who refuses to try the very food groups that would help overcome the underlying deficiency. Modern processed foods such as white bread and sugar lose much of their zinc content during processing.

Fatty Acids and Brain Development

Animal life first originated in the sea, where there was an abundance of Omega-3 fatty acids. These are the same fatty acids that now form the essential components of the photoreceptors of the eyes and the brain's cell membranes. The membranes of neurons are made up of a thin double layer of fatty acid molecules, which the brain uses to assemble the special types of fat it incorporates into its cell membranes. *Myelin* is also made up of at least 70% fat of which the most common fatty acid is oleic acid. (Oleic acid is abundant in human breast milk).

Anomalies in the availability and metabolism of fatty acids have been implicated in lower educational performance, hyperactivity, depression Alzheimer's and Parkinson's disease and Schizophrenia. Interestingly at least 3 of these conditions have also been linked to abnormalities in the availability of dopamine – a neurotransmitter involved in the regulation of motor movements and reward centres in the brain.

David Horrobin in his book The Madness of Adam and Eve[16] suggested that fats, particularly fatty acids found in abundance in coastal regions where inhabitants have a large proportion of marine food in their diet probably played a major role in human evolution. 'We became human because of quite small genetic changes of the fat inside our skulls . . . the brain is an organ which is mostly made of fat and requires a lot of energy to run. Although by weight it is only about 2% of the body, it uses about 20% of the energy. I believe that the rich food supplies of the aquatic/marginal environment, together with mutations of lipid metabolism which enabled

Myelin – the white cells composed of lipids and proteins that form a protective sheath around some types of nerve fibres and help facilitate electrical impulse transmission. Myelin also acts as an electrical insulator, increasing the efficiency of nerve conduction and preventing interference or 'cross chatter' from neighbouring pathways.

the brain to change and become more effective were the prime causes which allowed the development of hunting and all its associated skills. These food supplies also allowed our guts to become smaller as our brain grew.'

Omega-3 fats are necessary for the complete development of the human brain during pregnancy and the first two years of life. 'The Omega-3 fat and its derivative, DHA (docosahexaenoic acid), is so essential to a child's development that if a mother and infant are deficient in it, the child's nervous system and immune system may never fully develop, and it can cause a lifetime of unexplained emotional, learning, and immune system disorders.'[17]

Researchers in Adelaide, Australia, have suggested that fish oil supplements may be better than Ritalin in treating attention deficit hyperactivity disorder (ADHD). 'It is estimated that 5–10% of school-age children (mostly boys) in Europe suffer from ADHD. Comparative figures for the USA and Australia are 3–7% and 11%. Major symptoms of the disorder are difficulty in sustaining attention, hyperactivity, and impulsivity. ADHD is also associated with learning difficulties in reading, spelling, and math and may involve psychiatric problems that follow the child into adulthood. There is considerable evidence that ADHD is linked to a fatty acid deficiency or imbalance. Long-chain fatty acids such as eicosapentaenoic acid (EPA) and docosahexaenoic acid (DHA) are essential to proper brain functioning and several studies involving children with ADHD have shown that they are deficient in these essential fatty acids. Researchers at the University of South Australia report that an EPA and DHA containing supplement is effective in reducing ADHD symptoms.'[18]

Other studies have found fish oils to be effective in reducing the symptoms of ADHD. Researchers at Oxford University investigated whether supplementation with fish oils would help children with developmental coordination disorder (DCD) and ADHD. 'Neurodevelopmental disorders are becoming increasingly common among school-age children. It is estimated that about 5% of British school children suffer from developmental coordination disorder (DCD), while 1–2% suffer from attention deficit/hyperactivity disorder syndrome (ADHD). In the United States the prevalence of ADHD is estimated at 4%. DCD is characterized by problems with motor function (manual dexterity, ball skills and balance) and difficulties in learning, behavioural problems, and lack of social skills. The main symptoms of ADHD are cognitive problems (problems with thinking, learning and remembering), hyperactivity, anxiousness, shyness, perfectionism, opposition, social problems, excessive talkativeness, restlessness and noisiness.'[19]

The clinical trial involved 100 children between the ages of 5 and 12 years who had been diagnosed with DCD and who showed symptoms of ADHD as well. The children were randomized to receive six placebo (olive oil) capsules a day or six capsules a day of an essential fatty acid (EFA) mixture. Half the children received the EFA mixture for six months, while the other half received the placebo for three months, and then the EFA mixture for the remaining three months of the trial.

Improvements in the EFA groups were substantial. While no improvement was noted in motor skills, both reading and spelling skills improved significantly. The mean increase in reading age for the first three months was 9.5 months in the EFA group versus 3.3 months in the placebo group. Similarly, the increase in spelling age during the first three months of the trial was 6.6 months in the EFA group versus 1.2 months in the placebo group. Symptoms of ADHD also showed substantial improvement, particularly in children who had exhibited hyperactivity, cognitive problems, anxiousness, and shyness. The rate of improvements noted for the first three months continued for the subsequent three months of the trial. The researchers concluded that the EFA supplement may be a safe, tolerable, and effective treatment for improving academic progress and behaviour among children with DCD (but not necessarily the impaired motor skills which are a feature of DCD).

In addition to fatty acids, certain fish oils provide an important source of vitamin D. The main source of vitamin D is through ultraviolet radiation in sunlight, although it can be supplemented from dietary sources such as cod liver oil. As mentioned in Chapter 7, vitamin D is crucial for the absorption of calcium, which is key to the formation of healthy bones. Deficiencies can lead not only to rickets, but also to poor tooth formation, stunted growth, and general ill health. People with darker skin are at greater risk of vitamin D deficiencies in cool temperate zones because increased pigmentation reduces the capacity of the skin to manufacture the vitamin from sunlight. In northern regions such as Scandinavia where levels of sunlight are low in winter, fish forms a staple part of the diet. In the UK, this is no longer the case, and rickets, which was thought to have been eliminated with generally improved diet and other signs of vitamin D deficiency, is reappearing.

Previously, hypovitaminosis D has been considered to be a public health problem that affects mainly ethnic minority groups living in Britain, but a recent study has shown that the problem is very real also among the Caucasian population. Participants living in Scotland were twice as likely to have low vitamin D concentrations compared to others, and obese participants were twice as likely to have hypovitaminosis D (less than optimal levels of vitamin D) compared to others. Vitamin D deficiency can be avoided by an outdoor lifestyle and by not being completely shielded from all sun, eating oily fish and controlling weight.[20]

A study of middle-aged British adults[20] showed that the majority, 60 per cent, has hypovitaminosis D, and 90 per cent have less than optimal levels during winter and spring. People living south of Birmingham in the UK receive just enough sunlight with sufficient strength in winter to maintain levels of vitamin D. Those living north of Birmingham do not, unless an additional dietary source is provided. As the average age of the population rises, it is possible that diseases such as osteoporosis in the aged may be linked to hypovitaminosis in earlier life, and there is some evidence to suggest that arthritis (both osteoarthritis and inflammatory types) progresses faster in people who are low in vitamin D.

The link between vitamin D and calcium absorption is important because calcium is also necessary for electrical signalling by neurons. Several different kinds of ions appear in the brain, four of which are particularly involved in electrical signalling. These are sodium, potassium, chloride, and calcium. Sodium is responsible for initiation of the nerve impulse, involved in excitatory postsynaptic potential; potassium is responsible for restoration of resting potential during nerve impulse, involved in inhibitory postsynaptic potentials; chloride is involved in inhibitory postsynaptic

potentials, and calcium is necessary for the release of neurotransmitters at the synapse. An imbalance in any of the
electrolytes can affect excitability of the nervous system,
also affecting the functioning of essential organs such as
the heart.

Eating habits are not simply about food. Many other factors
are involved, including genetic determination of metabolic
rate, early feeding patterns, diet selection, and, in some
cases, emotional problems and peer, parental, and media
pressures, all of which can influence eating *habits*. However,
food is also strongly linked to *social context*, and this is one
area over which parents and educators can exert an influence throughout the learning years by providing *regular*,
nutritionally balanced, and *supervised* meals, thereby helping
to maintain stable levels of blood sugar throughout the
day.

Maintaining a stable blood sugar level is important because
glucose is essential for cortical functioning. Foods which
have a high sugar/fat/carbohydrate content cause an
immediate and sharp rise in blood glucose and insulin levels.
If too much insulin is produced, the blood glucose falls too
low, which then results in a craving for more glucose. It is
at this stage that a child will demand a 'quick fix' snack such
as a fizzy drink, packet of crisps, or candy bar (one fizzy
drink contains the equivalent of seven teaspoons of sugar).
This will temporarily solve the immediate sugar crisis,
but a similar pattern will recur within two to three hours.
Sugar craving cycles also increase the likelihood of obesity.

It takes up to 20 minutes for the hypothalamus (a specific
area of the brain involved in the perception of hunger and
satiety, sexual behaviour, and temperature control) to register signals from the stomach and the gut, which indicate
when enough food has been eaten, and for a child to become
conscious of a sense of satiety (fullness). 'Fast' food, food
eaten 'on the hoof' and even cafeteria-style feeding can all
encourage rapid consumption, meaning that more food is
selected and eaten than is actually required *before* satiety
centres have had time to register 'enough'.

Many secondary school children in the UK start the day
without breakfast, which means that they have a low over-
night fasting level of blood glucose. The body's natural reaction to low blood sugar is to compensate *by increasing*

Adrenaline, *also* *referred to as* *epinephrine, acts* *as a stimulant to* *the sympathetic* *nervous system,* *raising blood* *pressure,* *increasing the* *amount of glucose* *in the blood, and* *constricting* *smaller blood* *vessels.*

adrenaline output. Such a biochemical combination can affect attention, concentration, and impulse control. In the long term, a pendulum pattern of high/low blood sugar levels increases irritability, fatigue, and bouts of hyperactivity, reduced energy, and impaired cooperation. Symptoms of reactive hypoglycaemia include increased nervousness, irritability, weakness, extreme hunger, sugar craving, tremors, tearfulness, impatience, headache, drowsiness, impaired concentration, dizziness, confusion, fainting, and, in extreme cases, seizures.

Evidence supports the theory that obesity is invariably associated with insulin resistance.[21] Insulin resistance describes the body's inability to respond to and use the insulin it produces, resulting in a condition in which the blood glucose level remains higher than it should despite increased insulin secretion. Increased insulin secretion in response to food and food-related cues, which is thought to take place more in obese than in non-obese individuals, renders them more sensitive to sensations of hunger, with a tendency to eat more of the very food groups which ultimately exacerbate the problem. Rapidly changing blood sugar levels can also affect the body's ability to respond to insulin in the long term, which may be one reason why children of 10 and 12 years of age in the UK are now developing the type of diabetes which used to be found only in middle-aged adults.

Food allergies and intolerances (which are often a symptom of depleted vitamins, minerals, and EFAs needed for proper synthesis and absorption), or overconsumption of a particular food type, result in the release of opiate-like substances into the bloodstream, resulting in a child who feels, and often behaves, as if mildly 'stoned', affecting motivation, concentration, and learning.

A history of allergies, impaired immune functioning, excessive fatigue with dark circles under the eyes, and poor impulse control in the absence of obvious causal factors may all point to underlying nutritional imbalance which, in an ideal world, should be investigated and corrected by a doctor specializing in nutritional and environmental medicine. While this is often not possible within a general educational setting, there is much that could be done to reduce the amount of 'junk' food consumed and to ensure that the child eats at regular intervals.

The brain is often likened to a computer, but the human brain is far more than this. It is also a chemical factory, which responds to all the physical functions of the body affecting general well being, thoughts, moods, and performance. The mind – the product of the relationship between the brain and body and its interaction with the environment – cannot be separated from the chemical status of the body from one moment to the next. Because electrical communication within the nervous system is dependent on the release of neurotransmitters and nutrition provides the building blocks for many of the substances that ultimately make up neurotransmitters, nutritional status can affect concentration, intelligence, attention span, problem solving, and emotional lability.

USE OF PHYSICAL TESTS TO ASSESS NEUROLOGICAL READINESS IN SCHOOLS

The authors acknowledge that abnormal primitive and postural reflexes are not present in *all* children with specific learning difficulties and behavioural or emotional problems, and that the aetiology of these disorders is multifactorial. Nevertheless, within modern education, there is often a greater willingness to assume that the environment and/or social factors must be the primary causes of specific learning difficulties rather than being willing to investigate whether the child has the physical equipment necessary to achieve. Superficially, manipulating the learning environment of the child appears to be an easier option than correcting underlying problems of a physical nature, but in the longer term, this is not always the case. This does not mean to say that specialist teaching is not also essential to provide support for learning deficits that have arisen as a result of environmental factors, and to support students who have had learning difficulties as a result of physical problems in the past. Neuro-developmental therapy does not seek to replace specialist or supportive teaching in any way. However, teaching could become more effective if equal attention is given to identifying and resolving underlying physical problems.

A neuro-developmental approach and special educational measures are not mutually exclusive.

The following illustrations show examples of children's drawing of the human figure before and after the use of the INPP Developmental Exercises in schools. This is a programme of developmental exercises adapted to be used in schools for 10 minutes per day over the course of one academic year.[22] In the following examples, two drawings are shown for each child. The first drawing was carried out at the beginning of the school year, before the INPP exercises were introduced; the second drawing was done eight to nine months later, as the class was nearing the end of the exercise programme. Both drawings have a score of 'neurological readiness' based on the physical tests carried out at the beginning and at the end of the programme, and a percentile score for the drawing of the human figure (a measure of non-verbal cognitive performance).

The physical tests were carried out using The INPP Test Battery for Schools.[22] This comprises simple tests for balance, coordination, and three primitive reflexes (ATNR, STNR, and TLR), which have consistently been shown to be present in a high percentage of children with specific learning difficulties. Each test is scored using a rating scale of 0–4:

0 = no abnormality detected (NAD);
1 = 25 per cent dysfunction (e.g. traces of a primitive reflex evident or minor problem with tests for balance and coordination);
2 = 50 per cent dysfunction;
3 = 75 per cent dysfunction;
4 = 100 per cent dysfunction (e.g. primitive reflex fully retained, or child cannot maintain balance on one of the balance tests).

At the end of the assessment, the child's individual scores are added up to achieve an individual score out of a possible total score of 40. This provides an indication of each child's level of physical maturity. A score of 0/40 shows that physical maturity is commensurate with chronological age (CA). Scores of greater than 10/40 indicate a significant degree of physical immaturity.

Figures 11.5–11.8 show the changes in both neurological and percentile scores before and after using the physical programme with a group of 8- to 10-year-old children in a mainstream school in the north of England.

The combined use of pre- and post-test neurological scores with percentile scores enables the teacher to identify chil-

Figure 11.5 Child 1.

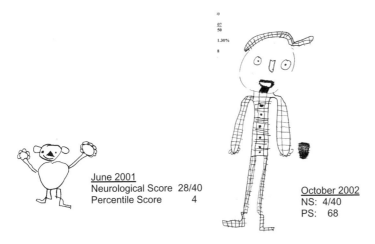

Figure 11.6 Child 2

dren who might be underachieving as a result of neurological immaturity. Figure 11.5 shows a child whose neurological score at the time of the first assessment indicates more than 50 per cent immaturity on the balance and reflex tests (21/40). The child's performance on the Draw-a-Person Test

---

[ii] Figures 11.5–11.8 reproduced with permission from Goddard Blythe SA. 2004. *The Well Balanced Child*. Hawthorn Press, Stroud.

June 2001
Neurological Score 23/40
Percentile Score   68

October 2002
Neurological Score 3.5/40
Percentile Score   99

Figure 11.7   Child 3

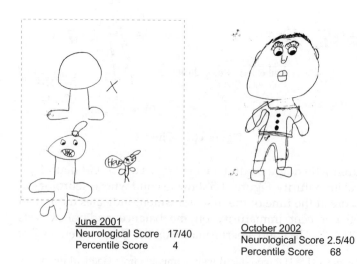

June 2001
Neurological Score   17/40
Percentile Score   4

October 2002
Neurological Score 2.5/40
Percentile Score   68

Figure 11.8   Child 4

(non-verbal cognitive performance) is on the low end of the percentile scale (14). Eight months later, the score for neurological dysfunction has decreased to 2/40, and performance on the Draw-a-Person Test has increased to 77. The improvement on the percentile scale indicates that in this case, something in addition to simply improving balance and coordination has taken place.

Child 2 had a significantly high score on the tests for neurological immaturity (28/40) and low performance on the Draw-a-Person Test (4) at the first assessment. This child had previously been identified as being in need of additional educational support. Following eight months on a physical programme, the Draw-a-Person Test still reveals some immaturity, but there is significantly improved performance on both the neurological tests (4/40) and the Draw-a-Person Test (68).

Child 3's drawings have been included to illustrate how combining neurological and cognitive tests can help to identify not only the children who are performing below their CA, but also children who are *underachieving*. Despite having a significant score on the neurological tests at the first assessment (23/40), because this child's performance on the Draw-a-Person Test was within an acceptable range (percentile score of 68), he or she could easily have been overlooked as not having any problems. However, the second drawing provides an example of how an intelligent child has learned to 'compensate' for underlying immaturities producing 'adequate' results while not performing to potential, in other words, underachieving. In this case, when neurological dysfunction was corrected (3.5/40), performance on the Draw-a-Person Test increased to above average (percentile score of 99).

Child 4 was in the same year group as Figures 11.5–11.7. He or she had also been identified as having special needs prior to assessment using the INPP tests. Note how this child's neurological score is not as high as some of the previous examples, where performance on the Draw-a-Person Test was higher despite significant neurological scores, indicating that there is probably more involved in this child's difficulties than just immature physical skills. In other words, in this case, the reflex abnormalities do not account for *all* of the presenting educational difficulties. Nevertheless, the neurological score was responsive to physical intervention, and although the Draw-a-Person Test still shows signs of immaturity at the second assessment for a child of 8–10 years of age, it has improved significantly.

Other schools using the INPP Developmental Programme have simply assessed the changes in scores using the Draw-a-Man test (Aston Index) before and after use of the exercise programme in school. Figures 11.9–11.11 show the increase in mental age (MA) on the Draw-a-Man Test compared to CA before and after using the programme for eight to nine months.

The results from use of The INPP Test Battery and Developmental Exercise Programme in Schools[23] and others[24] indicate that neurological immaturity confirmed by the presence of a cluster of abnormal primitive and postural reflexes in the school-aged child *is* responsive to specific developmental exercises carried out on a daily basis in many cases. Despite the growing body of evidence to support the use of developmental exercises on an individual basis or in schools, at the time of writing, these findings are still controversial, and the changes seen in reflex status, balance, and coordination,

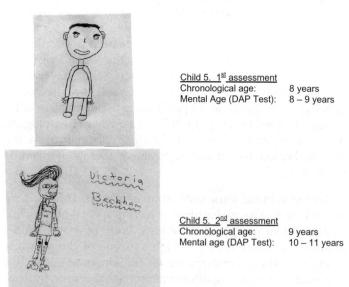

Child 5. 1st assessment
Chronological age: 8 years
Mental Age (DAP Test):   8 – 9 years

Child 5. 2nd assessment
Chronological age: 9 years
Mental age (DAP Test):   10 – 11 years

Figure 11.9   Child 5. Change in score for MA compared to CA before and after using the INPP (School) Exercise Programme. DAP, Draw a Person

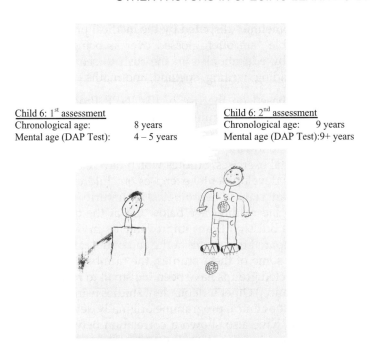

Child 6: 1st assessment
Chronological age: 8 years
Mental age (DAP Test):   4 – 5 years

Child 6: 2nd assessment
Chronological age: 9 years
Mental age (DAP Test):9+ years

Figure 11.10   Child 6. Change in score for MA compared to CA before and after using the INPP (School) Exercise Programme

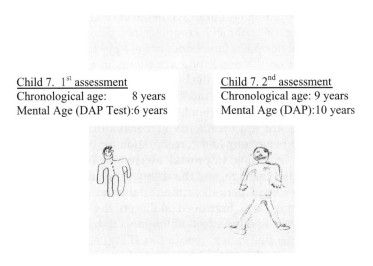

Child 7. 1st assessment
Chronological age: 8 years
Mental Age (DAP Test):6 years

Child 7. 2nd assessment
Chronological age: 9 years
Mental Age (DAP):10 years

Figure 11.11   Child 7. Change in score for MA compared to CA before and after using the INPP (School) Exercise Programme

while still sometimes disputed by the medical profession as being 'possible', are often glossed over as being of minor importance by educationists in the rush to see immediate effects on reading, writing, spelling, and maths.

All studies based on the use of the INPP Programme in Schools have shown significant improvement in tests for reflexes, balance, and coordination, and in the Draw-a-Person Test following the use of a daily programme of developmental exercises. Studies which have examined the effects of the developmental exercises on children who had both significant signs of neurological immaturity (more than 25 per cent) *and* reading age below CA at the outset have shown small but significant improvements in reading and spelling compared to controls at the end of the experimental period.[21] (In some of these studies, the numbers of participants in selected groups have been too small to reach statistical significance.) Other independent studies using exercises based upon the clinical programme originally devised by Dr Peter Blythe have also shown a correlation between reflex integration and improved reading scores.[22]

One of the problems in gaining recognition for the role of abnormal reflexes in educational underachievement, and the value of developmental perceptual-motor training programmes, may be because there tends to be an expectation of an immediate one-to-one relationship between motor-perceptual training and improvements in reading, spelling, handwriting, or arithmetic competencies. Successful remediation of abnormal reflexes does not always have an *immediate* impact on the presenting symptoms in the classroom but rather puts into place the building blocks that are necessary for academic achievement in the longer term. The first changes reported by schools using the INPP Schools' Programme are improvements in behaviour, particularly playground behaviour, and consideration for others; spatial awareness, including improved awareness of social distance, posture, carriage, and the ability to sit still; the ability to write for longer periods without the hand getting tired, neater writing, and improved skills on the sports field; self-confidence and increased willingness to try again if not successful the first time;[25] reading, spelling, and maths are usually the last things to show signs of improvement, and these continue for sometime *after* the programme has been concluded. In other words, improved physical skills need to be in place for some time before changes are seen in classroom measures of attainment on literacy and numeracy.

A study carried out at Swanwick School in Derbyshire[26] involving 93 children tested all children using The INPP Test Battery at the beginning of the project and then divided the participants into three groups:

1. Group 1 carried out the INPP Developmental Exercises every day in school under teacher supervision for one academic year (experimental group).
2. Group 2 carried out non-specific physical exercises [similar to physical education (PE) exercises] for the same time period each day as the experimental group.
3. Group 3 did not carry out physical exercises on a daily basis, but followed the normal PE syllabus.

The INPP neurological tests were carried out on all children at the end of the school year, and mean total scores for the neurological tests were calculated. Figure 11.12 shows the difference in mean scores between groups at the beginning and at the end of the school year.

The neurological scores of children in all three groups decreased over the course of the school year, showing that physical development continues to progress as part of normal development. The children who carried out non-

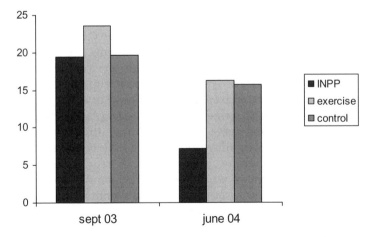

Figure 11.12 Changes in mean scores for neurological tests. Swanwick School, Derbyshire

specific physical exercises on a daily basis made almost twice as much improvement (decrease) in positive neurological scores compared to the children who did no formal daily exercises, indicating that regular exercise is important for maintaining and improving developmental 'fitness' for learning. However, the general exercise group made only *half* as much improvement as the children who carried out the specific developmental exercises, suggesting that the most improvement is achieved when physical exercise is matched to the developmental needs of the group.

The significance of these findings was summarized by a retired paediatrician in the north of England when he said that, 'as doctors, we used to carry out many of these tests as part of routine medical assessments on children more than 30 years ago. We then entered an era of evidence based medicine, when in addition to showing that a problem had been identified, it also became necessary to be able to provide an effective remedy. Because, at that time, we often did not know how to help children who failed these basic physical tests, routine testing was gradually phased out.'[27] He went on to say that 'children learn with the body not just with the brain. Because the Education Department is so focused on *cognitive* learning and the Health Service on *disease*, we have missed out on this vital transitional phase. This programme provides physical education in its truest sense.'[28]

The same delineation of professional domains has resulted in the child with neurological dysfunction often falling through the net of those professional services supposed to be in place to identify, assess, and provide effective remedial intervention. Children with severe problems are usually identified and treated within the health service, but those with mild to moderate dysfunction simply slip through the net and are not recognized as being in need of either investigation or support from the health service. (A child with a 30-decibel hearing curve would fall into this category.) While other services allied to medicine may be brought in such as physiotherapy, occupational therapy, or speech therapy, at the time of writing, in the UK, families can wait up to three years for assessment and intervention from these services, not because the individual professions are not aware of the need, but because of the way that these services are financed, allocated and managed, these children are not considered to be a priority. Physical or occupational therapy, when available, is often given in group sessions of one hour, once a week, over a period of six to eight weeks. Children make definite progress during and following intervention, but in many cases the intervention is not carried on for long enough for improvements to be sustained over time.

There are also important differences between the INPP programmes and other motor training programmes in the developmental level at which the physical exercises begin. For instance, movement programmes such as sensory integration (SI), developed by A. Jean Ayres, used by many occupational therapists specifically trained in the use of SI, work on principles of development and modulation through sensory-motor training. If there is over- or under-arousal in one sensory mode, stimulation of another sense can be used to calm or to excite. For example, proprioceptive stimulation can be used to dampen hyperarousal of the vestibular system; vestibular stimulation can be used to improve motor skills, etc. Clinical observation of patients seen at INPP in Chester and in Chicago indicates that while SI can be very effective in stimulating the postural reflexes and in improving balance, coordination, and self-confidence, abnormal primitive reflexes (developmentally earlier reflexes) sometimes remain active and continue to undermine academic performance.

Many other motor training programmes begin with balance training in the erect or quadruped position. These programmes appear to be successful in improving postural control, once again by stimulating postural reflexes and helping the cerebellum to function more efficiently. If this is the level from which the child's balance dysfunction stems, then these programmes will be successful. If, however, a cluster of primitive reflexes are present, although new skills emerge as a result of training, they do not necessarily become *integrated* and in these cases specific learning difficulties are likely to persist.

In other words, there are, in our view, no single 'miracle' cures for specific learning difficulties using motor-perceptual training programmes. Rather, there are many different methods of intervention which can be successful *if the intervention is matched to the developmental needs of the child*. Testing of primitive reflexes is useful in this respect, because primitive reflexes provide some of the earliest developmental markers of maturity in the control of balance, posture, motor skills, and the functioning of the CNS. As stated earlier, there are key stages in development when primitive reflexes should be present, when they should be inhibited, and when postural reflexes should develop. Reflex testing therefore provides a method whereby the trained professional can investigate whether the inner world of the child (CNS) is commensurate with CA, enabling the child to meet the expectations of the external world. It also provides evidence with which to decide what type and level of remedial intervention is suitable for the individual child.

Neuro-developmental assessment does not seek to replace the important role of the educational psychologist in assessing cognitive abilities and performance. Rather, it helps to explain in some cases when a specific learning difficulty has been identified *why* significant discrepancies show up on the Wechsler Intelligence Scale for Children (WISC); for example, if the ATNR is present – affecting visual-motor integration – it may explain why there are discrepancies between a child's verbal and performance score on the WISC; or, if vestibular and visual-perceptual problems have been identified on the INPP clinical assessment, why the child has problems with spatial tasks such as block design and picture assembly. Increased cooperation between professions investigating cognitive performance can only be in the long-term interest of the child as the source of various problems can be identified and remedial intervention can be aimed at the affected area(s).

APPLICATION OF THE INPP METHOD

Clinical assessment using the INPP Method is carried out on an individual basis and uses a range of tests to assess

- static balance;
- dynamic balance;
- soft signs of neurological dysfunction;
- cerebellar involvement;
- dysdiadochokinesia;
- primitive reflexes;
- postural reflexes;
- laterality;
- oculomotor functioning;
- visual perception;
- writing and copying;
- Draw-a-Person Test;
- audiometric assessment.

An individual programme of exercises designed to provide vestibular training and reflex stimulation and inhibition is prescribed on the basis of the individual assessment. Exercises must be carried out *every* day for an average of 12 months. The reflex profile is reassessed every eight weeks and the exercise programme adjusted according to progress.

The majority of exercises are based on infant movement patterns made during the first year of life, at the time when the primitive reflexes are normally inhibited. Exercises are based upon Blythe's theory of *replication*; that is, 'It is possible to give the brain a second chance to *register* the inhibitory movement patterns which should have been made at the appropriate stage of development, or, to recapitulate a stage of development which may have been omitted, or not completed during intra-uterine life, birth or infancy. All human babies make certain stereotyped movements during the first year of life.[29] These movements contain with them the natural antidote to the appropriate reflex at that stage in development, thus facilitating inhibition of a primitive reflex on the one hand, and the subsequent release of a postural reflex on the other.'[30] Because most infants do not learn to stand and walk until *after* the majority of primitive reflexes have been inhibited, usually from 9–12 months of age, the movement patterns used in the INPP clinical programme are largely floor-based exercises, which concentrate on training balance through the earliest developmental stages of movement capability.

The INPP Programme for Schools trains teachers how to administer a shortened battery of tests to identify children for whom retained reflexes and immature balance and coordination present. The intervention programme uses exercises put together in a developmental sequence, which can be used with a class of children or with selected groups. Teachers pace the programme according to the needs of the group but do not select individual exercises.

THE NEURO-EDUCATOR

The concept of neurological readiness for education is not new. The Quick Neurological Screening Test (QNST) was published 30 years ago in 1978. In their introduction, the authors of the QNST explained how this brief (approximately 20 minutes) individual test was designed to 'tap neurological integration as it relates to learning,'[31] and to 'enable a lay person to distinguish between normal and abnormal characteristics likely to affect the processes of learning and behaviour.'[31] When my eldest son was due to start school in the mid 1980s, all children in the UK were seen by the school doctor as a matter of routine for a pre-school medical examination. This involved standing on one leg, hopping to one end of the room and back, stacking a pile of bricks, etc., together with basic tests to assess eyesight and hearing. Since 1989, there has been a move away from routine developmental checks on all children to 'a more holistic, educational and problem solving approach to the needs of the child and the family.'[32] In effect, this has meant that many children who do not show up as having a medical problem simply slip through the net and are lost in the gaps between medicine, education and educational psychology. Failure to detect developmental disorders at an early stage can result in failure of early interventions.[33]

The overview of the Child Health Promotion Programme at the pre-school check (when it is carried out) should ideally ensure that appropriate interventions are available for any physical, developmental, or emotional problems that had previously been missed or had not been addressed. However, as the pre-school check is no longer carried out as a matter for routine but only on certain groups (for example, children in foster care, under the care of social services, or children already in contact with primary healthcare teams), the children who have not already been identified continue to remain 'lost in the system'.

In 1981, William Cruickshank wrote a paper entitled 'A New Perspective in Teacher Education. The Neuro-educator', in which he proposed that there was a need for a new profession trained to identify, assess, refer, and provide effective remedial intervention, and which bridged the existing gaps at the time between education, medicine and psychology. He said that 'Learning disabilities are inherent within the human organism. They are not something external to it. This being the case, the individual (neuro-educator) must understand the totality of *human anatomy* . . . since learning difficulties are, if correctly defined, neurological in nature, the student must have a solid course in *human neurology* and thus be able to understand the function of the neurological system . . . , and the student needs a course in *human neuro-physiology*.[34] All of these should be aimed at providing the neuro-educator with an understanding of physiological processes in relation to the development of the embryonic and foetal stages of human growth and how they relate to learning. He pointed out that, 'We do not and have not ever stated that there is a one to one relationship between perceptual-motor training and reading, spelling, handwriting or arithmetic competencies. From our clinical observations, however, there is a very real relationship in many children with learning disabilities between their motor deficiencies and their self-concepts'.[32]

ATTENTION, BALANCE, AND COORDINATION

Attention (linked to the French word meaning to stop) is the ability to direct and to maintain mental and physical faculties on one task while ceasing to attend to irrelevant environmental stimuli. This requires the ability to keep still, focused, and also poised or ready to respond to other stimuli if needed. It involves the ability to separate foreground from background and to selectively direct attention from one to the other. Although this is ultimately a conscious, cortically controlled ability, it requires the support of physical functions to facilitate it.

Visual attention, for example, involves the ability to maintain clear focus at one visual distance, e.g. near distance, while clear focus for information outside of the immediate point of visual attention recedes. Figure-ground problems occur when background information vies or interferes with foreground or vice versa. Clinical examples of this can be seen when a child is asked to visually 'fixate' on a stationary object at near distance, but he or she is unable to maintain visual attention because he or she is distracted by visual information in the background. Adults who have this problem describe experiencing acute anxiety when faced with visual information which requires depth perception such as having to walk across a slatted footbridge where there are spaces between the planks, or to climb a staircase where they can see the gaps between the treads.

attention deficit disorder (ADD) occurs when a person is unable to occlude irrelevant environmental stimuli to select and to maintain attention on one task. The term attention *deficit* disorder is misleading in this respect, because the deficit in ADD is specifically in *selective* attention, not in general attention. People with ADD usually pay attention to too many things at the same time, including, in some cases, their own bodily sensations.

Balance is the ability to hold stability and 'stillness' within the body, poised to respond in any way that is needed to changes in body position or to the environment. Balance and posture are interdependent, and both rely on integration and maturation of the underlying reflex system to function at a preconscious level. They provide the basis for being able to sit still, inhibit body movements to support concentration as well as the control of eye movements necessary for coordination, reading, and writing. Together, they provide the framework in which coordination can take place.

Coordination (formerly written as co-ordination, meaning 'to ordain together') is the outward expression of inner organization in terms of centres involved in balance, posture, and movement control all working together. Coordination affects skills at many levels – both gross and fine muscle – dexterity and adroitness. Problems with coordination both reflect and undermine the relationship between brain and body, resulting in discrepancy between intention and performance. In this sense, *attention, balance,* and *coordination* are the primary alphabet every child needs to have in order to be 'ready' to learn. This ABC of the body is but the beginning of learning success.

REFERENCES

1 American Speech-Language-Hearing Association. 2006. www.asha.org/members/deskref-journals/deskref/default. Ref. adapted from *Handbook of Auditory Processing Disorder*. Comprehensive Intervention Vol. 2, p. 3.
2 Madaule P. 2001. Seminar on The Ear-Voice Connection, November 2001. Chester.
3 Madaule P. 1994. *When Listening Comes Alive*. Moulin Publishing, Norval, Ontario.
4 Tomatis A. 1991. *The Conscious Ear*. The Talman Company, New York.

5 Berard G. 1993. *Hearing Equals Behaviour.* Keats Publishing Inc., New Canaan, CT.

6 Shaywitz SE. 1996. Dyslexia. *Scientific American,* November 1996, pp. 98–104.

7 Tallal P et al. 1996. Language comprehension in language-learning impaired children improved with acoustically modifed speech. *Science* 271:81–84.

8 Johansen KV. 2002. Dyslexia, auditory laterality and hemispheric-specific auditory stimulation. *Nordisk Tidsskrift for Spesialpedagogikk* 80:258–271..

9 The Listening Fitness Trainer (LiFT). www.listeningfitness. com

10 Goddard Blythe SA. 2008. *What Babies and Children Really Need. How Mothers and Fathers Can Nurture Children's Growth for Health and Well Being.* Hawthorn Press, Stroud.

11 ARROW. http://www.self-voice.co.uk/

12 Biederman H. 1992. Kinematic imbalance due to suboccipital strain. *Journal of Manual Medicine* 6:151–156.

13 Gershon MD. 1998. *The Second Brain. The Scientific Basis of Gut Instinct.* Harper Collins, New York.

14 Goddard Blythe SA. 2004. *The Well Balanced Child.* Hawthorn Press, Stroud.

15 Crawford M. 1994. Cited in: Morgan E. 1994. *The Descent of the Child.* Souvenir Press, London.

16 Horrobin D. 2001. *The Madness of Adam and Eve. How Schizophrenia Shaped Humanity.* Corgi Books, London.

17 Finnegan J. 1993. The vital role of essential fatty acids for pregnant and nursing women. *Celestial Arts.* http://www.thorne. com/townsend/dec/efas.html

18 Sinn N, Bryan J. 2007. Effect of supplementation with polyunsaturated fatty acids and micronutrients on learning and behavior problems associated with child ADHD. *Journal of Developmental and Behavioral Pediatrics* 28:82–91.

19 Richardson AJ, Montgomery P. 2005. The Oxford–Durham study: a randomized, controlled trial of dietary supplementation with fatty acids in children with developmental coordination disorder. *Pediatrics* 115:1360–1366.

20 Hyppönen E, Power C. 2007. Hypovitaminosis D in British adults at age 45y: nationwide cohort study on dietary and lifestyle predictors. *American Journal of Clinical Nutrition* 85/3: 860–868.

21 Boden G. 2001. Free fatty acids (FFA) – the link between obesity and insulin resistance. *Endocrine Practice* 7/1:44–51.

22 Goddard Blythe SA. 1996. *The Developmental Test Battery and Exercise Programme for Use in Schools with Children with Special Needs.* The Institute for Neuro-Physiological Psychology. Chester.

23 Goddard Blythe SA. 2005. Releasing educational potential through movement. A summary of individual studies carried

out using the INPP Test Battery and Developmental Exercise Programme for use in Schools with Children with Special Needs. *Child Care in Practice* 11/4:415–432.

24 McPhillips M et al. 2000. Effects of replicating primary reflex movements on specific reading difficulties in children: a randomised, double-blind, controlled trial. *Lancet* 355/2:537–541.

25 Smith G. 2006. In: Learn to move, move to learn. St Aidan's School Sports Partnership. Inspiring Partnerships. DVD produced by Youth Sport Trust. Learning Through Sharing Publication Series. http://www.youthsporttrust.org/

26 Micklethwaite J. 2004. A report of a study into the efficacy of the INPP School Programme at Swanwick Primary School, Derbyshire. A controlled study of 93 children. Department for Education and Employment Best Practice Scholarship. http://www.teachernet.gov.uk/, December 2004.

27 Paynter A. 2003. Personal communication.

28 Paynter A. 2006. In: Learn to move, move to learn. St Aidan's School Sports Partnership. Inspiring Partnerships. DVD produced by Youth Sport Trust. Learning Through Sharing Publication Series. http://www.youthsporttrust.org/

29 Thelan E. 1979. Rhythmical stereotypes on normal human infants. *Animal Behaviour* 27:699–715.

30 Goddard SA. 1990. *The Developmental Basis for Learning Difficulties and Language Disorders*. INPP Monograph Series 1/1990.

31 Mutti M et al. 1978. *QNST Quick Neurological Screening Test*. Academic Therapy Publications. Inc., Novato, CA.

32 http://www.patient.co.uk/

33 Tebruegge M et al. 2004. Does routine child health surveillance contribute to the early detection of children with pervasive developmental disorders? An epidemiological study in Kent, U.K. *BMC Pediatrics* 3/4:4. [abstract]

34 Cruickshank WM. 1981. A new perspective in teacher education: the neuroeducator. *Journal of Learning Disabilities* 14/6:337–341, 367.

SCREENING FOR NEUROLOGICAL DYSFUNCTION IN THE SPECIFIC LEARNING DIFFICULTY CHILD

Abridged version of study originally published in *The British Journal of Occupational Therapy*, October 1998

ABSTRACT

A developmental questionnaire was given to the parents of 140 children. Seventy of the children had a history of specific learning difficulties, which had not responded to normal remedial education. The remaining 70 had no history of specific learning difficulties. The research was undertaken to ascertain whether the developmental questionnaire could be used as a reliable instrument to detect the neuro-developmental delay (NDD) underlying the specific learning difficulties and preventing remedial intervention from being effective.

The results revealed that the screening questionnaire did discriminate between the two populations. At a 98 per cent confidence level, a child with a score of 7 or more belonged to the specific learning difficulty group, and a child scoring

2 or less did not. A score of 7 or more is therefore necessary to identify a neuro-developmentally based specific learning difficulty. The two populations were also compared on individual questions to identify which early developmental factors were significant in predicting later learning difficulties when viewed as part of a developmental profile.

INTRODUCTION

It is a recognized fact that the majority of specific learning difficulties[i] have their origin in neurological dysfunction and that neurological dysfunction will affect various aspects of development. Dyslexia is one such developmental disorder. The World Federation of Neurology defined dyslexia in 1968 as 'a disorder in children who, despite conventional classroom experience, fail to attain the language skills of reading, writing and spelling commensurate with their intellectual abilities.'[1]

The last 25 years of research into dyslexia have highlighted four main areas of difficulty:

1. automatic balance – the vestibular-cerebellar loop;[2–5]
2. motor skills;[6–9]
3. auditory processing;[8,10–16]
4. processing of visual information.[17–19]

Nicolson and Fawcett[20] and Nicolson et al.[21] concluded that 'children with dyslexia have deficits in phonological skill, speed of processing and motor skill. These deficits are well characterised as problems in skill automization, which are normally masked by the process of conscious compensation' (Fawcett et al. 1996, p. 280[5]). These four areas may also be linked in cases of underlying neurological dysfunction.

---

[i]Definition of specific learning difficulties in this context: dyslexia, dyspraxia, attention deficit disorder (ADD), specific writing difficulties, specific spelling difficulties, specific math difficulties, auditory discrimination and auditory processing difficulties.
The British Journal of Occupational Therapy, October 1998, 61(10).

EARLY IDENTIFICATION

There are a large number of school-aged children of average to above-average intelligence who fail to benefit from normal remedial education. Extra tuition in reading, writing, and spelling does not result in sustained improvement. In these cases, failure to respond can be the result of underlying NDD.

NDD is defined as the continued presence of a cluster of *primitive reflexes* above the age of one year, and the absence or underdevelopment of *postural reflexes* above the age of three and a half years.[6] Primitive reflexes that persist in this way and underdeveloped postural reflexes are said to be aberrant, and represent a structural weakness in the central nervous system, which will affect the development of later complex skills such as balance, motor control, oculomotor functioning, and perception.

There is evidence that NDD responds to remediation based upon a regime of physical exercises.[22-25] If NDD can be identified before a child enters junior school at around seven years of age, appropriate intervention in the form of a physical programme of remediation can be given and teaching can become effective.

With this in mind, it was decided to review the efficacy of the Blythe–McGlown Developmental Screening Questionnaire,[26] devised and used at the Institute for Neuro-Physiological Psychology (INPP), for the purpose of identifying those children whose learning difficulties stem directly from NDD. The screening questionnaire was compiled after a literature search through medical and other appropriate sources for factors that might either *cause* neurological dysfunction or *indicate* later neurological dysfunction.

Although the questionnaire has been in use for over 20 years, hitherto it has been employed as a screening device by only a small number of INPP-trained therapists in the UK and overseas who are directly involved in the testing and remediation of aberrant reflexes. The questionnaire's reliability was reassessed to determine whether it could be used more widely by other professionals involved in the diagnosis and remediation of specific learning difficulties.

AIM OF THE STUDY

The aim of the study was to compare the developmental history of a group of children with specific learning difficulties with that of a group of children with no specific learning difficulties, to see whether the INPP developmental questionnaire identified a tendency towards specific learning difficulties on the basis of early developmental history.

METHOD

A developmental questionnaire comprising 26 criteria (Table A.1[26]) was given to the parents of 70 children who had a history of specific learning difficulties who had failed to respond to remedial intervention and to the parents of 70 children who had no history of specific learning difficulties.

Answers were categorised into yes/no; for example, later than 16 months in learning to walk would be categorised as yes.

The specific learning difficulty group was selected at random from several hundred questionnaires returned to INPP by parents who had sought advice from INPP for their child's problem. The control group was selected from a Cheshire primary school, with the consent of the headmistress and the parents. In every case, the questionnaire was completed by the parents.

Seventy children were then selected for the control group on the basis of three questions:

1. Does your child have any history of reading difficulties?
2. Does your child have any history of writing difficulties?
3. Does your child have any history of copying difficulties?

Only those children who had *no* history of either reading, writing, or copying difficulties were included in the no specific learning difficulty group. All the children in both groups were between 8 and 10 years of age.

Table A.1   The Developmental Screening Questionnaire[26]

1. Is there any history of learning difficulties in your immediate family?

2. Were there any medical problems during your pregnancy?

3. Was the birth process unusual or prolonged in any way?

4. Was your child born early or late for term? (more than 2 weeks early or more than 10 days late)

5. What was your child's weight at birth? (less than 5 lb = low birth weight).

6. Did your child have any difficulty feeding in the first weeks of life, or in keeping food down?

7. Was your child extremely demanding in the first 6 months of life?

8. Did your child miss out the motor stages of crawling on his or her tummy and creeping on hands and knees?

9. At what age did your child learn to walk? (16 months or later would be considered late.)

10. At what age did your child learn to talk? (two to three word phrases at 18 months or later would be considered late.)

11. Did your child have difficulty in, for example, learning to dress himself or herself, do up buttons or tie shoelaces beyond the age of 6–7 years?

12. Does your child suffer from allergies?

13. Did your child have an adverse reaction to any of his or her vaccinations?

14. Did he or she suck his or her thumb up to age of 5 years or beyond?

15. Did your child continue to wet the bed, albeit occasionally, above the age of 5 years?

16. Does your child suffer from travel sickness?

17. Has your child found it very difficult to learn to tell the time from a traditional clock?

18. Did your child have an unusual degree of difficulty learning to ride a bicycle?

19. Did your child suffer from frequent ear, nose, throat, or chest infections?

20. In the first 3 years of life, did your child suffer from any illnesses involving extremely high temperature, delirium, or convulsions?

21. Does your child have difficulty catching a ball and stand out as 'awkward' in PE classes?

22. Does your child have difficulty sitting still for even a short period of time?

23. If there is a sudden unexpected noise, does your child overreact?

24. Does your child have reading difficulties?

25. Does your child have writing difficulties?

26. Does your child have copying difficulties?

The questionnaires were then submitted to independent statistical analysis[ii] and responses to the questionnaire were compared on two fronts:

1. to see if there was a significant difference between the two populations in early developmental history; that is, did the questionnaire differentiate between those with specific learning difficulties and those without on the basis of the total score of positive responses over the 23 criteria (excluding the questions on reading, writing, and copying difficulties which were used to select the control group)?

2. examination of each criterion to determine which individual factors (questions) could be used reliably to identify a tendency towards a developmentally based learning difficulty.

ANALYSIS OF THE QUESTIONNAIRE AS A MEANS OF IDENTIFYING SPECIFIC LEARNING DIFFICULTIES

Null hypothesis (H1): There is no difference between the population means of the specific learning difficulty group and the control group in terms of the criteria used in the screening questionnaire.

Statistical test: As two sample means presumed to be drawn from normally distributed populations with equal variances were being compared, the Student t ratio two-sample test was appropriate. The test criteria were $t = 3.291$, df = 138, $p = 0.001$.

Calculation: The questionnaire consisted of 26 criteria; of these, three criteria (reading, writing, and copying difficulties) could be construed as being the definition of specific learning difficulty and thus could bias the results. For this reason, the value of t was calculated for the 23 criteria set (excluding the questions on reading, writing, and copying difficulties).

ANALYSIS OF INDIVIDUAL QUESTIONS

Null hypothesis (H1): There is a difference between the children with specific learning difficulties and those without specific learning difficulties in terms of the criteria under evaluation.

[ii] David Hyland, MSc MBA, Hyland 3, 3090 Overijse, Belgium.

Statistical test: Since the two groups were independent, and the data were in terms of frequencies in discrete categories, the chi-square test of independence was the appropriate statistical test. The test criteria were $p = 0.05$, df $= 1$, $\chi^2 = 3.841$; $p = 0.01$, df $= 1$, $\chi^2 = 6.635$.

RESULTS

Analysis of the Questionnaire

23 criteria set, $t = 5.190393$, df $= 138$, $p = 0.001$.

Since the obtained t value fell within the critical regions ($t > 3.291$ and $t < -3.291$), H0 was rejected. Thus, there was strong evidence that the screening questionnaire did identify a tendency towards specific learning difficulty.

The mean of the control group over 23 criteria was 2.93, with a standard deviation of 1.73. The mean of the specific learning difficulty group was 9.76, with a standardized deviation of 3.59. The region of uncertainty was between 2.5 and 6.4. Therefore, at a 98 per cent confidence level, a score of 7 or above was necessary to identify a child belonging to the specific learning difficulty group.

Analysis of Individual Questions

At $p = 0.05$, the following criteria viewed in isolation *did not* appear to identify a tendency towards specific learning difficulty:

- less than two weeks premature/post-mature birth;
- low birth weight;
- adverse reaction to vaccination;
- motion sickness (among this age group);
- thumb sucking up to the age of five years or beyond (Figures A.1 and A.2).

DISCUSSION

Analysis of the questionnaire on the Student t test demonstrated that the questionnaire did discriminate between the

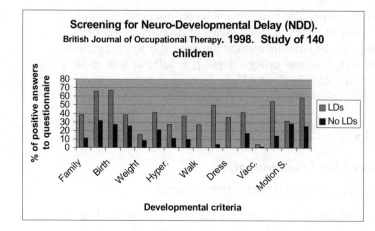

	Family	Pregnancy	Birth	Term	Weight	Feeding	Hyper.	Crawl	Walk	Talk	Dress	Allergies	Vacc.	Temps.	Motion S.	ENT
LDs	38.6	65.7	67.1	38.6	15.7	41.4	27.1	37.1	27.1	50	35.7	41.4	4.3	54.3	31.4	58.6
No LDs	11.4	31.4	27.1	25.7	8.6	21.4	11.4	10	0	4.3	0	17.1	1.4	14.3	28.6	25.7

copyright SGB 2004

Figure A.1   Differences in developmental criteria between children with and without reading, writing and spelling problems
Reproduced with permission from *The British Journal of Occupational Therapy.*

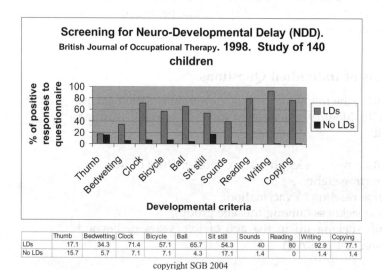

	Thumb	Bedwetting	Clock	Bicycle	Ball	Sit still	Sounds	Reading	Writing	Copying
LDs	17.1	34.3	71.4	57.1	65.7	54.3	40	80	92.9	77.1
No LDs	15.7	5.7	7.1	7.1	4.3	17.1	1.4	0	1.4	1.4

copyright SGB 2004

Figure A.2   Differences in developmental criteria between children with and without reading, writing and spelling problems
Reproduced with permission from *The British Journal of Occupational Therapy.*

specific learning difficulty group and the control group on the basis of total score.

At a 98 per cent confidence level, a child with a score of 7 or more belonged to the specific learning difficulty group and a child scoring 2 or less did not. Therefore, the area between and including 3 and 6 is uncertain, and it is necessary to obtain a score of 7 or more in order to identify a possible neurological basis to a child's specific learning difficulty. Further assessments for the presence of aberrant reflexes should then be carried out.

Analysis of the questionnaire on individual criteria demonstrated that that the following were significant indicators of later specific learning difficulties:

1. family history of learning difficulties;
2. medical problems during pregnancy;
3. complications during the birth process;
4. failure to pass through the motor stages of crawling on the tummy or creeping on hands and knees;
5. late at learning to talk (18 months or later);
6. late at learning to walk (16 months or later);
7. difficulty with, for example, dressing, buttons, or shoelaces beyond six and a half years of age;
8. allergies;
9. illness involving very high temperature in the first three years of life;
10. history of frequent ear, nose, throat, or chest infections in the first five years of life;
11. bed-wetting beyond the age of five years;
12. difficulty learning to ride a bicycle;
13. difficulty catching a ball above the age of five years;
14. difficulty sitting still;
15. difficulty learning to read an analogue clock above the age of seven years;
16. hypersensitivity to sound.

However, caution should be exercised in interpreting individual criteria. One factor taken in isolation would not be predictive of later specific learning difficulties. A profile of seven or more factors together may be used as an indication of underlying NDD.

The criteria that did reveal a marked difference between the two groups may be divided into two categories:

1. Factors that relate to motor development and vestibular functioning:
   - late at learning to walk;
   - omission of the developmental stages of crawling and/or creeping;
   - difficulty dressing (fine muscle coordination);
   - difficulty learning to ride a bicycle (vestibular);
   - difficulty catching a ball (eye/hand coordination);
   - difficulty sitting still;
   - bed-wetting above five years of age.
2. Factors that relate to the development of phonological skills:
   - late at learning to talk;
   - history of frequent ear, nose, throat, or chest infections in the first three years of life;
   - hypersensitive/overreacts to sound.

Delays in both motor development and/or auditory processing can affect subsequent language-based skills.

Mention should also be made of the criteria excluded by the chi-square test. While premature/post-mature birth was not significant in this sample, no child in the sample was more than two weeks early or one week late. Other studies[27] have revealed that premature birth and/or very low birth weight can underlie a number of other disorders. Adverse reaction to vaccination or inoculation has been linked to autism and attention deficit hyperactive disorder (ADHD),[28] which were not viewed as a discrete category in this sample.

The sample in this study suggests that motion sickness is developmentally normal up to 10 years of age. However, Beuret (seminar paper presented for INPP, 1993) found a history of continued motion sickness beyond puberty to be a factor among first and second year college students who started to experience educational and emotional difficulties for the first time at further education level. He also found a high incidence of continued motion sickness beyond puberty in students who experienced severe headaches when faced with an increased volume of reading. Motion sickness may therefore be pertinent if it continues beyond puberty.

CONCLUSIONS

The results of the Student t test suggest that the INPP Developmental Screening Questionnaire does discriminate between children with specific learning difficulties and those without specific learning difficulties on the basis of a cluster of factors in early development, a score of 7 or more differentiating the two groups.

This simple screening device could be of use to teachers, educational psychologists, occupational therapists, and other professionals in the initial assessment stages of a child's needs, to determine whether neurological/developmental factors lie beneath a child's presenting difficulties. Children who have NDD, as defined by the continued presence of a cluster of aberrant reflexes, respond to a physical/sensory programme of remediation, and this should be taken into account in any recommendations that are made to address their specific learning difficulties.

REFERENCES

1 World Federation of Neurology. 1968. Report of research group on developmental dyslexia and world illiteracy. *Bulletin of the Orton Society* 18:21–22.
2 Levinson HN. 1974. Dyslexia: does this unusual childhood syndrome begin as an ear infection? *Infectious Diseases* 15: 15.
3 De Quirós JB, Schrager O. 1978. *Neurophysiological Fundamentals in Learning Disabilities*. Academic Therapy, San Rafael, CA.
4 Nicolson RI, Fawcett AJ. 1990. A new framework for dyslexia research? *Cognition* 35:159–182.
5 Fawcett AJ et al. 1996. Impaired performance of children with dyslexia on a range of cerebellar tests. *Annals of Dyslexia* 46:259–283.
6 Blythe P, McGlown DJ. 1979. *An Organic Basis for Neuroses and Educational Difficulties*. Insight Publications, Chester.
7 Augur J. 1985. Guidelines for teachers, parents and learners. In: Snowling M (Ed.). *Children's Written Language Difficulties*. NFER Nelson, Windsor.
8 Denckla MB et al. 1985. Motor performance in dyslexic children with and without attentional disorders. *Archives of Neurology* 42:228–231.
9 Goddard SA. 1996. *A Teacher's Window into the Child's Mind*. Fern Ridge Press, Eugene, OR.

10 Geschwind N, Levitsky W. 1968. Left-right asymmetries in the temporal speech region. *Science* 161:186–187.

11 Tallal P, Piercy M. 1974. Developmental aphasia: rate of auditory processing and selective impairment of consonant perception. *Neuro-psychologia* 12:83–93.

12 Geschwind N, Galaburda AM. 1985. *Cerebral Lateralisation.* MIT Press, Cambridge, MA.

13 Dalby MA. 1986. Aspects in reading processes. In: Troudhjem K (Ed.). *12th Danavox Symposium.* Danavox, Denmark.

14 Johansen KV. 1988. *Sensory Deprivation – a Possible Cause of Dyslexia.* Nordisk Tidsskrift for Spesialpedagogikk, Scandinavian University Press, Abonementssekjonen, Postboks 2959, Toyen, N-0608 Oslo, Norge.

15 Shayvitz SE. 1996. Dyslexia. *Scientific American,* November, pp. 77–83.

16 Tallal P. 1996. Language learning impairment: integrating research and remediation. *Orton Dyslexia Society 47th Annual Conference Commemorative Booklet.* Orton Dyslexia Society, Boston, MA.

17 Galaburda AM et al. 1986. Histological asymmetry in the primary visual cortex of the rat; implications of mechanism of cerebral asymmetry. *Cortex* 22:151–160.

18 Pavlidis G, Miles T. 1987. *Dyslexia Research and its Applications to Education.* Wiley, Chichester.

19 Chase C, Jenner A. 1993. *Magnocular visual deficits affect temporal processing of dyslexics.* In: Tallal P, Galaburda AM, Linas R, von Euler C (Eds.). *Temporal Information Processing in the Nervous System, with Special Reference to Dyslexia and Dysphasia.* New York Academy of Sciences, New York.

20 Nicolson RI, Fawcett AJ. 1994. Reaction times and dyslexia. *Quarterly Journal of Experimental Psychology* 47A:29–48.

21 Nicolson RI et al. 1995. Time estimation deficits in developmental dyslexia; evidence for cerebellar involvement. *Proceedings of the Royal Society* 259:43–47.

22 Ayres AJ. 1973. *Sensory Integration and Learning Disorders.* Western Psychological Services, Los Angeles, CA.

23 Ayres AJ. 1982. *Sensory Integration and the Child.* Western Psychological Services, Los Angeles, CA.

24 Bender ML. 1976. *The Bender-Purdue Reflex Test.* Academic Therapy Publications, San Rafael, CA.

25 Bernhardsson K, Davidson K. 1983. *A Different Way of Helping Children with Learning Difficulties – A Final Report from the Dala Clinic.* Gothenburg Educational Psychology Service, Gothenburg, Sweden.

26 Blythe P, McGlown DJ. 1978. *Developmental Screening Questionnaire for Organic Brain Dysfunction.* Institute for Neuro-Physiological Psychology, Chester.

27 Roberts BL. 1989. Motor problems among children of very low birth weight. *The British Journal of Occupational Therapy* 52(3):97–99.

28 Coulter HL. 1990 *Vaccination, Social Violence and Criminality. The Medical Assault on the American Brain.* North Atlantic Books, Berkeley, CA.

APPENDIX 2

FREQUENCY RANGE OF VOCALS AND MUSICAL INSTRUMENTS

Reproduced with permission of: Brown S. www.listenhear.co.uk

VOCAL	Approximate Frequency Range
Soprano	250Hz - 1K
Contralto	200Hz - 700Hz
Baritone	110Hz - 425Hz
Bass	80Hz - 350Hz
WOODWIND	Top
Piccolo	630Hz - 5K
Flute	250Hz - 2.5K
Oboe	250Hz - 1.5K
Clarinet (B flat or A)	125Hz - 2K
Clarinet (E flat)	200Hz - 2K
Bass Clarinet	75Hz - 800Hz
Basset Horn	90Hz - 1K
Cor Anglais	160Hz - 1K
Bassoon	55Hz - 575Hz
Double Bassoon	25Hz - 200Hz
Soprano Saxophone	225Hz - 1K
Alto Saxophone	125Hz - 900Hz
Tenor Saxophone	110Hz - 630Hz
Baritone Saxophone	70Hz - 450Hz
Bass Saxophone	55Hz - 315Hz
BRASS	Top
Trumpet (C)	170Hz - 1K
Trumpet (F)	300Hz - 1K
Alto Trombone	110Hz - 630Hz
Tenor Trombone	80Hz - 600Hz
Bass Trombone	63Hz - 400Hz
Tuba	45Hz - 375Hz
Valve Horn	63Hz - 700Hz
STRINGS	Top
Violin	200Hz - 3.5K
Viola	125Hz -1K
Cello	63Hz - 630Hz
Double Bass	40Hz - 200Hz
Guitar	80Hz - 630Hz
KEYBOARDS	Top
Piano	28Hz - 4.1K
Organ	20Hz - 7K
PERCUSSION	Top
Celeste	260Hz - 3.5K
Timpani	90Hz - 180Hz
Glockenspiel	63Hz - 180Hz
Xylophone	700Hz - 3.5K

GLOSSARY OF TERMS

Action potential – the change in membrane potential occurring in nerve, muscle, or other excitable tissue when excitation occurs.

Adrenaline – also referred to as epinephrine; acts as a stimulant to the sympathetic nervous system, raising blood pressure, increasing the amount of glucose in the blood, and constricting smaller blood vessels.

Antinociception – a reduction in pain sensitivity produced within neurons when an endorphin or similar opium-containing substance, opioid, combines with a receptor, tending to reduce the perception and behavioural effects of nociceptive stimuli.

Apgar score – a method of assessing the general status of the newborn immediately after birth.

Archi – ancient.

Attitude – the result of reflexes that lead to the return to a species-specific position.

Bender–Gestalt Test – a neurological test, designed to help in the diagnosis of loss of function and organic brain damage in children and in adults, consisting of nine geometric figures that are copied, the drawings being evaluated according to the overall quality of the reproductions, their organization in relation to Gestalt *grouping laws*, and the errors made.

Bilateral integration – the ability to carry out movements on one side of the body independently of the other and the ability to coordinate both sides of the body in many different combinations.

Bradycardia – slowness of the heart rate, usually measured as fewer than 60 beats per minute in an adult.

Catecholamines – a group of physiologically important substances including adrenaline, noradrenaline, and dopamine, which have various different roles (mainly as *neurotransmitters*) in the functioning of the sympathetic and central nervous system.

Catecholamine surge – sudden increase in catecholamine levels, particularly adrenaline, which occurs when birth is imminent. This surge of hormones is thought to activate the foetal ejection reflex – the final powerful contraction which expels the baby at the moment of birth and prepares the baby for the change from a state of inhibition before birth to arousal after birth.

Cerebellum – the control centre for balance and movement coordination. As part of the nervous system, it receives two types of input: one locating the body's position in space, and the other indicating whether the muscle is contracted or relaxed. Based on this information, and depending on the desired action (move forward, grasp, etc.), the cerebellum triggers, adjusts, or stops a movement.

Cervical – pertaining to the neck.

Cochlea – part of the hearing apparatus. A spiral structure in the inner ear that looks like a snail shell and contains tiny hair cells whose movement is interpreted by the brain as sound.

Corpus callosum – the bundle of nerve fibres which allow for the exchange of information between the two cerebral hemispheres.

Cranio – relating to the skull.

Crawling and creeping – In the USA, crawling refers to commando-style crawling with the tummy in contact with the ground; creeping refers to creeping on hands and knees. In the UK, the term crawling is more often used to describe crawling on hands and knees, and the term creeping is rarely used. In this context, we have used the definition of the terms used in the USA.

Dendrite – branched extension of a nerve cell neuron that receives electrical signals from other neurons and conducts those signals to the cell body.

Dorsal – situated on the back.

Dynamic balance – ability to maintain equilibrium while moving.

Dysdiadochokinesis – difficulty with rapid alternate movements. Can affect the fingers, hands, feet, and speech apparatus.

Dysfunction – *dys* = difficulty; difficulty of functioning.

Dysmetria (Greek: 'difficult to measure') is a symptom exhibited by patients after cerebellar injury or injury to proprioceptive nerves (nerves that carry information about the position of joints and extremities) resulting in an inability to fix the range of movement in muscular activity. Rapid and brisk movements are made with more force than necessary.

Equilibrium – the interplay between forces enabling the maintenance and control of postures and attitudes.

Electronystagmography – electrical recording of eye movements.

Erb's palsy – involves a varying amount of injury to the fifth and sixth cranial nerves as they pass through the brachial plexus.

Fixed action patterns – stereotyped and often complex series of movements in response to a stimulus.

Fovea – a small pit or central depression in the macula retinae where the retina is very thin so that rays of light have free passage to the layer of photoreceptors, mostly cones. This is the area of most distinct vision to which the visual axis is directed.

Homologous – Greek: in agreement, corresponding. In the context of movement patterns such as crawling, this refers to use of the arms together to pull forward while either dragging the legs or attempting to push with the two legs at the same time. This is a primitive method of crawling.

Hydramnios – the presence of an abnormally large amount of amniotic fluid for a particular stage in pregnancy. Commonly associated with foetal abnormality, particularly neuromuscular disorders of prenatal onset.

Hyperacusis is defined as an inability to tolerate everyday sounds. People with hyperacusis may find that certain sounds are more difficult to listen to than others, and some sounds may cause pain in the ears, even when those sounds do not bother others. Often, the most disturbing or painful sounds can be sudden high-pitched noises like alarms, bus brakes, silverware and dishes, children's screams, and clapping. Sometimes, hyperacusis can be so severe that people avoid public or social settings.

Hz – hertz – unit of frequency. The SI unit of frequency equal to one cycle per second. Low frequency such as 100 Hz is detected as low-pitch sound; high frequency such as 12,000 is perceived as high pitch.

Kernicterus – the staining with bile of the basal nuclei of the brain, with toxic degeneration of the nerve cells which sometimes occurs in haemolytic disease of the newborn.

Kineses – the organism changes the *speed* of its movements in response to an environmental stimulus.

Libido – psychic energy.

Lordosis – bending of the body forwards and inwards.

Lunacy – a form of insanity once believed to come with changes of the moon.

MCV – measles-containing vaccine.

Microsomy – general smallness.

Myelin – the white cells composed of lipids and proteins that form a protective sheath around some types of nerve fibres and help facilitate electrical impulse transmission. Myelin also acts as an electrical insulator, increasing the efficiency of nerve conduction and preventing interference or 'cross chatter' from neighbouring pathways.

Neo – new.

Neuro-developmental delay – sometimes also referred to as *neurological dysfunction*, is defined by INPP as:

1. the continued presence of a *cluster* of aberrant primitive reflexes above six months of age and
2. absent or underdeveloped postural reflexes above the age of three and a half years.

Neurotransmitter – a chemical substance released from nerve endings to other nerves and across *synapses* to other nerves and across minute gaps between the nerves and muscles or glands that they supply.

Nystagmus – describes spontaneous, rapid, rhythmic movements of the eyes which occur during fixation or on ocular movement.

Occipital – refers to the back of the head.

Occiput – the lower and hind part of the head where it merges into the neck.

Ontogeny – the development of an individual from a fertilized ovum to maturity.

Otolith – Greek: 'ear-stone'. Minute calcium carbonate 'stones' associated with neuromast organs in the labyrinth. The 'stones' deform the villi of the hair cells in response to changes in orientation in the gravity field.

Otolithic organs – there are two on each side:

1. the utricle;
2. the saccule.

The otoconia crystals in the *otoconia layer* rest on the viscous gel layer and are heavier than their surroundings. During linear *acceleration*, they are displaced, which in turn deflects the hair cells, thereby producing a sensory signal.

Most of the utricular signals elicit eye movements, while the majority of the saccular signals project to muscles that control posture.

Pain gate control theory – proposed by Melzack and Wall (1962 and 1965) is the idea that the perception of physical pain does not occur as a direct result of activation of pain receptor neurons, but is modulated by interaction between different neurons, which are pain-transmitting and non-pain-transmitting. The theory asserts that activation of nerves that do not transmit pain signals can interfere with/ block signals from pain fibres and can inhibit an individual's perception of pain.

Paleo – old.

Phobia – fear.

Phylogeny – the evolutionary history of a species, genus, or group, as contrasted with development of an individual (ontogeny).

Positron emission tomography (PET) – a highly specialized imaging technique that uses short-lived radioactive substances to produce three-dimensional coloured images of those substances functioning within the body. These images are called PET scans.

PET scanning provides information about the body's chemistry not available through other procedures. PET studies metabolic activity or body function. PET has been used primarily in cardiology, neurology, and oncology.

Proprioception – feedback from muscles, tendons, and joints concerning position, movement, or balance of the body or any of its parts. Proprioception and balance provide *internal* information about the body's status relating to balance and position in space (intereceptors). Touch, vision, hearing, and smell inform us about the *external* environment (exteroceptors).

Pyramidal tract – either of two bundles of nerve fibres, shaped like inverted pyramids, running from each cerebral hemisphere down the spinal cord to all voluntary muscles of the body.

Reflexes – stereotyped movement of a body part in response to a stimulus.

Reticular formation – a network of nerves extending from the medulla oblongata in the brainstem to the midbrain. It receives information from all over the body. The ascending reticular activating system connects to areas in the thalamus, hypothalamus, and cortex, while the descending reticular activating system connects to the cerebellum and sensory nerves.

Sensory integration (SI) therapy – a theory developed more than 30 years ago by occupational therapist A. Jean Ayres. Ayres (1972) defined sensory integration as 'the neurological process that organizes sensation from one's own body and from the environment and makes it possible to use the body effectively within the environment.'

Soft signs – with the help of a standardized and age-adequate neurological examination technique, various forms of minor neurological dysfunction (MND), such as mild dysfunctions in muscle tone regulation, choreiform dyskinesia, or fine manipulative disability, can be diagnosed. Soft signs provide evidence of minor neurological dysfunction but do not necessarily point to the cause of the dysfunction.

Somatoform – relating to a group of psychologically induced conditions that have the characteristics of physical disease but for which no organic cause can be found.

Static balance – ability to maintain a fixed position. When control of static balance is unstable, more movement or involvement of other body parts is involved in the maintenance of stability.

Stimulus-bound effect – describes the inability to ignore irrelevant visual stimuli within a given visual field.

Synapse – the minute gap at the end of a nerve fibre across which nerve impulses pass from one neuron to the next

Taxes – are *directed* movements towards or away from a stimulus. They are a type of innate behaviour.

Tetrapod – any four-limbed animal.

Vagus nerve – the 10th cranial nerve, taking its name from the word 'vagrant', meaning 'wanderer'. So called because it is the longest of all the cranial nerves and affects many vital functions including innervation of the parasympathetic nervous system.

Vertigo – the physical characteristics of vertigo include disorientation and loss of postural and ocular control accompanied by ancillary autonomic symptoms such as cold, nausea, vomiting, and cold sweating stemming from a primary *dysfunction in the balance system.*

Vestibular reflexes – include tonic labyrinthine reflex, asymmetrical tonic neck reflex, symmetrical tonic neck reflex and labyrinthine head righting reflexes.

Vestibular system – a system responsible for maintaining *balance, posture,* and the body's orientation in space. This system also regulates locomotion and other movements, and keeps objects in visual focus as the body moves. The vestibular system comprises two components:

1. the semicircular canals, which detect rotational movements;
2. the otoliths, which detect linear translations.

Viscera – are the soft internal organs of the body, including the lungs, the heart, and the organs of the digestive system. Visceral functions are functions involving these systems.

BIBLIOGRAPHY

Alexopoulos EI et al. (2006). Association between primary nocturnal enuresis and habitual snoring in children. *Urology* **68**(2),
406–409.

Alhazen BC. Cited in: Arnheim R (1969). *Visual Thinking*. Berkeley,
CA, University of California Press.

Allen AC (1991). Preterm development. In AJ Camute & PJ Accardo
(eds), *Developmental Disabilities in Infancy and Childhood*. Baltimore, MD, Paul H Brookes Publishing Co.

Allen MC (1987). The symmetric tonic neck reflex (STNR) as a
normal finding in premature infants prior to term. *Pediatric
Research* **20**, 208A.

Allman J (2000). *Evolving Brains*. New York, Scientific American
Library.

American Speech-Language-Hearing Association. (2006). http://
www.asha.org/members/deskref-journals/deskref/default/.
Ref. adapted from *Handbook of Auditory Processing Disorder*. Comprehensive Intervention Vol. 2, p. 3.

Anderson UM (1996). *The Psalms of Children*. Ellicottville, NY,
She-Bear Publications.

Anderson UM. (2004). www.andersonbeyondgenome.com

Annett M (1972). The distribution of manual symmetry. *British
Journal of Psychology* **63**, 343–358.

Annett M (1985). *Left, Right, Hand and Brain. The Right Shift Theory*.
London, Lawrence Erlbaum.

Annett M (1995). The right shift theory of a genetic balanced polymorphism for cerebral dominance and cognitive processing.
Cahiers de Psychologie Cognitive **14**(5), 427–623.

ARROW. http://www.self-voice.co.uk/

Arvedson JC (2006). Swallowing and feeding in infants and young
children. GI Motility online. www.bioinfo.pl/ [auth:Arvedson].

Aslin RN (1985). Oculo-motor measures of visual development. In
G Gottlieb & N Krasnegor (eds), *Measurement of Audition and
Vision During the First Year of Life: a Methodological Overview*.
Norwood, NJ, Ablex, pp. 391–417.

Audesirk T & Audesirk G (1996). *Biology. Life on Earth*. Upper
Saddle River, NJ, Prentice-Hall Inc.

Augur J (1985). Guidelines for teachers, parents and learners. In M Snowling (ed.), *Children's Written Language Difficulties*. Windsor, NFER Nelson.

Ayres AJ (1972). Improving academic scores through sensory integration. *Journal of Learning Disabilities* 5, 338–343.

Ayres AJ (1973). *Sensory Integration and Learning Disorders*. Los Angeles, CA, Western Psychological Services.

Ayres AJ (1989). *Sensory Integration and Praxis Tests*. Los Angeles, CA, Western Psychological Services.

Ayto J (1990). *Dictionary of Word Origins*. St Ives, Cambridgeshire, Columbia Marketing.

Babinski I (1915). *Revue Neurologique* (Fr) **28**(2), 145; (1922):1049.

Badian NA (1983). Developmental dyscalculia. In HR Mykelbost (ed.), *Progress in Learning Disabilities*. New York, Grune and Stratton.

Barkley RA (1995). *Taking Charge of ADHD: the Complete, Authoritative Guide for Parents*. New York, Guilford.

Barnes DE & Walker DW (1981). Prenatal ethanol exposure permanently alters the rat hippocampus. Cited in: (1981) Mechanisms of alcohol damage in utero. *CIBA Foundation Symposium*, Vol. 105. London, Pitman.

Barsch RH. (1968). Achieving motor perception efficiency. A self-oriented approach to learning. Vol. 1 of *A Perceptual-Motor Curriculum*. Seattle, WA, Special Child Publications.

Bateman BD (1973). Educational implications of minimal brain dysfunction. *Annals of the New York Academy of Sciences* **205**, 245–250.

Bauer J (1916). Der Baranusche Zeigeveruch etc. bie traumatischen neurosen. *Wiener Klinisch Wochenschrift* **40**.

Bauer J & Schilder P (1919). Ubereinige psycholphysiologischen mechanismen funtioneller neurosen. *Zeitschrift für Nervenheilkunde* **164**, 279.

Bax M & MacKeith R (eds) (1962). *Minimal Cerebral Dysfunction*. London, The National Spastics Society. Education and Information Unit in association with William Heinemann Medical Books, Ltd.

Becker RD (1974). Minimal brain dysfunction – clinical fact, neurological fiction? *The Israel Annals of Psychiatry and Related Disciplines* **12**, 87.

Bein-Wierzbinski W (2001). Persistent primitive reflexes in elementary school children. Effect on oculomotor and visual perception. Paper presented at the 13th European Conference of Neuro-Developmental Delay in Children with Specific Learning Difficulties, Chester, UK.

Bellis Waller M (1993). *Crack Affected Children. A Teacher's Guide*. Newbury Park, CA, Corwin Press, Inc.

Bender L (1938). *A Visual Motor Gestalt Test and its Clinical Uses*. New York, American Orthopsychiatric Association.

Bender ML (1976). *Bender-Purdue Reflex Test and Training Manual*. San Rafael, CA, Academic Publications.

Bennett RV & Brown LK (1989). *Myles Textbook for Midwives.* Edinburgh, Churchill Livingstone.

Benson AJ (1998). Motion sickness. In JM Stellman et al. (eds), *Encyclopaedia of Occupational Health and Safety*, 4th ed. Vol. 50. Geneva, International Labour Office, pp. 12–14.

Berard G (1993). *Hearing Equals Behaviour.* New Canaan, CT, Keats Publishing Inc.

Bernhardsson K & Davidson K (1983). *A Different Way of Helping Children with Learning Difficulties – A Final Report from the Dala Clinic.* Gothenburg, Sweden, Gothenburg Educational.

Berthoz A (2000). *The Brain's Sense of Movement.* Cambridge, MA, Harvard University Press.

Berthoz A (2003). *Emotion and reason. The Cognitive Science of Decision Making.* Oxford, Oxford University Press.

Berthoz A (2007). Development and function of the balance system in the early years. *The 19th European Conference of Neuro-Developmental Delay in Children with Specific Learning Difficulties.* Pisa, September 2007.

Bertolotti M (1904). *Revue Neurologique* **12**, 1160.

Beuret LJ (1992). The role of neuro-developmental delays in advanced academic failure. *The 4th European Conference of Neuro-Developmental Delay in Children with Specific Learning Difficulties.* Chester, UK, March 1992.

Beuret LJ (1994). Seminar paper delivered to The Institute for Neuro-Physiological Psychology Supervision, Chester, 1994.

Beuret LJ (2000). The role of postural reflexes in learning. Part 2. Paper presented at the 12th European Conference of Neuro-developmental Delay in Children with Specific Learning Difficulties, Chester, UK, March 2000.

Biederman H (1992). Kinematic imbalance due to suboccipital strain. *Journal of Manual Medicine* **6**, 151–156.

Biguer B et al. (1982). The coordination of eye, head and arm movements during reaching at a single target. *Experimental Brain Research* **46**, 301–304.

Birth Choice UK website. http://www.BirthChoiceUK.com

Bloedal JR & Bracha V (1997). Duality of the cerebellar motor and cognitive function. *International Review of Neurobiology*, **41**(6), 613–634.

Blythe P (1972). *Stress Disease.* London, Arthur Baker.

Blythe P (1974a). *A Somatogenic Basis for Neurosis and the Effect Upon Health.* Chester, The Institute for Psychosomatic Therapy.

Blythe P (1974b). Somatogenic neuroses and the effect upon health. Monograph. Chester, Institute of Psychosomatic Therapy, August 1974.

Blythe P (1978). Minimal brain dysfunction and the treatment of psychoneuroses. *Journal of Psychomatic Research* **22**(4), 247–255.

Blythe P (1987). Oculo-motor dysfunctions and the effect on functioning. *Reflex Newsletter*, Chester, INPP.

Blythe P (1988a). An analysis of the developmental history of 103 patients diagnosed with agoraphobia and/or panic disorder. *The 2nd International Conference of Neuro-Developmental Delay.* Stockholm, October 1988.

Blythe P (1988b). *A New Approach that Explains Specific Learning Difficulties and Provides an Effective Treatment.* Chester, INPP.

Blythe P (1990a). Lecture for INPP Supervision, October 1990, Chester.

Blythe P (1990b). *The History of The Institute for Neuro-Physiological Psychology (INPP).* Chester, INPP.

Blythe P & McGlown DJ (1978). *Developmental Screening Questionnaire for Organic Brain Dysfunction.* Chester, INPP.

Blythe P & McGlown DJ (1979). *An Organic Basis for Neuroses and Educational Difficulties.* Chester, Insight Publications.

Blythe P & McGlown DJ (1980). *An Organic Basis for Neuroses and the Existence, Detection and Treatment of Secondary Neuroses.* Göteborg, Svenska Institutet för Neurofysiologisk Psykologi.

Blythe P & McGlown DJ (1981). MBD and OBD. *Swedish Medical Journal* **78**(1), 45–48.

Blythe P & McGlown D (1982). Agoraphobia – is it organic? *World Medicine,* July 1982, pp. 57–59.

Bobath B (1971). *Abnormal Postural Reflex Activity Caused by Brain Lesions.* (2nd ed). London, William Heinemann Medical Books, Ltd.

Bobath B (1978). *Abnormal Postural Reflex Activity Caused by Brain Lesions.* (3rd ed). London, William Heinemann Medical Books Ltd.

Bobath K. (1991). *A Neurophysiological Basis for the Treatment of Cerebral Palsy.* Cambridge, Cambridge University Press.

Bobath K & Bobath B (1965). *Abnormal Postural Reflex Activity Caused by Brain Lesions.* London, William Heinemann.

Boden G (2001). Free fatty acids-the link between obesity and insulin resistance. *Endocrine Practice* **7**(1), 8–54.

Bower B (1987). Images of obsession. *Science News* **131**, 236–237.

Bowlby R (2007). Babies and toddlers in non-parental daycare can avoid stress and anxiety if they develop a lasting secondary attachment bond with one carer who is consistently accessible to them. *Attachment and Human Development* **4**(4), 307–319.

Brambell FWR (1948). Prenatal mortality in mammals. *Biological Review* **23**, 379–407.

Breuer J (1874). Über die funktion der bogengängen des ohrlabyrinthes. *Wiener Medizinisch Jahrbuch* **4**, 72–124.

Breuer J (1875). Beitrage zur lehre vom statischen sinne (gleichgewichtsorgan, vestibularapparat des ohrlabyrinths). Zweite Mitteleilung. *Wiener Medizinisch Jahrbuch* **5**, 87–156.

Breuer J (1889). Neue Versuche and den ohrbogengängen. *Arch. ges. Physiol.* **44**, 135–152.

Breuer J (1891). Über die Funktion der Otolithenapparate. *Pflügers Archiv* **48**, 195–306.

Briggs Myers I et al. (1998). *MBTI Manual (A guide to the development and use of the Myers Briggs type indicator)*. (3rd ed). Washington, DC, Consulting Psychologists Press.

British Dyslexia Association (1998). *The Dyslexia Handbook*. Reading, The British Dyslexia Association.

Brodal P (1998). *The Central Nervous System. Structure and Function*. Oxford, Oxford University Press.

Brooks VB (1986). *The Neural Bases of Motor Control*. New York, Oxford University Press.

Buckley SJ (2005). *Gentle Birth, Gentle Mothering*. Brisbane, One Moon Press.

Bull J (2005). The possible role of primitive reflexes in the birth process. Midwifery Lecture delivered to students attending The Institute for Neuro-Physiological Psychology Training Course in Identification, Assessment and Treatment of Neuro-Developmental Delay, Chester, November 2005.

Burne J (2006). IVF: why we must be told the truth over birth defects. *Good Health Daily Mail*, 12 December 2006.

Butcher JN & Williams CL (2000). *Essentials of MMPI-2 and MMPI-A Interpretation*. (2nd ed). Minneapolis, MN, University of Minnesota Press.

Butler Hall B (1998). Discovering the hidden treasures in the ear. Paper presented at the 10th European Conference of Neuro-Developmental Delay in Children with Specific Learning Difficulties, Chester, March 1998.

Cantrell RW et al. (1979). Stapedius muscle function tests in the diagnosis of neuromuscular disorders. *Otolaryngology and Head and Neck Surgery* **87**, 261–265.

Capute AJ & Accardo PJ (1991). *Developmental Disabilities in Infancy and Childhood*. Baltimore, MD, Paul H Brookes Publishing Co.

Capute AJ et al. (1980). *Primitive Reflex Profile*. Baltimore, MD, University Park Press.

Capute AJ et al. (1981). Primitive reflexes: a factor in non-verbal language in early infancy. In Stark (ed.), *Language Behaviour in Infancy and Early Childhood*. New York, Elsevier.

Carbonell J & Perez JPM. Cited in: O'Doherty N (1986). *Neurological Examination of the Newborn*. Lancaster, MTP Press Limited.

Cawthorne T (1944). The physiological basis for head exercises. *The Journal of the Chartered Society of Physiotherapy* **30**, 106.

Cawthorne T. (1946). Vestibular injuries. *Proceedings of the Royal Society of Medicine* **39**, 270–272.

Chalfant JC & Scheffelin M (1969). *Central Processing Dysfunctions in Children*. Bethesda, MD, National Institute of Neurological Disorders and Stroke, National Institute of Health.

Chase C & Jenner A (1993). Magnocellular visual deficits affect temporal processing of dyslexics. In P Tallal, AM Galaburda, R

Llinas & C von Euler (eds), *Temporal Information Processing in the Nervous System, with Special Reference to Dyslexia and Dysphasia.* New York, New York Academy of Sciences.

Chasnoff IL & Burns WJ (1984). The Moro reaction: a scoring system for neonatal narcotic withdrawal. *Developmental Medicine and Child Neurology* **26**, 484–489.

Chasnoff IJ et al. (1985). Cocaine use in pregnancy. *New England Journal of Medicine* **313**, 666–669.

Chasnoff IJ et al. (1986). Prenatal drug exposure: effects of neonatal and infant growth development. *Neurobehavioral Toxicology and Teratology* **8**, 357–362.

Christiansen C & Baum C (eds) (1991). *Occupational Therapy. Overcoming Human Performance Deficits.* Thorofare, NJ, Slack Incorporated.

Chyi LJ et al. (2007). Cognitive school outcomes of infants born at 32 to 36 weeks gestation. *Pediatric Academies Society's Annual Meeting.* Toronto, Canada.

Clements S (1966). *Minimal Brain Dysfunction in Children: Terminology and Identification.* Task Force 1. Washington, DC, U.S. Department of Health, Education and Welfare.

Cohen AS (1973). Minimal brain dysfunction and practical matters such as teaching kids to read. *Annals of The New York Academy of Sciences* **205**, 251–261.

Compston A (2007). From the archives. *Brain* 2005 **128**(7), 1475–1477; doi:10.1093/brain/awh566.

Conger K (2007). Slightly early birth may still spell trouble later in school. Stanford Report. Stanford News Service. 9 May 2007. http://www.news-service.stanford.edu/news/2007/may9/med-premature

Cooksey FS (1946). Rehabilitation in vestibular injuries. *Proceedings of the Royal Society of Medicine* **39**, 273–275.

Coryell J & Henderson A (1979). Role of the asymmetrical tonic neck reflex in hand visualization in normal infants. *American Journal of Occupational Therapy* **33**(4), 255–260.

Cottrell S (1988). Aetiology, diagnosis and treatment of asthma through primitive reflex inhibition. Paper presented at the 2nd International Conference of Neurological Dysfunction, Stockholm, October 1988.

Coulter HL (1990). *Vaccination, Social Violence and Criminality. The Medical Assault on the American Brain.* Berkeley, CA, North Atlantic Books.

Courchesne E et al. (1994). Impairment in shifting attention in autistic and cerebellar patients. *Behavioral Neuroscience* **108**, 848–865.

Cox JM (1804). *Practical Observations in Insanity.* London, Baldwin and Murray.

Crawford M (1994). Cited in: Morgan E (1994). *The Descent of the Child.* London, Souvenir Press.

Croucher T & Hindmarch I (1973). The spiral after effect (SAE) as a measure of motion sickness susceptibility and the effect on the SAE of an antimotion sickness drug and a central nervous system depressant. *Psychopharmacology* **32**, 2.

Cruickshank WM (1981). A new perspective in teacher education: the neuroeducator. *Journal of Learning Disabilities* **14**(6), 337–341, 367.

Crutchfield CA & Barnes MR (1993). *Motor Control and Motor Learning in Rehabilitation*. Atlanta, GA, Stokesville Publishing Company.

Dalby MA (1986). Aspects in reading processes. In K Troudhjem (ed.), *12th Danavox Symposium*. Denmark, Danavox.

Dean P (1994). Cited in: A wobble now means less work later. *The Independent*, 26 April 1994, London.

Delacato CH (1959). *The Treatment and Prevention of Reading Problems*. Springfield, IL, Charles C Thomas.

Delacato C (1970). *The Diagnosis and Treatment of Speech and Reading Problems*. Springfield, IL, Charles C Thomas.

Delacato C (1981). *A New Start for the Child with Reading Problems*. New York, David McKay.

DeMause L (1982). *Foundations of Psychohistory*. New York, Creative Roots.

Denckla MB et al. (1985). Motor performance in dyslexic children with and without attentional disorders. *Archives of Neurology* **42**, 228–231.

De Quirós JB & Schrager OL (1978). *Neurological Fundamentals in Learning Disabilities*. Novato, CA, Academic Therapy Publications Inc.

Deuschl G et al. (2001). The pathophysiology of tremor. *Muscles and Nerves* **24**(6), 716–735.

Devries JIP et al. (1985). The emergence of fetal behavior: II. Quantitative aspects. *Early Human Development* **12**, 99–120.

Diagnostic and Statistical Manual of Mental Disorders IV (DSM IV) (1994). Washington, DC, American Psychiatric Association.

Draper IT (1993). *Lecture Notes on Neurology*. Oxford, Blackwell Scientific Publications.

Drillien CM & Drummond MB (1977). *Neurodevelopmental Problems in Early Childhood*. Oxford, Blackwell Scientific Publications.

Eggesbø M et al. (2005). Cesarean delivery and cow milk allergy/intolerance. *Allergy* **60**(9), 1172.

El-Chaar D. (2007). Fertility treatment raises birth defect risk. Presented at Conference hosted by The Society for Maternal-Fetal Medicine, San Francisco, 9 February 2007.

Eustis RS (1947). The primary origin of the specific language disabilities. *Journal of Pediatrics* **XXXI**, 455–488.

Eyeson-Annan M et al. (1996). Visual and vestibular components of motion sickness. *Aviation, Space, and Environmental Medicine* **67**(10), 955–962.

Fawcett AJ (1994). Cited in: A wobble now means less work later. *The Independent*, 26 April 1994, London.

Fawcett AJ et al. (1996). Impaired performance of children with dyslexia on a range of cerebellar tests. *Annals of Dyslexia* **46**, 259–283.

Fay T (1948). Neuromuscular reflex therapy for spastic disorders. *The Journal of the Florida Medical Association* **44**, 1234–1240.

Finnegan J (1993). The vital role of essential fatty acids for pregnant and nursing women. *Celestial Arts*. http://www.thorne.com/townsend/dec/efas.html

Fiorentino MR (1981a). *A Basis for Sensorimotor Development – Normal and Abnormal*. Springfield, IL, Charles C Thomas.

Fiorentino MR (1981b). *Reflex Testing Methods for Evaluating CNS Development*. Springfield, IL, Charles C Thomas.

Fitzgibbon J (2002). *Feeling Tired All The Time*. Dublin, Gill & Macmillan.

Flourens MJP (1824). *Recherches experimentales sur les propriétés et les functions du système nerveux dans les animaux vertébrés*. Paris, Crevot.

Flourens MJP (1830). Experiences sur les canaux semi circulaires de l'oreille. *Memoire Académie Royale Sciences* (Paris) **9**, 455–477.

Foresight. http://www.foresight-preconception.org.uk/

Forrest DS (2002). Prevalence of primitive reflexes in patients with anxiety disorders. Thesis submitted to the University of Edinburgh in part fulfilment of Doctorate in Clinical Psychology.

Frank J & Levinson H (1973). Dysmetric dyslexia and dyspraxia. Hypothesis and study. *The Journal of the American Academy of Child Psychiatry* **12**(4), 690–701.

Frank J & Levinson HN (1976). Compensatory mechanisms in cerebellar-vestibular dysfunction, dysmetric dyslexia and dyspraxia. *Academic Therapy* **12**, 1–14.

French TM (1930). Beziehungen des Unbewussten zur Funktion der Bogengänge. *International Journal of Psychoanalysis* **16**, 73–86.

Freud S. Cited in: Brown JAC. (1991). *Freud and the Post Freudians*. Harmondsworth, Penguin Books.

Gahlinger PM (1999). How to help your patients avoid travel travail. *Postgraduate Medicine online*. **106**(4), 1 October. http://www.postgraduate.com/issues.

Galaburda AL (2001). Dyslexia and the brain. *The 5th International BDA Conference Proceedings*. University of York, April 2001.

Galaburda AM & Kemper TL (1979). Cytoarchitectonic abnormalities in developmental dyslexia: A case study. *Annals of Neurology* **6**, 94–100.

Galaburda AM et al. (1985). Developmental dyslexia: four consecutive patients with cortical anomalies. *Annals of Neurology* **18**, 222, 223.

Galaburda AM et al. (1986). Histological asymmetry in the primary visual cortex of the rat: implications for mechanisms of cerebral asymmetry. *Cortex* **22**, 151–160.

Galant S (1917). Der Rückgratreflex: ein neuer Reflex im Säuglingsalter mit besonderer Berücksichtigung der anderen Reflexvorgänge bei den Säuglingen. Doctoral Dissertation, Basel, Basler.

Gale CR & Martyn CN (2004). Birth weight and later risk of depression in a national birth cohort. *British Journal of Psychiatry* **184**, 28–33.

Gallahue DL & Ozmun JC (1998). *Understanding Motor Development*. Singapore, McGraw-Hill Book Company.

Gershon MD (1998). *The Second Brain. The Scientific Basis of Gut Instinct*. New York, Harper Collins.

Geschwind N & Galaburda AM (1985). *Cerebral Lateralisation*. Cambridge, MA, MIT Press.

Geschwind N & Levitsky W (1968). Left-right asymmetries in the temporal speech region. *Science* **161**, 186–187.

Gesell A (1954). The ontogenesis of infant behavior. In L Carmichael (ed.), *Manual of Child Psychology*. New York, NY, Wiley pp. 295–331.

Gibbs RB (1994). Estrogen and nerve growth factor-related systems in the brain. Effects on basal forebrain cholinergic neurons and implications for learning and memory processes and aging. In VN Luine & CF Harding (eds), *Hormonal restructuring of the adult brain. Basic and clinical perspectives. Annals of The New York Academy of Sciences* Vol. 743, pp. 165–199.

Giordano GG (1953). *Acta Neurologica* **III**, Quaderno, 313. Cited in Peiper A (1963). *Cerebral Function in Infancy and Childhood*. New York, Consultants Bureau.

Goddard SA (1989). *The Fear Paralysis and its Interaction with the Primitive Reflexes*. INPP monograph Series **1**, Chester.

Goddard S (1990a). *The Developmental Basis for Learning Difficulties and Language Disorders*. INPP Monograph Series **1**.

Goddard SA (1990b). *Developmental Milestones: a Blueprint for Survival*. INPP Monograph Series **2**, Chester.

Goddard SA (1991). Elective mutism; the unchosen silence. Paper presented at The 5th European Conference of Neuro-Developmental Delay in Children with Specific Learning Difficulties, March 1991. In: Goddard SA (1996). *A Teacher's Window into the Child's Mind*. Eugene, OR, Fern Ridge Press.

Goddard SA (1996). *A Teacher's Window into the Child's Mind*. Eugene, OR, Fern Ridge Press.

Goddard SA (2002). *Reflexes, Learning and Behavior*. Eugene, OR, Fern Ridge Press.

Goddard SA & Hyland D (1998). Screening for neurological dysfunction in the specific learning difficulty child. *The British Journal of Occupational Therapy* **10**, 459–464.

Goddard Blythe SA (1996). *The Developmental Test Battery and Exercise Programme for Use in Schools with Children with Special Needs.* Chester, The Institute for Neuro-Physiological Psychology.

Goddard Blythe SA (2001). Neurological dysfunction as a significant factor in children diagnosed with dyslexia. *Proceedings of The 5th International British Dyslexia Association Conference.* University of York, April 2001.

Goddard Blythe SA (2004). *The Well Balanced Child.* Stroud, Hawthorn Press.

Goddard Blythe SA (2005). Releasing educational potential through movement. A summary of individual studies carried out using the INPP Test Battery and Developmental Exercise Programme for use in Schools with Children with Special Needs. *Child Care in Practice* 11(4), 415–432.

Goddard Blythe SA (2008). *What Babies and Children Really Need. How Mothers and Fathers Can Nurture Children's Growth for Health and Well Being.* Stroud, Hawthorn Press.

Goddard Blythe SA & Hyland D (1998). Screening for neurological dysfunction in the specific learning difficulty child. *The British Journal of Occupational Therapy* 61(10).

Golan H & Huleihel M (2006). The effect of prenatal hypoxia on brain development: short- and long-term consequences demonstrated in rodent models. *Developmental Science* 9(4), 338–349.

Gold SJ (2006). Using the head righting reflex to check for warning symptoms that something is wrong with the child's 'gaze control' and how to proceed from there. Svea Gold. Speech for AAHD conference October 2006.sjgold22@comcast.net

Golding J (2007). Motion sickness: friend or foe? The Inaugural Lecture of John Golding, March 2007, London.

Goldstein. Cited in: Schilder P (1933). The vestibular apparatus in neurosis and psychosis. *The Journal of Nervous and Mental Disease* 78(1), 1–23.

Goltz F (1870). Über der physiologische Bedeutung der Bogengänge des Ohrlabyrinthes. *Pflügers Arch. ges. Physiol.* 3, 172–192.

Goodenough F (1926). *Measurement of Intelligence by Drawings.* New York, World Book Co.

Gordon CR et al. (1994). Seasickness susceptibility, personality factors and salivation. *Aviation, Space, and Environmental Medicine* 65(7), 610–614.

Gustafsson D (1971). A comparison of basis reflexes with the subtests of the Purdue-Perceptual-Motor Survey. Unpublished Master's Thesis, University of Kansas.

Hadders Algra M et al. (1986). Neurologically deviant newborn: neurological and behavioural developments at the age of six years. *Developmental Medicine and Child Neurology* 28, 569–578.

Hadders Algra M et al. (1988). Perinatal correlates of major and minor neurological dysfunction at school-age – a multivariate analysis. *Developmental Medicine and Child Neurology* **30**, 482–491.

Hallaran WS (1810). *An Enquiry into the Causes Producing the Extraordinary Addition to the Number of Insane, Together with Extended Observations on the Care of Insanity: with Hints as to the Better Management of Public Asylums.* Cork, Edwards & Savage.

Halleck RP (1898). *Education of the Nervous System.* New York, Macmillan and Company Ltd.

Hallett M & Grafman J (1997). Executive function and motor skill learning. *International Review of Neurobiology* **41**, 297–323.

Halverson HM (1927). Studies of the grasp response in early infancy. *The Journal of Genetic Psychology* **51**, 371–449.

Harris DB. (1963). *Children's Drawings as Measures of Intellectual Maturity.* New York, Harcourt Brace and World Inc.

Hava G & Mahmoud H (2006). The effect of prenatal hypoxia on brain development: short- and long-term consequences demonstrated in rodent models. *Developmental Science* **9**(4), 338–349.

Hawkins JE & Schacht J (2005). Sketches of Otohistory. Part 7: The nineteenth-century rise of laryngology. *Audiology and Neurootology* **10**(3), 130–133.

Helmerhorst FM et al. (2004). Perinatal outcome of singletons and twins after assisted conception: a systematic review of controlled studies. *BMJ* **328**, 261.

Hertig AT et al. (1959). Thirty-four fertilised human ova, good, bad and indifferent, recovered from women of known fertility. A study of biologic wastage in early human pregnancy. *Pediatrics* **23**, 202–211.

Hippocrates. In *Hippocrates VII.* (1994). Epidemics 2/4–7. *The Nature of Man.* Vol. 4. (1994). Loeb Classical Library. Cambridge, MA, Harvard University Press.

Hobson AJ (1988). *The Dreaming Brain.* New York, Basic Books.

Holle B (1981). *Motor Development in Children. Normal and Retarded.* Oxford, Blackwell Scientific Publications.

Holmes TH & Rahe RH (1967). Social readjustment rating scale. *Journal of Psychosomatic Research* **11**, 213–18.

Hooker D (1938). *Proceedings of the American Philosophical Society* **79**, 597.

Hooker D (1952). *The Prenatal Origin of Behaviour.* Lawrence, KS, University of Kansas Press.

Hooker D & Hare C (1954). Early human fetal behaviour with a preliminary note on double simultaneous fetal stimulation. In D Hooker & C Hare (eds), *Genetics and Inheritance of Neuropsychiatric Patterns*, Vol. 33. Research Publications – Association for Research in Nervous and Mental Disease, pp. 98–113.

Horrobin D (2001). *The Madness of Adam and Eve. How Schizophrenia Shaped Humanity.* London, Corgi Books.

Horvath K et al. (1999). Gastrointestinal abnormalities in children with autistic disorder. *Journal of Pediatrics* **135**(5), 559–563.

http://www.balametrics.com

http://www.merck.com/

http://www.patient.co.uk/

http://www.vestibular.org/vestibular

Hughlings Jackson J (1946). Cited in: Walshe FMR (1923). On certain tonic or postural reflexes in hemiplegia with special reference to the so-called associated movements. *Brain* Part 1.46/2, **14**, 16–23.

Humphrey T (1964). Some correlations between the appearance of human fetal reflexes and the development of the nervous system. *Progress in Brain Research* **4**, 93–135.

Humphreys P et al. (1990). Developmental dyslexia in women: neuropathological findings in three cases. *Annals of Neurology* **28**, 727–738.

Hyppönen E & Power C (2007). Hypovitaminosis D in British adults at age 45y: nationwide cohort study on dietary and lifestyle predictors. *American Journal of Clinical Nutrition.* **85**, 860–868.

Ingram TTS (1973). Soft signs. *Developmental Medicine and Child Neurology* **15**, 527.

Isbert H & Peiper A (1963). Cited in: Peiper A & Isbert H (1963). *Cerebral Function in Infancy and Childhood.* The International Behavioral Sciences Series. New York, Consultants Bureau.

James W (1882). The sense of dizziness in deaf mutes. *The American Journal of Otology* **4**, 239–254.

Jenike et al. (1989). Obsessive compulsive disorder: a double blind, placebo controlled trial of clomiprimine in 27 patients. *American Journal of Psychiatry* **146**, 1328–1330.

Jensen TK et al. (2007). Fertility treatment and reproductive health of male offspring: a study of 1925 young men from the general population. *American Journal of Epidemiology* **165**(5), 583–590.

Johansen KV (1988). Sensory deprivation – a possible cause of dyslexia. In *Nordisk Tidsskrift for Spesialpedagogikk.* Oslo, Scandinavian University Press.

Johansen KV (2002). Dyslexia, auditory laterality and hemispheric-specific auditory stimulation. *Nordisk Tidsskrift for Spesialpedogogikk* **80**, 258–271. Oslo, Universitetsforlaget.

Johnson DL et al. (1999). Cerebral blood flow and personality: a positron emission tomography study. *American Journal of Psychiatry* **156**, 252–257.

Kaada B (1986). *Sudden Infant Death Syndrome. The Possible Role of the Fear Paralysis Reflex.* Oslo, Scandinavian University Press.

Kaye K (1977). Toward the origin of dialogue. In HR Schaffer (ed.), *Studies in Mother-Infant Interaction.* London, Academic Press.

Kelly YJ et al. (2001). Birth weight and behavioural problems in children: a modifiable effect? *International Journal of Epidemiology* **30**, 88–94.

Kennard MA (1996). Value of equivocal signs in neurologic diagnosis. *Neurology* **10**, 753–764.

Kohen-Raz R (1986). *Learning Disabilities and Postural Control.* London, Freund Publishing House.

Kohen-Raz R (2004). Postural correlates of learning and disabilities and communication disorders. The European Conference of Neuro-developmental delay in children with specific learning difficulties, Chester, March 2004.

Lack of vitamin D made worse in winter. 28 October 2003. http://www.CNN.com./HEALTH

Lagercrantz H (1989). Neurochemical modulation of fetal behaviour and excitation at birth. In E Euler, H Forssberg & H Lagercrantz (eds), *Neurobiology of Early Infant Behaviour.* Wenner-Gren International Symposium Series. Vol. 55. New York, Stockton Press.

Lawton Brown R (1990). Dyslexia and maths. Paper presented at the 2nd European Conference of Neuro-developmental Delay in Children with Specific Learning Difficulties, Chester, UK, March 1990.

Leidler & Loewy (1923). Der Swindel der Neurosen. *Monatschrift für Ohrenheilkunde und Laryngo Rhinologie* **57**(1).

Leiner HC et al. (1986). Does the cerebellum contribute to mental skills? *Behavioral Neuroscience* **100**, 443–454.

Leiner HC et al. (1991). The human cerebro-cerebellar system: its computing, cognitive and language skills. *Behavioral Brain Research* **44**, 113–128.

Leiner HC et al. (1993). Cognitive and language functions of the human cerebellum. *Trends in Neuroscience* **16**, 444–447.

Levinson HN (1974). Dyslexia: does this unusual childhood syndrome begin as an ear infection? *Infectious Diseases* **15**(15).

Levinson HN (1980). *A Solution to the Riddle – Dyslexia.* New York Springer-Verlag.

Levinson HN (1984). *Smart but Feeling Dumb.* New York, Warner Books Inc.

Levinson HN (1986). *Phobia Free.* New York, M Evans and Company Inc.

Levinson HN (1990). *Total Concentration.* New York, M Evans and Company.

Levinson HN (1992). *Turning Around the Upside Down Kids.* New York, M Evans and Company.

Levinson HN (1994). *A Scientific Watergate.* Lake Success, NY Stonebridge Publishing Ltd.

Levinson HN (2000). *Feeling Smarter and Smarter.* Lake Success, NY, Stonebridge Publishing Ltd.

Levinson HN & Sanders A (1991). *The Upside Down Kids.* New York, M Evans and Company.

Levitt S (1984). *Treatment of Cerebral Palsy and Motor Delay.* Oxford, Blackwell Scientific Publications.

Lipsitt LP (1980). Conditioning the rage to live. *Psychology Today*, February.

Ljunggren M (1982). Agoraphobia – an organic basis? An explanatory neuropsychological approach. Unpublished Master's Thesis. Universitet Göteborg, Psychologiska Institutionen.

Luckett PW (1974). Reproductive development and evolution of the placenta in primates. *Contributions of Primatology* **3**, 142–234.

Mach E (1873). Physikalische Versuche uber den Gleichgewichtssinn des Menschen, Sitzungsberickte der kaiserl. *Akademie der Wissenschaften*. **68**, 124–140.

Macnair T (2006). Febrile convulsions. http://www.bbc.co.uk/health

Madaule P (1994). *When Listening Comes Alive*. Norval, Ontario, Moulin Publishing.

Madaule P (2001). Seminar on The Ear-Voice Connection, November 2001, Chester.

Mahoney D (2003). Cited in: *Pediatric News*, 31 July 2003.

Manor O & Amir N (1995). Developmental right hemisphere syndrome: clinical spectrum of the non-verbal learning disability. *Journal of Learning Disabilities* **28**, 80–86.

Manor O et al. (1993). The acquisition of arithmetic in normal children: assessment by a cognitive model of dyscalculia. *Developmental Medicine and Child Neurology* **35**, 593–601.

Maurer D (1983). The scanning of compound figures by young infants. *Journal of Experimental Child Psychology* **35**, 437–448.

Maurer D & Maurer C (1988). *The World of the Newborn*. London, Viking.

McGraw M (1945). *The Neuromuscular Maturation of the Human Infant*. New York, Hafner Press.

McKeever TM et al. (2002). A birth cohort study using the West Midlands General Practice Database. *American Journal of Respiratory and Critical Care Medicine* **166**, 827–832.

McPhillips M (2006). The role of movement in early development and long-term implications for educational progress. Paper presented at The Vision, Basic Skills Development and Bridging the Skills Gap Conference, BABO, University of London, November 2006.

McPhillips M & Sheehy N (2004). Prevalence of persistent primary reflexes and motor problems in children with reading difficulties. *Dyslexia* **10**(4), 316–338.

McPhillips M et al. (2000). Effects of replicating primary reflex movements on specific reading difficulties in children: a randomised, double-blind, controlled trial. *Lancet* **355**(2), 537–541.

Medical references: drinking alchohol during pregnancy. http://www.marchofdimes.com/

Melillo R & Leisman G (2004). *Neurobehavioral disorders of childhood. An evolutionary perspective.* New York, Kluwer Avademic/Plenum Publishers.

Melzack R & Wall P (1965). Pain mechanisms: a new theory. *Science* **150**, 171–179.

Members of the Department of Neurology and the Department of Physiology and Biophysics, Mayo Clinic and Mayo Foundation for Medical Education and Research, Graduate School, University of Minnesota, Rochester, MN (1976). *Clinical examinations in neurology.* Philadelphia, PA, WB Saunders Company.

Ménière P (1861). Mémoire sur des lesions de l'oreille interne donnant lieu à des symptômes de congestion cérébrale apoplectiforme. *Gazette Médicale de Paris* **55**, 17–32.

Mereu G et al. (2003). Prenatal exposure to a cannabinoid agonist produces memory deficits linked to dysfunction in hippocampal long-term potentiation and glutamate release. *Proceedings of the National Academy of Sciences of the United States of America* **100**(8), 4915–4920.

Micklethwaite J (2004). A report of a study into the efficacy of the INPP School Programme at Swanwick Primary School, Derbyshire. A controlled study of 93 children. Department for Education and Employment Best Practice Scholarship. http://www.teachernet.gov.uk, December 2004.

Milani-Comparetti A (1981). The neurophysiological and clinical implications of studies on fetal motor behaviour. *Seminars in Perinatology* **5**, 183–189.

Miller JL et al. (2003). Emergence of oropharyngeal, laryngeal and swallowing activity in the developing fetal upper aerodigestive tract: an ultrasound evaluation. *Early Human Development* **71**(1), 61–87.

Minowski A (Ed.) (1967). *Regional Development of the Brain in Early Life.* Davis FA, Philadelphia, PA, pp. 3–70.

Mitchell RG (1960). The Moro reflex. *Cerebral Palsy Bulletin* **2**, 135–141.

Moir A & Jessel D (1991). *Brain Sex. The Real Difference Between Men and Women.* London, Mandarin.

Montagu A (1971). *Touching. The Human Significance of Skin.* New York, Columbia University Press.

Morris SE (1978). Oral motor development: Normal and abnormal. In JM Wilson (ed.), *Oral Motor Function and Dysfunction in Children.* Proceedings of a conference on oral-motor dysfunction in children, Chapel Hill, NC. Chapel Hill, NC, University of North Carolina, Department of Medical Allied Health Professionals, Division of Physical Therapy, pp. 114–206.

Moscowitz-Cook A (1979). The development of photopic spectral sensitivity in human infants. *Vision Research* **19**, 1133–1142.

Mutti M et al. (1978). *QNST Quick neurological screening test.* Novato, CA, Academic Therapy Publications Inc.

National Library for Health. (1982), http://www.cks.library. nhs.uk.

Nicolson RI & Fawcett AJ (1990). A new framework for dyslexia research? *Cognition* **35**, 159–182.

Nicolson RI & Fawcett AJ (1994). Reaction times and dyslexia. *Quarterly Journal of Experimental Psychology* **47A**, 29–48.

Nicolson RI et al. (1995). Time estimation deficits in developmental dyslexia: evidence for cerebellar involvement. *Proceedings of the Royal Society* **259**, 43–47.

Noica (1912). *Revue Neurologique.* **20**(1), 134.

Nopola-Hemme et al. (2001). A dominant gene for developmental dyslexia on chromosome 3. *Journal of Medical Genetics* **38**, 658–664.

Nordtveit TI et al. (2008). Maternal and paternal contribution to intergenerational recurrence of breech delivery: population based cohort study. *BMJ* doi: 10. 1136/bmj.39505.436539.BE

North Eastern Education and Library Board (NEELB) (2004). An evaluation of the pilot INPP movement programme in primary schools in the North Eastern Education and Library Board, Northern Ireland. Final Report. Prepared by Brainbox Research Ltd for the NEELB. www.neeelb.org.uk

O'Connor TG et al. (2002). Maternal antenatal anxiety and children's behavioural/emotional problems at 4 years: report from the Avon Longitudinal Study of Parents and Children. *British Journal of Psychiatry* **180**, 502–508.

O'Dell NE & Cook PA (2004). *Stopping ADHD. A Unique and Proven Drug-free Program for Treating ADHD in Children and Adults.* New York, Avery.

Odent M (1991). The early expression of the rooting reflex. Paper presented at The European Conference of Neuro-Developmental Delay in Children with Specific Learning Difficulties, Chester, UK.

O'Hare A (1999). Dysgraphia and dyscalculia. In K Whitmore, H Hart & G Willems (eds), *A Neurodevelopmental Approach to Specific Learning Disorders.* London, MacKeith Press.

O'Keane V & Scott J (2005). From obstetric complications to a maternal-foetal origin hypothesis of mood disorder. *British Journal of Psychiatry* **18**, 367, 368.

Ott P (1997). *How to Detect and Manage Dyslexia. A Resource Manual.* Oxford, Heinemann.

Parmelee AH (1964). A critical evaluation of the Moro reflex. *Pediatrics* **33**, 773–788.

Parmenter C (1975). The asymmetric tonic neck reflex in normal first and third grade children. *The American Journal of Occupational Therapy* **29**, 463–468.

Passingham RE (1975). Changes in the size and organisation of the brain in man and his ancestors. *Brain, Behavior and Evolution* **11**, 73–90.

Pavlidis G & Miles T (1981). *Dyslexia Research and its Application to Education*. New York, John Wiley and Sons, Ltd.

Pavlidis G & Miles T (1987). *Dyslexia Research and its Applications to Education*. Chichester, Wiley.

Paynter A (2006). Learn to move, move to learn. St Aidan's School Sports Partnership. Inspiring Partnerships. DVD produced by Youth Sport Trust. Learning Through Sharing Publication Series. http://www.youthsporttrust.org/

Peiper A (1963). *Cerebral Function in Infancy and Childhood*. The International Behavioral Sciences Series. New York, Consultants Bureau.

Pellionisz A (1985). Tensorial aspects of the multidimensional approach to the vestibule-oculo-motor reflex and gaze. In A Berthoz & M Jones (eds), *Adaptive Mechanisms in Gaze Control. Facts and Theories*. Amsterdam, Elsevier Science Publishers BV.

Peto A (1970). To cast away. *Pyschoanalytic Study of the Child* **25**, 401.

Philip Rice F (1992). *Human Development. A Life Span Approach*. London, Prentice-Hall International.

Portions of brain are smaller in children born prematurely. Genetics, hormones may shield girls' brains from adverse effects of early birth. *Stanford Report*, 18 August 2004.

Posner MI & Raichle ME (1994). *Images of Mind*. New York, Freeman.

Prechtl HFR (1953). Über die Koppelung von Saugen und Greifreflex beim Säugling. *Naturwissenschaften* **12**, 347.

Profet M (1992). Cited in: *The Adapted Mind*. JH Barkow et al. (ed.). New York, Oxford University Press.

Profet M (1995). *Protecting Your Baby-to-be: Preventing Birth Defects in the First Trimester*. Reading, Addison-Wesley.

Pucher G et al. (1987). Quantitative assessment of the Moro reflex: an attempt to identify infants at risk for SIDS? *Biomedizinische Technik. Biomedical Engineering* **32**(5), 112–117.

Pulgar Marx I (1955). *Revista Espanola de Pediatria* **11**, 317; also see (1957) *Zentralblatt für Kinderheilkunde* **58**, 220.

Purkinje J (1820). Beyträge zur näheren Kenntniss des Schwindels aus heautognostischen Daten. *Medicinische Jahrbücher des kaiserlich-königlichen österreichischen Staates* **6**, 79–125.

Reason JT & Brand JJ (1975). *Motion Sickness*. London, Academic Press.

Reiss A et al. (2004). Sex differences in cerebral volumes of 8-year-olds born preterm. *The Journal of Pediatrics* **145**(2), 242–249.

Richardson AJ & Montgomery P (2005). The Oxford-Durham study: a randomized, controlled trial of dietary supplementation with fatty acids in children with developmental coordination disorder. *Pediatrics* **115**, 1360–1366.

Richter CP (1931). *Archives of Neurology and Psychiatry* **26**, 748.

Rider B (1976). Relationship of postural reflexes to learning disabilities. *American Journal of Occupational Therapy* **26**(5), 239–243.

Righard L & Alade MO (1990). Effect of delivery room routine on success of first breast-feed. *Lancet* **3**/**336**(8723), 1105–1107.

Risey J & Briner W (1990). Dyscalculia in patients with vertigo. *Journal of Vestibular Research* **1**, 31–37.

Roberts BL et al. (1989). Motor problems among children of very low birth weight. *The British Journal of Occupational Therapy* **52**(3), 97–99.

Robinson R (1891). The nineteenth century. **30**, 831. Cited in: Peiper A (1963). *Cerebral Function in Infancy, and Early Childhood.* New York, Consultants Bureau.

Roeckelein JE (1998). *Dictionary of Theories, Laws, and Concepts in Psychology.* Westport, CT, Greenwood Press.

Rosen GD et al. (1993). Dyslexia and brain pathology: experimental animal models. In AM Galaburda (ed.), *Dyslexia and Development. Neurobiological Aspects of Extraordinary Brains.* Cambridge MA, Harvard University Press.

Rosenberg K & Trevathen WR (2001). The evolution of human birth. *Scientific American*, November, pp. 77–81.

Sarkar P et al. (2007). Ontogeny of foetal exposure to maternal cortisol using midtrimester amniotic fluid as a biomarker. *Clinical Endocrinology* **66**(5), 636.

Schaughnecy EA & Hynd GW (1989). Attention and impulse control in attention deficit disorders (ADD). *Learning and Individual Differences* **1**, 423–449.

Schilder P (1920). Uber hallucinationen. *Zeitschrift für Neurologie.* **53**, 169–173.

Schilder P (1933). The vestibular apparatus in neurosis and psychosis. *Journal of Nervous and Mental Disease* **78**, 1–23, 137–164.

Schmidt RA & Lee TD (1999). *Motor Control and Learning. A Behavioural Emphasis.* Champagne, IL, Human Kinetics.

Schrager OL (2000). Balance, control, age and language development. Paper presented at the 12th European Conference on Neuro-Developmental Delay in Children with Specific Learning Difficulties, Chester, March 2000.

Selye H (1956). *The Stress of Life.* New York, McGraw-Hill Book Co.

Shalev RS et al. (1988). Developmental dyscalculia. *Cortex* **24**, 555–561.

Shaskan DA & Roller WL (1985). *Paul Schilder. Mind Explorer.* New York, Human Sciences Press.

Shaywitz SE (1996). Dyslexia. *Scientific American*, November, pp. 77–104.

Shepherd R (1980). *Physiotherapy in Paediatrics.* Oxford, Butterworth-Heinemann Limited.

Sherrington C (1906). *The Integrative Function of the Nervous System.* Cambridge, Cambridge University Press.

Singhal A et al. (2007). Infant nutrition and stereoacuity at age 4–6 years. *American Journal of Clinical Nutrition* **85**(1), 152–159.

Sinn N & Bryan J (2007). Effect of supplementation with polyunsaturated fatty acids and micronutrients on learning and behavior problems associated with child ADHD. *Journal of Developmental & Behavioral Pediatrics* **28**, 82–91.

Smith G (2006). Learn to move, move to learn. St Aidan's School Sports Partnership. Inspiring Partnerships. DVD produced by Youth Sport Trust. Learning Through Sharing Publication Series. http://www.youthsporttrust.org/

Sontag LW (1944). War and the foetal maternal relationship. *Marriage and Family Living* **6**, 1–5.

Steinbach I (1994). How does sound therapy work? Paper presented at the 6th European Conference of Neuro-Developmental Delay in Children with Specific Learning Difficulties, Chester, UK.

Stephan H & Andy OJ (1969). Quantitive comparative neuroanatomy of primates: an attempt at a phylogenetic interpretation. In JM Petras & CR Noback (eds), *Comparative and Evolutionary Aspects of the Vertebrate Nervous System.* Annals 167. New York, New York Academy of Sciences, pp. 370–387.

Stoodley CJ et al. (2005). Impaired balancing ability in dyslexic children. *Experimental Brain Research* **167**(3), 370–380.

Strauss H (1929). *Journal of Psychology* **38**, 111.

Swamy G (2008). Cited in: Preterm birth linked to lifelong health issues. *Science Daily.* http://www.sciencedaily.com/releases/2008/03.

Swamy GK et al. (2008). Association of preterm birth with long-term survival, reproduction, and next-generation preterm birth. *JAMA* **299**, 1429–1436.

Tallal P (1996). Language learning impairment: integrating research and remediation. In *Orton Dyslexia Society 47th Annual Conference Commemorative Booklet.* Boston, MA, Orton Dyslexia Society.

Tallal P & Piercy M (1974). Developmental aphasia: rate of auditory processing and selective impairment of consonant perception. *Neuropsychologia* **12**, 83–98.

Tallal P et al. (1996). Language comprehension in language-learning impaired children improved with acoustically modifed speech. *Science* **271**, 81–84.

Tansley AE (1967). *Reading and Remedial Reading.* London, Routledge and Kegan Paul Ltd.

Taylor M et al. (2004). Primitive reflexes and attention-deficit/hyperactivity disorder: developmental origins of classroom dysfunction. *International Journal of Special Education* **19**(1), 23–37.

Tebruegge et al. (2004). Does routine child health surveillance contribute to the early detection of children with pervasive developmental disorders? An epidemiological study in Kent, U.K. *BMC Pediatrics* **3**(4), 4. [abstract]

Telleus C (1980). En kompararitiv studie av neurologisk skillnader hos born medoch utan Isoch skrivovarigheter. Unpublished Master's Thesis, Göteborg Universitet Psychologisker Instituktionen.

Thelan E (1979). Rhythmical stereotypes in normal human infants. *Animal Behaviour* **27**, 699–715.

The Listening Fitness Trainer (LiFT). www.listeningfitness.com

The Merck Manual of Diagnosis and Therapy (1999). Whitehouse Station, NJ, Merck Research Laboratories.

The New England Journal of Medicine **355**, 992–1005. Cited in: New Scientist.com.news service, 22 September 2006.

Thomas A et al. (1954). *La Presse Médicale* **146**, 885.

Thompson C et al. (2001). Birth weight and the risk of depressive disorder in late life. *British Journal of Psychiatry* **179**, 450–455.

Tomatis A (1991). *The Conscious Ear*. New York, The Talman Company.

Tomlinson DR (1988). Gaze shifts and vestibular-ocular reflex. In OH Barber & JA Sharpe (eds), *Vestibular Disorders*. Chicago, IL, Year Book Medical Publishers, Inc.

Tong S et al. (2004). Serum concentrations of macrophage inhibitory cytokine 1 (MIC 1) as a predictor of miscarriage. *Lancet* **363**, 129–130.

Towen B (1976). *Neurological Development in Infancy*. London, William Heinemann Medical Books Ltd.

Trevathan WR (1987). *Human Birth. An Evolutionary Perspective*. New York, Aldine de Gruyter.

Tuormaa TE (1994). The adverse effects of alcohol on reproduction. *International Journal of Biosocial and Medical Research* **14**(2). Reproduced for Foresight, The Association for the Promotion of Preconceptual Care.

Underwood R (1976). Learning disability as a predisposing cause of criminality. *Canada's Mental Health* **24**(4), 11–16.

Van Allen MW & Rodnitzky RL (1981). *Pictorial Manual of Neurological Tests*. Chicago, IL, Year Book Medical Publishers Inc.

Van Dongen GR & Goudie EG (1980). Fetal movements in the first trimester of pregnancy. *British Journal of Obstetrics and Gynecology* **87**, 191–193.

Van Woerkom W (1912). *Revue Neurologique* **20**(II), 285.

Veraguth (1918). *Neurologisches Zentralblatt* **7**.

Verny T (1982). *The Secret Life of the Unborn Child*. London, Sphere Books Ltd.

von Weizsäcker V. Cited in: Schilder P (1933). The vestibular apparatus in neurosis and psychosis. *The Journal of Nervous and Mental Disease* **78**(1), 1–23.

Vose RH. (1981). *Agoraphobia*. London, Faber & Faber.

Wakefield AJ et al. (1998). Ileal-lymphoid hyperplasia non-specific colitis, and pervasive developmental disorder in children. *Lancet* **351**(9103), 637–641.

Wakefield AJ et al. (2006). Gastrointestinal comorbidity, autistic regression and measles-containing vaccines: positive re-challenge and biological gradient. *Medical Veritas* **3**, 796–802.

Walk RD & Gibson EJ (1961). A comparative and analytical study of visual depth perception. *Psychological Monographs* **75**.

Walker C et al. (1998). Balance in the cat: role of the tail and effects of sacrocaudal transaction. *Behavioral Brain Research* **91**(1–2), 41–47.

Wall PD & Melzack R (1962). On nature of cutaneous sensory mechanisms. *Brain* **85**, 331.

Wartenberg R (1952). *Die Untersuchung der reflexe*. (*The Examination of Reflexes*), p. 163 of German translation. Stuttgart, Thieme.

Webster DB (1995). *Neuroscience of Communication*. San Diego, CA, Singular Publishing Group Inc.

Weider D et al. (1991). Nocturnal enuresis with upper airway obstruction. *Otolaryngology Head and Neck Surgery* **105**, 427–432.

Werner EE et al. (1971). *The Children of Kauai. A Longitudinal Study from the Prenatal Period to Age Ten*. Honolulu, University of Hawaii Press.

Wertmanelad R & Gross-Tsur V (1995). Developmental dyscalculia and brain laterality. *Cortex* **31**, 357–365.

West JR et al. (1984). Prenatal and early postnatal exposure to ethanol permanently alters the rat hippocampus. Cited in: (1984) Mechanisms of alcohol damage in utero. *CIBA Foundation Symposium*, Vol. 105. London, Pitman.

Westman JC & Walters JR (1981). Noise and stress: a comparative approach. *Environmental Health Perspectives* **41**, 291–309.

Wiest G & Baloh RW (2002). The pioneering work of Josef Breuer on the vestibular system. *Archives of Neurology* **59**, 1647–1653.

Wiles NJ et al. (2005). Birth weight and psychological distress at 45–51 years. *British Journal of Psychiatry* **187**, 21–28.

Wilkinson G (1994). The relationship of primitive and postural reflexes to learning difficulty and under-achievement. Unpublished MEd Thesis, University of Newcastle-upon-Tyne.

Willis T (1971). *The Anatomy of the Brain*. New York, Tuckhoe.

Witkin HA et al. (1971). *Children's Embedded Figures Test*. Palo Alto, CA, Consulting Pyschologists Press. Inc.

Wolff P (1968). Sucking patterns of infant mammals. *Brain, Behavior and Evolution* **1**, 354–367.

World Federation of Neurology (1968). Report of research group on developmental dyslexia and world illiteracy. *Bulletin of the Orton Society* **18**, 21, 22.

Yakoylev A & Lecours AR (1967). Myelogenetic cycles of regional maturation in the brain. In A Minowski (ed.), *Regional*

Development of the Brain in Early Life. Philadelphia, PA, Davis FA, pp. 3–70.

Zagon IS et al. (1977). Neural populations in the human cerebellum: estimations from isolated cell nuclei. *Brain Research* **127**, 279–282.

Zangwill OL (1960). *Cerebral Dominance in its Relation to Psychological Function*. Edinburgh, Oliver & Boyd.

INDEX

abnormalities, congenital 158, 162–4
acoustic stapedius reflex 64–5, 233, 330, 331
  underdeveloped 331
adenoidectomy and bed-wetting 221
  see also ear, nose and throat infections
adrenaline
  maternal, effect on foetus 176
  output 49, 346
  and retained Moro reflex
  see also stress, maternal; trauma, maternal
agoraphobia 286–9
Ajuriaguerre, J. de 317
alarm reaction 175
alcohol 179–81
  and birth defects 179
  see also foetal alcohol syndrome
allergies 163, 205, 214–16, 346
  associated with caesarean delivery 190
  and immune function 59, 346
  and Moro reflex 59
  and pregnancy 168
Alzheimer's disease and regression of reflex integration 6, 39
ambidexterity 317
ambulation *see* walking
amphibian reflex 150–1
Anderson, U. 162
animal hypnosis 50–1
ANS division 49
antibiotics, effect on foetus 174
antinociception 54
anxiety, adult 2, 59, 141, 223, 266, 285, 286
  anticipatory 58
  disorders (DSM IV classification) 289–92
  exogenous and indigenous 286
  maternal, effect on foetus 177
Apgar score 202
apnoea *see* sleep
arousal 44, 49
  over-arousal 230
articulation 337

asymmetrical tonic neck reflex 39, 41, 72, 80–2, 189, 219, 143, 315
  inhibition 84, 85
  retained 85, 89
attention 4, 9, 44, 248, 285, 361
  shifting 260
  sustained 285
  visual 361
attention deficit disorder 3, 21–3, 31, 362
  clinical criteria 21–2
attention deficit hyperactivity disorder 10, 21, 278, 311
  and omega-3 fatty acids 3412
  and right hemisphere dysfunction 278
  and sleep disorders 208
  symptom criteria 22
  and symmetrical tonic neck reflex 100
auditory confusion 330–1
auditory delay 329
auditory discrimination 225, 233, 277, 325
  and frequency-specific stimulation/ hemisphere-specific discrimination 332
auditory image 326
auditory integrative training 63–4, 129, 229, 332
auditory learning and retention 299
auditory memory 330
auditory orienting response 65
auditory perception 11
auditory processing 12, 21, 63–5, 128, 233, 330, 374
  disorders 325–37; central 326
  stimulus-bound effect 330
auditory retention 299
auditory stimulus-bound effect 330
autistic spectrum disorders 3, 10, 209
  and hyperacusis 63, 233, 332
  effect of inoculations 219
autonomic nervous system 44, 49
avoidance 48, 286, 292, 298
Avon Longitudinal Study of Parents and Children 177
Ayres, J. 18, 87, 357

Also by Sally Goddard Blythe

What Babies and Children Really Need

Psychologist Sally Goddard Blythe draws on the latest scientific research to show how the first few years determine the way children develop – body and mind – for the rest of their lives. She sets out the cornerstones which underpin the raising of healthy, happy children, including:

- how good pre-conceptual and pre-natal care prepare the ground for healthy child development
- how events during birth can affect later educational achievement
- why mother, movement and music are the 3 M's of pre-school education
- the importance of 'rough and tumble' play for emotional and social development
- the special and essential roles of mothers and fathers

'An excellent book which I highly recommend. Sally Goddard Blythe's book reflects her knowledge, passion and dedication to this very important subject.'
Professor Ursula Anderson, international consultant in maternal and child health

'A compelling account of the journey from conception to individuated person, and a valuable reference for all who work with children and special needs children.'
Mary Waller, Professor Emeritus, University of Wisconsin

What Babies and Children Really Need, published by Hawthorn Press in the Early Years Series
£16.99 ISBN: 978-1-903458-76-1 (pbk) www.hawthornpress.com